D0853000

The Knopf Collectors' Guides
to American Antiques

Robert Bishop, Series Consultant

A Chanticleer Press Edition

Chests, Cupboards, Desks & Other Pieces

William C. Ketchum, Jr.

With photographs by Chun Y. Lai

Alfred A. Knopf, New York

This is a Borzoi Book
Published by Alfred A. Knopf, Inc.

Published in the United States by Alfred A. Knopf, Inc., New
York, and simultaneously in Canada by Random House of
Canada Limited, Toronto. Distributed by Random House, Inc.,
New York.

Prepared and produced by
Chanticleer Press, Inc., New York.

Color reproductions by Nievergelt Repro AG, Zurich,
Switzerland. Type set in Century Expanded by Dix Type Inc.,
Syracuse, New York. Printed and bound by Dai Nippon Printing
Co., Ltd., Tokyo, Japan.

Published September 1982
Second Printing, January 1987

Library of Congress Catalog Number: 82-47847
ISBN: 0-394-71270-6

Contents

Acknowledgments

Many people have helped to make this book possible and assisted in its preparation. Special thanks are due to all the individuals and institutions who made their collections available to us, particularly Bernard and S. Dean Levy, and John Ott, Director of the Shaker Community in Pittsfield, Massachusetts. I am especially grateful to Holman J. Swinney, Director of the Margaret Woodbury Strong Museum, who allowed us to photograph objects in the museum's collection, and to Lawrence L. Belles, former chief curator of collections, who helped in the preparation for photography at the museum. Chun Y. Lai spent months photographing almost all of the objects in this book. Robert Bishop's encouragement was invaluable; he also read the manuscript and made many helpful suggestions. My appreciation also goes to Judith Reiter Weissman for her substantial editorial contributions. Amelia Weiss copy-edited the text. The following individuals were kind enough to assist in the preparation of the price guide: Frederick DiMaio of Inglenook Antiques in New York City; Dean Failey of Christie's, New York; and Chris Kennedy of American Decorative Arts in Northampton, Massachusetts. I am especially grateful to Paul Steiner and the staff at Chanticleer Press: Gudrun Buettner and Susan Costello, who developed the idea for this series; Mary Beth Brewer, who, with the help of Cathy Peck, edited and coordinated the project; Carol Nehring, who supervised the art and layouts; and Helga Lose and John Holliday, who directed the production of the book. Finally, I want to thank Charles Elliott, Senior Editor at Alfred A. Knopf, who supported the book throughout its preparation.

About the Author, Photographer, and Consultants

William C. Ketchum, Jr.

A member of the faculty of The New School for Social Research, author William C. Ketchum, Jr., is also a guest curator at the Museum of American Folk Art in New York City and a consultant to the Phillips gallery. Dr. Ketchum has written 17 books, including *The Catalog of American Antiques*, and is a contributing editor of *Antique Monthly*.

Chun Y. Lai

Chun Y. Lai is a New York-based freelance photographer specializing in antiques and architecture. His photographs have been featured in many national magazines, including *Antiques*, and in *The Catalog of World Antiques*.

Robert Bishop

Director of the Museum of American Folk Art in New York City, consultant Robert Bishop is author of more than 30 books, among them *How to Know American Antique Furniture*. He established the first master's degree program in folk art studies at New York University. Dr. Bishop is on the editorial boards of *Art & Antiques*, *Horizon Magazine*, and *Antique Monthly*.

Marvin D. Schwartz

Consultant Marvin D. Schwartz is the author of several books, including *The Furniture of John Henry Belter and the Rococo Revival*, and a frequent contributor to antiques magazines. He has served as curator of decorative arts at the Brooklyn Museum and has lectured and organized exhibitions at The Metropolitan Museum of Art, the Detroit Institute of Arts, and other museums throughout the country.

Preface

In the 20th century, interest in American antiques has grown immensely, and no area within the field has attracted more attention than furniture. This is hardly surprising, for what is closer to us or more directly associated with our lives than the furnishings that surround us? Collecting furniture is fascinating and appeals to all ages, tastes, and budgets.

Furniture collections are as diverse as the people who assemble them. For some, the nucleus of a collection consists of 1 or 2 treasured heirlooms; for others, it is an inexpensive cupboard purchased at a country auction. Although connoisseurs have traditionally limited their collections to high-style pieces from the late 17th and early 18th centuries, today's discriminating collector is just as likely to specialize in 20th-century Art Deco or Mission-style furniture. Some may argue that pieces produced in this century do not qualify as antiques, yet many dealers carry a wide range of objects made as recently as 1950. Given the escalating popularity of American furniture, these pieces may be the antiques of tomorrow, and are more than likely to increase in value.

This volume covers case furniture—that is, pieces that enclose a space, such as desks, chests, and cupboards—made from the Colonial era to the present day. In addition, miscellaneous furnishings such as fire screens, hall racks, and planters are included. A companion volume presents chairs, sofas, stools, and other forms of seating, as well as beds and tables. To help collectors identify American furniture, this guide is organized by function and size rather than by chronology, method of manufacture, or decorative style. Each illustrated entry fully describes a representative object, tells where and when it was made, lists important variations, and provides historical background along with practical hints on what to look for and what to avoid.

To help determine what you may expect to pay, the Price Guide lists current prices for the types of furniture illustrated; many pieces are no more expensive than quality furniture being manufactured today. Those collectors who prefer more traditional examples made before the turn of the century, yet who cannot afford most Colonial pieces, will find a variety of 19th-century furnishings available in almost every price range. Those who want a genuine 17th- or 18th-century piece will find that some of the smaller objects and country furnishings included here are priced at more affordable levels. Using this guide, anyone can wisely build a distinctive and beautiful collection of fine American furniture.

A Simple Way to Identify Furniture

Chests, desks, cupboards, and other types of case furniture are incredibly varied, ranging from elaborately carved, handcrafted pieces to those that are plain and factory made, and from those fashioned during the Colonial era to those manufactured today. To help you identify, date, and assess the style and value of the furniture you encounter, we have chosen 334 representative objects for full picture-and-text coverage. These include the most common, reasonably priced pieces available, as well as some rare, costly examples that are important for an understanding of the development of American furniture. The color plates and accompanying text are organized visually and according to function and size so that beginners can find a piece quickly without knowing its style, maker, or date. Knowledgeable collectors who may want to refer directly to an entry can turn to the List of Plates by Style or the Index.

Because it is impossible to illustrate every type of case furniture made in America, this guide is also designed to assist you in identifying pieces that are not shown. An introductory essay— American Furniture Styles—provides background information and drawings that will help you determine the style of any piece you encounter. In addition, a Checklist for Identifying Styles lists in brief the most important elements of each major period. The illustrated Glossary defines specialized terms used in this book. The essay on Construction and Connoisseurship explains how furniture is made, and discusses how to determine the condition of a piece and how to tell if a piece has been altered or restored, or if it is a reproduction. Finally, the up-to-date Price Guide lists current prices for all the types of furniture illustrated.

Using all of these tools, both the beginner and the connoisseur— whether collector, dealer, decorator, or designer—will find that this guide enhances the joy of collecting.

American Furniture Styles

Throughout the past 350 years, American furniture has changed tremendously. Substantial differences in appearance, construction, and materials mark each stylistic period. Dominating each period is a "high style"—an American adaptation of an English or European style, and the mode followed by the most fashionable American cabinetmakers. In a sense, the dates assigned to any one period are arbitrary. For example, long after the William and Mary period is said to have ended (c. 1725), some cabinetmakers continued to craft pieces that were influenced by that style. This was especially true in rural areas. Pieces made in a style no longer in vogue are sometimes termed survivals. Most country furniture falls into this category. Especially in the 17th and 18th centuries, American cabinetmakers relied heavily on English prototypes, adapting them to create forms more suitable to their new country and employing native woods in place of the traditional timbers. At first the styles available in America lagged behind those that were fashionable abroad, but as travel and communications improved, the time gap lessened.

Pilgrim Style: 1630–1690

In the early 17th century, English furniture was massive, rectilinear, and usually made of oak. Since oak was plentiful in America, the colonists used it to make similar forms. Pine was sometimes employed for concealed elements.

Like 17th-century English furniture, Pilgrim-style furniture (as it is called, although little of it was made by Pilgrims) is simple and strong. Many case pieces are composed of grooved stiles and rails that form a frame into which panels are set. The panels usually have carved decoration. Many of these early pieces were painted, but few today have traces of their original paint. Some Pilgrim-style furnishings were embellished with applied spindles and egg-shaped wooden ornaments called bosses. Both were

Pilgrim-century court cupboard

Pilgrim-century carved chest

often painted black in imitation of ebony.

Homes in the 17th century were usually small and had only a few utilitarian objects. The most common case pieces executed in the Pilgrim style are chests and Bible boxes, and the massive court and press cupboards that only a few wealthy individuals could afford.

William and Mary Style: 1690–1725

Named after the king and queen of England who reigned jointly from 1689 to 1694, the English William and Mary style is an interpretation of the Baroque mode that had swept through Europe earlier in the century. When it reached the colonies it had a profound effect on American furniture design. Unlike the massive pieces in the Pilgrim style, William and Mary furniture is graceful, with elegant lines. The most important new forms introduced during the period, the highboy and lowboy, clearly illustrate the stylistic change that had taken place: these pieces rest on high, elaborately turned legs, and contrast sharply with the squat, blocklike furniture made in the 17th century. Cabinetmakers soon favored walnut, maple, and fruitwoods rather than oak. Veneer became common, especially in fancy, grained woods. Legs were turned in elaborate trumpet or spiral shapes, and even simple chests were adorned with bulbous ball, bun, or turnip feet. Hardware, which was usually imported, became decorative as well as functional. Made of cast brass rather than wood, pulls and escutcheons are primarily scrolled plates; handles are teardrop-shaped.

William and Mary trumpet-leg highboy

William and Mary desk-on-frame

Queen Anne Style: 1725–1750

In the early 18th century, following the shift in European taste
from the monumental Baroque to a more intimate mode, English
cabinetmakers created their own interpretation of the style,
which they named after England's Queen Anne (1702–1714). It
was not until 10 years after Queen Anne's death that the style
began to influence American furniture design.

The Queen Anne style is characterized by delicacy, restrained
decoration, and curvilinear forms. These curving lines are best
seen in the cabriole leg, a new development of the period.
Modeled after an animal's leg, the S-shaped cabriole leg gives
furniture a more intimate, human quality than the massive
turned legs of the William and Mary style. The cabriole leg is
also extremely practical; the balance it achieves makes it possible
to support heavy pieces of case furniture on slim legs, without
the use of stretchers. An exotic foreign wood, mahogany, was
introduced to America during the Queen Anne period. Of a rich
brown hue and easily carved, it was an immediate favorite;
however, because of its expense, most cabinetmakers continued
to use native walnut and maple.

American Queen Anne furniture was small and delicate, with
richly polished wooden surfaces that were either undecorated or
embellished with simple shell- or fan-shaped carving. The heavy
ball feet used during the William and Mary period were replaced
by small, graceful pad, spade, or trifid feet. Elegant batwing
brasses took the place of teardrop pulls.

Queen Anne flat-top highboy

Queen Anne desk-on-frame

Chippendale Style: 1750–1780

In 1754, the Englishman Thomas Chippendale published the first edition of his *The Gentleman and Cabinet-Maker's Director*. Within a short time of its publication, this book of furniture patterns was being used in America, where it had a profound effect on furniture design. Chippendale furniture has the light proportions of Queen Anne pieces, but is generally more opulent. Fashionable examples were made of richly carved mahogany, and adorned with ornate willow brasses. Although more extravagant than American Queen Anne pieces, American Chippendale furniture is more conservative than its English counterpart. For example, when Chippendale published his book, he considered the claw-and-ball foot too old-fashioned to include, yet in America it was featured.

American Chippendale pieces typically have cabriole legs terminating in claw-and-ball feet, or straight square Marlborough legs. Chests and desks often have plain, scrolled, or molded bracket feet. Although mahogany was the preferred wood, walnut, maple, and cherry appeared in less expensive examples. Chests of drawers and desks often have bowed, serpentine, or oxbow fronts; some swell-front, or bombé, pieces were made as well. And a form almost unique to America—the block front—emerged. Chippendale highboys and secretaries are taller than they were in the Queen Anne era, and their pediments are frequently more elaborately carved.

Chippendale lowboy

Chippendale block-front secretary

Federal Style (Hepplewhite and Sheraton): 1780–1820

Cut off from England during the Revolution, it was not until the last 20 years of the century that America became familiar with Neoclassicism, the style that had swept through Europe after 1760. Prompted in part by the excavations at the classical sites of Herculaneum (begun in 1738) and Pompeii (1748), Neoclassicism rejected the innovation and pomp of the Baroque and Rococo. Instead it was based on a new vision of antiquity that stressed simplicity, clarity of line, and delicate, restrained ornament.

In England, the architect and designer Robert Adam was the chief proponent of the style. Beginning in the 1750s, he created furnishings remarkable for their light proportions, geometric lines, and use of classical decoration. In America, the style was called Federal, in deference to the country's new independence. In both America and England, pieces were embellished with classical decorative devices, including the bellflower and urn; in America, patriotic motifs, such as the eagle, were popular as well. Decoration was often executed in inlay, but also appeared in paint or low relief carving.

The American interpretation of Neoclassicism relied substantially on 2 English design books, George Hepplewhite's *Cabinet-Maker and Upholsterer's Guide* (1788) and Thomas Sheraton's *Cabinet-Maker and Upholsterer's Drawing Book* (1791–94). Both Hepplewhite and Sheraton favored light, rectangular forms. They differed, however, in their treatment of decorative details and legs. Hepplewhite pieces usually have square, tapered legs, while Sheraton examples have reeded, slightly vase-shaped legs. American designers freely mixed elements of both styles, and it is rare to find a piece that is purely Hepplewhite or Sheraton.

Hepplewhite sideboard

Sheraton dressing table

The Empire Style: 1815–1840

The Empire style became popular in America around 1815. Developed in Paris at the end of the 18th and beginning of the 19th century, it was the official style of the Napoleonic Empire and relied heavily on the revival of antique Roman forms. In this it resembles English Neoclassicism and American Federalism, but unlike these movements, the Empire style was literal in its interpretation of antiquity. The furniture is heavier and more ornate than that made in the preceding period.

Inspiration for Empire forms was derived from ancient models illustrated in a number of contemporary French and English publications. Even as late as the 1840s, when Victorian taste had begun to take hold, American design books included a number of Empire models. In the country, the style lasted throughout the 19th century.

Mahogany continued to be the preferred wood; walnut was substituted when the more costly wood was not available. Veneer was also common, especially in inexpensive pieces. Inlay, which had been so important during the Federal period, was replaced by carving in high relief, stenciling, gilding, and stamped-brass plaques. Empire pieces are typically massive and often supported by lyre-shaped legs; feet may be scroll-shaped or carved to resemble animal paws. In this period, industrialization began to affect furniture manufacture. The introduction of the circular saw and machinery that could cut thin sheets of veneer allowed manufacturers to increase their output. Because of mass production, Empire furnishings could be made at every price level. By the 1830s the expanding middle-class market had created a nationwide furniture industry that began to replace the craftsman's workshop.

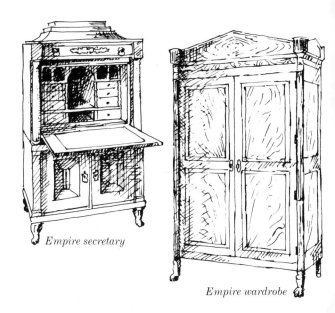

Empire secretary

Empire wardrobe

Country Furniture: 1690–1900

The term country furniture is usually applied to simple, somewhat rustic pieces produced by cabinetmakers who worked outside the high style of the period in which they were active. These pieces are generally made of native hardwoods rather than imported timbers that were favored by sophisticated city cabinetmakers. A single piece of country furniture was usually made of several different woods since each was more suitable for a given purpose. However, since the grain and color of the woods differed, most country pieces were painted, some so elaborately that they reach the level of folk art.

Country pieces often combine elements of several different styles. For example, it is common to find Victorian chests of drawers that incorporate the broad surfaces and scrolled feet of the late Empire mode. Moreover, since most country cabinetmakers were conservative, and worked for a clientele whose tastes changed slowly, their pieces would often be in a style that was out of date by the standards of city manufacturers. Thus it is common to find country craftsmen working in the Federal style in the mid-19th century, 30 or 40 years after their more sophisticated brethren had moved on to other styles.

The term country furniture is also applied to pieces made by city cabinetmakers that are simple, less costly versions of high-style pieces. There was a demand for both simple and elaborate examples, and urban workers supplied them. Country furniture was made throughout the 19th century, particularly in frontier areas, remote from the major furniture centers. The most interesting pieces date from the first half of the 19th century.

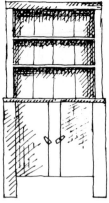

Country open cupboard

Pie safe

Shaker Furniture: 1790–1900

Perhaps the finest examples of country furniture are those produced by the Shakers. The sect was most active from 1800 to the Civil War and had communities scattered from New England to Kentucky and Indiana. The Shakers, who believed in celibacy, lived in communities that were largely self-supporting, and tended to be very traditional. Simplicity and conservatism were heightened by religious strictures against any sort of unnecessary decoration. As a consequence, Shaker furniture is characterized by its severity of line and high level of craftsmanship. Until the late 19th century, most pieces were modeled after Federal examples and 18th-century country furniture.

Most Shaker pieces have simple, geometric lines; many have complex drawer arrangements and ingenious features. Long after other manufacturers had turned to machine production, the Shakers continued to fashion their work by hand. Most often, surfaces were left unpainted, although some were covered with a thin coat of red, yellow, or blue stain.

Before 1860 almost all Shaker furniture was made for use within the community. After 1860 Shakers produced furniture (mostly chairs) for the outside world. Most Shaker furniture became available to collectors only when the communities began to close in the late 19th and early 20th centuries. While later examples, especially those made in the South and West, show the influence of contemporary Empire and Victorian taste, pieces made before 1870 are remarkably consistent in their simplified style.

Shaker blanket chest

Shaker cupboard-chest

Victorian Revival Styles 1840–1880

By 1840, factory production made it possible to manufacture a huge variety of furnishings for a growing number of buyers. At the same time, designers in America and abroad abandoned their traditional reliance on one style. Instead, they turned to various styles from the past, which they mixed in a free and experimental fashion. Furniture made between 1840 and 1900 is often termed Victorian, but there is no one Victorian style. The term refers, of course, to the reign of England's Queen Victoria and the different styles and substyles that arose during her reign.

The Rococo Revival style was introduced to America around 1840 and remained dominant throughout the 1860s. Although it is based on the 18th-century European Rococo style, it is much bolder than its model. Ornament is carved in higher relief, and decorative detail is usually far more realistic. The furniture types follow the taste of the 19th century. Rococo Revival examples are usually smaller than 18th-century prototypes. Many pieces are supported on curving cabriole legs, and topped by marble. Most examples have exuberant, curvilinear floral decoration. Some of these pieces are intricately carved and pierced, made possible by a new technique introduced by John Henry Belter of New York. His use of lamination on Rococo Revival pieces was widely imitated.

In the 1830s the Gothic taste swept through England, and by the 1840s it was popular in America. The style uses decorative elements such as Gothic arches, tracery, quatrefoils, and trefoils to suggest a medieval feeling. Designers also turned to other historic revival styles, such as Romanesque and Elizabethan, especially in the 1850s. Although Gothic-style furnishings fell out of fashion by the 1860s, a limited amount of Gothic-style work was produced as late as the early 20th century.

Gothic Revival washstand

Rococo Revival cupboard-base étagère

The Renaissance Revival style existed side by side with the Rococo Revival style and is sometimes considered a reaction to it. Instead of the carved embellishments and the curving, flowing, foliate lines of Rococo, Renaissance pieces are characterized by their rectilinear forms, heavy proportions, turned elements, and emphatic decoration. Many pieces incorporate porcelain, bronze, or mother-of-pearl plaques, as well as decorative motifs such as cartouches and caryatids and architectural elements such as pediments and columns.

Cottage Style: 1860–1910

At the same time that the Victorian revival styles flourished, Cottage-style furnishings became popular in America. They were intended for the homes, or "cottages," of the working class. Made of inexpensive pine, then painted and decorated, these pieces were mass-produced and sold throughout the United States. Bedroom sets were among the pieces most often made in the Cottage style. Most Cottage pieces have plain lines and a blocky appearance; they resemble examples in the Empire, Rococo, and Renaissance modes, although they lack the ornate touches that characterize those three styles. Their visual effect relies almost entirely on their painted decoration. The most interesting pieces have applied molding, splashboards, and gilding, or simple stenciled landscapes or floral motifs.

Cottage-style commode

*Renaissance Revival
dressing table*

Eastlake Style: 1870–1890

In 1872, Charles Lock Eastlake's book *Hints on Household Taste* was published in America. Eastlake, a prominent English architect, author, and lecturer, advocated the reform of furniture design. In particular, he called for a return to high-quality craftsmanship, an honest use of materials, and an integration of form and function—goals shared by the English Arts and Crafts movement, with which he is sometimes associated. Eastlake was reacting to what he saw as the decorative excesses of the prevalent Victorian revival styles. He urged a return to simple, sturdy furniture; instead of the overly familiar classical motifs, he sought new inspiration in medieval, Middle Eastern, and Far Eastern patterns. He emphasized the beauty of natural wood grain. Simple rectilinear shapes were to replace the curving lines that characterized so many of the revival styles. In essence, Eastlake was decrying the decline in quality that accompanied the mass production of Victorian furniture. In America, furniture manufacturers seized Eastlake's ideas; unfortunately, few of them honored his insistence on the integrity of materials and honest design. Many shoddily made pieces were marketed as Eastlake, and often these furnishings incorporated motifs he would have frowned upon. Although Eastlake's ideas were altered—at times to the point that nothing was left of what he had proposed—he remained important in his insistence on a return to fundamentals. In both his outlook and his designs, he looked forward to many 20th-century developments.

Eastlake pier mirror

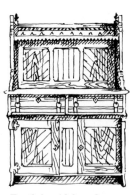

Eastlake sideboard

Anglo-Japanese Style: 1880–1910

In England and on the Continent, Japanese influence was felt as early as 1850. To a limited extent, Americans became familiar with Oriental motifs through the work of Eastlake and others. However, it was not until 1876 that a vast number of Americans became acquainted with the decorative arts of the Far East. It was then, at the Centennial Exhibition in Philadelphia, that Japanese furnishings captured the fancy of America. Furniture manufacturers began to produce pieces that were reminiscent of those that had been exhibited at the Japanese Pavilion; some examples had bamboo-turned legs or applied molding, and others incorporated Oriental motifs such as fans. Ebonizing was the preferred finish. Unlike most American furnishings, which are almost invariably symmetrical, Anglo-Japanese pieces are asymmetrical.

Art Nouveau Style: 1895–1910

Although the Art Nouveau style was a major force in European design, it had only a limited following in the United States. Characterized by its use of fluid, sinuous lines and organic, elongated forms, the style became prominent in Europe in the 1890s, affecting virtually every branch of design from glassmaking to architecture. In America, a few disciplines, such as glassmaking, fell under its sway, but furniture designers rarely adopted the style as a whole. Instead they employed isolated motifs. In 1904, at the Saint Louis fair, the French Pavilion exhibited numerous pieces executed in the Art Nouveau style. Shortly afterward, major midwestern manufacturers, especially those in Grand Rapids, Michigan, began to produce furniture somewhat reminiscent of the French prototypes. These American examples generally combine an Eastlake or Rococo Revival form with applied floral decoration in a vaguely Art Nouveau manner.

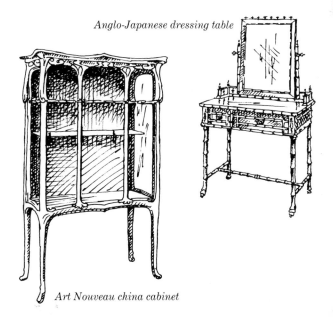

Anglo-Japanese dressing table

Art Nouveau china cabinet

Colonial Revival Style: 1890–1925
In the 1880s and 1890s, colonial furniture began to capture the imagination of America, and this led, particularly after 1890, to the manufacture of reproductions of early American furnishings. This was prompted, in part, by the patriotic fervor that had swept through the country as it celebrated its centennial. Although a few discriminating people had begun to collect 17th- and 18th-century American furniture as early as the 1850s, few Americans were actually familiar with the furniture of their forefathers. What most wanted, and got, were furnishings that suggested days gone by, rather than literal copies of actual pieces. A few cabinetmakers, such as Wallace Nutting, produced high-quality reproductions of American colonial furniture. Nutting worked from actual pieces in his own collection, and achieved so authentic a look that it can still occasionally deceive. More often, however, inexpensive reproductions were mass-produced; they usually relied on thin veneer rather than solid wood, pressed rather than carved decoration, and stamped- rather than cast-brass hardware. For most Americans, this was enough. Some of the more interesting pieces of Colonial Revival furniture combine elements from more than one style, or incorporate colonial motifs onto 19th- and 20th-century forms.

Colonial Revival desk-on-frame

Colonial Revival china cabinet

Arts and Crafts and Mission Styles: 1900–1920

The Arts and Crafts movement was founded in England by William Morris, who denounced the poor quality of mass-produced goods and advocated a return to the handcraft tradition. In the 1860s Morris opened his own firm, where high-quality fabrics, wallpapers, and furnishings were produced. By the 1890s the Arts and Crafts movement was a major force in European design, and by the turn of the century it was also influential in America, as American designers traveled to England to become more closely acquainted with the movement's precepts.

The basic problem posed by the Arts and Crafts group was how to produce handcrafted pieces at prices that the average person could afford. Although a number of Americans had begun small crafts studios, the pieces produced in them were usually expensive since they were made by hand and in limited quantities. It was Gustav Stickley, in the early years of the 20th century, who attempted to reconcile the Arts and Crafts emphasis on handcraftsmanship with mass production. Working from several crafts studios, and using machines, Stickley produced handsome pieces, mostly of oak, that are characterized by their simple, rectilinear forms and exposed construction elements, such as pegs. Elbert Hubbard, in his various Roycroft enterprises, also manufactured simple oak furniture that resembles that made by Stickley. Although Stickley and Hubbard were, in fact, working within the Arts and Crafts movement, their work took on the name "Mission" and came to be associated with the furniture from the old Franciscan missions of California, although, in fact, the types have little in common.

Mission-style magazine pedestal

Arts and Crafts sideboard

Art Deco Style: 1925–1945
Just as the Mission style had its roots abroad, the American Art
Deco style was an interpretation of a French movement. Art
Deco is, in spirit, closely tied to the earlier Art Nouveau style,
both emphasizing bold decorative elements. Named for the
influential *L'Exposition Internationale des Arts Décoratifs et
Industriels Modernes*, which was held in 1925, Art Deco was a
French response to the postwar demand for luxurious objects
and fine craftsmanship. With its streamlined simplification of
traditional forms and, in France, its lavish use of costly
materials, inlays, and veneers, the Art Deco aesthetic was
applied to every branch of the decorative arts.

In America, Art Deco became immensely popular in the 1920s
and 1930s and immediately became an integral part of the
decorative scene. Many of its elements were derived from the
new, mechanized age, and suggested the streamlined automobile,
airplane, and ocean liner. Unlike its French counterpart, the
American Art Deco style used relatively ordinary materials, such
as paint, lacquer, and Bakelite, which made it possible to
produce furnishings that sold for a relatively modest price. The
most advanced American Art Deco designs were developed by
leading architects and industrial and interior designers. Although
Art Deco's heyday was in the 1930s, the basic elements of the
style lingered on as late as 1945.

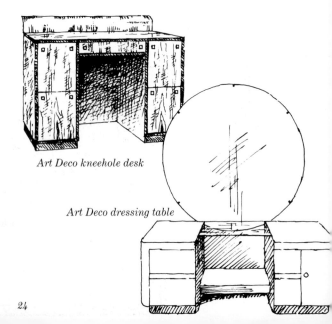

Art Deco kneehole desk

Art Deco dressing table

The Modern Style: 1925–1950

Developing simultaneously with Art Deco, the modern movement was largely dominated by architects such as Marcel Breuer and Corbusier. They were motivated by a desire to create furnishings that were functional and made of materials used in modern architecture and that could be mass-produced while remaining attractive and comfortable.

The founders of the modern movement were related to or part of the Bauhaus, a school of art and design founded in Germany in 1919. The Bauhaus movement was concerned not only with design but also with materials. It recognized that mass production was most suited to industrial products such as chrome, steel, plastic, and glass. Slim lines, a bold streamlined look, and a highly functional character typify modern furniture. The rise of Hitler caused many of the foremost European architects and designers to flee to the United States, which after 1940 became the center for this movement.

The modern style remains the dominant theme in interior design even today, although the movement has undergone various modifications over the years. Wood, largely repudiated in the 1930s, is once more popular, spurred on by new designs and the sophisticated use of lamination. The introduction after World War II of new plastics and molding techniques has resulted in a generation of molded plastic furnishings. Finally, while the earliest designers in the modern vein were concerned with mass-produced works, craftsmen after World War II have turned again to handmade, highly individualistic pieces. Produced in small quantities, these are already attracting collectors' attention.

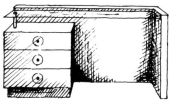

Modern glass-top dressing table

Skyscraper bookcase

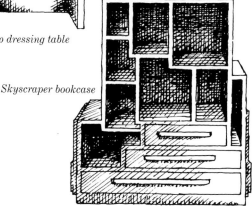

Parts of Furniture

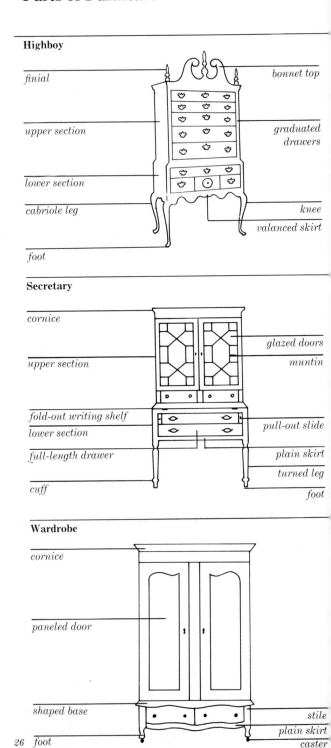

Highboy

finial

bonnet top

upper section

graduated drawers

lower section

cabriole leg

knee

valanced skirt

foot

Secretary

cornice

glazed doors

upper section

muntin

fold-out writing shelf

lower section

pull-out slide

full-length drawer

plain skirt

turned leg

cuff

foot

Wardrobe

cornice

paneled door

shaped base

stile

plain skirt

foot

caster

Sideboard

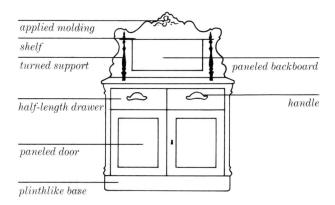

applied molding

shelf

turned support

paneled backboard

half-length drawer

handle

paneled door

plinthlike base

Shaving Stand

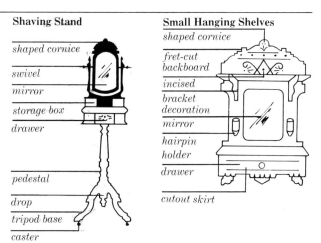

shaped cornice

swivel

mirror

storage box

drawer

pedestal

drop

tripod base

caster

Small Hanging Shelves

shaped cornice

fret-cut backboard

incised

bracket decoration

mirror

hairpin holder

drawer

cutout skirt

Chest-over-drawers

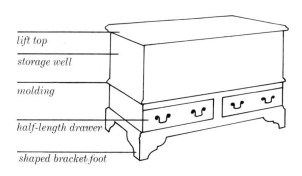

lift top

storage well

molding

half-length drawer

shaped bracket foot

Parts of Furniture

Feet

spade   *blunt arrow*   *pad*   *snake*

bun   *turnip*   *ball*   *C-scroll*

Turnings

sausage   *spool*   *spiral*   *vase-and-ring*

Pediments

pediment   *broken pediment*

Skirts

plain   *arched*

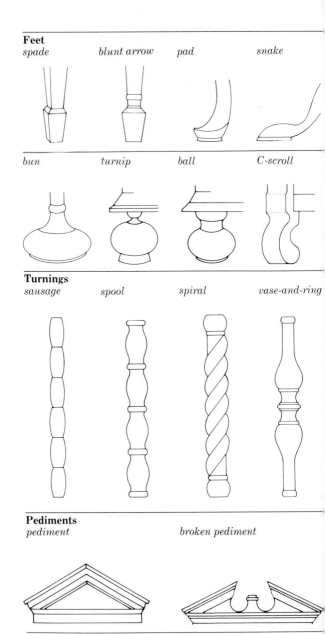

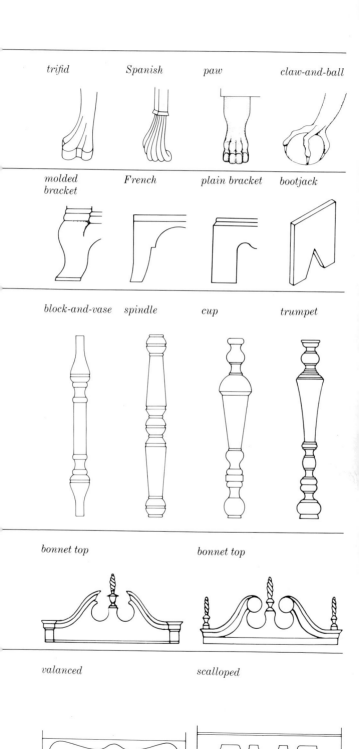

trifid　　　*Spanish*　　　*paw*　　　*claw-and-ball*

molded bracket　　*French*　　*plain bracket*　　*bootjack*

block-and-vase　　*spindle*　　*cup*　　*trumpet*

bonnet top　　　　　　*bonnet top*

valanced　　　　　　*scalloped*

Hardware

Like feet, legs, and moldings, most types of hardware were
made during particular periods. Learning to recognize the
varieties of hardware and the materials from which they were
made will provide clues to dating the furniture you encounter.
The most common types of hinges, escutcheons, and pulls are
illustrated here and defined in the Glossary. The illustrations are
arranged visually, with similar objects grouped together.

Hinges

Until the 20th century, most hinges were made of either wrought
iron or cast brass. The most common wrought-iron types include:
the cotter-pin or snipe hinge (used from the mid-18th to early
19th centuries); the butterfly (early 18th century); the strap (18th
and early 19th centuries); and the rattail (mid-18th century). The
butt hinge, also made of wrought iron, was used in America as
early as the 1600s, although it became common only around 1800;
it is still in use today but is now made of steel. H and HL hinges,
popular in the mid-18th century, were usually made of cast
brass.

Escutcheons

Escutcheons were uncommon until the 18th century; most were
heavy wrought-iron plates. In the William and Mary, Queen
Anne, and Chippendale periods, escutcheons most often matched
pulls. These matching, or conforming, plates were also used
during the Federal era, although inset bone or wooden plates
were also employed. Keyhole surrounds are thin cast-iron or
brass plates that are inset into wood to surround the keyhole;
favored in the Federal period, they are still used today.

Pulls

In the Pilgrim century, most pulls consisted of turned or carved
wooden knobs. By around 1690, cast brass was introduced; it
remained popular well into the 19th century. At first, in the
William and Mary period, the pulls were either diamond-shaped
mounts with teardrop handles or oblong mounts with bail
handles. In the Queen Anne era, batwing mounts with bail
handles were standard; the similar willow mounts with bail
handles were favored in the Chippendale period, although
rosettes with bail handles were also employed. Some willow
mounts were pierced; others were solid. In the Federal era, pulls
became more varied. Cabinetmakers working in the Hepplewhite
style fashioned oval mounts with bail handles. Sheraton mounts
were either oblong plates with bail handles, or rosettes with
pendant rings; occasionally cast-brass lion's-head mounts with
pendant rings were employed. In the Federal period and in
earlier periods, interior pulls were typically small cast-brass
knobs. The Empire era also employed lion's-head mounts; in
addition, pressed-glass and turned wooden knobs, which had first
appeared during the Sheraton period, were sometimes
utilized.

Many Victorian pieces sport leaf-, fruit-, or floral-carved wooden
handles with finger grips; occasionally, plain wooden knobs
appear. In addition, stamped brass began to replace the heavier
and more expensive cast brass at this time. Both oblong and
round shapes are common; occasionally, brass plates are
combined with ebonized wooden pulls. Some 20th-century pulls
recall earlier types; these are usually made of light stamped
brass. The most interesting modern pulls are simple but made in
new materials such as steel, aluminum, and fiberglass.

Hinges

butterfly

butt

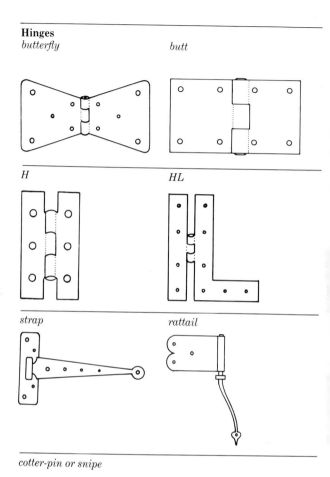

H

HL

strap

rattail

cotter-pin or snipe

Escutcheons

keyhole surround

oval plate

Pulls

rosette knob

turned wooden knob

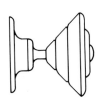

rosette with pendant ring

lion's-head mount with pendant ring

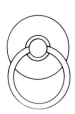

rosette mounts with bail handle

rectangular mount with bail handle

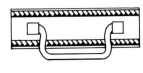

oval mount with bail handle

oblong mount with bail handle

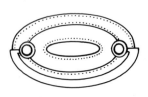

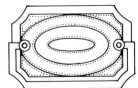

circular plate

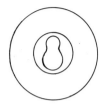

diamond-shaped plate

pressed-glass knob

circular mount with pear-shaped handle

diamond-shaped mount with teardrop handle

batwing mount with bail handle

willow mount with bail handle

fruit-carved wooden handle

How to Use This Guide

Successful collectors utilize a number of related skills: a knowledge of the major periods and styles, an understanding of how furniture is made, and an awareness of current market activity. The simple steps outlined below should help you acquire these skills and make it easy to identify, date, and evaluate furniture.

Preparation
1. Turn to the Visual Key to become acquainted with how the furniture in this book is organized. Based on size and function, the objects are divided into 13 groups; similar objects within each division are grouped together.
2. Read the brief introduction that precedes each group; it discusses the history of the forms illustrated.

Using the Color Plates to Identify Your Piece
1. Compare the piece of furniture you have found with the drawings in the Visual Key. Find the drawing that most closely resembles your object and then turn to the entries listed above the drawing.
2. Continue the visual comparison by narrowing your choice to a single color plate. Remember that your piece may not match it exactly. For example, the feet, skirt, or hardware may differ from those in the illustration; your piece may be made of a different wood, or it may be painted while the example shown is not; detachable parts, such as splashboards and mirrors, may be missing. The text account lists the most common variations.
3. Read the text account to check your identification. Here you will find a detailed description of the piece as well as collecting hints.
4. After you have verified your identification, turn to the Price Guide for an estimate of the current market value of the piece. Choose a figure toward the low end of the range if your object is damaged and toward the high end of the range if the piece is an exceptional example.

Developing Expertise
1. Begin by reading the brief history of American Furniture Styles. Major styles are illustrated with drawings of representative objects, making it easy for you to see the elements characteristic of each style, how the styles are related, and how they differ. In addition, a Checklist for Identifying Styles summarizes the most important features of each. Experience will enable you to determine the style of most of the pieces you encounter.
2. Familiarize yourself with the basic terminology. The illustrated Glossary explains cabinetmakers' terms, and labeled drawings in the Introduction cover the parts of typical pieces of case furniture.
3. Learn how furniture is constructed. The section on Construction and Connoisseurship will make it much easier for you to detect alterations, reproductions, and outright fakes.
4. One of the best ways to learn about furniture is to visit museum collections. The section Public Collections lists those near you. Familiarity with the best examples will help you to develop a sense of style and to recognize outstanding pieces.
5. Consult the Bibliography for major books.
6. The sections Where to Buy Antique Furniture and Buying at Auction describe the major sources of antiques, how an auction works, and how to bid most effectively.

Information-at-a-Glance

Each color plate in this book is accompanied by a full text description. At a glance, you can recognize the type of object you are looking at and then find the information you need to identify and date it.

Description
This covers the most prominent features of the type of object illustrated, moving from top to bottom and including parts that are not visible. It lists elements that may vary, such as feet and moldings. The descriptions usually conclude with the method of construction. Technical terms are defined in the Glossary.

Materials and Dimensions
This section lists the woods and hardware most often used in the type of furniture illustrated. Primary woods are given first, then the secondary woods used for concealed elements. For painted or lacquered furniture, the colors most frequently employed are listed. Next the hardware is discussed, beginning with hinges, then moving on to pulls, latches, and escutcheons. Since size varies from piece to piece, a measurement range is provided. Height is measured from the top of the piece (excluding splashboards or extensions of backboards) to the floor, width from end to end, and depth from front to back.

Locality and Period
This category indicates where and when furniture of the type illustrated was made. Whenever possible, the geographic range reflects all the places where a particular type was manufactured, and indicates whether the type was factory made. Even if the example illustrated is dated, we provide a range of dates, showing when the type was produced.

Comment
The history of the furniture type is related here, typically including its uses, popularity, and influence. Also mentioned are the common variations you may expect to find and brief descriptions of important related pieces.

Hints for Collectors
These tips point out what to look for and what to avoid, how to detect fakes, alterations, and reproductions, the most reliable signs of age, what type of wear you should find, and the factors that influence price.

Visual Key

The furniture included in this guide has been divided into 13 groups. For each group, a symbol appears on the left, along with a brief explanation of the types of furniture in that group. Drawings of representative objects in the group are shown on the right. The plate numbers are indicated above each shape. The group symbol is repeated on the opening page of the section concerning that group and again in the Price Guide.

Dry Sinks, Washstands, and Commodes (*Plates 1–18*)
These utilitarian objects may include a recessed sink, a cutout in the top for a washbowl, or a flat working surface. Most have a cupboard that held a chamber pot or other personal items; some have drawers for additional storage. Washstands and commodes sometimes have a splashboard or marble top to protect their wood from water damage.

Servers, Serving Tables, and Sideboards (*Plates 19–38*)
All of the pieces in this section were designed to display and serve food. Serving tables may have 1 drawer for storage; servers generally have 1 or more drawers, sometimes a lower shelf, and often a splashboard. Sideboards always have 1 or more cupboards; those included here range widely in styles, from long, elegant Federal examples to heavy Victorian pieces that may include a splashboard. 20th-century sideboards and serving tables tend to be simple and often resemble long tables.

Desks and Low Secretaries (*Plates 39–76*)
Desks, which consist of a writing surface and storage area, range from simple Bible boxes to elaborate slant-front bureau desks that include numerous pigeonholes and drawers. Some of the most common types are desk-on-frames and kneehole and rolltop desks. Low secretaries, which have a small storage cabinet mounted on the rear of the writing surface, are also included here.

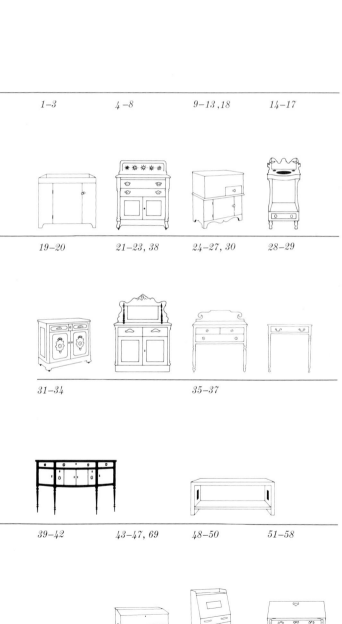

1–3   4–8   9–13,18   14–17

19–20   21–23, 38   24–27, 30   28–29

31–34   35–37

39–42   43–47, 69   48–50   51–58

Desks and Low Secretaries *(Plates 39–76)*
Continued.

Secretaries and Tall Desks *(Plates 77–90)*
These tall pieces all combine a desk with a storage area for books
and writing necessities. In some, the lower section has a fold-out
writing flap and the upper section has glazed doors. Others
consist of a bureau desk beneath a cupboard. Secretaries and tall
desks from the late 19th century often incorporate shaped
backboards, mirrors, or tall glass-enclosed bookshelves.

Cupboards, Cabinets, and Other Large Storage Pieces
(Plates 91–132)
These storage and display pieces range from simple pine
cupboards to elaborate étagères. Cupboards are usually made in
2 pieces; the upper and lower sections may be open or enclosed
by glazed or wooden doors. On most china cabinets, the fronts
are composed almost entirely of glass. Etagères, also meant for
display, typically combine a variety of shelves with 1 or more
cupboards. Wardrobes have a tall storage area enclosed by 2
doors; some have 1 or 2 drawers at the bottom. Smaller storage
pieces, such as bedside and music cabinets, are also included in
this group.

Highboys and Tall Chests of Drawers *(Plates 133–148)*
The large pieces in this section provide storage areas for clothing
and other personal articles. Highboys are always made in 2
pieces and typically have long thin legs. Chest-on-chests, also
made in 2 pieces, rest on shorter legs. Both highboys and chest-
on-chests may have a flat top or be crowned with a pediment or
bonnet top. Tall 1-piece chests of drawers have short legs or rest
on a plinthlike base or detachable frame; those made in the 20th
century are usually streamlined and have minimal decoration.

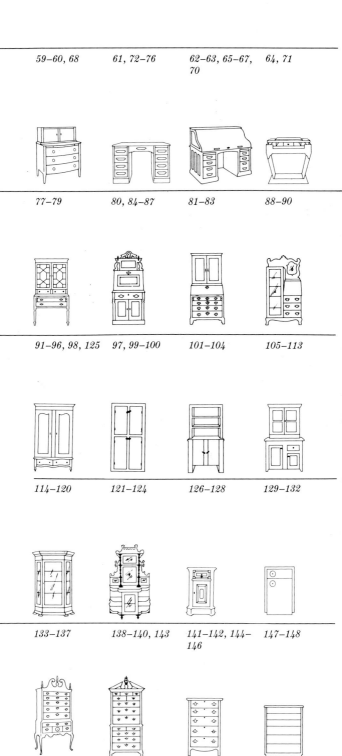

| 59–60, 68 | 61, 72–76 | 62–63, 65–67, 70 | 64, 71 |

| 77–79 | 80, 84–87 | 81–83 | 88–90 |

| 91–96, 98, 125 | 97, 99–100 | 101–104 | 105–113 |

| 114–120 | 121–124 | 126–128 | 129–132 |

| 133–137 | 138–140, 143 | 141–142, 144–146 | 147–148 |

Lowboys, Dressing Tables, Dressers, and Shaving Stands
(*Plates 149–178*)

The pieces in this section all provide a place for storing and applying toiletries. The lowboy, which resembles the base of a highboy, and early dressing tables, which may have a kneehole, lack mirrors. Later dressing tables, ranging from simple country pieces to 20th-century examples, have a permanently attached mirror. Shaving stands consist of a mirror and drawers or a shelf, all usually mounted on a pedestal-type base. Dressers resemble chests of drawers but always have a mirror.

Mirrors (*Plates 179–202*)

Although most of the mirrors in this section are meant to be hung on walls, a few are intended for tabletops. Of the wall mirrors, most have simple rectangular, square, oval, or round frames. In some, the glass consists of 2 panes, which are often divided by a thin wooden strip. Some early mirrors have fret-cut frames; others are embellished with patriotic motifs or applied metal decoration. Some tabletop mirrors rest on trestlelike feet; others lift up from a dressing box or rest on a solid or tubular base.

Chests of Drawers (*Plates 203–230*)

The chest of drawers consists of 3 to 5 full-length drawers; occasionally the top drawer is replaced by 2 or more smaller drawers. Some examples have a plain skirt; others have a skirt with a valance. In the 18th and 19th centuries, many chests had shaped fronts; these include serpentine, oxbow, bowed, bombé, and block forms. 20th-century chests of drawers often rest on a plinthlike base; most have clean, simple lines.

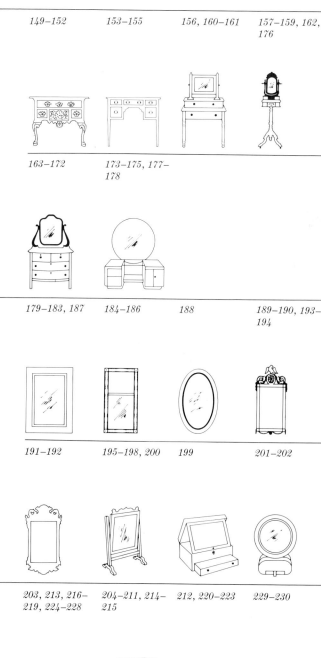

| 149–152 | 153–155 | 156, 160–161 | 157–159, 162, 176 |

| 163–172 | 173–175, 177–178 |

| 179–183, 187 | 184–186 | 188 | 189–190, 193–194 |

| 191–192 | 195–198, 200 | 199 | 201–202 |

| 203, 213, 216–219, 224–228 | 204–211, 214–215 | 212, 220–223 | 229–230 |

Chests and Blanket Chests (*Plates 231–252*)
The simplest chest consists of 6 plain boards that are either nailed or dovetailed together; the top is hinged, and lifts up to reveal a storage well. In some examples, the side boards are extended to form feet; in others, feet are carved or turned separately, and then applied. Some low chests have a single tier of 1 to 3 drawers at their base. Blanket chests are taller and consist of several full-length drawers beneath a storage well.

Small Storage Units (*Plates 253–272*)
The storage units in this section either rest on a tabletop or hang from a wall. Some pieces, intended for the display and storage of pipes, candles, tobacco, or pewter, have 1 or more exposed shelves or shallow compartments; in addition, a few have 1 or more drawers. Victorian storage units are incredibly varied. Designed either to fit into a corner or to rest flat against a wall, they often have mirrors and elaborate fret-cut or inscribed decoration. There are also a variety of small, simple pieces that have various arrangements of drawers and cupboards.

Miscellaneous Furnishings (*Plates 273–326*)
The objects in this group range from simple wooden umbrella racks to metal smoking stands. Most date from the 19th and 20th centuries, and many are made of unusual materials, including steel, glass, fiberglass, bamboo, and wicker. Some types, such as bookshelves, plant stands, and hall racks, are well known, while others, such as display stands and tea carts, are less common. Gun racks, fish tanks, and other objects are also included in this group.

Fire Screens (*Plates 327–334*)
These decorative objects were meant to shield the occupants of a room from the blazing fires necessary before the introduction of central heating. There are 2 basic types. In one, the panel is mounted on a long pole and can be moved up or down; the pole is attached to a tripodlike base. In the second type, the panel is larger, lower, and permanently attached to 2 sets of hooflike feet. In both types, the panel may consist of needlework, printed paper or fabric, or other decorative material.

| 231–233 | 234–237, 239–240 | 238, 241–243 | 244–252 |

| 253–260 | 261–262, 266–269 | 263–265 | 270–272 |

| 276–280 | 281–284 | 285–290, 292–294 | 295–296 |

| 298–299 | 300–312 | 314–320 | 321–322 |

| 327–331 | 332–334 |

Dry Sinks, Washstands, and Commodes

Before the introduction of indoor plumbing, almost every American home had a dry sink and a washstand or commode. The dry sink was the forerunner of today's kitchen sink, and it was used to wash virtually everything from the baby to the dinner dishes. The washstand and commode were used for personal hygiene; they were made for the bedroom or an adjoining chamber and held a pitcher and bowl, as well as soap and brushes. In addition, the commode had a cupboard, which was often used to store the chamber pot.

Although the early settlers must have had dry sinks and washstands, few examples made before the 19th century have survived. These utilitarian objects were easy to build and not especially decorative, and most were probably broken up for firewood once they became damaged or obsolete.

All dry sinks have a shallow well that is lined with tin or zinc. Dirty water is discharged through a drain hole or pipe, either into a bucket or through other pipes to the outdoors. The earliest examples date from around 1800. The simplest type (1) consists of a well on legs, often with a shelf below for storing buckets. In a later, more common version (2), there is a 1- or 2-door cupboard beneath the well; some of these pieces have splashboards, drawers, lift tops, or other additional features. In some pieces (3), the well extends about two-thirds across the top; a short top and drawer takes up the remaining third, and there is a 2-door cupboard below. The finest examples of this type have shelves or double drawers above the well.

Washstands are smaller than dry sinks and have flat tops backed by splashboards or galleries. There is an open space below that is high enough to accommodate a ceramic pitcher and washbowl on a low shelf. The shelf may also incorporate a drawer. Some of the earliest washstands date from around 1790 and are in the Federal style. They can be divided into 2 types: high-style examples (17), usually with solid tops, and later country pieces (16), with cutouts in the top to accommodate washbowls, glasses, and soap dishes. Some are triangular, allowing them to be placed in a corner, and a few have applied brass decoration.

By 1820, washstands began to appear in the Empire mode. Heavier than their Federal relatives, these pieces had Sheraton-style legs, which were eventually replaced by the scroll-cut legs typical of the Empire style. From 1820–50, rural craftsmen, such as the Shakers, built plain washstands, usually of pine. These often incorporated a cupboard (4), and thus stand midway between the washstand and commode.

Because they have a cupboard, commodes are more practical than washstands. The first examples appeared in the late 18th century. These rare Federal pieces (18) are usually demilune in shape, and have long, turned legs. By 1820, boxlike Empire commodes with 1 cupboard door and ball feet (13) were fairly common. But it was in the Victorian era that commodes reached their greatest popularity. The majority were factory made. The most common form (5) had a flat top with a splashboard; below were 1 or 2 full-length drawers, then a 1- or 2-door cupboard. A lift-top version with a concealed stepped well (11) was also widespread.

Dry sinks, washstands, and commodes are immensely popular with collectors today. Many fine examples of washstands and commodes are available; however, good dry sinks are less common and, because of the high prices they bring, are often faked.

1 Primitive dry sink

Description
Tablelike dry sink with unlined well 7–10″ high. Well composed
of 4 boards that rest on square legs tapering out slightly from top
to bottom. Below, 2 stretchers, 4–6″ from floor, support wide,
flat shelf. Nailed or dovetailed construction.

Materials and Dimensions
Usually pine, sometimes with ash, hickory, or maple legs; rarely
pine and walnut. May be stained red, green, blue, or brown.
Height: 30–34″. Width: 32–36″. Depth: 20–22″.

Locality and Period
Throughout the United States. c. 1800–1900.

Comment
The crudest of dry sinks and perhaps the earliest, these simple,
tablelike pieces were made by farmers and householders
throughout the United States. Most were simply old boards
nailed together and are of little interest to the collector. They are
as uncomplicated as their original purpose, which was to serve as
a storage place for buckets of water and as a spot where personal
objects might be washed. Since they were so ordinary, most
were chopped up for firewood when something better became
available.

Hints for Collectors
This sort of primitive dry sink can often be purchased for very
little, and would make a good flower or fern stand. Look for
something different when choosing one. Dovetailing, old paint,
good lines and construction, and an appealing history could all be
pluses.

Description
Plain sink with well recessed 8–12″ below sink rim, usually without molding. Single central door, plain or paneled; interior with 1–2 shelves. Plain skirt. Feet, when present, short and turned in Federal manner or tapered extensions of stiles. Nailed or, less frequently, dovetailed construction.

Materials and Dimensions
Pine, poplar, or mixed softwoods; rarely cherry or maple. Typically painted solid red, blue, gray, or yellow. Zinc- or tin-lined well, with iron or tin drainpipe. Hinges: iron butt. Pulls, when present: brass, porcelain, or turned wooden knobs. Latches: iron, brass, or shaped wood. Height: 30–38″. Width: 34–48″. Depth: 17–20″.

Locality and Period
New England west to Texas and California, and throughout the South. c. 1810–80.

Comment
Simple dry sinks, like the one shown here, were found in almost every kitchen, especially in rural areas. Before indoor plumbing, all washing was done in the dry sink. When the cork or corncob plug blocking the drain was removed, the water went down a pipe into a bucket, or through a pipe to the outdoors and into the ground.

Hints for Collectors
Be wary of dry sinks. Despite the large quantity made, the demand has outstripped the supply, and reproductions and alterations are common. Sometimes a new top and sink well are added to an old, low cupboard. Beware of new wood or paint; there should be uniform wear and construction.

Double-door dry sink

Description
2-door sink, sometimes with lift top, with well recessed 8–12″ below sink rim; well may extend only partially across top. Back may extend upward to form small gallery or, rarely, a cupboard. 2 large paneled or board doors below sink conceal 1–2 shelves. 1–2 drawers sometimes present above cupboard. Skirt plain or valanced, sometimes with central drop. Feet plain bracket, turned in Federal manner, or tapered extensions of stiles. Nailed or dovetailed construction.

Materials and Dimensions
Pine, poplar, walnut, maple, cherry, or mixed softwoods. Softwood examples usually painted red, blue, yellow, or gray, or grained in earth tones. Zinc-, tin-, or enamel-lined well. Hinges: iron butt. Pulls: brass, porcelain, or turned wooden knobs. Latches: iron, brass, or shaped wood. Height: 32–38″. Width: 42–54″. Depth: 18–22″.

Locality and Period
New England west to California; also the South and Southwest. c. 1810–80.

Comment
This is a more elaborate version of the common 1-door dry sink. The most complex is the rare Pennsylvania type, which has 2 large cupboards above the well and 3 to 5 drawers below.

Hints for Collectors
Because the addition of drawers or a cupboard top to a dry sink greatly enhances its value, a number of altered pieces turn up on the market. Check to see if a drawer has been added by removing the drawer and examining the frame around it. If the frame looks raw and new, the drawer is probably not original.

Shaker washstand

Description
Washstand with galleried top, slightly canted and overhanging 2″. Gallery flat at front, rising in curve at sides to higher (5–7″) straight back. Below, full-length drawer over paneled, central 1-door cupboard with shelfless interior. Horizontal board under base of door. Plain board sides. No skirt or feet. Dovetailed, nailed, and pegged construction.

Materials and Dimensions
Pine or maple. Usually natural; also stained pale blue or yellow. Hinges: iron butt. Pulls: turned wooden knobs. Latch: shaped wood. Height: 36–38″. Width: 26–28″. Depth: 19–20″.

Locality and Period
Shaker communities in New England and New York. c. 1820–50.

Comment
The Shaker stand shown here is a simplified version of the Federal washstand, which was common throughout much of the United States. Like most Shaker pieces, however, this one has its own character. Unlike most washstands, it has a cupboard and consequently resembles a commode.

Hints for Collectors
Like any piece offered as Shaker, a washstand should be compared with other examples known to be from the same community to establish its authenticity. Good clues to Shaker origin in the piece illustrated here are the slightly sloping sides and back, the fine dovetailing, and the paneled cupboard door. By recognizing these characteristics, you may even be able to detect Shaker pieces disguised by coats of paint. Although the Shakers never painted their furniture, pieces were sometimes decorated by later owners.

5 Eastlake commode

Description
Commode with flat, overhanging molded top; splashboard (5–7″ high) has rounded corners and stamped, starlike decoration in Eastlake manner. Applied molding at juncture of splashboard and top. Below, 2 full-length drawers, the upper protruding 1–2″ to reach applied, turned columns mounted on each front stile. 2 paneled doors below open on cupboard divided by vertical board. Paneled sides. Molded base with plain skirt. Front feet scrolled, rear feet extensions of stiles, all usually mounted on casters. Nailed and glued construction.

Materials and Dimensions
Oak; sometimes walnut with pine secondary wood. Hinges: iron or brass butt. Pulls: oblong brass plates with bail handles; also brass rosette plates with ring handles or turned wooden knobs. Casters: iron. Height: 36–40″. Width: 29–32″. Depth: 15–18″.

Locality and Period
Large factories in the East and Midwest. c. 1875–1905.

Comment
Many Eastlake-style commodes show a relatively early use of oak, which was most in demand after 1890. Despite its starlike decoration, the illustrated piece is not pure Eastlake; the combination of pillars and scrolled feet is more in the classical or Empire Revival mode.

Hints for Collectors
Early oak commodes should not be confused with the more common "golden oak" examples that were produced from about 1900 to 1920. The latter often have bowed or serpentine fronts and are frequently veneered. They are also made of thinner boards, often nailed together in a slapdash manner.

6 Cottage-style commode

Description
Commode with elaborate painting or graining. Molded top with
curved corners terminating in scallop-cut splashboard (5–7″ high)
with turned candle bracket on each side. Full-length drawer over
2-door cupboard. Cupboard doors plain or paneled. Interior may
have 1–2 shelves on left or right. Paneled sides. Plain or
valanced skirt and plinthlike base. Square pad feet; may have
casters. Always painted. Nailed and glued construction.

Materials and Dimensions
Pine. Elaborately painted or grained; gilt striping often present;
doors may have freehand painting of floral or landscape designs.
Hinges: iron or brass butt. Pulls: brass plates with pendant ring
handles; also leaf-carved wooden handles or turned wooden
knobs. Escutcheons: iron keyhole surrounds or applied wood.
Casters, when present: iron and wood. Height: 29–33″. Width:
36–39″. Depth: 15–17″.

Locality and Period
Large factories in the East and Midwest. c. 1875–1910.

Comment
Commodes like the one shown here were generally part of an
entire bedroom set, some of which can still be found complete.
Unfortunately, many commodes show water damage, a serious
problem with painted pieces.

Hints for Collectors
Look for Cottage-style commodes with rich decoration; avoid
poorly decorated pieces and those with damaged surfaces. In the
illustrated example, the holes on both sides of the pulls indicate
that the original pulls have been replaced. This common problem
slightly decreases value.

Victorian marble-top commode

Description

Commode with removable, overhanging, molded top and splashboard (8–10″ high) of figured marble. 2 demilune marble candle brackets may be attached to splashboard. Full-length drawer with 2-door cupboard below. Doors molded and paneled. Interior has 1 fixed shelf. Paneled side boards. Reeded corner posts. Plain skirt and molded plinthlike base; casters often present. Nailed and glued construction.

Materials and Dimensions

Oak, walnut, or ash. Secondary wood pine. Top white to dark blue-gray marble. Hinges: iron butt. Pulls: oblong brass plates with bail handles; also brass pendant ring handles or leaf-carved wooden handles. Escutcheons: brass plates or applied wood. Casters: brass or iron and wood. Height: 44–48″. Width: 36–39″. Depth: 16–18″.

Locality and Period

Large factories throughout the East and Midwest. c. 1860–90.

Comment

Though more expensive than all-wood pieces, marble-top commodes were popular and sold in substantial quantities. Commodes were constantly getting wet, and a marble top protected the wood. Such pieces were usually part of bedroom sets, which might also have included marble-top tables and bureaus.

Hints for Collectors

Marble-top commodes are still popular and fairly easy to find. Be sure, however, that the top is not a recent replacement, for this will lessen the value 30% to 40%. It should show stains and fine scratches from the pitchers and bowls that constantly slid back and forth across its surface.

8 Victorian single-door commode

Description
Commode with overhanging, molded top and paneled
splashboard (6–9″ high) with incised dentil trim. Full-length
drawer, with 1-door cupboard below. Paneled cupboard door
conceals 1 fixed shelf or none. To left or right of cupboard, 2–3
half-length drawers, separated by heavy molding. Paneled sides.
Plain skirt and molded base. Shaped stiles, decorated with
incised geometric or floral forms and terminating in block feet,
usually with casters. Glued, nailed, and dovetailed construction.

Materials and Dimensions
Oak or walnut; walnut examples may have pine secondary wood;
rarely, as shown here, mahogany with pine secondary wood.
Splashboard and door panel may have walnut or mahogany
veneer. Hinges: iron or brass butt. Pulls: oblong brass plates
with bail handles; also brass pendant ring handles or floral-
carved wooden handles. Escutcheons: brass plates or applied
wood. Casters: brass or iron and wood. Height: 36–38″. Width:
30–32″. Depth: 16–17″.

Locality and Period
Large factories throughout the East and Midwest. c. 1860–90.

Comment
Single-door commodes are somewhat less common than those
with 2 doors, but with their extra drawers they seem more
practical. Like other commodes, they were normally part of a
bedroom set.

Hints for Collectors
The piece shown here is made of mahogany, a wood seldom used
for commodes, and is thus especially desirable. Other sought-
after features are good painted or incised decoration and good
lines.

9 Victorian commode

Description
Commode with overhanging, serpentine, molded top. 2 full-length drawers below top; upper drawer serpentine fronted. 2 paneled doors below drawers; interior with 1–2 fixed shelves. Sides paneled. Skirt plain or slightly valanced. Feet square extensions of stiles; front feet tapered. Nailed and glued construction.

Materials and Dimensions
Oak and quartersawed oak with strong grain. Shelves sometimes pine; top occasionally marble. Hinges: brass or iron butt. Pulls: brass plates with bail handles; also pendant ring handles or brass rosette knobs. Height: 29–32″. Width: 28–30″. Depth: 18–19″.

Locality and Period
Large factories throughout the United States. c. 1890–1920.

Comment
This is the last form of the once popular commode. With their serpentine design and elaborate brasses, these pieces are reminiscent of the romantic aspect of the Victorian era, yet the plain cupboard and base belong to the later Mission style. Since turn-of-the-century oak furnishings bridged both styles, such transitional pieces are not unusual.

Hints for Collectors
Oak commodes are extremely common but not inexpensive, since many collectors use them as bars or for television or stereo units. Altering the basic form of a piece by taking off the doors or cutting holes in the back, however, destroys its value as an antique.

Cottage-style "necessary"

Description
Cabinet with concealed toilet seat and removable, overhanging, molded top. Upper front panel is hinged and folds up and back; it conceals wooden toilet seat with space below for chamber pot. Lower compartment also hinged. Interior walls often covered with cloth or wallpaper. Plain board sides. Plain skirt. Block feet, usually with casters. Always painted. Nailed and glued construction.

Materials and Dimensions
Pine or poplar. Painted white, gray, or blue. Often decorated with gilt; also freehand oil painting with floral and scenic motifs. Hinges: brass or iron butt. Casters: brass or iron and wood. Height: 32–34″. Width: 28–30″. Depth: 18–20″.

Locality and Period
Factories in the East and Midwest. c. 1860–90.

Comment
Like the far more common oak "necessaries" produced at the turn of the century, these painted and decorated pieces were destroyed in large numbers once indoor plumbing became common. Though some were one-of-a-kind home creations, the great majority were made in furniture factories. Period factory catalogues indicate that most Victorian bedroom sets included these pieces, but not many remain today.

Hints for Collectors
"Necessaries" have little appeal for most collectors, although some like them precisely because they are curiosities. Even though they are no longer useful, they should be preserved for their historic value. Museums and local historical societies are usually glad to have them.

Decorated lift-top commode

Description
2-part commode with molded, overhanging, hinged lift top
concealing stepped interior. Rectangular drawer in lower left
corner of upper section. Lower section has plain, unmolded top
and central, paneled, 1-door cupboard; interior shelfless. Applied
molding separates upper and lower sections. Plain board sides.
Skirt valanced in balanced cyma curves. Plain bracket feet.
Nailed and glued or, rarely, dovetailed construction.

Materials and Dimensions
Pine or poplar. Painted red, blue, or gray; also sponged or grain-
painted. Hinges: iron butt. Pulls: turned wooden knobs. Height:
29–31″. Width: 27–29″. Depth: 18–19″.

Locality and Period
Small cabinet shops and factories throughout the East and
Midwest. c. 1840–70.

Comment
This piece superficially resembles a Cottage-type lift-top
commode, but it lacks the applied serpentine band and typical
Cottage decoration. Sometimes shops made a basic form, which
was then elaborated (with graining, applied decoration, etc.) for
the well-to-do. At the same time, country cabinetmakers might
copy a popular factory piece almost detail for detail and grain-
paint or sponge it to please their customers.

Hints for Collectors
Some grained or sponged pieces are factory-made. Handmade
construction must be determined from other characteristics, such
as saw marks, wood thickness, and hardware. For example, a
piece from a small shop would have thicker boards and might
show signs of hand sawing. The piece illustrated here represents
the late Empire style.

Description
2-part commode with molded, overhanging, hinged lift top concealing stepped interior. Applied, serpentine wooden band across front, directly below lid. Rectangular drawer in lower left corner of upper section. Applied molding, separating upper section from lower, looks like overhang. Lower section has central, solid-panel 1-door cupboard; interior shelfless. Plain board or paneled sides. Skirt plain or valanced in balanced cyma curves. Plain bracket feet. Usually painted. Nailed and glued construction.

Materials and Dimensions
Pine, poplar, or ash; rarely walnut. Secondary wood pine or poplar. Painted, grained, and decorated in Cottage style; walnut examples unpainted. Hinges: iron butt. Pulls: turned wooden knobs. Height: 31–33″. Width: 28–30″. Depth: 17–18″.

Locality and Period
Factories throughout the East and Midwest. c. 1850–90.

Comment
The lift-top commode concealed toilet articles. The stepped interior provided space for a pitcher and bowl, the small drawer could be used for smaller items like soap and toothbrushes, and the lower cupboard hid the chamber pot.

Hints for Collectors
These popular Cottage-style pieces are often subject to abuse. Removing the top and covering the well with tin or copper makes a reasonable facsimile of the dry sink, but dry sinks do not have stepped interiors and are usually wider than commodes.

Empire lift-top commode

Description
Narrow commode with slightly molded, hinged lift top.
Concealed well has perforated platform for storing toilet articles
and space for pitcher and bowl. Below well, large, paneled 1-door
cupboard without shelves. Full-length drawer beneath cupboard.
Paneled sides. Plain skirt. Large, turned, turniplike feet.
Dovetailed construction.

Materials and Dimensions
Mahogany or mahogany veneer; also walnut or walnut veneer.
Secondary wood pine. Hinges: brass or iron butt. Pulls: turned
wooden knobs, brass pendant ring handles, or brass rosettes.
Height: 33–36″. Width: 18–20″. Depth: 18–20″.

Locality and Period
New England west and south to New Orleans. c. 1820–40.

Comment
Among the first of what may properly be called commodes, these
pieces combine storage areas for washing and toilet articles with
a surface on which to use them, along with a place to store a
chamber pot. A late development of the washstand, Empire
examples were relatively small, and early in the Victorian era
were replaced by larger, more practical commodes.

Hints for Collectors
Empire commodes like the one shown here are rare and may be
confused with the more common Empire-style bedside table. The
lift top and perforated storage area identify a piece as a
commode. Such examples are small enough to serve as bedside
tables, speaker housings, or even liquor cabinets. The best are
solid mahogany and have wide dovetails.

14 Shaker child's commode-washstand

Description
Unusual small commode with slightly molded, overhanging top and hole at left for washbowl. Splashboard (5–7″ high) with rounded corners supported on extensions of rear stiles. Across upper quarter of splashboard is shallow, pierced shelf for glasses and toothbrushes. Below left: low shelf for water pitcher. Below right: 2 half-length drawers above 1-door cupboard without shelves. Plain skirt. Legs square, slightly tapered extensions of front stiles. Dovetailed and nailed construction.

Materials and Dimensions
Pine, ash, or maple. Secondary wood pine. Usually natural, but may have yellow or red stain. Hinges: iron butt. Pulls: small, turned wooden knobs. Height: 32–34″. Width: 28–30″. Depth: 17–18″.

Locality and Period
Shaker communities from New England west to Indiana. c. 1820–60.

Comment
The Shakers were fond of children and concerned about their health and welfare. Every community had furniture designed for young believers, especially beds, chairs, and tables. Small desks, cupboards, and commodes are somewhat less common. The piece shown here combines a washstand with a commode.

Hints for Collectors
The inexperienced collector may easily fail to recognize this piece as Shaker since its form is similar to that of many mid-19th-century country commodes. But the skillful dovetailing, rare by this time in non-Shaker pieces, the perforated shelf, and the delicate, turned knobs mark the piece as Shaker, and its small proportions indicate it was made for children.

Late Federal transitional washstand

Description
Narrow stand with galleried top. Gallery 3-sided, scalloped, rising 5–7″ at rear, and fitted at each rear corner with wedge-shaped storage shelf. Molded, bowed upper shelf with central circular cutout for washbowl; at each side, circular cutout for a glass or soap dish. Rear gallery and plain skirt below cutout top have applied metal rosettes. Sides below have semicircular cutout sweeping out at base. Plain skirt. Short, turned Sheraton legs. Ball feet. Dovetailed or nailed construction.

Materials and Dimensions
Pine painted or grained in contrasting colors; also walnut, mahogany, or maple with pine secondary wood. Applied rosettes: Federal-style brass. Pulls: brass rosettes or Sandwich glass knobs. Height: 35–37″. Width: 16–18″. Depth: 18–19″.

Locality and Period
New England west to Ohio, south to the Carolinas and Georgia. c. 1800–25.

Comment
This attractive piece reflects the change from earlier Federal washstands, which usually had open bases and lacked washbowl cutouts, to the Empire form with a bulkier silhouette and heavier feet. Here, the applied brass decoration common on Federal pieces is still in evidence, as well as the cutout and floor-level drawer associated with later pieces.

Hints for Collectors
Washstands are often reproduced, so make sure you are buying an original piece. Look for the wear and loss of paint on the back and lower shelf caused by the pitcher and bowl resting against them and for the wear around the edge of the circular cutout where the washbowl rested.

Country Sheraton washstand

Description
Narrow, sometimes triangular stand with galleried top. Gallery sides (3–5″ high) slope toward front. Splashboard (6–8″ high) scalloped or symmetrically shaped. Upper shelf with swelling, sometimes molded edge and cutout for washbowl; may also have smaller cutouts for glasses or soap dish. Plain board sides curve inward, then out at lower shelf used to store pitcher and bowl. Below, 1 or, rarely, 2 full-length drawers. Plain skirt. Simple turned Sheraton legs. Blunt arrow or ball feet. Dovetailed or nailed construction.

Materials and Dimensions
Pine; legs sometimes maple. May be painted red, blue, or green, or elaborately grained or sponged in 2 contrasting colors. Occasionally decorated with brass rosettes. Pulls: turned wooden knobs or brass rosettes. Height: 33–37″. Width: 16–18″. Depth: 14–16″.

Locality and Period
Throughout the Northeast and Middle Atlantic states, west to Ohio and Indiana. c. 1800–40.

Comment
Though examples in the Hepplewhite and later Empire modes can be found, most washstands are Sheraton in feeling. Smaller than commodes, they were designed for use in bedrooms, and customarily held a pitcher, bowl, soap dish, and glass, and provided a drawer or shelves for toilet articles.

Hints for Collectors
The cutout top for the washbowl limits the use of these pieces. Still, they can be purely ornamental or adapted for use as plant stands. Look for good form and original paint; grain-painted examples are especially desirable.

Sheraton washstand

Description
Triangular, 4-legged stand with molded, wedge-shaped top.
Scallop-edged gallery on 2 sides rises 6–8″ at back. Below,
wedge-shaped shelf (3–4″ high) with central drawer (6–7″ wide).
Both top and shelf have plain or, sometimes, valanced skirts.
Stiles, 2 at front, 1 at rear, turned, blocked at top and shelf level,
terminating in Sheraton legs and ball feet. Separate, matching
leg and foot at front, attached directly below lower shelf.
Dovetailed or nailed and glued construction.

Materials and Dimensions
Mahogany or mahogany veneer; sometimes cherry or walnut.
Secondary wood pine. Pulls: brass willow mounts with bail
handles; also brass rosettes with ring handles or turned wooden
knobs. Height: 39–43″. Width: 26–29″. Depth: 17–19″.

Locality and Period
New England west to Ohio, south to Georgia. c. 1790–1820.

Comment
High-style washstands like this did not customarily have cutouts
for pitcher and bowl, and were often simpler than their country
cousins. The use of the fourth, freestanding leg here is a
sophisticated touch, since anchoring it requires skills usually
beyond those of the country cabinetmaker.

Hints for Collectors
The kind of wood as well as the cabinetmaking techniques can be
a clue to both origin and period. Mahogany was mostly used by
cabinet shops in larger cities, especially before 1830. Rural shops
often substituted walnut, cherry, or stained pine. Inlay,
stringing, and sophisticated veneer work were much more likely
to be found on early Federal city-made pieces.

Federal marble-top commode

Description
Demilune-shaped stand with removable, shaped and molded marble top. Carcass bowed at front, with 1 full-length drawer above a 2-door cupboard; no interior shelves. At each side, 1 quadrant-shaped cupboard with false drawer on upper portion. Plain skirt with scrolled corner brackets. Turned legs extensions of stiles, reeded above tapered feet. Dovetailed, nailed, and glued construction.

Materials and Dimensions
Mahogany and mahogany veneer over pine. Secondary wood pine. Hinges: brass butt. Pulls: brass rosettes with ring handles. Escutcheons: scrolled and decorated brass ovals mounted vertically. Height: 35–37″. Width: 44–46″. Depth: 25–26″.

Locality and Period
A few sophisticated furniture makers in Boston, New York, and Philadelphia. c. 1790–1810.

Comment
The first American commodes appeared during the Federal period. Just when they began to be used for chamber pots is unclear, but it was probably after 1820. Early pieces, such as the one shown here, resemble sideboards. The French used the term commode loosely to describe chests and cabinets, and it seems likely that the example illustrated was used to store personal effects rather than as a storage area for a chamber pot.

Hints for Collectors
Federal commodes are not only rare but may also be confused with English examples. The commode shown here is believed to have been made in Boston, but its sophisticated look would be compatible with an imported piece. When in doubt, be sure to get a guarantee that the piece you are buying is American.

Serving Tables, Servers, and Sideboards

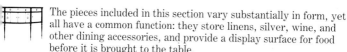

The pieces included in this section vary substantially in form, yet all have a common function: they store linens, silver, wine, and other dining accessories, and provide a display surface for food before it is brought to the table.

Of these, serving tables (29) are the plainest. They can easily be confused with the side tables and utility tables covered in the companion volume to this guide. However, serving tables are very shallow in relation to their width, much more so than are side tables and utility tables. All 3 types may have 1 drawer, either at the front or at an end. Serving tables in the Queen Anne style are rare. Although a number of Chippendale examples exist, the form became common only during the Federal period, around 1790. While examples from the late 18th and 19th centuries are never very large, some 20th-century pieces are 6' long.

Servers (25) are closely related to serving tables, but slightly more complex. Like serving tables, they became common in the late 18th century and are rarely more than 4' long. They typically have 2 to 4 drawers; many have an additional case of 2 or 3 shallow drawers attached to the top rear, or they may have a splashboard. Empire examples are slightly more elaborate than their Federal predecessors and may include a lower shelf. The few Victorian servers have several drawers; they are found in Eastlake and Renaissance Revival styles. The form persisted in the 20th century, mostly in the Mission, Art Deco, and Colonial Revival styles.

Sideboards are the most complex of the pieces included here: in addition to drawers, they have 1 or more cupboards. In America, they first appeared in the Federal period, when they reached their most spectacular form. A typical Federal sideboard (34) may be 7' long; it is usually mounted on 6 long, thin legs, with 4 in the front and 2 in the rear. The front legs divide the piece into 3 sections, and each section contains a variety of cupboards and drawers. The front may be straight, bowed, serpentine, or oxbow, or a combination of these, and it often has elaborate inlay and stringing.

Because of their size and cost, Federal sideboards were impractical for most Americans. By 1820, a smaller, simpler form appeared. These Empire pieces (20) typically have a large 2-door storage area below 1 full-length drawer or lift top, or a 1-door cupboard flanked by narrow bottle drawers. Many have a high splashboard that extends around the sides to form a gallery.

Victorian sideboards are similar in structure to Empire pieces, but reflect the many substyles of the Victorian period, such as Renaissance Revival and Rococco Revival. In some examples, the backboards extend high above the top and may be elaborately shaped and decorated with mirrors and applied carving. Although most have straight fronts, when oak became popular after 1880, bowfront and serpentine examples appeared. In the 20th century, sideboards became less common. Of those made, among the most interesting are the inventive Art Deco pieces, the handcrafted Arts and Crafts examples, and others that reflect the development of new materials or the continuation of traditional styles. For most collectors, the smaller Empire, Victorian, and Colonial Revival sideboards are the most practical. Many are reasonably priced, and they often appear on the market.

19 Renaissance Revival sideboard

Description
Low, massive sideboard with removable, molded marble top slightly shaped at rear. Below top, 2 half-length drawers, with paneled fronts and lozenge-shaped raised molding, separated by vertical panel. Interiors sometimes divided into 2–4 spaces. Paneled 2-door cupboard below, with applied, saw-cut devices in Renaissance mode. Interior sometimes has 1 shelf. Paneled sides. Heavy, molded base. Block feet, often with casters. Dovetailed and nailed and glued construction.

Materials and Dimensions
Walnut; sometimes mahogany or rosewood. Secondary wood pine. Hinges: iron butt. Pulls: turned wooden knobs or fruit- or floral-carved wooden handles. Escutcheons: applied, carved wood or iron keyhole surrounds. Casters: iron or iron and wood. Height: 38–42″. Width: 43–46″. Depth: 20–23″.

Locality and Period
Better factories and cabinet shops in the East and Midwest. c. 1855–80.

Comment
Smaller sideboards began to appear during the Empire era, and increased in popularity throughout the Victorian period. Their size made them especially useful in the crowded Victorian home, where an average-size room often held as many as a dozen chairs and half a dozen tables.

Hints for Collectors
In the modern home, smaller Victorian sideboards like the one shown here can provide excellent storage for stereo and television sets, and can also be used as bars or for buffet serving. An original marble top increases the desirability of these pieces.

Empire sideboard

Description
Sideboard with hinged lift top concealing interior storage area.
Alternatively, there may be 1–3 tiered drawers of varying sizes
below top. 1–3 large cupboards beneath, each with 1–2 shelves.
Front corners finished with massive turned pillars. Plain skirt.
Lion's-paw or short, turned feet. Dovetailed construction.

Materials and Dimensions
Mahogany or pine, both with mahogany veneer; also walnut,
occasionally with drawer fronts in figured maple veneer.
Secondary wood pine or poplar. Hinges: iron or brass butt. Pulls:
brass pendant ring handles; also brass, pressed-glass, or turned
wooden knobs. Escutcheons: brass plates. Height: 32–35″.
Width: 36–50″. Depth: 19–21″.

Locality and Period
New England, the Midwest, and throughout the South.
c. 1830–50.

Comment
Empire sideboards are considerably less ornate than those of the
Federal era. Like much Empire furniture, they also reflect the
development of machine production and the gradual decline of
craftsmanship. Early examples may have elaborate, well-carved
legs and pillars, while mid-century pieces are plain and
undistinguished. As a rule, Empire pieces vary little and have
few drawers and cupboards.

Hints for Collectors
Empire sideboards are usually available at reasonable prices.
Avoid pieces with missing veneer, since replacing it is difficult
and costly.

Oak bowfront sideboard

Description
Sideboard with flat, molded top bowed at front. Splashboard
(5–7″ high) with molded architectural cornice. 2–3 bowfront
drawers directly below top, with 2 large, flat 1-door cupboards
underneath. Interior sometimes has 1 shelf. Large, full-length
drawer below cupboards. Skirt often reeded, rarely shaped.
Stiles, sometimes reeded, terminate in square feet. Skirt, legs,
and feet sometimes have carved or applied decoration. Nailed
and glued construction.

Materials and Dimensions
Oak and quartersawed oak. Secondary wood, when present,
pine. Applied decoration oak. Hinges: brass or iron butt. Pulls:
brass rosette knobs, turned wooden knobs, or brass pierced
willow mounts with bail handles. Escutcheons: brass keyhole
surrounds. Height: 42–45″. Width: 47–55″. Depth: 22–25″.

Locality and Period
Large factories throughout most of the United States.
c. 1880–1930.

Comment
Less elaborate than earlier Victorian sideboards, these pieces
were designed for sale to the working classes, whose homes
could rarely accommodate the fancier specimens. Most, however,
were sturdy, well made, and more durable than their
predecessors.

Hints for Collectors
Oak sideboards like the one illustrated provide excellent storage
space with their combination of drawers and cupboards. Not
much in demand, they can often be bought for a reasonable price,
particularly in country or small-town shops.

Rococo Revival sideboard

Description
Sideboard with removable, shaped marble top. Removable, paneled backboard has scroll-cut edges and applied floral and fruit carving. Slim turned columns in front of backboard support molded, shaped shelf attached to backboard. 2 half-length drawers below top; 1 interior divided into 4 sections, the other into 2. Paneled 2-door cupboard, sometimes with 1–2 shelves. Blocked base without feet. Top corners of stiles shaped and carved in floral motif. Dovetailed, doweled, and nailed construction.

Materials and Dimensions
Walnut; sometimes rosewood or mahogany. Secondary wood pine. Hinges: iron butt. Pulls: leaf- or fruit-carved wooden handles. Escutcheons: carved, applied wood or iron keyhole surrounds. Height: 60–65″. Width: 46–50″. Depth: 18–21″.

Locality and Period
Better factories and smaller shops in the East and Midwest. c. 1850–75.

Comment
Most Victorian sideboards are in a vaguely Rococo style typified by the shaped corner stiles and, when present, the scrolled backboard.

Hints for Collectors
Because the dowels that secured them often broke off, the backboards of many Victorian sideboards have been lost. Look for 3–4 round holes at the back of the top. Even if filled, they indicate that a backboard was once attached. Another clue is a marble top not quite deep enough for the top of the sideboard. Without the original backboard, value decreases substantially.

Painted country Empire sideboard

Description
2-door sideboard with flat, molded top. Elaborate, scrolled splashboard (6–8″ high) and side boards form 3-sided gallery. Full-length drawer with S-scroll face but no handle; instead, finger grooves on underside. Large, paneled, 2-door cupboard with gadrooned moldings. No interior shelves. Plain skirt. Saw-cut S-scroll legs applied to front stiles. Front feet C-scroll form; back feet square, tapered extensions of back stiles. Dovetailed and nailed construction.

Materials and Dimensions
Pine or, rarely, poplar. Secondary wood pine or poplar. Painted and grained to imitate mahogany or rosewood. Hinges: iron butt. Pulls, when present: turned wooden knobs. Escutcheons: brass keyhole surrounds. Height: 29–31″. Width: 36–40″. Depth: 16–19″.

Locality and Period
New England west to Missouri, Texas, and most of the South. c. 1830–55.

Comment
For the most part, Empire sideboards were a good deal shorter and bulkier than their Federal counterparts. This was especially true of country versions, which usually lacked such luxurious elements as drawers for wine bottles and silver.

Hints for Collectors
Note the finely preserved graining on the piece shown here, as well as the unusual and appealing gallery. Sideboards of this sort go well with modern furnishings and are useful for storage. Unfortunately, such pieces are rather uncommon.

Description
Server with slightly overhanging top and with splashboard (4–6″ high) that is sometimes elaborately shaped. 2 full-length drawers or 2 half-length drawers over a full-length one. Low, full-length shelf below drawers slightly cut out for leg room. Turned legs extensions of stiles. Small casters or ball feet. Dovetailed and nailed construction.

Materials and Dimensions
Maple, walnut, cherry, or pine; tiger or bird's-eye maple less common. Occasionally, drawer fronts in crotch mahogany or burl walnut. Secondary wood pine or poplar. Pine examples may be stained; pine or poplar pieces may be painted red, yellow, blue, or gray, or sponged or grained. Pulls: turned wooden knobs; occasionally round brass or pressed-glass knobs. Casters, when present: brass. Height: 37–42″. Width: 34–44″. Depth: 18–22″.

Locality and Period
New England west to the Mississippi River and throughout the South. c. 1820–50.

Comment
Servers or serving tables of this type were produced by many rural cabinetmakers. Early examples reflect Sheraton influence, while mid-century pieces begin to take on a Victorian appearance.

Hints for Collectors
Empire servers are relatively easy to find and not too expensive, so look for the best examples, those with highly grained woods or original paint, particularly sponging or graining. Many servers had no splashboard or only a simple, curved one, so make sure the splashboard is original and not a later addition. Raw wood, nails, or uneven wear may indicate that it is new.

Empire square-leg server

Description
Small server with flat, slightly overhanging top and shaped splashboard (5–7″ high). 2 half-length drawers over slightly deeper full-length drawer. Sides solid panels; back single nailed-on board. Legs turned block-and-disk extensions of end posts. Short blunt arrow feet. Dovetailed and nailed construction.

Materials and Dimensions
Cherry or walnut; also pine with cherry or walnut veneer. Drawer fronts often with curly maple or bird's-eye veneer. Secondary wood pine. Pulls: pressed-glass or turned wooden knobs. Escutcheons, when present: brass keyhole surrounds. Height: 33–36″. Width: 36–38″. Depth: 16–18″.

Locality and Period
New England, New York, and Pennsylvania west to Ohio, south to Maryland. c. 1825–55.

Comment
The turned block-and-disk leg is characteristic of much Empire furniture, especially the tables, desks, and servers made in the Northeast during the second quarter of the 19th century. The thicker legs balance the heavy bodies characteristic of Empire pieces and add interest to otherwise ordinary forms.

Hints for Collectors
Examples with a light-figured veneer and glass knobs against a darker background are often the most attractive. Similar pieces in solid cherry or walnut are usually far less interesting. But be sure the veneered drawers are original. If they fit poorly or show signs of having been shortened or reworked, they may have come from another piece.

Painted country Federal server

Description
Small server with overhanging top and splashboard. Top with elaborately shaped front edge; splashboard (4–6″ high) similarly shaped. Deep, plain skirt has centered rectangular drawer. Very thin, square, tapered legs. Dovetailed and nailed construction.

Materials and Dimensions
Usually maple, birch, or other hardwood. Top pine. Better examples elaborately grained or painted to imitate period inlay and veneer; less often, painted solid colors. Pulls: round wooden knobs or brass rosette knobs. Escutcheons, when present: brass keyhole surrounds. Height: 33–36″. Width: 26–29″. Depth: 18–20″.

Locality and Period
New England, New York, and Pennsylvania. c. 1810–40.

Comment
The piece shown here is far too fine to be considered typical of painted country Federal servers. However, it typically reflects the country cabinetmaker's efforts to duplicate with paint the satinwood veneers and boxwood or holly stringing often found on Hepplewhite and Sheraton serving pieces. Especially noteworthy in the example illustrated are the oblong medallions at each side of the front drawer. They not only imitate satinwood but also reflect the placement of the wine cupboards in a large sideboard.

Hints for Collectors
The piece shown, with its finely executed, well-preserved paint, is an example of the best in painted furniture. Such a piece is generally one of a kind, and an owner can often name the price. Less valuable examples may be painted in solid colors or refinished, and will lack the quality of line and construction seen in this piece.

Mission-style server

Description
Shallow server with flat, unmolded, square-cornered top.
Splashboard (3–4″ high) mortised into square extensions of back
posts. 2–3 drawers across front, directly beneath top. Plain,
open shelf supported by stretchers 6–8″ above floor. Square-cut
legs extensions of corner stiles. Mortise-and-tenon construction.

Materials and Dimensions
Oak and quartersawed oak. Pulls: brass or copper oblong or
rectangular mounts with bail handles. Height: 35–37″. Width:
37–40″. Depth: 15–16″.

Locality and Period
Small shops and larger factories in New York and Michigan.
c. 1900–25.

Comment
In their extreme simplicity of line, these servers have far more
in common with similar pieces from the Federal era than with
the elaborate servers of the Empire and Victorian periods. And
like Federal serving tables, their function is serving rather than
storage.

Hints for Collectors
While oak furniture in this style might have been fumed or given
a dark finish, it would never have been painted. It might,
however, have acquired several coats of paint later on. To
recognize a piece of Mission oak under all that paint and perhaps
with replacement hardware requires a knowledge of its basic
forms: the square blocky shapes, the mortise-and-tenon
construction, and the lack of screws and nails so common on
other oak.

Hepplewhite serving table

Description
Shallow serving table with overhanging, plain or shaped and molded top; rare examples have serpentine front. Single drawer across front. Alternatively, single drawer across 1 end, with matching false drawer in opposite end. Drawer fronts and frames may have inlaid oval panels. Plain skirt. Square, tapered legs, often with stringing. Feet square extensions of legs. Dovetailed construction.

Materials and Dimensions
Mahogany, walnut, cherry, or maple; veneer, when present, satinwood, rosewood, or figured maple. Secondary wood pine or poplar. Drawer fronts and legs with boxwood or holly stringing. Pulls: round or oval brass mounts with bail handles. Escutcheons: brass plates or keyhole surrounds. Height: 29–31″. Width: 38–44″. Depth: 19–21″.

Locality and Period
New England west to Ohio, south to the Carolinas. c. 1785–1815.

Comment
Most serving tables had a single full-length drawer. In the piece shown here, the narrow drawer in 1 end is an interesting variation, especially with its matching, false-drawer front at the opposite end. With the bodies of these pieces so shallow, there is little room for decoration, and most Hepplewhite serving tables show only a simple oval inlay and the usual stringing.

Hints for Collectors
Distinguishing a serving table from the common side table may be difficult, particularly since there is often little information about how a piece was used. The term "serving table" is usually applied to a piece that has only a single tier of drawers and is much longer than it is deep.

Sheraton serving table

Description
Narrow serving table with overhanging, plain or shaped and molded top. Single full-length or 2 half-length drawers across front. Drawer fronts may be veneered but not inlaid. Ring-turned and reeded legs, tapered or swelling gently at bottom. Small ball feet, sometimes with brass casters. Dovetailed construction.

Materials and Dimensions
Mahogany, cherry, walnut, or curly or tiger maple. Occasionally cherry body with drawers in curly maple veneer. Secondary wood pine or poplar. Pulls: plain brass rosettes or oblong mounts, both with bail handles. Escutcheons: matching brass. Height: 34–36″. Width: 36–40″. Depth: 18–21″.

Locality
New England, New York, and Pennsylvania, south to Maryland. c. 1790–1810.

Comment
The serving table antedates both the sideboard and the server, having first appeared in the Queen Anne era, though such early examples are very rare. By the Chippendale period, serving tables were fairly numerous, and most had Chinese-style square legs. The tables attained their greatest popularity during the Federal epoch, and many, in both Hepplewhite and Sheraton forms, may be found today.

Hints for Collectors
The serving table is an attractive and handy dining room piece. Since it is relatively unfamiliar to many collectors, it can often be purchased quite reasonably. Look for the more delicate examples, such as the one shown here, with long, tapered legs, but make sure the legs have not been broken and repaired.

Sheraton server

Description
Small server with square-cornered, overhanging, stepped top with 3 small drawers. Base has 2–3 full-length drawers. Skirt plain or slightly valanced. Legs plain or turned and reeded in Sheraton manner. Turned ball feet or casters. Dovetailed construction.

Materials and Dimensions
Mahogany, cherry, walnut, apple, or flame maple; occasionally cherry and maple in combination. Drawer fronts may have burl walnut or bird's-eye maple veneer. Secondary wood pine, cedar, or poplar. Pulls: oval brass mounts with bail handles or brass rosettes with loop handles. Escutcheons: brass plates. Casters, when present: brass. Height: 36–40″. Width: 32–36″. Depth: 18–22″.

Locality and Period
New England west to Ohio, south to Virginia. c. 1790–1820.

Comment
These servers stand midway between the simple serving table with 1 or no drawers and the complex Federal sideboard with numerous drawers, cupboards, and other storage spaces. Linens and silver were kept in the drawers, while dishes were put on top. Sheraton servers were relatively small, allowing them to fit in the dining rooms of the growing merchant class.

Hints for Collectors
Most modern homes have no room for a large Federal sideboard, but the smaller servers like this one are well suited to contemporary settings. Relatively common, these pieces are worth looking for, especially when they retain their original brasses and veneer. Examples with bird's-eye maple veneer on the drawer fronts are particularly desirable today.

31 Colonial Revival sideboard

Description
Small sideboard with unmolded, overhanging, flat top, shaped to conform to front stiles and drawers. Short center drawer bowed and flanked by 1-door cupboards. Interiors without shelves. Below drawer, simple scrolled skirt. Plain board sides. 6 square legs taper to block or Marlborough feet. Nailed and glued construction, sometimes with dovetails.

Materials and Dimensions
Mahogany with flame mahogany veneer over pine. Secondary wood oak. Hinges: iron or brass butt. Pulls: brass rosettes with circular handles. Escutcheons: brass plates. Height: 33–35″. Width: 46–49″. Depth: 23–25″.

Locality and Period
Large factories in the East and Midwest. c. 1900–30.

Comment
Small Colonial Revival sideboards like this one were a kind of compromise between the desire for 18th-century styling and the limited space in many 20th-century homes. The sideboards had a vaguely Federal look and, with their cupboards and drawers, were extremely practical.

Hints for Collectors
A Colonial Revival piece, as opposed to an authentic period one, will be made with much thinner boards, often bearing the marks from a circular saw, which was introduced around 1840. In addition, it will have thin brass pulls and will be joined with wire nails. Where dovetails exist, they will be narrow, uniform, and machine-made.

Hepplewhite tambour sideboard

Description
Sideboard with slightly overhanging, unmolded top that
conforms to shape of bowed center section. Central bowfront
drawer over 2 tambour doors, set in an arch, and opening on
interior storage space. At right, 1 deep drawer, made to look like
2, with interior divided into 12 bottle storage units. At left, 1
shallow, rectangular drawer above 1 deeper drawer of equal
width. Drawer fronts decorated with oval designs in light-colored
wood. Plain skirt. 6 square, tapered, inlaid legs. Spade feet.
Dovetailed and mortise-and-tenon construction.

Materials and Dimensions
Mahogany. Secondary wood pine. Tambour rods mahogany.
Inlay and stringing boxwood. Hinges: brass butt. Pulls: oval
brass mounts with bail handles and small brass knobs.
Escutcheons: brass keyhole surrounds. Height: 40–42″. Width:
67–71″. Depth: 24–27″.

Locality and Period
New England west to Ohio and throughout the South Atlantic
states. c. 1790–1810.

Comment
Most Hepplewhite sideboards do not have tambour doors. Of
those that do, the most common form has doors in the center, but
the doors may also flank the central cupboard. The 6-legged
support system is usual, and necessary, with all but the smallest
sideboards.

Hints for Collectors
Smaller sideboards like this are far more suited to contemporary
needs and homes than larger ones. With any tambour-doored
piece, avoid examples with extensive damage to the tambours;
repairs can be very expensive.

Hepplewhite serpentine and bowfront sideboard

Description
Sideboard with serpentine center, bowed ends, and molded top. Center section with long, shallow drawer over 2-door cupboard, flanked by 2 tall bottle drawers; side sections with shallow drawer over 1-door cupboard. In some examples, 1 side drawer and cupboard are replaced by large, deep drawer. Plain skirt. 6 or, rarely, 8 square, tapered legs, often with bellflower inlay. Feet square extensions of legs. Inlays include oval, fan, and eagle forms. Dovetailed construction.

Materials and Dimensions
Light and dark mahogany or satinwood veneer and mahogany; rarely maple or walnut. Secondary wood pine or poplar. Inlay satinwood or bird's-eye maple; stringing holly or boxwood. Hinges: brass butt. Pulls: oval or oblong brass mounts or oval rosettes, both with bail handles. Escutcheons: brass plates. Height: 40–43″. Width: 72–80″. Depth: 27–29″.

Locality and Period
Southern New England west to Pennsylvania, south to Maryland. c. 1790–1815.

Comment
Complex sideboards were much in style at the close of the 18th century. Serpentine, oxbow, and bowed fronts were available, as well as examples combining all 3 types. All, however, conformed to the basic pattern of drawers over cupboards, with smaller versions often omitting the bottle drawers.

Hints for Collectors
Elaborate Federal sideboards, such as the one shown here, are rare. Do not confuse them with the many reproductions made between 1880 and 1930. The latter have machine-cut boards, wire nails, and factory-stamped brasses.

Description
Sideboard with bowed front and slightly overhanging, flat top.
Center section has long drawer above 2-door cupboard, flanked
by tall bottle drawers. Rarely, center cupboard has tambour
slide. Both end sections have shorter drawer above 1-door
cupboard. Plain skirt. 6 tapered, turned, and reeded legs with
blunt feet. May have inlay and stringing. Dovetailed construction.

Materials and Dimensions
Mahogany with crotch mahogany veneer; also mahogany with
satinwood veneer or cherry with curly maple veneer; rarely
maple with mahogany veneer. Secondary wood pine or maple.
Inlay satinwood; stringing boxwood or holly. Hinges: brass butt.
Pulls: brass lion's-head pendant rings or rosette knobs.
Escutcheons: brass plates or keyhole surrounds. Height: 40–43″.
Width: 60–68″. Depth: 24–26″.

Locality and Period
New England, New York, and Pennsylvania, south to Maryland
and Virginia. c. 1795–1820.

Comment
Sideboards reached their greatest popularity during the half
century from 1790 to 1840. Early examples were relatively small
in size, but by the end of the Federal period they had become
both complex and massive, with various drawers and cupboards
for the many necessities of the sophisticated and well-to-do
diner.

Hints for Collectors
Sideboards vary greatly in length. Not all are 5′ long or more,
and the shorter ones often have 4 legs, rather than the
customary 6. Note that sideboards differ from servers in that
they always have at least 1 cupboard.

Arts and Crafts sideboard

Description
Long sideboard with flat, molded top, battened at each end.
Low, shaped splashboard at rear. 2 long, graduated central
drawers flanked by 1-door cupboards. Front has decorative
inserts in ebonized wood; cupboard doors ebony-bordered, with
decorative inlay of flowering plants. 8 legs extensions of stiles.
Feet slightly tapered, square, joined by box stretchers of wide
boards pierced with horizontal slots and mounted vertically.
Pegged mortise-and-tenon construction.

Materials and Dimensions
Mahogany. Ebony pegs and decorative banding. Inlay fruitwood
and gemstone fragments. Hinges: metal butt. Pulls: rectangular
mahogany handles with ebony inlay. Latches: bronze. Height:
39–40″. Width: 79–81″. Depth: 23–24″.

Locality and Period
Southern California. c. 1908–10.

Comment
This piece was designed by Charles Sumner Greene and Henry
Mather Greene. They were greatly influenced by the English
Arts and Crafts movement, which emphasized fine workmanship
and the use of superior materials. As West Coast designers,
however, Greene and Greene were also influenced by Oriental
taste, and in its general lines, this piece owes a debt to the East.

Hints for Collectors
This sideboard was custom-made and an exact duplicate will not
be found. However, it reflects a school of West Coast design that
spawned a variety of imitators. Although few pieces are as fine
as the one illustrated here, West Coast collectors should be on
the lookout for related examples that stress quality
workmanship.

Description
Plain serving table with flat, unmolded top. Low, full-length shelf rests on shaped battens protruding from sides. Rectangular sides have square center cutouts. No skirt. Steel caps on base; no feet. Glued and screwed construction.

Materials and Dimensions
Pine; shelf solid mahogany. Lacquered white, except shelf. Height: 28–29″. Width: 72–74″. Depth: 21–23″.

Locality and Period
Better-quality manufacturers in the East and Midwest. c. 1930–45.

Comment
When serving tables fell out of fashion in this country, they were replaced by sideboards and servers. They all but disappeared during the 19th century, only to reappear in the 20th. The example illustrated is characteristic of the very plain but elegant pieces from the Art Deco epoch. Particularly sophisticated is the combination of white lacquer and mahogany.

Hints for Collectors
Tables this size are usually too large for the modern home, so be sure to check the space you have available before buying one. Since most have extremely plain lines, better pieces are distinguished by the use of rare woods, such as mahogany, and the quality of the lacquer work. As with all 20th-century furniture, the name of the designer and the manufacturer are often important in evaluating a given piece. Serving tables by designers like Frankl or from companies like Herman Miller bring a premium. Look for makers' paper or metal labels or stamped marks underneath the top.

Description
Long, shallow sideboard with flat top; on each end, tall
columnlike storage units terminating in open cornice. Storage
units have 2 open shelves above 4 shallow drawers and narrow
2-door cupboard below, all resting on ebonized, plinthlike base.
Large central 2-door cupboard below serving area has 2–3
interior shelves. Smaller, flanking cupboards have 1–2 shelves.
Nailed and glued construction.

Materials and Dimensions
Gray maple and gray maple veneer over pine. Secondary wood
pine. Plywood back. Serving area surface and edges of some
stiles and stretchers finished in green lacquer. Hinges: brass
butt. Pulls: rectangular brass handles. Height: 70–72″. Width:
94–98″. Depth: 14–17″.

Locality and Period
Major factories in the East and Midwest. c. 1925–40.

Comment
The piece illustrated here was designed for mass production by
Jules Bouy, one of the many European furniture designers who
came to the United States after World War I. Though it has a
somewhat spectacular, towerlike design, its purpose is
thoroughly conventional. Like 19th-century sideboards, it
combines a flat, unencumbered serving area with a combination
of storage cupboards and drawers.

Hints for Collectors
Twentieth-century Art Deco sideboards are relatively rare,
especially good-size examples. Examples by known designers,
like Bouy, whose work is identifiable, are worth more than pieces
by unknown designers, and some can fetch substantial sums.

Modern molded-plywood sideboard

Description
Curvilinear sideboard with unmolded, slightly overhanging top.
Backboard (2″ high) has 2 graduated, rectangular shelves with
curved corners. Both supported by D-shaped brackets. Body is a
single piece of steamed and bent plywood cut into 3 flush doors.
Narrow center door opens on 3 drawers lined with green baize.
Side doors conceal cupboards, each with 4 removable shelves.
Molded and slightly overhanging base with plain skirt. Legs
splayed and tapered toward ground. Glued and screwed
construction.

Materials and Dimensions
Plywood (maple) steamed, bent, and cut to shape. Hinges: steel
butt. Pulls: rectangular maple blocks. Height: 52–54″. Width:
47–49″. Depth: 18–19″.

Locality and Period
A limited number of factories in the East and Midwest.
c. 1940–50.

Comment
The development of molded plywood allowed for the creation of
sleek, modern furniture that was both strong and lightweight.
The example illustrated was made by Thayer-Jordan, but similar
pieces came from a number of different factories.

Hints for Collectors
Though of relatively recent vintage, molded-plywood furniture is
already attracting collector interest, in part because of the
attention given designer Charles Eames's laminated chairs. As
with all fairly recent designs, the most sought after are the early
prototypes. Later pieces are usually not as valuable.

Desks and Low Secretaries

The earliest American desks evolved from simple, sturdy boxes made in the 17th century by the first settlers. Most of these are constructed from 6 or 7 plain boards, although more elaborate examples have geometric or floral carving or painted decoration (41). These pieces are often referred to as Bible boxes because the treasured family Bible might be kept in them, but it seems likely that important papers and other small valuables were also stored there. These boxes have either flat or slanting tops and were placed for convenient use on tables or benches. The top of the slanting form could be used as a writing surface.

As the colonists gradually settled into more permanent homes, their furnishings took on increasingly substantial forms. Typical of this evolution was the addition of legs to the slant-top box to form the desk-on-frame (46). Perhaps the best-known example of this form, the schoolmaster's desk (45), developed later in the 19th century. Many 20th-century variations, including a Mission-style version (48), are based on this simple desk.

An even larger form, known as the bureau desk, developed during the William and Mary period (55). It combines the slant-top box with a lower chest of drawers. At first the lid of the box was hinged at the top, but later the hinges were moved to the bottom so that the lid could fall forward to provide a convenient writing surface. Initially, pull-out slides supported the open lid, but later chains or folding hinges served the same purpose. Besides the writing area, the interior of each box houses numerous useful pigeonholes and small drawers. The bureau desk proved so practical that it remains the basic desk form today. While most have straight fronts, others have serpentine, oxbow, block, or bowed fronts.

During the Chippendale period, the kneehole desk (66) developed. This innovative form, which made it easier to sit close to the desk, was especially popular in the Victorian period. Most Victorian examples have a flat top resting on 2 pedestals that contain drawers and storage areas. A variation of the kneehole desk that is much sought after today is the rolltop desk (64), which developed from the tambour models (68) of the Federal period. In the Federal pieces, the storage area above the writing surface was occasionally concealed by tambour doors, composed of thin wooden slats mounted vertically on a cloth backing. In a tambour piece, the doors open toward the sides, and in the rolltop desk, the door rolls up.

In the 20th century, desks differ more in the use of new materials than in design innovations. They are sometimes lacquered (76) and incorporate a host of modern materials, including tubular steel and glass. Yet most modern forms are in fact adaptations of late 19th-century designs. For the most part, 20th-century desks are smaller and less complex than those from the 19th century, reflecting a society in which the telephone, typewriter, and computer have made writing and file-keeping a less arduous task.

Most of the desks available to the collector today are either handcrafted high-style pieces or factory-made examples from the 19th and 20th centuries; the few that were made by rural carpenters are chiefly variations of the desk-on-frame. Collectors interested in country furnishings, however, can seek out Shaker desks (60), marked by the characteristic Shaker simplicity and ingenuity.

Desk or Bible box

Description
Low box with hinged, slightly overhanging top that has molded edge. Top lifts to reveal well. Plain board front, sides, and bottom. Almost always decorated. Dovetailed or nailed 6-board construction.

Materials and Dimensions
Oak; sometimes walnut. Top and/or bottom pine. Typically painted, as shown here, with scalloped border, heart motifs, date, and initials; may also have geometric designs. Hinges: iron snipe. Escutcheons: brass plates. Height: 9–12″. Width: 24–26″. Depth: 16–18″.

Locality and Period
New England to Pennsylvania. c. 1700–1835.

Comment
This type of plain, flat-topped box endured well into the 19th century. Such pieces are sometimes called survivals because they are a late form of a much earlier type. The date, initials, and decoration indicate that the piece illustrated here was made as a special order rather than as part of the cabinetmaker's regular stock.

Hints for Collectors
This interesting old box illustrates a typical collector's dilemma. The decoration, date, and paint are in excellent condition and make the piece highly desirable. On the other hand, the unbattened top is warped, possibly beyond repair, and the bottom is badly affected with dry rot. These problems, which would require a substantial amount of restoration, need to be reflected in the price paid for such a piece.

William and Mary inlaid desk box

Description
Low table-top box with hinged, slightly overhanging lift top that has molded edge. Top and sides inlaid with compass-drawn vine and berry motifs in contrasting, light-colored wood. Protruding, molded base. Feet, when present, ball-shaped. Nailed or dovetailed 6-board construction.

Materials and Dimensions
Usually walnut; also maple or pine, the latter stained red, or walnut with pine top. Inlay birch, apple, or boxwood. Hinges: iron butt or snipe; rarely, butterfly. Escutcheons: iron or brass circles. Height: 6–8″. Width: 20–22″. Depth: 16–18″.

Locality and Period
New England west to Pennsylvania, south to Delaware. c. 1690–1750.

Comment
These large, flat-topped boxes, commonly referred to as Bible boxes, may have been used to store the family Bible and, probably, important papers as well. Some examples have the ball-shaped feet associated with the William and Mary period. The use of inlay similar to that found on period chests indicates the importance of these boxes in the home; inlay was time-consuming, expensive work reserved for the most valued pieces.

Hints for Collectors
Many boxes and small chests that originally had feet have lost them over the years. Holes at the bottom corners of a box, or differences in the way the wood has aged, may mark the location of the feet. By examining those holes, a knowledgeable restorer can even identify the type of feet the piece had.

Carved desk or Bible box

Description
Low storage box with hinged, overhanging lid. Lid has
thumbnail molding and a molded batten on underside of each
end. Front and sometimes sides and top decorated with notch- or
gouge-carved lunettes, stars, and vine and floral forms; box may
also be inscribed with initials and/or dates. Dovetailed or nailed
6-board construction.

Materials and Dimensions
Oak with pine lid and bottom; sometimes entirely pine, or oak
with maple top. Originally may have been stained red, green,
black, or brown. Hinges: iron snipe or butt, or wooden pins
attached through battens. Escutcheons, when present: iron
oblongs or diamonds. Height: 8–10″. Width: 25–27″. Depth:
14–15″.

Locality and Period
New England, primarily Massachusetts and Connecticut.
c. 1640–1700.

Comment
The flat-top desk box was an earlier development than the slope-
lid form and was generally more difficult to work at. Although
these pieces are often referred to as Bible boxes, the almost
invariable presence of a lock may indicate that more often they
were used to store money and valuables.

Hints for Collectors
Flat-top boxes decorated with the type of carving seen here were
made in Europe as well as America and have been imported in
substantial numbers. Foreign pieces often have unusually
elaborate decoration and are, of course, made of foreign woods.
17th-century desk boxes are expensive; don't buy one without a
guarantee of American origin.

42 Slope-lid desk box

Description
Low box with molded, slightly overhanging, sloped lid. Lid
hinged at rear to flat top 3–4″ deep, and opens to reveal storage
well. Flared, molded base. May be decorated with gouge-carved
stars, interlacing lunettes, or geometric devices; rare examples
bear dates and initials. Nailed or dovetailed construction.

Materials and Dimensions
Oak with pine lid and bottom; rarely oak with maple top; some
examples all oak. Some may have red or black stain. Hinges: iron
butterfly (as here) or snipe, or wooden pins. Escutcheons, when
present: iron oblongs. Height: 8–10″. Width: 18–20″. Depth:
14–16″.

Locality and Period
New England, primarily Massachusetts and Connecticut.
c. 1650–1700.

Comment
The slope-lid writing desk is the forerunner of the modern slant-
front desk and was for many years the only writing surface
available in most homes. Later, similar boxes were supported by
legs, creating the desk-on-frame.

Hints for Collectors
Note the distinction between the slope-lid and the slant-front
desk. The former is hinged at the top and lifts up. The latter is
hinged at the bottom and falls forward to form a writing surface.
The slant-front desk is clearly more practical. Slope-lid boxes
from the 17th century are extremely rare today, and most are
now in museum collections.

Countinghouse desk

Description
Large, boxlike desk with 2-piece, sloped (25–30° angle) lift top. Large writing flap hinged at back to wide (5–8″), full-length board. Interior well without dividers or with 2–4 large pigeonholes. Often 1 full-length drawer below well. Plain board sides. Plain skirt. Turned legs are extensions of stiles; no stretchers. Ball feet. Dovetailed or nailed construction.

Materials and Dimensions
Pine or, less often, pine body and maple or other hardwood legs; later and rarely, oak or walnut. Typically painted red, blue, brown, or black; also sponged, oak-grained, or varnished. Hinges: iron butt. Escutcheons, when present: iron keyhole surrounds. Height: 30–37″. Width: 33–42″. Depth: 27–32″.

Locality and Period
The East. c. 1820–80. Rarely the West and Southwest. c. 1870–1900.

Comment
Countinghouse (that is, office) or store desks were once common in almost every shop and office. The addition of a large cupboard converted them into the more unusual plantation desks. Although they resemble schoolmaster's desks, countinghouse desks are distinguished by being substantially taller and wider. The writer must usually use a high stool.

Hints for Collectors
Because they are large and not particularly useful—except in restaurants, where they can serve as a host's or head waiter's post—these are among the more reasonably priced desks. Look for the better examples, which will have divided interiors and a single drawer below the well. Original paint, particularly sponging or graining, will also enhance desirability.

Shaker child's desk

Description
Small, delicately made desk with slightly angled lift top, hinged at back to a 3–4″ wide, full-length board. Molded desk top lifts to reveal undivided well. Single shallow, full-length drawer on both sides. Skirt plain or slightly valanced at front, plain on sides. Square, tapered legs. Dovetailed, pegged, and nailed construction.

Materials and Dimensions
Pine; occasionally walnut, cherry, maple, or butternut. Secondary wood pine. Natural finish or stained red or yellow. Hinges: iron butt. Pulls: brass or turned wooden knobs. Escutcheons: iron keyhole surrounds. Height: 28–33″. Width: 25–29″. Depth: 18–20″.

Locality and Period
Shaker communities from New England west to Indiana. c. 1815–75.

Comment
Although it resembles a schoolmaster's desk, this Shaker piece has the characteristic Shaker touches. With most schoolmaster's desks, the writer must move back after opening the single full-length drawer across the front; here the typical Shaker side drawers make that unnecessary.

Hints for Collectors
Unusual drawer arrangements may mark an otherwise unidentified piece as Shaker. Since the Shakers disliked clutter, their furniture had many drawers, some in quite unexpected places.

Schoolmaster's desk

Description
Tall desk with 2-part lift top: sloping lid attached by hinges at rear to a 3–5″ wide horizontal board fastened to sides. Lift top may have molding at lower edge to hold papers and a low gallery at top rear. Interior may contain 2–5 pigeonholes. 1 full-length drawer usually present. Legs square and tapered from top or turned. Square or flattened ball feet. Stretchers, when present, are of box variety. Decorative molding occasionally present. Nailed or dovetailed construction.

Materials and Dimensions
Pine; rarely walnut. Legs maple or cherry. Often painted red, brown, black, or green. Hinges: iron butt. Pulls, when present: turned wooden pins or simple brass knobs. Escutcheons, when present: brass or cut bone plates. Height: 36–46″. Width: 26–32″. Depth: 21–27″.

Locality and Period
Maine west to Missouri and throughout the South. c. 1800–1900.

Comment
This desk takes its name from its widespread use in rural schoolhouses. Designed to be worked at from a stool or while standing, it is essentially late Federal in style with Victorian touches. Most were plainly made by rural craftsmen.

Hints for Collectors
This common and relatively inexpensive desk form is impractical unless you plan to use a high stool with it. Look for good, original paint. And like many desk-on-frames, well-formed examples are relatively uncommon; most appear top-heavy.

William and Mary desk-on-frame

Description
Slant-top writing box on turned frame. Box either attached to frame or removable from base molding. Lift top hinged at rear to fold back or at front to fall forward and rest on 2 pull-out slides, and may conceal 3–4 interior compartments. Base of box with 1–3 storage drawers. Legs turned in vase-and-disk or trumpet style, with box or X-shaped stretchers. Early examples have carved front and may have applied bosses and spindles; later examples stained red or, rarely, painted in floral motifs. Early boxes paneled; later examples dovetailed or nailed.

Materials and Dimensions
Oak; rarely walnut. Secondary wood pine or tulip poplar. Spindles and bosses ebonized maple. Hinges: iron snipe or iron or brass butt. Pulls: turned wooden pins; also brass teardrop pulls or batwing mounts with bail handles. Escutcheons: matching brass. Height: 32–36″. Width: 30–34″. Depth: 28–33″.

Locality and Period
New England and Pennsylvania. c. 1700–20.

Comment
This rare desk-on-frame was a logical extension of the desk box. The example shown, which is attached to a base similar to that of a period tavern table, is an especially good example of the transition. In many desk-on-frames the writing box is flush with the base.

Hints for Collectors
Carefully examine the construction of any desk-on-frame. Wear on the bottom of the box section may indicate that the writing box was not originally attached to the frame. There are only a few dozen known William and Mary desk-on-frames, so each one should have an authenticated history.

Description
Slant-top writing-box-on-frame. Lift top folds back or drops
forward onto 2 pull-out slides to reveal 5–8 drawers and
compartments. Writing box usually made in 1 piece with base,
although 2-piece examples are known. Base or frame may have a
drawer. Legs straight or reeded; stretchers, when present, box
or H type. Dovetailed or nailed construction.

Materials and Dimensions
Maple, walnut, or cherry. Secondary wood pine, cedar, or
poplar. Originally painted red, black, or green; occasionally with
floral decoration. Hinges: brass or iron butt. Pulls: turned
wooden pins; also brass rosettes or willow mounts, both with bail
handles. Escutcheons: matching brass. Interior pulls: small brass
knobs. Height: 37–40″. Width: 30–34″. Depth: 17–19″.

Locality and Period
New England south to Maryland and Virginia, west to Ohio.
c. 1770–1800.

Comment
The desk-on-frame survived long in rural areas, where tastes
changed slowly. Queen Anne and Federal examples are similarly
constructed and usually made by country cabinetmakers, who
used native woods that were often stained. Most are rather
crudely constructed.

Hints for Collectors
As with all desk-on-frames, beware of made-up pieces. Quality of
construction is the key to value. Look for well-turned legs, good
structure, and fine dovetailing. Proportions are very important:
many of these pieces are poorly balanced and look crude. A
delicate piece with old paint is a true find.

Mission-style slant-front desk

Description
Shallow desk on stand. Flat, unmolded top surrounded on 3 sides
by low (1–2″) gallery. Rear stiles, tapering to blunt-pointed ends,
rise 2–3″ above gallery. Steeply pitched desk lid falls forward
and is supported by interior hinges. Well has 5–7 pigeonholes
and 2 drawers. Front stiles frame a full-length drawer and
terminate above it in blunt points. Slightly arched skirt. Legs
extensions of square stiles; stretchers at sides and rear. Shaped
trestle feet. Mortise-and-tenon, nailed, and glued construction.

Materials and Dimensions
Oak. Sometimes pine secondary wood present. Hinges: brass or
iron butt. Pulls: copper or brass plates with circular bail handles.
Escutcheons: copper or brass plates. Applied decorative
elements (as seen here): matching copper or brass. Height:
44–48″. Width: 29–32″. Depth: 16–18″.

Locality and Period
Factories in the East and Midwest. c. 1905–25.

Comment
The use of purely decorative metal elements, such as the
straplike pieces on the front of this desk, is characteristic of
earlier and better-quality Mission-style furnishings. Later pieces
tend to be much plainer.

Hints for Collectors
Beware of plain pieces that have had decoration added to make
them look like more expensive examples. Pulls that do not match
the holes in the drawers and accessories that look new or out of
character are clues to this kind of deception.

Mission-style slant-front desk

Description
Tall, shallow desk with flat top surrounded by 3-sided gallery.
Solid board sides, 5–7″ deep at top, angle out to depth of 25–27″
where paneled lid is attached. Lid falls forward on metal hinges
to reveal well. Interior has 1 central drawer and 4–6
pigeonholes. Full-length drawer below fall front. Recessed (1–2″)
bookshelf directly above feet, which are cutout extensions of side
boards. Glued and screwed construction.

Materials and Dimensions
Ebonized maple, oak, or ash; also other hardwoods. Secondary
wood pine or maple. Hinges: brass or iron butt. Pulls: brass
handles or turned wooden knobs. Escutcheons: brass ovals,
applied vertically. Folding lid hinges: brass. Height: 45–48″.
Width: 25–27″. Depth: 13–15″.

Locality and Period
Manufacturers in the East and Midwest. c. 1900–20.

Comment
Tall, shallow desks like this one reflect the Arts and Crafts style
popular in England at the turn of the century and influential in
the designs of American furniture makers like Elbert Hubbard
and Gustav Stickley. Combining simplicity of construction with
sophisticated design, such pieces were too advanced for most
contemporary consumers.

Hints for Collectors
The desk shown here was designed by Gustav Stickley and sold
by the Boston firm of Cobb Eastman. Although signed pieces by
Stickley are fairly expensive, desks like this one from mass
producers are usually good buys.

Arts and Crafts slant-front desk

Description
Tall, shallow desk with flat, unmolded top. Slightly slanted battened front falls forward to reveal interior well with pigeonholes of various sizes. Below, full-length drawer above 2-door cupboard. Cupboard doors have applied decorative boards. Boards, front battens, and sides have small, round wooden bosses. Sides: 2 boards joined with Dutch patches rise above top. Plain skirt. Feet, with shallow cutouts, extensions of side boards. Screwed construction.

Materials and Dimensions
Ash. Natural finish. Hinges: steel butt. Pulls: horizontal wooden bars. Escutcheons: rectangular wooden blocks placed horizontally or vertically. Height: 50–51″. Width: 31–32″. Depth: 16–17″.

Locality and Period
California. c. 1900–1910.

Comment
The piece illustrated here was made by the California designer Charles Sumner Greene. It represents a blending of English Arts and Crafts theory with the work of Gustav Stickley, as well as Greene's own concern with Chinese furniture design. Although a one-of-a-kind piece, it reflects advanced design concepts that later influenced mass-produced furnishings.

Hints for Collectors
Note Greene's use of small, round wooden bosses to cover the heads of the screws holding this piece together. At a later date almost all factory-made Mission-style furniture was designed in this way—giving the illusion of handcrafting where none actually existed.

Queen Anne slant-front desk

Description
Flat-top bureau desk with battened lid that falls forward onto 2 pull-out slides to reveal well. Interior has 6–10 pigeonholes with scrolled tops, in varying sizes, above 2 rows of 8–12 small drawers with molded fronts. Occasionally, central locker or cupboard, with paneled or sunburst-carved door, concealing 4–6 small, plain drawers. Below well, 3–4 equal or graduated drawers. Base molded, protruding 1–2″. Skirt plain or, occasionally, with carved central finial. Plain bracket feet. Dovetailed, pegged, and nailed construction.

Materials and Dimensions
Cherry, maple, curly maple, birch, or walnut. Secondary wood pine or poplar. Sometimes stained red. Hinges: iron butt. Pulls: brass batwing or willow mounts with bail handles. Escutcheons: matching or circular brass. Interior pulls: small brass knobs. Height: 38–43″. Width: 35–42″. Depth: 20–21″.

Locality and Period
New England west to Pennsylvania, south to Georgia. c. 1730–60.

Comment
Much plainer than its William and Mary predecessor, the Queen Anne slant-front desk was the prototype for writing desks well into the Empire period. Prior to the 1830s most changes were primarily cosmetic rather than structural.

Hints for Collectors
Queen Anne desks are often similar on the outside, but the interior work distinguishes exceptional pieces from the ordinary Well-carved lockers and scrolled pigeonholes mark the outstanding examples, provided, of course, that the work is original to the piece.

Description
Miniature slant-front bureau desk with hinged lid that falls forward onto 2 disproportionately large pull-out slides to form writing surface. Plain interior has 6–10 drawers and arched pigeonholes. Below well, 2–3 drawers. Base heavily molded. Plain bracket feet meet on sides to form skirt. Dovetailed or nailed construction.

Materials and Dimensions
Walnut, cherry, or maple; sometimes curly maple. Secondary wood pine or cedar. Occasionally stained red. Hinges: brass or iron butt. Pulls: brass willow mounts with bail handles. Escutcheons: brass keyhole surrounds or matching brass. Interior pulls: small brass knobs. Height: 20–22″. Width: 19–21″. Depth: 10–12″.

Locality and Period
New England, New York, and Pennsylvania. c. 1730–50.

Comment
Though dating as early as the William and Mary period, miniature desks are relatively uncommon. Like all miniatures, they resemble the full-size pieces of their period, although their proportions are often changed. While the piece shown here has full-size brasses, others have scaled-down hardware. A desk such as this may have been a salesman's sample, a child's toy, or simply something for the amusement of adults.

Hints for Collectors
Miniatures have always been popular and have been collected and duplicated for generations. Late Victorian reproductions of Queen Anne miniatures can be very deceptive. The originals were made by hand with attention to detail and show the patina of age.

53 Chippendale slant-front desk

Description
Slant-front bureau desk with plain, unmolded top. Battened lid
with thumbnail molding falls forward onto 2 pull-out slides.
Interior well sometimes has central locker flanked by fluted
columns. At each side, 3–4 pigeonholes with shaped dividers
above 1 full-length and 2 half-length drawers. Straight front with
4 graduated, full-length drawers flanked by fluted quarter-
columns. Protruding, molded base. Plain skirt. Plain or molded
bracket feet. Dovetailed and pegged construction.

Materials and Dimensions
Mahogany, cherry, or walnut; rarely maple. Secondary wood
pine or poplar. Hinges: brass or iron butt. Pulls: brass willow
mounts with bail handles. Escutcheons: matching brass. Interior
pulls: small brass knobs. Height: 41–44″. Width: 41–44″. Depth:
20–23″.

Locality and Period
New England west to Ohio, south to Georgia. c. 1760–90.

Comment
The straight-front version is the most typical of the Chippendale
slant-front desks and the one most often available to collectors.
Country examples or those made for sale to the less affluent of
the period will lack the fluted quarter-columns and the interior
details.

Hints for Collectors
Woods can make a difference in price. It is often possible to buy
a nice Chippendale slant-front desk in cherry or walnut for much
less than a mahogany example. Since the details are often quite
similar, keep an eye out for pieces in native woods; they are
frequently better buys, and of comparable quality.

Chippendale oxbow slant-front desk

Description
Slant-front bureau desk with oxbow-shaped drawer fronts. Lid falls forward onto 2 pull-out slides. Interior well contains 10–18 drawers and pigeonholes: drawers may be plain, shell-carved, molded, incised with reeding, or have applied pilasters; pigeonholes may have arched or scalloped tops. 4 full-length drawers, often graduated. Front corners from base of lid to feet may be chamfered and reeded. Molded base may be plain or decorated with a central shell-carved pendant. Short cabriole legs. Claw-and-ball or molded bracket feet. Dovetailed and pegged construction.

Materials and Dimensions
Mahogany, walnut, or maple. Secondary wood pine or poplar. Hinges: brass or iron butt. Pulls: brass willow mounts or rosettes, both with bail handles. Escutcheons: matching brass. Interior pulls: small brass knobs. Height: 44–47″. Width: 40–43″. Depth: 20–23″.

Locality and Period
New England, New York, and Pennsylvania, south to Maryland and Virginia. c. 1760–85.

Comment
Like the serpentine front, the oxbow front was hard to achieve, and few cabinetmakers attempted it. As a result, examples in this style are much harder to find and more expensive than the typical straight-front variety. Oxbow fronts may also be found on chests of drawers, chest-on-chests, and secretaries.

Hints for Collectors
Look for oxbow-front desks in New England, where most of them were made. A more or less matching set of desk and chest of drawers or chest-on-chest is an appealing combination.

William and Mary slant-front desk

Description
Slant-front bureau desk with 3–4 often graduated drawers
separated by single- or double-arch molding. Lid usually falls
forward to rest on 2 pull-out slides; rare early examples have lift
top. Interior has shaped and molded drawers and pigeonholes,
and occasionally a central locker with architectural door
concealing additional drawers. Slide in base of desk interior
encloses well, or secret compartment. Base heavily molded. Ball
or turnip feet. Early examples paneled; later ones nailed or
dovetailed.

Materials and Dimensions
Walnut or maple. Secondary wood pine or poplar. Lid and
drawer fronts may be veneered in burl walnut or bird's-eye
maple. Sometimes stained red. Hinges: iron butt. Pulls: brass
teardrops or batwings. Escutcheons: matching brass. Interior
pulls: small brass knobs. Height: 40–44″. Width: 34–37″. Depth:
19–22″.

Locality and Period
New England, New York, New Jersey, and Pennsylvania.
c. 1700–20.

Comment
A combination of a desk and a chest of drawers, this is the first
practical desk form, useful for writing in a seated position and for
storage. It became the prototype for most later desks.

Hints for Collectors
Desk interiors often separate the common from the above-
average example. The interior of the desk illustrated includes the
uncommon central locker. To be sure the interior is not a
replacement, look for matching wood, wear, and ink stains.

Late Victorian oak slant-front desk

Description
Bureau desk with slanting lid, decorated with applied, pressed designs that imitate carving. Interior well with 4–6 pigeonholes flanking 2 central drawers. Below, 3 full-length drawers, all with pressed-work decoration; top drawer slightly narrower than other 2. Plain board sides. Plain skirt. Short cabriole front legs terminating in squared-off, pad feet. Back legs square. Nailed and glued construction.

Materials and Dimensions
Oak and quartersawed oak, with machine-pressed decorative carving. Sometimes darkened or fumed to highlight decoration. Hinges: iron or brass butt. Pulls: brass rosette knobs. Escutcheons: brass or iron keyhole surrounds. Height: 41–44″. Width: 35–38″. Depth: 18–20″.

Locality and Period
Large factories throughout the East and Midwest. c. 1900–30.

Comment
Though somewhat in the Colonial Revival style, this piece is best placed in the general category of oak furniture. There is no attempt to imitate 18th-century woods or manufacturing techniques, and it simply represents a 20th-century continuation of the long-popular slant-front desk.

Hints for Collectors
A better-quality piece of oak furniture like the one shown here has thicker wood, better construction, fine brasses, and more detailed decoration than ordinary examples. A piece of this sort was fairly expensive when it was new, and is still expensive today.

Description
Slant-front desk on low, removable frame. Battened desk lid drops forward onto 2 pull-out slides to provide writing surface. Interior contains 5–14 pigeonholes and drawers, sometimes shell-carved or with curving fronts. 3–5 drawers, sometimes graduated, below desk section. Frame has molded top and plain or elaborately scalloped skirt, rarely with drops. Short (8–12″) cabriole legs. Pad, slipper, or trifid feet. Dovetailed, pegged, or, rarely, nailed construction.

Materials and Dimensions
Cherry, maple, or walnut. Secondary wood pine, cedar, or poplar. Hinges: iron or brass butt. Pulls: brass willow mounts with bail handles. Escutcheons: matching brass. Interior pulls: small brass knobs. Height: 44–50″. Width: 37–45″. Depth: 19–22″.

Locality and Period
New England, primarily Connecticut. c. 1730–50.

Comment
The earliest Queen Anne desk-on-frames have long, turned legs ending in slipper or button feet; the desks rest on shallow frames containing a drawer. Later examples may have lowboy-type frames with cabriole legs and 3–5 small drawers. The example illustrated is the latest and most common form, providing greater storage space beneath the writing box.

Hints for Collectors
Examine the desk frame closely to see whether it is a recent addition to a bureau desk that has lost its original feet. Make sure there are no signs of missing feet on the bottom of the desk proper: look for variations in wood color and nail or screw holes at the corners. The base should also match the top in wood type, color, and age.

Colonial Revival desk-on-frame

Description

Slant-front desk-on-frame with battened lid that falls forward to
rest on 2 pull-out slides. Well of desk contains 5–7 pigeonholes
above 3 shallow drawers with curved fronts. 3 graduated or
equal-size drawers below desk top. Permanently attached base
contains full-length drawer. Skirt valanced. Short cabriole legs.
Dutch feet. Top: dovetailed and glued construction. Base:
mortise-and-tenon construction.

Materials and Dimensions

Mahogany or pine with mahogany veneer. Secondary wood pine.
In less expensive examples, back is plywood. Hinges: iron or
brass butt. Pulls: brass willow mounts with bail handles.
Escutcheons: matching brass. Interior pulls: small brass knobs.
Height: 39–42″. Width: 23–26″. Depth: 14–17″.

Locality and Period

Better factories throughout the United States. c. 1920–35.

Comment

This well-proportioned example of the Colonial Revival style has
reasonably accurate brasses and an attractive interior. In the
1920s and 1930s, the demand for furnishings in the "Colonial
manner" led to such factory reproductions as this one. Today
these pieces are popular and considered a good investment.

Hints for Collectors

There are obvious signs that this is a reproduction. Unlike 18th-
century desk-on-frames, in this piece the upper and lower
sections are permanently attached. A close inspection also
reveals wire nails, uniform machine-cut dovetails, and modern
iron hinges. Finally, the drawer bottoms are square-cut to fit
into slots rather than chamfered as they are in 18th-century
pieces.

Description

Low, 2-part secretary. Upper section: shallow and set back, with slightly overhanging top and sliding tambour shutters; interior with 4 drawers and 6 pigeonholes. Lower section: bowfront chest of drawers with conforming, overhanging top. Pull-out writing slide below; 3 full-length drawers of equal size with inlaid borders. Stiles decorated with line inlay of flowers. Plain skirt. Square, tapered legs are extensions of stiles. Dovetailed construction.

Materials and Dimensions

Mahogany; also bird's-eye maple, satinwood, or crotch grain mahogany veneer. Secondary wood pine. Inlay and stringing holly or boxwood. Pulls: brass knobs, rings, rosettes, or oblong plates with bail handles. Escutcheons: matching brass, brass keyhole surrounds, or diamond-shaped bone. Height: 42–51″. Width: 37–42″. Depth: 22–25″.

Locality and Period

New England, particularly around Boston. c. 1785–1805.

Comment

Sometimes referred to as bureau secretaries, these small pieces combine the functions of a desk and a chest of drawers and were frequently used in bedrooms. A similar straight-front form substitutes a fold-over writing flap for the pull-out slide.

Hints for Collectors

Be careful in handling tambour pieces. The cloth on which the wooden strips of the tambour are mounted is often very fragile. Better examples will have unrestored shutters and the original finish. New finish or restored veneer or inlay will decrease the value.

Shaker sewing desk

Description
Blocky work desk with slightly overhanging top. Upper section:
central cupboard with 3 small, rectangular drawers on each side.
Single paneled door and 1 interior shelf. Lower section: wide,
overhanging work surface with pull-out slide of almost equal
width beneath it. Below work surface, 3 small drawers on left.
On right side, 3 deep, full-length drawers. Paneled back, front,
and sides. Plain skirt. Legs turned extensions of stiles. Paneled,
pegged, and dovetailed construction.

Materials and Dimensions
Maple or bird's-eye maple with pine panels; rarely cherry.
Secondary wood pine. Natural finish or stained, usually red or
yellow. Hinges: iron butt. Pulls: turned wooden knobs. Latches:
brass or iron. Height: 37–39″. Width: 31–34″. Depth: 25–27″.

Locality and Period
Shaker communities in New England and New York. c. 1840–60.

Comment
These pieces are referred to as desks, and no doubt were often
used for writing or storage of writing materials. Their primary
use, however, was for sewing, which explains the large pull-out
surface, essential for cutting and basting fabric.

Hints for Collectors
The unique drawer arrangement reflects Shaker practicality and
is a mark of a Shaker piece. Full-length drawers beneath the
slide would have been hard to reach with the slide extended, so
the drawers were put at one end and on the side of the piece.
The use of the same piece as a desk and a sewing table further
illustrates the Shaker concern with utility.

61 Art Deco secretary

Description
Small, asymmetrical secretary in Chinese manner with slightly molded top. Open cupboard on upper left. Upper right, desk top, hinged at bottom and supported on chains, swings down to become writing surface. Interior well has 4–6 plain pigeonholes. Lower left, 2-door cupboard with 1–2 shelves protrudes 2–3″ beyond upper cupboard. Lower right, 2 open bookshelves. Plain base. Lacquered. Glued, nailed, and screwed construction.

Materials and Dimensions
Pine. Plywood back. Lacquered pearl-gray, blue, red, or black. Hinges: steel butt. Pulls: applied, lacquered wooden circles. Chains: brass. Height: 42–44″. Width: 50–52″. Depth: 15–16″.

Locality and Period
Better factories in the East and Midwest. c. 1925–45.

Comment
The influence of the Chinese style is visible in much Art Deco furniture and is reflected in the lacquer finish, styling, and color schemes. In the example shown, the lines are clearly those of a Chinese cabinet, and the red and black combination and the circular pulls are characteristic of Oriental taste.

Hints for Collectors
This secretary resembles the work of Paul T. Frankl, a major designer of modern furniture. Marked or otherwise identifiable examples (known by their form or from catalogue pictures), such as Frankl pieces, are in demand and increasing in value. With 20th-century furniture, always look for the manufacturer's mark, usually found in drawers or on the bottom or back of the piece.

Description
Kneehole desk with flat, molded top. Full-length drawer without pulls. Below left, single drawer above 1 deep double drawer made to look like 2. Right, solid pedestal with 1–2 adjustable bookshelves on side, mounted on movable brackets. Turned feet, sometimes with steel caps, at an angle to base of pedestals. Nailed, screwed, and glued construction.

Materials and Dimensions
Maple or pine with maple veneer. Secondary wood pine. Pulls: shaped solid maple. Height: 30–31″. Width: 43–45″. Depth: 30–31″.

Locality and Period
Large factories throughout the East and Midwest. c. 1930–50.

Comment
Made by Heywood-Wakefield, a well-known furniture manufacturer, the example illustrated is similar to desks made by a number of other companies. Better-quality pieces were solid maple rather than veneered. Most were designed for use in the home; office examples were larger.

Hints for Collectors
The blond look of maple or birch was very popular in the 1930s and 1940s and is attracting attention again. Today, light-colored pieces, especially of solid wood, can be a good investment. Look for good lines, good condition, and examples with the maker's mark. Heywood-Wakefield usually stamped its factory logo inside a drawer, while other companies often put their marks on the back or bottom of a piece.

Description
Pedestal desk with flat, molded top. Writing surface plain or covered with baize or leather. Top center drawer flanked by 2 writing slides or 2 half-size drawers. Each pedestal support contains 3–4 drawers or large, paneled door cupboards; rarely a cupboard on 1 side and drawers on the other. Cupboards, when present, contain 2–3 movable shelves. Sides paneled. Molded pedestal base. Plain skirt. Paneled, nailed, and glued construction.

Materials and Dimensions
Mahogany, walnut, cherry, rosewood, or maple. Secondary wood oak or, less commonly, pine or poplar. Shellacked or varnished; occasionally ebonized. Early examples sometimes with inlay or carved or incised. Pulls: oblong or turned wooden knobs or leaf-carved wooden grips. Escutcheons: iron keyhole surrounds or wooden rosettes. Height: 29–32″. Width: 40–48″. Depth: 26–36″.

Locality and Period
Throughout the United States, first in small shops, then mass-produced in factories. c. 1870–1930.

Comment
This popular form has a less common variant, the so-called partners' desk, which has matching sets of drawers and cupboards on the front and back, enabling 2 people to work facing each other.

Hints for Collectors
These desks are often reasonably priced. Look for the appealing variations—a child's desk or early examples that may have burl inlay and other decoration rare on mass-produced pieces. Pedestal desks are among the oak pieces being reproduced today, so be sure to check for signs of age.

Description
Massive 2-piece desk with quarter-round cover of turned louvers on canvas backing that rolls up and back to reveal well with 20–24 pigeonholes and 4–6 drawers. Narrow top (6–8"), molded and slightly overhanging, parallels writing surface that divides well from lower pedestals. Each pedestal has 3–4 drawers of equal size topped by narrow pull-out writing slide. Plain skirt and molded, plinthlike base. Sides and back paneled; sides in several sections. Nailed, glued, and screwed construction.

Materials and Dimensions
Oak; early examples rarely cherry or walnut. Secondary wood oak or pine. Louvers oak. Natural or fumed finish. Pulls: oblong wooden finger grips or dumbbell-shaped brass handles. Escutcheons: brass oblongs. Height: 49–52". Width: 60–64". Depth: 31–33".

Locality and Period
Large factories throughout the East and Midwest. c. 1880–1930.

Comment
For more than 50 years the rolltop was the standard office desk throughout the United States. Many thousands of desks were produced, and many still remain. The earliest were made of walnut or cherry, but by 1900 oak was used almost exclusively.

Hints for Collectors
It seems that everybody wants a rolltop desk, and the demand has led not only to high prices but also to reproductions in substantial numbers. The new desks look very much like the older ones, so check for wear, staining (particularly on the interior), and damage, such as chipped louvers and worn or bent pulls and escutcheons.

65 Eastlake rotary cylinder desk

Description
Pedestal desk with flat top and molded edge. 3 inset leather panels on top; center panel adjustable to desired height for reading or writing. Below, a tier of 3 drawers. Molded cupboard doors on each pedestal open on quadrant-shaped storage areas of 20–30 pigeonholes and 5–7 drawers. Pedestals swivel to provide access to interior. Sides and back paneled. Molded base. Glued, dovetailed, and nailed construction.

Materials and Dimensions
Walnut or walnut veneer with burl veneer panels. Secondary wood pine or chestnut. Hinges: brass butt. Pulls: brass plates with pendant rings. Interior pulls: brass or carved wooden knobs. Escutcheons: brass plates or keyhole surrounds. Height: 30–33″. Width: 55–57″. Depth: 33–34″.

Locality and Period
Primarily W.S. Wooton of Indianapolis, Indiana. c. 1875–85. Variations by other midwestern and eastern manufacturers.

Comment
Created by Wooton as a smaller version of his famous "Wooton desk," the rotary cylinder desk also has substantial storage space combined with the practical innovation of an adjustable writing surface.

Hints for Collectors
While the larger Wooton desks are practically unobtainable, it is possible to find the smaller cylinder desks. Look for well-made examples with a variety of pigeonholes, drawers, and adjustable writing surfaces. In general, the more complex the piece, the more desirable it is.

Chippendale kneehole desk

Description
Block- or straight-front desk with recessed center cabinet. Desk top serves as writing surface. 1 long central drawer and 6 or, rarely, 8 short side drawers; drawers may be shell-carved. Cabinet with molded door conceals interior bookshelves. Corners may be chamfered and fluted. Heavily molded base. Plain or molded bracket feet or claw-and-ball feet. Long top drawer front occasionally hinged to fall forward and provide shallow writing surface; behind this are 6–10 plain or molded drawers and pigeonholes. Dovetailed construction.

Materials and Dimensions
Mahogany or walnut. Secondary wood pine or poplar. Pulls: brass willow mounts or rosettes with bail handles. Escutcheons: matching brass. Interior pulls, when present: small brass knobs. Height: 25–34″. Width: 34–42″. Depth: 21–23″.

Locality and Period
New England and New York. c. 1760–80.

Comment
Although they appeared first in the Queen Anne era, kneehole desks, particularly blocked examples, are rather uncommon. Block-front pieces required great skill to produce and were never as popular in this country as fall-front desks.

Hints for Collectors
These beautiful and costly desks are not necessarily practical. The kneehole area is quite narrow, often only about 16″ wide, and many people today are too large to sit at an 18th-century piece. On the other hand, they make rather nice dressing tables, and, indeed, some once served this purpose.

Empire kneehole desk

Description
Massive 2-piece desk. Upper section: slightly overhanging, molded top; below, 4 small rectangular drawers above center 2-door cupboard with 2–3 interior shelves. Long cupboard on each side of center cupboard and drawers; interiors have 4–5 shelves above a small drawer. All doors paneled. Gently sloping writing surface galleried. Leather-covered, hinged central section swings up to reveal shallow well. Lower section: base with paneled sides and 2 pedestals, each with 3 graduated drawers. Valanced skirt. Plain bracket feet. Paneled, dovetailed, nailed, and glued construction.

Materials and Dimensions
Mahogany or walnut; also mahogany veneer over pine. Secondary wood pine. Hinges: iron or brass butt. Pulls: turned wooden knobs. Escutcheons: oblong brass plates or small brass circles. Height: 59–62″. Width: 44–48″. Depth: 28–32″ (at base).

Locality and Period
Larger shops in the East and Southeast. c. 1820–45.

Comment
There are relatively few Empire desk forms. The one shown here could almost be called a secretary, although the kneehole base and lower height make the term "desk" more appropriate.

Hints for Collectors
A desk of this sort, unfortunately too large for many homes or apartments, is nevertheless extremely practical, with space for just about anything. In addition, the form is relatively rare and more appealing than others of the Empire period.

Description
Desk with fold-out writing shelf resting on 2 pull-out slides.
Writing shelf sometimes covered with leather or cloth. Upper
section sometimes removable, with tambour doors that open to
reveal 6–10 small drawers and arched pigeonholes. 2–3 full-
length drawers below. Plain skirt. Legs square and tapered.
Spade feet sometimes present. Often elaborately decorated:
veneered drawer fronts; stringing around drawers and on legs;
pendant bellflower inlay on legs. Dovetailed construction.

Materials and Dimensions
Mahogany. Secondary wood pine or cedar. Tambour rods often
alternating mahogany and satinwood. Veneer and inlay
satinwood or bird's-eye maple; stringing boxwood or holly.
Hinges: brass butt. Pulls: oval or round brass mounts with bail
handles; also rosettes. Interior pulls: brass, ivory, or turned
wood. Escutcheons: brass keyhole surrounds. Height: 42–50″.
Width: 36–40″. Depth: 11–20″.

Locality and Period
New England, primarily Massachusetts. c. 1790–1810.

Comment
The tambour front, an early version of the rolltop desk, is
composed of many vertical rods, which are usually glued to a
flexible cloth backing. Occasionally the tambour doors will be
inlaid with various Federal motifs, such as the swag, tassel,
husk, and urn. These pieces are sometimes called secretaries,
which is misleading since they have no upper book storage area.

Hints for Collectors
Look for good proportions, attractive veneer and inlay, and the
amount of veneer that has been replaced. A loss of original
veneer and inlay reduces the worth of a piece.

Hepplewhite fold-out writing desk

Description
Boxlike desk with unmolded 2-part top. Front section of top folds
out and forward to form a baize-covered writing surface. Interior
contains 3 shallow full-length drawers; writing surface lifts back
to reveal 2 storage compartments. 1 full-length drawer below
well. Arched skirt tapers to meet legs. Legs square, tapered
extensions of stiles. Sides have metal carrying handles.
Decorated with veneer and stringing. Dovetailed construction.

Materials and Dimensions
Mahogany with birch veneer. Secondary wood pine. Stringing
boxwood. Hinges: brass butt. Pulls: oval Federal-style brass
plates with bail handles or rosettes. Interior pulls: brass loops or
small brass knobs. Escutcheons: brass keyhole surrounds or
carved ivory diamonds. Carrying handles: brass plates with bail
handles. Height: 32–35″. Width: 28–31″. Depth: 17–18″.

Locality and Period
New England to Ohio and south to Maryland. c. 1790–1810.

Comment
Small desks of this sort are descendants of the earlier desk-on-
frames. The handles on the sides may indicate that they were
intended to be carried from place to place while in use. Such
pieces are sometimes referred to as ladies' desks because of their
small size, although they were no doubt used by both men and
women.

Hints for Collectors
These desks are rare. Don't confuse them with common Federal
writing boxes mounted on separate frames, usually of later date.
This desk and its frame are all of 1 piece. The made-up pieces
have a framework or set of legs attached to a desk box.

Mission-style kneehole desk

Description
Low kneehole desk with unmolded, overhanging top. Half-length center drawer flanked by rectangular, quarter-length drawers, below which are slightly taller ones, equal in width. Skirt cut in simple, semicircular form with kneehole area below. Paneled back and sides. 8 legs, tapered extensions of stiles, the center 4 flanking kneehole at front and back. Feet blunt terminals of legs, capped with metal shoes. Glued mortise-and-tenon construction.

Materials and Dimensions
Oak and quartersawed oak. Pulls: brass bail handles or turned wooden knobs. Escutcheons: brass circles. Height: 28–29″. Width: 47–50″. Depth: 29–32″.

Locality and Period
Factories in the East and Midwest. c. 1905–20.

Comment
Although this example was made by the well-known firm of L. & J. G. Stickley, similar kneehole desks were produced in many different factories, both large and small. Used mainly in homes, they were found in offices as well.

Hints for Collectors
Look for plain desks like these in small shops in the country and used furniture stores in the city. Unmarked pieces are worth buying if they are sturdy and well preserved. However, examples bearing the marks of well-known designers are true finds. Look for a paper label or a brand stamped into the wood inside drawers, on the bottom of the carcass, or on the inside of the legs. The Stickley brothers produced catalogues of their furniture designs, and an unmarked piece may sometimes be identified by reference to these.

Child's rolltop desk-on-frame

Description
Small, plain rolltop desk-on-frame with slightly overhanging, unmolded top. Rolltop of flexible, molded wooden slats forms a quarter-circle. Slats, set into runners at sides of desk, slide up and back. Interior with 4–6 plain pigeonholes and shallow writing surface. Single full-length drawer below well. Back is single piece of plywood. Sides plain or paneled. Plain skirt. Simple, sticklike rectangular legs joined at back and sides by sticklike stretchers. Nailed and glued construction.

Materials and Dimensions
Oak. Pine secondary wood sometimes present. Back plywood. Unpainted or fumed. Pulls: brass or turned wooden knobs. Escutcheons, when present: brass or iron keyhole surrounds. Height: 32–35″. Width: 19–22″. Depth: 15–16″.

Locality and Period
Large factories throughout the United States. c. 1880–1930.

Comment
Small desks of this sort were once found in almost every child's bedroom or playroom. Although made by many manufacturers, they vary surprisingly little. Some have locks, others a lower shelf between the stretchers; otherwise, the example illustrated is typical.

Hints for Collectors
Children's rolltop desks are popular today and still being made. Since the basic form has changed little over the years, make sure a piece is actually old. Look for signs of age: wear on the bottom of the legs, scratches and stains in the interior, and wear from friction at the sides and base of the rolltop.

Description

Small wicker writing table with slightly overhanging, kidney-shaped wooden top edged with woven wicker ropework. Gallery of woven wicker extends halfway around top, rising in splashboard (4–6″) at rear. Rectangular storage area in front of splashboard. Woven wicker base with single wooden drawer. Wicker-wrapped, tapered wooden legs support a wooden shelf with wicker-wrapped edge and triangular wooden supports. Blunt, tin-capped feet. Woven, glued, and nailed construction.

Materials and Dimensions

Woven wicker with oak, ash, or hickory drawer, top, legs, and shelf. May be painted white, green, brown, or black; sometimes other colors. Pulls: turned wooden knobs. Height: 37–39″. Width: 37–40″. Depth: 21–23″.

Locality and Period

Large manufacturers throughout the East and Midwest. c. 1880–1910.

Comment

Often referred to as ladies' desks because of their diminutive size and delicate appearance, these small desks or writing tables were very popular at the turn of the century. They were often part of a suite of parlor or porch furniture and were also found in the bedroom.

Hints for Collectors

Early wicker can be distinguished from pieces being made today not only by signs of age, such as worn feet, frayed pieces of wicker, or surface wear, but also by the method of construction. Most modern manufacturers use staples somewhere on every piece, while early makers used only nails. At present, this sort of wicker desk is not being reproduced.

Mission-style writing table

Description
Small desk with flat, unmolded top above 1 full-length drawer. Square corner posts project slightly above writing surface. On sides, 3–4 flat slats joined to top with flat, horizontal stretcher. Shallow shelf supported by same stretchers. Corner posts taper slightly toward floor to form square legs and square, blunt feet. Glued mortise-and-tenon construction.

Materials and Dimensions
Oak and quartersawed oak. Pulls: brass plates with circular handles or turned wooden knobs. Height: 29–31″. Width: 23–26″. Depth: 21–23″.

Locality and Period
New York and Michigan. c. 1905–15.

Comment
Small tablelike desks such as this were advertised in the catalogues of Gustav Stickley, the leading designer of Mission-style furniture. This piece although unmarked, is attributed to him, but similar examples were also made by his brothers, L. and J. G. Stickley. As the 3 Stickleys and others all produced similar designs, it is often difficult to attribute a piece. This piece, with its straight lines, overall severity, and solid construction, typifies better-quality Mission-style furniture.

Hints for Collectors
Although called desks, these pieces have limited storage space and are more practical as tables. Small and compact, they are ideal for modern apartments and in great demand among collectors of Mission-style oak. Look for them in used furniture stores and other out-of-the-way shops in smaller towns, where they may not yet be recognized as collector's pieces.

Mission-style desk with writing boxes

Description
Simple desk with flat, unmolded top. At the rear of top are 2 storage boxes with curving lift tops and an interior shelf. Boxes backed with and connected by simple flat-top splashboard incised with diamond design. Square legs joined by 2 stretchers; top stretcher supports 3 flat, vertical slats that run parallel to legs. Trestle-type, carved feet terminate in spiral ovals above iron and wood casters. Glued mortise-and-tenon construction; some nailing.

Materials and Dimensions
Oak. Boxes mahogany and pine. Hinges: brass butt. Pulls: small brass knobs. Height: 43–45″. Width: 35–37″. Depth: 25–26″.

Locality and Period
Factories, primarily in New York and Michigan. c. 1905–25.

Comment
A transitional piece, the desk shown here combines the appealing simplicity of Mission-style furniture with characteristics of less expensive, mass-produced golden oak pieces. However, it lacks the quality of construction found in the work of leading designers. Their pieces would be pegged together where this one is only glued.

Hints for Collectors
Look for well-made and attractive Mission-style furnishings by larger factories. As the enthusiasm for Mission grows, pieces by the leading makers, such as Stickley, Roycroft, and Limbert, become harder to find and more expensive. However, examples by lesser-known producers remain reasonable. Many of these are attractive by themselves or blend well with pieces by better-known designers.

Art Deco pedestal-base desk

Description
Modern desk on angled frame, with shallow, boxlike body.
Hinged top folds back to reveal shallow well with narrow writing
surface in front of central drawer (5–7″ wide); 2 pigeonholes at
each side of drawer. When desk top is closed, hinged section
swings down to cover well front. Skirt plain with slight valance
at corners. Legs flat, boardlike stiles tapering toward bottom
and terminating in rectangular, chamfered, platformlike base.
Lacquered. Nailed, glued, and screwed construction.

Materials and Dimensions
Pine or ash. Interior drawer bird's-eye maple veneer. Lacquered
black or white. Hinges: steel butt. Pulls: plastic oblongs. Height:
32–34″. Width: 36–38″. Depth: 19–20″.

Locality and Period
Better factories in the East and Midwest. c. 1925–40.

Comment
Never made in large quantity, these spectacular desks were
often part of Art Deco bedroom suites. The combination of
veneer and lacquer is unusual for the period and indicates a
sophistication often lacking in factory-produced furniture.

Hints for Collectors
Like the example shown here, the best Art Deco pieces have
strong lines and handsome finishes, and are worth looking for.
Lacquered furniture, however, can be a problem. If the finish is
chipped or worn away, it detracts from the piece, and restoring
lacquer is quite expensive. As a general rule, one should avoid
buying anything with damaged lacquer unless it is a good enough
example to warrant the high cost of restoration.

Description
Simple, almost kidney-shaped free-form writing table with thick
(6″) top, supported by 1 round and 2 semicircular, curved legs. 2
small, rectangular drawers set side by side in front edge,
midway between front legs. Entire piece lacquered, usually with
contrasting color scheme. Glued, screwed, and factory-cut
dovetailed construction.

Materials and Dimensions
Pine. Top lacquered dark brown; legs white. Height: 28–29″.
Width: 47–50″. Depth: 23–24″.

Locality and Period
Major factories in the East and Midwest. c. 1930–45.

Comment
Initially, the modern movement led to the construction of desks
in conventional forms but in new materials, such as metal and
plastic. Later, designers created organic forms like this one. The
body of this piece is almost kidney-shaped, a form well suited to
a writing desk. However, the small drawers provide limited
storage space for writing materials.

Hints for Collectors
The example illustrated was designed by Paul Frankl for the
Johnson Furniture Company. Although factory made, desks like
this were produced in limited numbers, and they were
expensive. Because of their rarity and elegant forms, they have
become highly collectible. Be sure to check for damage to the
legs, as they are fragile and may have been broken and repaired.
Also, as with all lacquered examples, the lacquer should be in
good condition.

Secretaries and Tall Desks

A secretary combines a desk with a storage unit for books and writing materials. Probably because of the scarcity of books in Colonial America, the combination did not develop until the mid-18th century. The first examples, in the Queen Anne style (82), consist of 2 sections: a slant-front desk topped by a 2-door cupboard that opens to reveal bookshelves, drawers, and pigeonholes. Secretaries of this period are either flat-topped or crowned by an elaborately carved bonnet top. Chippendale secretaries (81) have the same basic form, but are usually much larger and may be crowned by a massive cornice.

Although large slant-front secretaries continued to be made throughout the Federal period, smaller types developed as well. In one of the most common forms (78), a writing surface is created when a hinged flap folds outward to rest on slides or a drawer. Other innovations include the pull-out writing shelf and the tambour secretary. In the latter, tambour slides, consisting of thin wooden strips attached to fabric, roll into recessed areas in each side of the desk section.

In some Federal pieces, the upper section was also modified to include glazed doors (77), made possible by the greater availability of glass. Federal cabinetmakers separated the glass panes by thin wooden strips, or muntins, often arranged in complex geometric patterns. Empire-style secretaries (79) are less varied than their Federal predecessors and almost always incorporate heavy Empire-style pillars and massive feet. Doors are often glazed, and the arrangement of shelves and cupboards is simplified.

Typically, variety flourished during the Victorian period. Although traditional forms like the slant-front secretary were still made, more extravagant pieces (89) incorporated elaborate bookshelves, china cabinets, clothes hooks, and even mirrors. Also produced in this period was the Wooton desk (90), an oversize piece with a number of drawers and as many as 100 pigeonholes that swing out from behind an ornate front.

At the turn of the century, a conservative trend set in. Arts and Crafts secretaries (86) are austere, as are Mission-style pieces. Surface decoration is minimal, and the pigeonholes and drawers that are commonly found behind desk lids of earlier periods are often replaced by plain exposed shelves. After 1920, the secretary became something of a rarity, and of those that were made, most hark back to earlier Colonial styles. As bookcases became increasingly common, there was less need for a combination desk and storage area, and the form underwent a reduction in size as well as a decline in popularity.

Sheraton secretary

Description
Small secretary, usually in 2 pieces. Flat top with molded edge or low, shaped pediment, usually without finials. Upper section: glazed cabinet with geometric panes set in latticework or Gothic pattern; interior containing 3–4 bookshelves. 2–3 small drawers are set into base. Fold-out writing shelf covered in leather or cloth and supported by 2 pull-out slides. Lower section: 2 full-length drawers, which may be veneered. Skirt plain or valanced. Tapered, turned, and reeded legs with cuff and blunt-arrow feet. Dovetailed construction.

Materials and Dimensions
Mahogany, sometimes with crotch mahogany veneer; also cherry or maple. Secondary wood pine or poplar. Hinges: brass butt. Pulls: oval or oblong brass mounts with bail handles, or rosette knobs. Interior pulls: small brass knobs. Height: 64–74″. Width: 36–42″. Depth: 17–21″.

Locality and Period
New England west to the Mississippi River, south to Georgia. c. 1790–1820.

Comment
Sheraton secretaries may be distinguished from their Hepplewhite counterparts by the characteristic reeded leg, which in later examples becomes quite squat and bulbous. In addition, the elaborate veneering in light woods, stringing, and bellflower inlay associated with most Hepplewhite examples are often lacking in Sheraton pieces.

Hints for Collectors
Examine the legs on Federal pieces for repaired fractures or even restoration of a whole leg. Signs of saw cuts, differences in wood color, and fresh paint are all clues to new additions.

Description
2-piece secretary with flat top or shaped pediment with finials, typically with eagle in center flanked by 2 spheres. Upper section: removable, with glass doors in Gothic arch or latticework design; interior containing 8–14 small drawers and pigeonholes with bookshelves above. Fold-out writing surface covered in cloth or leather and supported by 2 pull-out slides. Lower section: 3–4 full-length, usually graduated drawers, often veneered and decorated with inlay and stringing. Skirt plain or valanced with drop. French feet. Dovetailed construction.

Materials and Dimensions
Mahogany; rarely cherry or curly maple. Secondary wood pine. Veneer flame mahogany, rosewood, or satinwood. Stringing boxwood or holly; inlay satinwood. Hinges: brass butt. Pulls: oval brass mounts with bail handles. Interior pulls: small brass knobs or ivory rings. Escutcheons: brass plates or keyhole surrounds. Height: 64–66″. Width: 38–40″. Depth: 19–20″.

Locality and Period
New England west to Ohio, south to the Carolinas. c. 1790–1810.

Comment
Some versions of this secretary have paneled wooden, rather than glass, cabinet doors. The best examples display balance in form and delicacy in design, with features like oval satinwood inlay in the doors that may match the drawer fronts.

Hints for Collectors
Check the glazing on glass-door secretaries. Usually most of the original panes have been replaced. That is not a serious problem unless the pieces of wood between the panes look new or rearranged, which may indicate that a relatively plain design has been rebuilt to make the piece more attractive.

Description
2-piece secretary has broken pediment cornice with center block. Upper section: 2-door cupboard, each door with 4 panes of glass separated by wooden muntins. Below each cupboard, 1 half-length drawer. Lower section: protruding (7–9″), with fold-out, baize-covered writing flap that rests on 2 narrow pull-out slides. 3 full-length drawers, top one overhanging (4–6″), flanked by turned wooden pillars, which are block-and-disk-turned on bottom half. Pillars terminate in waferlike feet. Plain skirt. Nailed and glued construction with dovetailed drawers.

Materials and Dimensions
Mahogany or mahogany and mahogany veneer over pine or walnut. Secondary wood pine. Hinges: brass or iron butt. Pulls: turned wooden knobs; brass rosettes with bail handles or rosette knobs; or small brass knobs. Escutcheons: brass keyhole surrounds. Height: 62–66″. Width: 35–38″. Depth: 18–20″.

Locality and Period
New England west to Ohio and throughout much of the South to Texas. c. 1820–60.

Comment
There is less variety in Empire secretaries than in those of the Federal period. This example is typical of the most common type. Its protruding upper drawer is similar to those on some Empire chests of drawers.

Hints for Collectors
Examples in the Empire mode are the least expensive of all pre-1900 secretaries; however, many have heavy proportions. Look for the smaller, more delicate examples with good turnings and solid wood. Veneered pieces should be avoided unless the veneer is in excellent condition, as restoration is very expensive.

Description

2-piece desk with slanting lid; desk top has molded edge. Above, shelf with flaring edge supported by flat, scrolled uprights and paneled backboard. Above backboard is elaborately pierced and scroll-cut cornice and spindle-turned, acornlike finials. Paneled desk lid falls forward to rest on molded shelf above an overhanging full-length drawer. Below, 2 paneled doors conceal 2–3 shelves or, less often, 3 additional full-length shelves; sometimes 3 half-size drawers and half-size cupboard with single door present. Shaped and slightly protruding stiles terminate in projecting plinthlike base. Skirt plain or valanced, concealing iron casters. Paneled, dovetailed, and glued construction.

Materials and Dimensions

Walnut or oak. Secondary wood pine. Hinges: iron butt. Pulls: carved wooden fruit-and-flower handles, or brass plates with bail or loop handles. Escutcheons: brass or shaped wood. Height: 74–79″. Width: 31–34″. Depth: 16–18″.

Locality and Period

New England west to the Mississippi River and throughout most of the South. c. 1860–85.

Comment

These tall desks reflect the eclectic nature of Victorian design, incorporating Renaissance Revival, Eastlake, and Empire elements. Many Victorian pieces do not fall into a single stylistic category.

Hints for Collectors

This uncommon desk form is practical and desirable. The lower section provides ample storage space, while the overhanging design ensures ample leg room. Such pieces are usually less expensive than secretaries of the same period.

Chippendale block-front secretary

Description
Large 2-piece secretary consisting of removable cupboard on a slant-front bureau desk. Upper section: bonnet top has applied wood or metal finials and shell carving. Cupboard has paneled doors concealing 15–17 scalloped pigeonholes and 2–3 bookshelves. 2 candle slides below. Lower section: blocked and sometimes shell-carved slant-front desk. Lid falls forward onto 2 pull-out slides. Well with 12–17 molded and shell-carved drawers and scalloped pigeonholes. 4 graduated drawers. Top and bottom may have fluted quarter-columns. Molded base. Skirt valanced, with central drop. Claw-and-ball or plain or molded bracket feet. Paneled and dovetailed construction.

Materials and Dimensions
Usually mahogany; sometimes walnut, cherry, or maple. Secondary wood pine or poplar. Hinges: brass butt. Pulls: brass willow mounts or rosettes, both with bail handles. Escutcheons: matching brass. Interior pulls: small brass knobs. Height: 84–96″. Width: 38–46″. Depth: 27–30″.

Locality and Period
New England, New York, and Pennsylvania, south to Virginia. c. 1755–80.

Comment
Chippendale secretaries, like highboys, were so massive that they were customarily made in 2 pieces. The bottom section would often have a large brass carrying handle on each side.

Hints for Collectors
Anyone who wants a purely American piece should buy a block-front chest, highboy, or secretary. It is generally agreed that the style originated here. But block-fronts were not easy to create, and the available examples command extremely high prices.

Queen Anne flat-top secretary

Description
2-piece secretary with overhanging, molded cornice and flat top.
Upper section: 2-door cupboard with sunken panels. Interior has
10–14 pigeonholes and shelves of various sizes. Occasionally, 2
candle slides below. Lower section: slant-front desk. Lid with
battened ends falls forward onto 2 pull-out slides. Well with 8–10
plain or shaped pigeonholes, 4–6 varying drawers, and
sometimes a central locker. 4 graduated drawers. Molded base
with plain skirt. Plain or molded bracket feet. Paneled,
dovetailed, and pegged construction.

Materials and Dimensions
Maple, cherry, or walnut; rarely mahogany. Secondary wood
pine or chestnut. Sometimes stained red. Hinges: brass H or
strap, or iron butt. Pulls: brass willow mounts, plain or pierced,
with bail handles. Escutcheons: matching brass. Interior pulls:
small brass knobs. Height: 72–84″. Width: 34–38″. Depth: 19–22″.

Locality and Period
New England south to the Carolinas. c. 1740–60.

Comment
Flat-top secretaries are primarily country pieces. Most were
made by cabinetmakers unable or unwilling to deal with the
complexities of bonnet tops and broken pediments, or were built
for customers who would not pay for such details. Nevertheless,
the cabinetwork is generally of a high order.

Hints for Collectors
Be sure to examine these pieces carefully. Authentic examples
are rare, and a 2-door cupboard with a new interior can be added
easily to a Queen Anne slant-front desk to make a fairly
convincing piece. Check to see that the woods of the 2 sections
match and the interior pigeonhole unit shows age.

Country Sheraton secretary

Description

1- or 2-piece slant-front secretary with cupboard. Flat top with overhanging molding. Upper section: glazed, solid, or paneled doors conceal 3–5 bookshelves. Lower section: desk above case of drawers. Desk lid falls forward onto 2 pull-out slides to reveal 4–6 small drawers, valanced pigeonholes, and raised painted or leather-covered writing surface. Case has 3–4 drawers, with the top one shortened to accommodate slides. Short, turned Sheraton-type legs. Ball feet. Often painted. Paneled and nailed or dovetailed construction.

Materials and Dimensions

Cherry, walnut, birch, or maple. Secondary wood pine or poplar. Drawer fronts sometimes veneered in curly or bird's-eye maple. Most originally grain- or sponge-painted. Hinges: iron butt. Pulls: turned wooden knobs; also brass or, rarely, pressed-glass rosette knobs. Escutcheons: brass keyhole surrounds. Height: 69–78″. Width: 28–31″. Depth: 17–19″.

Locality and Period

New England west to Ohio, south to Maryland and Virginia. c. 1800–20.

Comment

The interior of the desk shown here is particularly well conceived; details like the cutout drops above the drawers are unusual since country secretaries were, for the most part, considered wholly functional.

Hints for Collectors

Maine and New Hampshire are good sources for country Sheraton secretaries, which were made over a wide area and for some years. Even after 1820, survival types were still produced in rural areas.

Shaker built-in secretary

Description
Shallow secretary desk, originally built in, with molded, slightly overhanging top. Above desk is cupboard with central, paneled door. Desk top paneled and hinged to fall forward on chain to form writing surface. Desk well has 6–7 pigeonholes. Below desk is large cupboard with single paneled door and 1–2 interior shelves. No skirt or feet. Paneled, nailed, and dovetailed construction.

Materials and Dimensions
Pine or maple. Secondary wood pine. Natural finish or, frequently, stained red, yellow, or blue. Interior may be stained red. Hinges: iron butt. Pulls: brass or turned wooden knobs. Escutcheons: iron keyhole surrounds. Chain: metal link. Height: 54–60″. Width: 23–24″. Depth: 8–9″.

Locality and Period
Shaker communities from New England west to Indiana, south to Kentucky. c. 1810–60.

Comment
These very small secretaries are fairly rare since many were destroyed along with the buildings of which they were a part. Usually built into the walls of kitchens or workshops, they provided a workspace for supervisors and, like much Shaker furniture, were often built for a particular individual.

Hints for Collectors
Many Shaker pieces that were originally built in have been altered and look freestanding. Backs have been added, as well as top and base molding, and even feet. Examine all these areas for new wood and incongruous materials, such as wire nails and fresh paint. New molding will often be much more elaborate than Shaker-made molding.

Description
Secretary with molded, overhanging top that has scalloped skirt. Upper section: 18–24 narrow, vertical pigeonholes with shaped dividers. Shallow writing surface (8–10″) has molded, protruding lip in front of 6–10 pigeonholes, cutout pen rack, and 3 drawers, 2 of them with locks. Lower section: 2-door cupboard conceals single shelf. Side boards solid and scalloped. Plain skirt. Elongated, plain bracket feet. Nailed and dovetailed construction.

Materials and Dimensions
Pine. Usually painted brown, yellow, red, or blue. Hinges: iron butt. Pulls: turned wooden knobs. Latch: carved wood. Escutcheons: iron keyhole surrounds or diamond-shaped carved bone or wood. Height: 60–62″. Width: 34–37″. Depth: 17–19″.

Locality and Period
New England west to Ohio, south to Georgia. c. 1820–50.

Comment
Country secretaries of this sort were one-of-a-kind pieces, and for that reason examples vary widely. The piece illustrated shows characteristics of the Empire pillar-and-scroll mode, but is also related to early 19th-century open cupboards with scalloped edges.

Hints for Collectors
Possibly used in a post office or general store, this secretary has a wonderful folksy quality. Its original finish is also appealing to the knowledgeable collector. Part of its charm is that, like many of the better country pieces, it does not fall easily into any category. A piece like this was made to meet specific storage needs, which makes it much more interesting than a traditional high-style Empire secretary.

Description
Shallow secretary with shaped and molded top with deep
overhang (4–6″). Directly below top, paneled skirt with 3
decorative brackets. Upper section: back and sides composed of
vertical slats. Narrow full-length shelf. Below shelf, paneled lid
of slant-front desk drops onto 2 pull-out slides; desk well with
6–8 pigeonholes. Lower section: 1 full-length drawer over 2 open
shelves. Sides have cutout decoration and demilune skirt.
Rectangular block feet. Paneled, nailed, glued, and dovetailed
construction.

Materials and Dimensions
Mixed hardwoods, often ash or oak. Secondary wood pine. Often
originally ebonized. Hinges: brass butt. Pulls: brass plates with
bail handles or round brass knobs. Escutcheons: brass or iron
keyhole surrounds. Height: 60–65″. Width: 36–38″. Depth:
15–17″.

Locality and Period
A few major factories, primarily in the East. c. 1890–1910.

Comment
The Arts and Crafts movement never attained the popularity in
this country that it had in Europe, and the amount of American
Arts and Crafts furniture is limited. Nevertheless, American
examples, such as the one shown, are very attractive and well
suited for contemporary homes.

Hints for Collectors
These pieces are easy to identify. The overhanging top, the
unusual construction, and the cutout decoration are
characteristics not likely to be found in other furnishings of the
period. Such pieces are rapidly increasing in value and well
worth searching for.

Description
Shallow desk with slant front that conceals 8–10 plain pigeonholes. Solid board sides join high splashboard with curvilinear mirror. Mirror flanked by small, shaped shelves supported on turned posts. 2 open bookshelves below desk top. Skirt has applied, shaped molding. Lid and splashboard have applied decorative motifs in Art Nouveau style. Feet are shaped bracket extensions of side boards. Nailed and glued construction.

Materials and Dimensions
Oak or quartersawed oak. Applied decoration ash or maple. Back plywood. Hinges: iron or brass butt. Escutcheons: brass keyhole surrounds or plates; also shaped wood. Height: 60–64". Width: 29–32". Depth: 12–14".

Locality and Period
Large factories throughout the East and Midwest. c. 1890–1910.

Comment
These inexpensive, rather flimsy desks were mass-produced and shipped throughout the United States. Since they could be put together with nails or screws, they were often transported in pieces and then assembled where they were sold. The Larkin Manufacturing Company of Buffalo, New York, a major producer of soaps and toiletries, gave away so many of these desks as premiums that they are often called Larkin desks.

Hints for Collectors
Look for simple, sturdily built examples made from well-grained oak. Avoid pieces with busy decoration, cracked mirrors, and missing lids or doors. These desks are common enough to be reasonably priced.

Victorian cylinder desk

Description
Tall cylinder desk with overhanging, molded top. At left rear, square fixed mirror in scroll-cut frame, with pressed, decorated cornice. At right, scrolled backboard behind small storage cabinet with paneled door and open gallery of rods with turned finials. Paneled cylinder rolls up and back to reveal well with 7 pigeonholes. Below are 2–3 full-length, graduated or equal drawers above molded, plinthlike base. Plain board sides with waist-level molding. Paneled, nailed, and glued construction.

Materials and Dimensions
Oak and quartersawed oak. Hinges: brass or iron butt. Pulls: pierced-brass plates with bail handles and/or turned wooden knobs. Escutcheons: diamond-shaped, carved wood, or brass plates. Height: 62–66″. Width: 30–33″. Depth: 19–20″.

Locality and Period
Large factories throughout the East and Midwest. c. 1880–1910.

Comment
One of the earliest forms to be made in oak, the cylinder desk was eventually replaced by the rolltop. The addition of the mirror and storage cabinet is reflective of the Victorian craving for multipurpose furnishings. Despite its cabinet and pigeonholes, however, the desk is not very functional; the shallow writing surface is recessed and difficult to use.

Hints for Collectors
While the piece shown here is in its original form, such desks are sometimes the result of a "marriage," where the cabinet, mirror, and even sets of shelves have been mounted on a plain oak desk. Always check for matching wood, proper aging, and original hardware to ensure that the piece has not been altered.

Description
Tall combination bookcase and desk. Scalloped backboard has applied floral decoration. At left, bookcase has unmolded, slightly overhanging top and glass door in plain frame. At right, shaped oblong mirror over slant-front desk. Desk has battened lid with applied floral decoration that opens to reveal 3–4 shaped pigeonholes and 1–2 small drawers. Below, 3 drawers. Plain board sides. Applied, molded base with shaped skirt. Squat cabriole front legs and feet; cutout bootjack rear feet. Screwed, glued, and nailed construction.

Materials and Dimensions
Oak, sometimes with pine secondary wood. Applied decoration stained maple or birch. Hinges: brass or iron butt. Pulls: oblong brass mounts with bail handles. Interior pulls: small turned wooden knobs. Escutcheons: round or oval brass disks. Height: 56–60″. Width: 33–36″. Depth: 12–14″.

Locality and Period
Large factories in the East and Midwest. c. 1880–1920.

Comment
The side-by-side was one of the most popular of Victorian desks and a premier example of the Victorian preference for furniture that could serve several purposes. In the example shown here, the drawers could serve as a dresser.

Hints for Collectors
Side-by-sides are no longer inexpensive. To find a reasonably priced example, advertise in rural papers and attend house sales. Beware of examples that are warped or those in which the different sections are separating, both common faults in these dual-purpose pieces.

Wooton desk

Description
Massive 3-unit desk with molded, overhanging top, crowned by
gallery or carved splashboard. Elaborately carved finials, the
center one often in shape of globe or cartouche. Divided into 3
units joined by hinges. Center section: fall-front desk below 12
pigeonholes and over 4–5 drawers flanked by 10–14 pigeonholes.
At each side of central unit, quadrant-topped storage units. Left
section: 5–6 full-length pigeonholes above 10–12 half-length
pigeonholes. Right section: 60–70 small pigeonholes. Molded base
with bracket-shaped feet mounted on casters. Paneled, glued,
screwed, nailed, and dovetailed construction.

Materials and Dimensions
Walnut or pine with burl walnut veneer. Inlay satinwood,
natural or stained. Hinges: brass butt. Pulls: rectangular brass
plates with bail handles, occasionally with cloisonné. Interior
pulls: black walnut rosettes. Escutcheons: brass plates. Height:
72–81″. Width: 42–48″. Depth: 31–32″ (closed).

Locality and Period
W.S. Wooton of Indianapolis, Indiana. c. 1874–82.

Comment
The Wooton desk is the crowning achievement of Victorian
patent furniture. Designed to be, in effect, a working office, the
piece was made almost exclusively to special order.
Consequently, no 2 desks are ever exactly alike.

Hints for Collectors
Only a decade ago these desks were white elephants: they were
seen as too big, ugly, and impractical to use. Today there are few
Wooton desks available, and prices go quite high. The moral is
clear: tastes change, and the smart collector can often make a
good investment by buying styles currently out of fashion.

Cupboards, Cabinets, and Other Large Storage Pieces

Cupboards, linen presses, wardrobes, and other large storage pieces were a necessity in American homes until the innovation of built-in closets and pantries in the late 19th century. Even after they were replaced by built-in storage areas, variations continued to flourish, built mostly for the display of treasured valuables and memorabilia.

In America, cupboards appeared in the mid-17th century. As their name suggests, these were originally merely "cup boards," or single shelves built to hold cups and other dishes. Soon they were used to store china, silver, and other household accessories. Two basic types evolved: a wedge-shaped cupboard (100) designed to fit into a corner and a flat-backed piece (101) that stood against a wall. Both types can either stand freely or be built into the woodwork. Most cupboards are constructed in 2 parts: the upper section for display and the lower for storage. Typically, the upper section consists of 3 to 4 full-length shelves within an open frame or behind solid or glazed doors. The lower section has a tier of 2 to 3 drawers above a storage area that often contains shelves and is usually enclosed by 1 or 2 doors.

The linen press (93) appeared in the 18th century. This massive piece consists of a cupboard, in which clothing can be hung, that rests on top of a chest of drawers. Linen presses are often highly architectural in form; the finest examples appeared during the Chippendale and Federal periods.

By the mid-19th century, smaller and less ornate wardrobes (95) had replaced the linen press. Most of these are country pine pieces with painted or grained surfaces. High-style Victorian taste preferred the larger and more decorative armoire (94), a wardrobe with several drawers and an interior fitted for storage of smaller items such as collars and shirts.

The Victorians owned many large display pieces. These included great glass-front cabinets and bookcases (113) for the storage and display of knickknacks and books. Elaborate sets of open shelves over cupboard bases, known as étagères (123), were also primarily for display. Throughout the Victorian era, cupboards remained popular, although by that time they were primarily country pieces, such as the jelly cupboard. A few high-style Renaissance Revival or Eastlake cupboards continued to be made; however, by the 1880s a new furniture form had taken the cupboard's place as a display piece—the china cabinet (118). With the front consisting almost entirely of glass, it contained several shelves; most were made of oak. Although some examples had straight fronts, elaborately curved forms were most favored. 20th-century types include Art Deco examples with flat fronts, inlay, and elongated legs.

In the 20th century, most tall pieces fell out of fashion, at least in part because homes were becoming smaller. Yet medium-size pieces like liquor cabinets remain popular today.

Jelly cupboard

Description
1-piece cupboard with overhanging, occasionally molded cornice.
Some examples have low gallery at rear. 2 drawers over 1–2
frequently paneled doors. Interior has 2–3 shelves. Skirt plain or
slightly valanced. Feet short, turned in Sheraton manner, or
cutout extensions of side boards, tapered or semicircular. Most
originally painted. Paneled and dovetailed or nailed construction.

Materials and Dimensions
Walnut, pine, cherry, or poplar; often mixed softwoods. Painted
red, blue, or gray. Hinges: iron butt or, less often, H. Pulls:
small brass, porcelain, or turned wooden knobs. Latches: brass
or iron. Escutcheons, when present: brass keyhole surrounds.
Height: 44–52″. Width: 38–43″. Depth: 12–16″.

Locality and Period
Primarily Pennsylvania; also New Jersey, Delaware, Maryland,
and Virginia. c. 1800–60.

Comment
Usually referred to as jelly or jam cupboards, these pieces were
undoubtedly used to store foodstuffs. Most were originally found
in the kitchen or dining area, and many bear holes left by hungry
mice. Most have a drawer that locks; tea and sugar, the most
valuable provisions, were kept there.

Hints for Collectors
Jelly cupboards are nice country pieces and easy to find, so look
for well-made examples with paneled doors, attractive moldings,
and well-shaped feet. Avoid those with mouseholes, especially in
the front.

Description
Massive wardrobe with deeply overhanging, heavily molded cornice. Tall 2-door cupboard with raised, molded panels. Doors separated and flanked by wide stiles with oblong, molded panels, sometimes inlaid with curly maple. Interior has 2–4 wide shelves, some only half the width of case. May also have central drawer hanging on rails below shelf. Beneath cupboard, single full-length drawer, often paneled to look like 2. Molded base occasionally with applied, diamond-shaped decoration. Plain skirt. Massive ball feet. Paneled, pegged, and dovetailed construction.

Materials and Dimensions
Walnut, sweet gum, maple, basswood, or pine. Secondary wood pine or poplar. May be painted with elaborate floral motifs, or in solid colors such as dark red or brown. Hinges: iron butt or H. Pulls: turned wooden knobs or brass rosettes with pendant rings. Escutcheons: scrolled brass plates. Height: 72–86″. Width: 60–96″. Depth: 25–30″.

Locality and Period
Hudson Valley region of New York. c. 1690–1820.

Comment
Made by Dutch settlers, the kas was styled after European cupboards of the Baroque period and held most of a family's possessions, particularly its clothing. Because of their great size and weight, the top, back, and base usually came apart, so they could be moved.

Hints for Collectors
Until fairly recently, these pieces were underpriced because their size made them impractical to move or display. Although they are currently attracting collector attention, they are too large to have more than a limited appeal.

93 Linen press

Description
2-piece storage unit with overhanging, molded cornice. Corners may be chamfered and reeded. Upper section: cupboard with 2 paneled doors concealing 3–5 shelves, possibly with sliding trays or drawers. Lower section: slightly wider than upper section, with 3–5 full-length, usually graduated drawers. Molded base with plain skirt. Simple bracket or claw-and-ball feet. Paneled, dovetailed, and pegged construction.

Materials and Dimensions
Mahogany, cherry, walnut, or birch. Rarely drawer fronts veneered in crotch mahogany or curly maple. Secondary wood pine or poplar. Hinges: brass or iron butt or H. Pulls: brass willow mounts or rosettes with bail handles. Escutcheons: matching brass or brass keyhole surrounds. Height: 72–84″. Width: 40–47″. Depth: 17–21″.

Locality and Period
New England, New York, Pennsylvania, and Maryland. c. 1770–1820.

Comment
Closely related to the chest-on-chest, the linen press appeared in the late Chippendale era and was popular throughout the Federal period. Though as large as the chest-on-chest and secretary, the linen press was usually much plainer.

Hints for Collectors
The linen press is not very popular with collectors and tends to cost considerably less than other large period pieces. Most show some restoration, particularly inside the cupboard. For example, in the 19th century, they were often fitted with hooks to serve as wardrobes. Make sure that you have a true linen press and not just a cupboard mounted on a chest of drawers.

Victorian wardrobe

Description
Massive storage piece with plain, overhanging cornice. Below, simple beaded molding over large, paneled 2-door cupboard. Applied, pressed-wood decorative elements in featherlike design across door tops. Interior has clothing hooks and horizontal rods for 3 removable shelves. Base plain or with serpentine or oxbow edge; protrudes 2–3″ over 2 similarly shaped half-length drawers. Paneled sides, top, and bottom. Plain skirt. Stiles terminate in shaped feet above casters. Paneled, nailed, and glued construction.

Materials and Dimensions
Oak and quartersawed oak. Applied decoration oak, ash, or hickory; stained to match. Hinges: brass or iron butt. Pulls: brass rosettes. Escutcheons: brass oblongs with finger grips. Casters: iron. Height: 80–86″. Width: 48–52″. Depth: 30–38″.

Locality and Period
Large factories in the East and Midwest. c. 1880–1920.

Comment
Since closets were rare in most houses and apartments until the late 19th century, a large wardrobe like this one was a necessity, and many homes might have had at least 6 of them. Being large and bulky, however, many were broken up once they went out of style, and they are no longer easy to find.

Hints for Collectors
Wardrobes similar to this one are being reproduced today, so be sure to examine each piece, particularly the frame, for signs of age, dirt, and wear. Start with the interior, as stains and dirt will remain there even after a piece has been refinished.

Description
Tall clothes cupboard with overhanging, sometimes molded cornice. 1 or, more often, 2 long doors, usually paneled. Interior has wooden pegs or iron hooks for clothing. Sides frequently paneled. May have 1 full-length drawer below doors. Skirt plain or valanced. Feet French-style or simple, tapered extensions of sides. Usually painted. Paneled and nailed construction.

Materials and Dimensions
Pine, poplar, cedar, walnut, or mixed softwoods. Usually stained or painted brown, black, red, or dark gray. Sponging and graining, usually in imitation of mahogany, less common. Hinges: iron or brass butt. Pulls: turned wooden, brass, porcelain, or pressed-glass knobs. Latches: carved wood. Height: 78–84″. Width: 42–46″. Depth: 22–24″.

Locality and Period
New England west to California and the Southwest, and throughout the South. c. 1870–90.

Comment
At first glance, the wardrobe shown here would seem to date from the Federal period, but wardrobes did not appear in this form until almost the middle of the 19th century. It actually dates from c. 1870, and is an example of the Victorian Federal Revival style.

Hints for Collectors
Although these wardrobes were made in quantity during the Victorian era, few have survived. Yet they often may be acquired inexpensively because their large size makes them impractical for most homes and consequently they are not in demand. Grained or sponged examples are particularly desirable.

Description
Tall clothes cupboard with overhanging, molded cornice. 2 long, paneled doors open on cupboard with wooden pegs and horizontal supports for 3–4 removable shelves. Below doors, 1 full-length drawer with applied, molded edge. Sides paneled in 2 sections. Back paneled. Plinthlike base. Paneled and nailed construction.

Materials and Dimensions
Pine or poplar. Natural, or stained red, blue, or green. Hinges: iron or brass butt. Pulls: turned wooden, iron, or pressed-glass knobs. Latches, when present: iron or carved wood. Escutcheons: brass or iron keyhole surrounds. Height: 72–76″. Width: 38–42″. Depth: 18–21″.

Locality and Period
New England west to Missouri and Texas, and throughout most of the South. c. 1790–1870.

Comment
Paneled wardrobes were always a mark of superior craftsmanship because they required more time and skill than nailed or dovetailed pieces. Although most were made in the late 18th and early 19th centuries, the demand for them survived well into the Victorian period.

Hints for Collectors
Any piece that could be used in several ways, like this one, is especially interesting to the serious collector. With its pegs and without the shelves, this was a wardrobe. When the shelves were added, it became a cupboard. The superior quality of the molding and cabinetwork also marks this piece as an especially good example of the country wardrobe.

Description
Boxlike cold-storage unit with slightly overhanging, molded top above 3 paneled 1-door cupboards. At upper left, ice compartment with drain tube leading to waste-water vessel at base. At lower left, small shelfless cupboard. At right, main storage cupboard with 1–2 shelves. Below, molded panel, hung on pivots, swings up to allow access to waste-water vessel. Plain skirt and plinthlike base. Paneled sides and back. Paneled and nailed construction.

Materials and Dimensions
Oak and quartersawed oak; occasionally pine. Secondary wood pine. Ice compartment lining: tin. Drain pipe: metal. Waste-water vessel: enamelware or tin. Hinges: brass or steel. Pulls: brass latches and handles in combination. Height: 40–48″. Width: 25–29″. Depth: 13–16″.

Locality and Period
Throughout the United States. c. 1890–1930.

Comment
Although ice refrigeration had been used in the 1800s, it only became popular around the turn of the century. Some iceboxes were quite ornate and, like the one shown here, had elaborate cast-brass fittings. Others, particularly those made after 1920, were plainly made and had industrial steel latches and hinges.

Hints for Collectors
Few people use iceboxes today for refrigeration, but they are extremely popular as liquor cabinets and storage units. At antiques stores they usually command a high price, but less expensive examples can be found at country house sales and auctions. Since they are extremely durable, iceboxes usually need little work other than a bit of cleaning up or paint stripping.

Description
Massive wardrobe with rough, unmolded top. 2 long, paneled
doors open on closet space with wooden pegs and shelving. Plain
board sides and stiles extend to floor and form crude, cutout feet.
Plain skirt. Back paneled in massive boards. Paneled, pegged,
and nailed construction.

Materials and Dimensions
Usually pine; rarely chestnut, poplar, or walnut. Pine examples
often stained red, blue, or green. Hinges: iron butt. Pulls: turned
wooden knobs or iron latches. Height: 70–74″. Width: 42–47″.
Depth: 18–24″.

Locality and Period
New England west to Texas and throughout the South.
c. 1800–80.

Comment
A large wardrobe or clothespress was often built into a 19th-
century bedroom or kitchen. It was originally used to store
clothing, but at a later date might have housed anything from
food to tools, or even animal fodder. An owner often altered the
interior of a piece to suit personal needs; here the shelving is a
later addition.

Hints for Collectors
Large, crude cupboards of this sort are sometimes a good buy,
particularly if, like the one shown here, they are pegged and
have paneled doors. Their look puts off some buyers, while their
size intimidates others. But with a bit of cleaning, and possibly
the addition of an appropriate molding at the top, a wardrobe
like this can become an attractive country piece.

Built-in side cupboard

Description
Tall built-in cupboard, usually shallow in relation to height and
width. 2–4 doors, plain, paneled, or battened to prevent
warping. Doors conceal 4–6 shelves, which may be adjustable.
Top, sides, and base plain or molded. Back often absent. Usually
lacks feet. Usually painted. Nailed or, occasionally, dovetailed
construction.

Materials and Dimensions
Pine or poplar; sometimes maple, walnut, or birch. Originally
painted 1–2 solid colors, such as red, blue, or white. Hinges: iron
butt; H or strap early and rare. Pulls: porcelain or turned
wooden knobs. Latches, when present: shaped wood or brass.
Height: 70–80″. Width: 38–46″. Depth: 12–18″.

Locality and Period
New England west to Ohio, south to the Carolinas. c. 1780–1830.

Comment
Since they were often designed to the homeowner's
specifications, there are many different types of built-in side
cupboards. Early pieces were sometimes designed to match
corner cupboards. Country examples can usually be dated only
by their original surroundings, if known, or by hardware and
construction. The best examples have finely paneled doors and
elaborate molding.

Hints for Collectors
As with corner cupboards, feet have sometimes been added to
these cupboards to make them more marketable; make sure they
match the piece in style and construction. If there is a back,
make sure it is original. The nails with which it is attached
should match those on the sides and shelves.

Description
Triangular 1- or 2-piece cupboard with molded cornice or flat, slightly overhanging top. Both upper and lower sections have 1- or 2-door paneled cupboard; interiors have 2–3 plain triangular shelves. Plain skirt. Feet tapered extensions of stiles or plain bracket. Paneled and nailed or dovetailed construction.

Materials and Dimensions
Pine or poplar; also maple, walnut, cherry, or apple. Secondary wood pine or poplar. Painted gray, red, blue, or brown; sometimes grained to imitate mahogany or sponged in earth tones. Hinges: iron butt or H. Pulls: brass, porcelain, or turned wooden knobs. Latches: brass or iron. Escutcheons, when present: brass or iron plates or keyhole surrounds. Height: 72–84″. Width: 37–44″. Depth: 19–22″.

Locality and Period
New England west to the Mississippi River, and into the South and Southwest. c. 1820–50.

Comment
As a rule, the earlier the corner cupboard, the more elaborate the molding and door panels. By the mid-19th century these pieces had moved from the dining room to the kitchen and had lost the characteristics of a specific style.

Hints for Collectors
The popularity of corner cupboards has made even the most ordinary examples expensive. As a result, brand-new cupboards made of old boards are appearing on the market. Watch out for new paint, 20th-century nails, and boards with nail holes, as well as signs of artificial aging and wear in unusual places; all are clues that the piece is not what it seems.

Open cupboard

Description
1- or 2-piece cupboard with plain or molded cornice. Upper section: 2–4 open shelves, 1 or more sometimes with grooves for plates or square holes for spoons. Set back from lower section 4–12″, forming countertop. Lower section: various arrangements of cupboards and drawers, most often with 1–2 paneled or plain-board doors concealing 1–3 shelves. Base molded and without feet, or with plain or valanced skirt and tapered or plain bracket feet. Often painted. Paneled and dovetailed or nailed construction.

Materials and Dimensions
Pine or poplar. Most painted 1–2 colors, usually red, blue, green, or gray; sponge- or grain-painting less common. Hinges: iron butt; rarely H or butterfly. Pulls: turned wooden, brass, pressed-glass, or porcelain knobs. Latches: shaped wood or brass. Escutcheons, when present: brass or iron keyhole surrounds. Height: 72–80″. Width: 37–42″. Depth: 15–19″.

Locality and Period
New England west to California and throughout the South. c. 1780–1880.

Comment
Many of these cupboards were originally built in and consequently lack feet. Most were made by country joiners, carpenters, or farmers, frequently from several kinds of scrap timber, and tend to be rather crude.

Hints for Collectors
Practical and homey, the open cupboard is a great favorite among collectors and, fortunately, still relatively easy to find. Look for quality construction, good proportions, and original paint.

Scalloped open cupboard

Description
1- or 2-piece cupboard with molded or plain cornice. Cornice board and upper front stiles cut in scalloped pattern. Upper section: 2–4 shelves, 1 frequently with notched plate rack or cutout holes for spoons. Set back from lower section 4–12″, forming countertop. Lower section: 1–2 paneled or plain-board doors concealing 1–3 shelves. 2–3 narrow drawers may be present directly below counter. Plain or scalloped skirt and plain bracket feet. Usually painted. Paneled and nailed or, less frequently, dovetailed construction.

Materials and Dimensions
Pine, poplar, or walnut; occasionally birch or cherry. Secondary wood pine or poplar. Most originally painted red, blue, or gray; rarely grained or sponge-painted. Hinges: iron butt; less often, H or butterfly. Pulls: brass, porcelain, or turned wooden knobs. Latches: shaped wood or brass. Height: 72–76″. Width: 39–42″. Depth: 9–13″.

Locality and Period
New England west to California, and into the South. c. 1800–70.

Comment
Scalloped open cupboards, sometimes called dressers, were most numerous in New England and Pennsylvania. The scalloping was an attempt to lend distinction to an otherwise prosaic form.

Hints for Collectors
Scalloped cupboards are easy to fake, so make sure you are getting the real thing. It is easy to make a plain open cupboard more desirable and much more expensive by cutting scallops into the stiles and cornice boards. Make sure the scallops are uneven and without sharp edges, as old hand-cut examples would be, and be wary of new wood or paint.

Low scalloped corner cupboard

Description
Triangular open cupboard with slightly overhanging, molded cornice. May have secret drawer in cornice. End boards elaborately scalloped and canted rather than flat. 2–3 interior shelves with cyma-curve edges. Base molding matches that of cornice. Skirt valanced. Plain bracket feet. Usually painted. Nailed or dovetailed construction.

Materials and Dimensions
Pine, including Southern hard pine, poplar, or walnut. Most examples originally painted; interior and exterior often contrasting colors, most commonly red/green or green/blue. Height: 47–50″. Width: 33–36″. Depth: 17–19″.

Locality and Period
Pennsylvania south to the Carolinas and Georgia. c. 1770–1820.

Comment
Low corner cupboards, such as the one shown here, which is barely 4′ high, might have originally stood on a table or in a wall niche, although their height also made them suitable for display at floor level. These cupboards are rare and seldom seen, even in museums or private collections, possibly because they were less practical than the larger types.

Hints for Collectors
Approach low corner cupboards with caution. Any good example should have well-worn feet and skirt. New paint, new wood, differences in color or wear on the cupboard bottom all indicate that the base may be new, and that the piece is only the top half of a larger cupboard.

Chippendale architectural built-in corner cupboard

Description
Triangular or bow-backed cupboard, originally built into corner of room. Upper section: 3–4 concave, scalloped shelves and shell-carved dome flanked by fluted pilasters with ornate capitals. Lower section: may have single matching shelf and pilasters flanking dome; doors, when present, paneled or glazed. Dovetailed or nailed construction.

Materials and Dimensions
Pine or poplar; rarely walnut. Painted to match woodwork of original room; usually several layers of paint; often white. Hinges: iron butt or H. Pulls: brass knobs or small brass pendant loop handles; occasionally turned wooden knobs. Escutcheons, when present: brass keyhole surrounds. Height: 84–100″. Width: 36–40″. Depth: 15–19″.

Locality and Period
New England west to Pennsylvania, south to Georgia.
c. 1750–75.

Comment
Since built-in corner cupboards were seen only from the front, the backs are usually rough or unfinished; they also lack the skirt and feet found on movable cupboards. Details such as the cornice and moldings usually match the architectural style of the room for which a piece was built.

Hints for Collectors
To increase their usability, built-in corner cupboards that have been removed from their original settings often have feet added to them. Examine the feet closely to determine whether they match the rest of the piece in wood, construction, and paint.

Description
Small cupboard and drawers with molded top. Plain pegged and paneled door concealing storage space, usually without shelves. Below, 3–5 drawers with molded thumbnail edges. Plain skirt. Feet extensions of side boards cut out in scalloped pattern. Paneled and dovetailed construction.

Materials and Dimensions
Pine or butternut; either natural or stained red, yellow, green, or blue. Hinges: iron butt. Pulls: turned wooden knobs, often walnut. Latches: iron or brass. Escutcheons, when present: iron keyhole surrounds. Height: 37–48″. Width: 14–18″. Depth: 15–17″.

Locality and Period
Shaker communities in New England, New York, and parts of the South and Midwest. c. 1800–80.

Comment
While all are similar in style, Shaker cupboards were used for many different purposes, and each example is unique. Individual pieces vary in size and number of drawers, in placement of doors, and in interior arrangements.

Hints for Collectors
Not all that is plain is Shaker. Many country cabinetmakers produced simple, vaguely Federal-style furnishings, which may be confused with Shaker pieces, especially since Shaker cupboards are one of a kind. But most Shaker pieces share common characteristics: fine cabinetwork, clean lines, and balanced composition. Studying Shaker pieces in museum collections or shops is the best way to become familiar with the style.

Description
Tall 2-piece kitchen cabinet. Upper section: at top left, tall paneled and glazed 1-door cupboard conceals flour sifter. At top right, shorter 2-door cupboard with 1 shelf. At lower left, 1 short drawer. At lower right, roll-up door conceals work space. Enamelware counter separates upper and lower sections. Lower section: 4–6″ wider than upper section. At left, 1-door cupboard with wire door rack and 3 shelves. At right, 2 short drawers over 1 taller drawer. Small casters beneath plain skirt. Paneled, glued, nailed, and screwed construction.

Materials and Dimensions
Oak; late examples may be painted pine or ash. Glass may be pebbled and tinted, as here; also clear or frosted. Hinges and latches: copper, brass, or iron. Pulls: brass, copper, or iron oblong finger grips. Casters: iron. Height: 66–72″. Width: 38–44″. Depth: 23–27″.

Locality and Period
Large factories in the Midwest, particularly Indiana. c. 1910–40.

Comment
The apartment-dweller's dream, the Hoosier cabinet, so-called because so many were made in Indiana, was designed to be a self-contained kitchen. Besides the flour sifter and rack for cooking tools, these cabinets often came with matching sets of canisters.

Hints for Collectors
A Hoosier cabinet is marvelous for a small kitchen; it provides an ideal storage and work space. Scout country shops and sales, where they sometimes sell for very little in "as is" condition; refinished examples in city stores will cost significantly more. Stripping and cleaning will take time, but will be well worth it.

Glazed setback cupboard

Description
1-piece cupboard with overhanging, molded cornice. Upper section: recessed (4–7″) 2-door cupboard. Each door with 2 panes separated by wooden muntins; interior with 2–3 shelves. Plain, overhanging workshelf over slide-out bread- or cutting-board separates upper and lower sections. Lower section: at left, paneled 1-door cupboard, sometimes with 1 shelf. At right, small drawer over paneled 1-door cupboard. Plain skirt and short bracket feet. Often painted. Paneled and nailed construction.

Materials and Dimensions
Pine or poplar; sometimes cherry or maple. Secondary wood pine. May be painted red, blue, gray, or white. Hinges: brass or iron butt. Pulls: turned wooden or pressed-glass knobs. Latches, when present: iron or brass. Escutcheons (rarely present): iron or brass keyhole surrounds. Height: 60–72″. Width: 26–38″. Depth: 18–21″.

Locality and Period
New England west to Missouri and Texas and throughout the South. c. 1820–80.

Comment
These practical country cupboards were produced throughout a wide area and over a long period of time. Though later examples may have Victorian hardware and decorative detail, the basic form remains remarkably constant. However, because many pieces were made to fit particular rooms, the arrangement of drawers and cupboards and the size may vary substantially.

Hints for Collectors
Plain cupboards are often made more elaborate by the addition of drawers or pull-out breadboards. Beware of new wood, new paint, a lack of wear, or unusual proportions.

Glazed corner cupboard

Description

Tall, triangular cupboard with slightly overhanging, molded cornice. Upper section: 1 door with 6–12 panes of glass divided by wooden muntins. Interior with 2–3 shelves, often with plate ridges. Lower section: permanently attached, deeper than top (1–2″). Full-length drawer above paneled 2-door cupboard, with no shelves or 1. Corners chamfered. Plain skirt. Bracket or chamfered feet. Paneled, pegged, and nailed construction.

Materials and Dimensions

Pine; sometimes poplar or maple with secondary wood pine. May be painted red, blue, or white. Hinges: iron or brass butt. Pulls: turned wooden, pressed-glass, or brass knobs. Latches: iron or brass. Escutcheons (rarely present): brass or iron keyhole surrounds or plates. Height: 86–90″. Width: 40–44″. Depth: 21–24″.

Locality and Period

New England west to Missouri and Texas and throughout the South. c. 1820–70.

Comment

Simple glazed corner cupboards owe something to Federal taste, but most are so plain as to be essentially without a style. Nevertheless, because glass was still relatively expensive, the original owners would have been people of some means.

Hints for Collectors

Solid doors are sometimes replaced with glass because glass-fronted corner cupboards bring a higher price. Look for fresh-cut wood or new paint at the edge of the glass, or for doors that do not match the rest of the piece. The absence of old, bubbly glass panes does not necessarily mean a piece has been altered recently; old panes might have been replaced much earlier.

Empire glass-front cupboard

Description
Tall 2-piece cupboard with heavy, overhanging, molded cornice. Upper section: 2-door cupboard, each door with 6 panes of glass separated by wooden muntins; interior with 3–4 shelves. Lower section: deeper and wider (6–8″) than upper section, with overhanging, molded top and paneled 2-door cupboard; interior with 2–3 shelves and 1–2 locked boxes. Turned balusters applied to front stiles rest on narrow shelf 3–4″ from floor. Plain board sides. Plain skirt. Turned front feet end in small ball. Blocklike rear feet cut out of plain board back. Paneled, dovetailed, and nailed construction.

Materials and Dimensions
Mahogany, walnut, or, as here, pine stained to imitate mahogany. Balusters stained maple. Secondary wood pine. Hinges: brass or iron butt. Pulls: turned wooden knobs. Latches: carved wood. Escutcheons: iron or brass keyhole surrounds or plates. Height: 84–108″. Width: 39–49″. Depth: 14–17″.

Locality and Period
Large factories in the East, South, and Midwest. c. 1825–55.

Comment
Less common than the corresponding corner cupboards, Empire cupboards of this sort are rather plain, being distinguished mainly by the large balusters applied to the front stiles.

Hints for Collectors
Look for the little touches that distinguish a cupboard. Here not only the baluster decoration but also the small, locked boxes inside the lower cupboard add character to the piece. Probably used for silver storage, the boxes also appeared in the Victorian period.

Empire corner cupboard

Description
Triangular 1- or 2-piece corner cupboard with molded,
overhanging cornice. Upper section: front corners have ring-and-
baluster-turned three-quarter-round pilasters on stiles. Glazed
door with muntins in geometric pattern and 2–3 interior shelves.
Lower section: 2 paneled doors conceal 1–2 shelves; turned
balusters and carved rosettes on stiles. Top and bottom
separated by molding. Simple base molding. Pilasters terminate
in square feet. Paneled, dovetailed, and nailed construction.

Materials and Dimensions
Pine, poplar, or walnut. Secondary wood pine. Sometimes
stained red or grained to imitate mahogany. Applied pilasters
usually maple. Hinges: iron butt. Pulls: small brass knobs.
Escutcheons: brass keyhole surrounds or plates. Height: 72–80″.
Width: 37–43″. Depth: 17–19″.

Locality and Period
New England, New Jersey, and Pennsylvania west to Ohio,
south to Maryland. c. 1820–40.

Comment
Many of these high-style cupboards were made around Bergen
County, New Jersey. Though this piece is basically Empire in
feeling, the muntins are set in a distinctly Federal pattern.

Hints for Collectors
Check corner cupboards to see that cornice, feet, backboard, and
paint, if present, are original. Glazed examples should have the
original muntin pattern; check for signs of age and fine wear.
Empire corner cupboards are relatively rare, and pieces as
charming as the one shown here are not easy to find.

Federal corner cupboard

Description
Tall, triangular 2-piece cupboard with molded, slightly overhanging cornice. Front ends chamfered. Upper section: cupboard with 2 glazed doors, each with 4–9 panes separated by wooden muntins and sometimes arranged in a geometric pattern. Interior has 2–3 shelves with molded edges. Narrow molding at juncture of 2 sections. Lower section: deep, paneled 2-door cupboard decorated with stringing. Plain board sides. Molded base above plain skirt. Slightly protruding, plain bracket feet. Paneled, dovetailed, and nailed construction.

Materials and Dimensions
Mahogany, cherry, or walnut. Secondary wood pine or poplar. Shelves pine or poplar; rarely, as here, birch. Stringing boxwood. Hinges: brass or iron butt. Pulls, when present: small brass knobs. Escutcheons: brass ovals or carved ivory diamonds. Height: 86–89″. Width: 48–52″. Depth: 22–25″.

Locality and Period
New England west to Ohio, south to Virginia. c. 1785–1810.

Comment
High-style Federal corner cupboards like the one shown here are rare, although country-made examples are common. Even the most sophisticated examples have relatively little inlay. Many such pieces were made to order for a particular house, so dimensions vary substantially.

Hints for Collectors
Whenever a piece has glass doors, they must be examined with care. The doors may be altered, or may be replacements for the less desirable solid panel doors. Early muntins and frames will show age and wear, and the wood should be the same as that of the cupboard.

Chippendale glazed cupboard

Description
Massive 2-piece cupboard with overhanging, molded cornice above narrow row of beading. Upper section: 2-door cupboard; each door has 6 panes of glass separated by wooden muntins. Interior with 1 full- and 2 half-depth shelves, deeper one with plate rail. Molded skirt and arched base. Lower section: 5–7″ deeper than upper section, with molded top. Tier of 3 drawers over 2 single-door, paneled cupboards that flank reeded center panel. Molded base. Plain or molded bracket feet. Paneled, dovetailed, pegged, and nailed construction.

Materials and Dimensions
Walnut, cherry, or maple; sometimes stained to imitate mahogany. Secondary wood pine. Hinges: brass or iron H or butt. Pulls: brass willow mounts with bail handles, or wooden or brass knobs. Escutcheons, when present: brass or iron plates or keyhole surrounds. Height: 78–82″. Width: 53–57″. Depth: 20–22″.

Locality and Period
New England west to Ohio; mostly Pennsylvania. c. 1780–1830.

Comment
Next to high-style pieces, these large, architectural cupboards were the finest examples of the cabinetmaker's art. The bracket feet and surface reeding are Chippendale characteristics that were used long after the period was over.

Hints for Collectors
The interior of the fine old cupboard shown here has unfortunately been repainted; the lack of wear or crazing and the shiny surface give away the paint's recent application. A fine coat of mellow old paint would enhance the value of such a piece, but new paint decreases its worth.

Eastlake bookcase and cabinet

Description
Massive storage unit. Upper section: high, sloping top has door concealing storage area. Below, 2 rows of applied decoration. Large cabinet with 2 glass-front doors contains 2 shelves. Scalloped molding with 2 pull-out writing slides separates upper and lower sections. Lower section: 2 half-length cupboards with carved decoration over 2 half-length drawers; below drawers, 2 additional half-length cupboards. Plain skirt. Block feet extensions of stiles; center stile extends to floor. Mortise-and-tenon and nailed and glued construction.

Materials and Dimensions
Walnut. Secondary wood pine and poplar. Hinges: brass butt. Pulls: oblong brass mounts with bail handles or brass or turned wooden knobs. Escutcheons: brass or iron keyhole surrounds. Height: 85–87″. Width: 60–63″. Depth: 31–33″.

Locality and Period
Major factories in the East and Midwest. c. 1875–90.

Comment
Though representative of many Eastlake-style bookcase and cabinet combinations produced in America, the piece shown here is probably unique. The upper cabinet closely resembles a "Library Book Case" shown in Eastlake's *Hints on Household Taste* (1872), but the base is totally different from the prototype and was no doubt made to suit a specific purpose.

Hints for Collectors
Pieces like the one illustrated here present a challenge. Although most unusual examples are probably just variations of common forms, a collector occasionally stumbles upon a unique design.

Mission-style glass-front cabinet

Description
Cabinet or bookcase with gallery (4–6″ high) formed from
extensions of back and side boards. Sides of gallery taper slightly
toward front. Glass-front door has 16 panes separated by plain,
rectangular wooden muntins. Interior contains 3–4 movable
shelves resting on adjustable brass pegs. Back and sides solid
boards. Plain skirt. Shallow bootjack feet. Mortise-and-tenon
construction fixed with wedges and pegs.

Materials and Dimensions
Oak and quartersawed oak. Hinges: brass butt with removable
pins. Pulls: brass plate combines escutcheon and bell-shaped
handle. Height: 54–57″. Width: 29–31″. Depth: 12–13″.

Locality and Period
Small shops and factories in the East and Midwest. c. 1900–20.

Comment
Glass-front cabinets such as this one by L. & J. G. Stickley of
Fayetteville, New York, one of several leading manufacturers,
were a favorite of the Mission-style designers. The pieces were
used as bookcases and cabinets for storing and displaying curios.

Hints for Collectors
Since there are many Mission-style cabinets similar to this one, a
collector should learn to distinguish those of better quality.
Ordinary pieces will be joined with nails or screws, often
concealed beneath wooden tabs glued to the surface of the case.
Better pieces will have mortise-and-tenon construction, pegged
or wedged together. Such construction indicates that the cabinet
was hand-assembled by skilled workmen.

115 Colonial Revival glass-front bookcase

Description
1-piece bookcase with molded, overhanging top above a veneered and inlaid frieze. 2 large glazed doors, each with 24–28 panes separated by wooden muntins. Interior has 2–4 unmolded shelves. Door frames decorated with black paint that mimics ebony stringing. Plain board sides. Protruding base has heavy molding and contains molded full-length drawer. Elaborately valanced skirt with applied decoration at center. Molded bracket feet. Nailed, screwed, and glued construction.

Materials and Dimensions
Walnut and burl walnut veneer over pine. Back plywood. Inlay birch. Hinges: brass or iron butt. Pulls: brass rosettes with teardrop handles. Height: 48–50″. Width: 40–41″. Depth: 16–17″.

Locality and Period
Large factories throughout the East and Midwest. c. 1910–30.

Comment
Like many Colonial Revival pieces, this bookcase does not really look like any piece of 18th-century furniture, but is a mélange of the Chippendale, Federal, and Empire styles, which are more or less artfully blended. Since those who purchased such furnishings were more interested in a feeling of bygone days than in historical accuracy, this was sufficient.

Hints for Collectors
The bookcase illustrated here has peeling veneer, a broken foot, and a damaged pull. Were it actually an 18th-century piece, restoration would be worth undertaking. However, because there are so many late Colonial Revival bookcases, and because they are relatively inexpensive, only buy an example that is in good condition.

Renaissance Revival corner cupboard

Description
Massive, 5-sided cupboard with broad front, narrow canted
sides, and wedge-shaped back. Overhanging, molded top has
band of rope-turned decoration beneath edge. Tall glass
cupboard door has molded frame with applied, floral-decorated
bow at top. At each side of door, narrow glass panel surrounded
by molded frame. Cupboard interior has 3 molded shelves, each
with a plate slot. Flanking door, 2 pilasterlike stiles, rope-turned
above, baluster-turned below. Molded, plinthlike base has full-
length drawer. Dovetailed and nailed construction.

Materials and Dimensions
Rosewood, mahogany, or walnut. Secondary wood pine. Hinges:
brass or iron butt. Pulls: oblong brass mounts with bail handles.
Escutcheons: brass oblongs set vertically. Height: 64–70″. Width:
41–45″. Depth: 27–29″.

Locality and Period
Better shops and factories in the East and Midwest. c. 1860–80.

Comment
During the Victorian era, corner cupboards declined in
popularity and glass-front china cabinets replaced them as
display units. Most are in the Gothic or Renaissance revival
styles. Cupboards in a simple country style, which were also
produced in the Victorian era, more closely resemble Federal
pieces.

Hints for Collectors
Although Victorian corner cupboards are relatively rare, they
have never captured much attention from collectors. Examples
with good molding and fine woods, such as mahogany or
rosewood, are the most desirable.

117 Gothic Revival vitrine

Description
Tall, 2-piece display cabinet. Upper section: large 2-door glass cabinet topped by elaborate, scrolled fretwork cornice with pierced foliate and geometric decoration. Doors have wooden frames with arched, fretwork-decorated tops. Interior with 3–4 adjustable shelves and mirrored back. Lower section: 2 half-length drawers set back 6–8″ above 1 full-length drawer, forming a shallow, galleried shelf. Solid board sides. Plain skirt. Short, turned legs with ball feet. Dovetailed, nailed, and glued construction.

Materials and Dimensions
Walnut or walnut veneer; rarely mahogany or rosewood. Secondary wood pine. Hinges: brass butt. Pulls: small turned wooden or brass knobs. Latches, when present: iron or brass. Escutcheons: circular brass. Height: 99–102″. Width: 43–47″. Depth: 17–19″.

Locality and Period
Several large eastern and midwestern factories. c. 1845–70.

Comment
Vitrines, used to display the many natural objects and souvenirs the middle- and upper-class Victorians were fond of accumulating, are not to be confused with bookshelves or cabinets. The mirrored back would be of no use in a bookcase, and the shelves are too light to support a row of books.

Hints for Collectors
Gothic Revival furniture is not easy to find. Much of the visual effect of a piece like the one shown here is in the pierced cornice, so be sure it is intact; significant damage will considerably lessen the value.

Description
Tall, shallow cupboard with molded, slightly overhanging top and glass front and sides. Shaped backboard has cutout cornice, applied floral decoration, and central oblong mirror. Flat glass door and curved glass sides framed by plain stiles; interior contains 3 shelves with molded edges and plate slots. Solid board back. Protruding, molded base has plain skirt. Flattened cabriole legs supported by shaped brackets. Glued, screwed, and nailed construction.

Materials and Dimensions
Oak and quartersawed oak, sometimes with pine secondary wood; rare, early examples walnut. Hinges: brass or iron butt. Pulls: brass handles that incorporate diamond-shaped escutcheons. Height: 65–70″. Width: 37–42″. Depth: 12–15″.

Locality and Period
Large factories throughout the East and Midwest. c. 1890–1920.

Comment
The china closet with curved sides was a late 19th-century innovation that reflected both the new abundance of inexpensive plate glass and the Victorian fondness for displaying knickknacks and china. Because they were produced just as oak became popular, most are made in that wood.

Hints for Collectors
Elaborate china closets with mirrors and shaped cornices bring high prices, while plainer examples are still reasonable. Whatever your choice, avoid pieces that have cracked or missing sections of curved glass, which is expensive and difficult to replace.

Colonial Revival china cabinet

Description
Tall, shallow, 2-piece cabinet. Upper section: molded, overhanging top has gallery that rises at center and 3 metal finials, the central one flanked by reeded pilasters. Below, burled frieze with molded bands, and 2-door cabinet. Doors, separated by panel, have 7–11 panes divided by wooden muntins. Interior has 2–3 adjustable shelves. Lower section: 4–6″ deeper than upper section, with molded, overhanging, serpentine top and 1 full-length serpentine drawer. Shaped skirt. Stylized inlay on drawer and skirt. Square, tapered legs and spade feet. Nailed, screwed, doweled, and glued construction.

Materials and Dimensions
Walnut and walnut burl veneer. Secondary wood pine. Inlay boxwood. Black paint imitates stringing. Hinges: brass butt. Pulls: oval brass mounts with bail handles and small brass knobs. Finials: brass. Height: 64–69″. Width: 36–39″. Depth: 13–15″.

Locality and Period
Large factories in the East and Midwest. c. 1890–1930.

Comment
Although the china cabinet seen here reflects the Hepplewhite style, other Colonial Revival cabinets may be in the Queen Anne, Chippendale, or Empire modes. All differ substantially from the period pieces they imitate in appearance and materials.

Hints for Collectors
The earlier examples of Colonial Revival furniture are usually better crafted than those made toward the end of the period. A china closet made between 1880 and 1910 may be dovetailed or even pegged, while the one shown here, made around 1930, is put together with wire nails, screws, and factory-cut dowels. Look for quality turn-of-the-century examples.

Art Deco china cabinet

Description
Blocky, 1-door cabinet mounted on thin legs. Flat top with thin band of inlay, veneer decorated edge, and chamfered front corners. Large square door has glass panes set in muntins to form a geometric pattern inside a narrow, molded frame. Full-length drawer below cabinet, and front corners decorated with painted cross-hatch and star designs to imitate inlaid ivory. Unvalanced skirt with thin band of inlay. Octagonal legs topped by finial-like turnings and joined at sides by slightly curved stretchers. Feet plain stumps. Nailed and glued construction.

Materials and Dimensions
Mahogany or walnut veneer over pine. Inlay rosewood. Legs ebonized. Muntins and frame: metal, painted. Hinges: steel butt. Pulls: plug-shaped celluloid knobs. Height: 52–55″. Width: 31–32″. Depth: 10–11″.

Locality and Period
Factories in the East. c. 1926–30.

Comment
Made to order for B. Altman & Co., the New York City department store, the example illustrated imitates, in less expensive materials, the fine Art Deco furniture made by French designers like Emile-Jacques Ruhlmann.

Hints for Collectors
Recognizing the design sources of a cabinet like the one shown here requires a familiarity with the Art Deco movement in Europe and its effect on American design. For example, here the use of white paint to imitate ivory reflects the influence of early French Art Deco designers, who frequently employed ivory for inlay. The use of mixed light and dark woods seen here is also characteristic of French examples.

Art Nouveau étagère

Description
Tall, slim display piece with overhanging, shaped and molded top. Mirrored backboard has molded, carved, and pierced frame and an overhanging shelf supported by a curvilinear, shell-carved bracket. Central cabinet has mirrored back, bowfront glass door, and 2 carved, leglike supports. On each side of cabinet, molded and carved oblong shelves with mirrored backboards rest on similar supports. Plain skirt. Cabriole legs end in small paw feet. Glued and screwed construction.

Materials and Dimensions
Mahogany, rosewood, or walnut. Secondary wood pine. Hinges: brass butt. Pulls, when present: small brass knobs. Escutcheons: brass oblong plates. Height: 63–66″. Width: 33–36″. Depth: 10–12″.

Locality and Period
Fine factories in the East and Midwest. c. 1900–10.

Comment
Though the Art Nouveau style was tremendously popular in Europe at the turn of the century, its flowing lines and rich carving had relatively little effect on American furniture design. American examples executed in the style were produced in relatively small quantities by a very limited number of manufacturers.

Hints for Collectors
Small, light étagères, such as the one shown here, are hard to come by and extremely desirable. Examine the wood carefully for cracks and repairs. Rosewood is very brittle and apt to split, especially when it is carved in thin pieces, as it is here.

Description

Set of open shelves over 1-door cabinet. Upper section: central shelf with molded edge below high, pagodalike backboard with 4 mirrors. Carved-fretwork supports at sides of backboard. Cornice in form of temple roof. At sides, shaped shelves braced by spindle-turned or carved supports. Lower section: glazed 1-door cupboard with interior shelf, flanked by 2 shaped shelves. Lower front stiles in Oriental style. Plain skirt below molded base. Square feet. Paneled back. Dovetailed, glued, nailed, and screwed construction.

Materials and Dimensions

Ash and pine, ebonized; occasionally other ebonized hardwoods. Secondary wood pine. Hinges: brass right angles, in Oriental style. Escutcheons: matching brass. Height: 76–80″. Width: 47–50″. Depth: 16–18″.

Locality and Period

A limited number of factories, primarily in New York and the Midwest. c. 1875–85.

Comment

Very few étagères in the Anglo-Japanese mode were made in America; most were made to order for the well-to-do, and all were slightly different. Though the basic form was rectilinear, some have flat rather than rooflike tops, and others have asymmetrically arranged shelves.

Hints for Collectors

An étagère like the one illustrated is very rare and will be priced accordingly. Although a piece with damaged fretwork and finials may sell for less, restoration is costly, and what looks like a bargain in "as is" condition may be quite expensive.

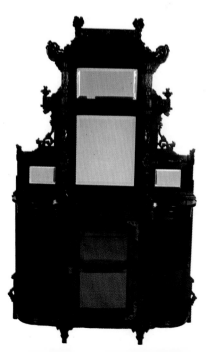

123 Renaissance Revival cupboard-base étagère

Description
Monumental 2-piece display shelves and cupboard. Upper section: tall backboard has 3 mirrors, with the largest in center. Back rises to curved, triangular pediment with molded edge, topped by urn-shaped finial. At each side of pediment, smaller, urnlike finials top turned spindles that support 3 shaped shelves. Lower section: removable, molded, and slightly overhanging marble top above central cupboard with 1 paneled door, inlaid with decorative banding and floral motif. At each side of cupboard, quadrant-shaped opening with 1 curving shelf. Plinthlike base with 4 square pilasters. Paneled, dovetailed, glued, and screwed construction.

Materials and Dimensions
Walnut. Secondary wood pine. Inlay and stringing boxwood and burl walnut. Applied decoration may be ebonized, gilded, or painted. Hinges: brass butt. Escutcheons: wooden circles. Height: 87–102″. Width: 47–56″. Depth: 18–22″.

Locality and Period
A few fine cabinet shops in large eastern cities; some examples English imports. c. 1860–75.

Comment
Since massive display pieces like this were almost always made to order, they were expensive and never common. While most differ in decorative details, they retain the same basic mirror and shelf arrangement. The example shown here is in the Renaissance Revival style, but Rococo pieces are also known.

Hints for Collectors
Because of their size, large étagères were often dismantled. A portion of any étagère is not of any great value, but a complete example is quite costly.

Description
Massive display piece with molded backboard and protruding
center cabinet flanked by 2 smaller cabinets. Backboard has 3
small, inset porcelain plaques, and center cabinet has additional
larger plaque of woman's head. Elaborately carved and scrolled
back rises in 2 steps to cartouchelike cornice. Cabinets flanked by
carved, turned, and gilded pillars. Cabinet interiors have single
shelves. Shaped and molded base conforms to cabinet front.
Large, flattened ball or paw feet. Paneled back. Glued, nailed,
and screwed construction.

Materials and Dimensions
Mixed hardwoods, including walnut, maple, and ash. Decorated
with painting, gilding, and satinwood inlay. Ebonized feet.
Hinges: inset brass butt. Escutcheons: brass keyhole surrounds.
Brass frame surrounds large plaque. Height: 71–75″. Width:
62–65″. Depth: 17–19″.

Locality and Period
Fine cabinetmakers in the East. c. 1860–80.

Comment
These large cabinets were intended primarily for the storage and
display of silver, trophies, and other memorabilia so dear to
Victorians and were made in limited quantities for use in the
parlor or drawing room. This example is in the Neo-Grec style, a
somewhat uncommon Victorian mode closely related to the
Renaissance Revival style.

Hints for Collectors
This is a good example of a piece of furniture that today is
primarily of historical interest. Too large for the average modern
home and not a practical storage piece, a cabinet like this is
better suited for display at a museum or historic site.

Renaissance Revival wardrobe

Description
Massive wardrobe with overhanging molding at top. At rear, short, rectangular splashboard with burl panel and shell-carved and molded cornice. Splashboard flanked by low railing of turned spindles; at each end, 1 block topped by metal, urn-shaped finial. Beneath top, full-length drawer with paneled burl front flanked by faceted blocks. Below, simple molding above paneled 2-door storage area, also with molding. At each side of storage area, elaborately turned pilasters terminate in turnip feet; block feet at rear. Sides solid pine. Plain skirt. Paneled, dovetailed, nailed, and glued construction.

Materials and Dimensions
Walnut and solid burl walnut; early examples mahogany. Secondary wood pine. Hinges: brass butt. Pulls: engraved brass oblongs with bail handles. Escutcheons: brass oblongs. Finials: brass. Height: 65–73″. Width: 38–43″. Depth: 17–19″.

Locality and Period
Better factories in the East and Midwest. c. 1860–80.

Comment
Early Victorian wardrobes were made in limited numbers and are seen less often today than the large oak examples from the turn of the century. Most were too heavy to move and were discarded when their usefulness declined.

Hints for Collectors
Although the example illustrated here is American, many Victorian wardrobes and armoires were made in England or the Continent. Foreign examples may be constructed of woods not native to America and also tend to be more elaborately designed and decorated than American pieces.

Victorian transitional bedside cabinet

Description
Pedestal-shaped cabinet with square, molded lift top. Top opens to reveal small compartment with sides tapering outward to a molded edge. Below compartment, full-length drawer. Large cupboard below has 1 paneled door flanked by ¾-turned pillars. Protruding, molded base rests on plinthlike foundation. Plain skirt. Often has casters. Paneled and glued construction.

Materials and Dimensions
Walnut or pine with burl walnut veneer. Secondary wood pine. Interior compartment lined with bird's-eye maple. Hinges: brass or iron butt. Pulls: brass mounts in dragonfly design, with brass pendant drops and crosspieces. Escutcheons: brass or wooden circular plates. Casters: iron and wood or brass. Height: 35–37″. Width: 21–23″. Depth: 20–22″.

Locality and Period
Major factories in the East and Midwest. c. 1850–80.

Comment
Though clearly Renaissance Revival in general appearance, the piece shown here also displays a revival of the Empire style, demonstrated by the symmetrical pillars and use of veneer. Other similar pieces will have Rococo or Eastlake details. The example shown is 1 of 2 types; the other has a flat, unhinged top, usually of white marble.

Hints for Collectors
Unusual details often distinguish the better Victorian pieces from run-of-the-mill examples. The use of bird's-eye maple as a lining in this cabinet indicates superior workmanship, as do the turning of the pillars and the paneling of door and sides. Note also the carefully matched veneer.

Renaissance Revival bedside cabinet

Description
Pedestal-shaped stand has marble or wooden top with molded edge. Front of top slightly inset to conform to pattern of canted, shaped, scrolled, and reeded stiles, which protrude over front and sides of cabinet. Paneled cupboard door has raised central oblong below full-length drawer decorated with veneer and corner bosses. Paneled sides. Massive plinthlike base, often with casters. Plain skirt. Paneled and glued construction.

Materials and Dimensions
Mahogany, rosewood, or walnut, with walnut veneer, both burl and crotch grain. Secondary wood pine. Hinges: brass butt. Pulls: brass rosettes with ebonized, turned wooden pendant drops, brass rosettes with brass rings, or leaf-carved wooden handles. Escutcheons: brass or carved wooden circular plates. Casters: brass or iron and wood. Height: 34–35″. Width: 18–20″. Depth: 20–22″.

Locality and Period
Better shops throughout the East and Midwest. c. 1860–90.

Comment
Small cabinets such as this one were often part of a Renaissance-style bedroom set, which would include a bed, dresser, chest of drawers, and 2 or more chairs. These cabinets are relatively common and well made. Less often seen is a lift-top version.

Hints for Collectors
Many Victorian pieces had iron or brass casters. Turn a piece over to see if it has holes for casters; if it does, you may want to restore them. Check a piece that is intact to determine the proper replacements. Period casters can often be found in old cabinet shops or even in junk or secondhand stores.

Renaissance Revival music cabinet

Description
Storage cabinet has removable marble top with molded edges. Canted stiles, scrolled at top and bottom, extend slightly beyond sides of chest. Cupboard with 1 paneled door decorated with applied carving of musical instruments. Interior divided by vertical wooden slats. Full-length drawer below. Plain skirt. Molded feet partially conceal casters. Paneled, glued, and nailed construction.

Materials and Dimensions
Walnut or rosewood; rarely oak. Walnut veneer on door. Secondary wood pine. Some portions ebonized. Top veined brown marble. Hinges: brass or iron butt. Pulls: turned and ebonized wooden handles on brass mounts. Escutcheons: brass keyhole surrounds. Casters: wood and metal. Height: 42–45″. Width: 30–32″. Depth: 17–18″.

Locality and Period
Major factories in the East and Midwest. c. 1865–85.

Comment
Early music cabinets are not common. The cupboard and drawer combination is similar to that found in other Victorian pieces, such as commodes and bedside cabinets. But even without the identifying decoration, the function of the piece shown here is evident from the vertical dividers in the interior of the cabinet.

Hints for Collectors
Marble tops are sometimes added to Victorian pieces to increase desirability, so make sure the marble is original and in good condition. Remove the top and see if the rough frame beneath it looks old and shows the wear caused by shifting of the heavy marble top. The underside of the top may also be discolored on those sections that touch the frame.

Art Nouveau–Art Deco cabinet

Description
Storage cabinet with flat, molded top. Slightly overhanging full-length drawer with compartments over 2-door cupboard with 4 fixed shelves. Doors decorated in marquetry with stylized design in form of floral wreath against background of geometric devices. Plain skirt. Short, turned feet extend from stiles. Glued and screwed construction with nailed backboard.

Materials and Dimensions
Gumwood with walnut veneer; also mahogany veneer. Sometimes lacquered blue or green. Hinges: brass butt with removable pins. Pulls: octagonal brass drawer knobs and small, round brass cupboard knobs. Height: 34–36″. Width: 21–23″. Depth: 12–14″.

Locality and Period
Large factories throughout the United States. c. 1925–40.

Comment
In the 20th century, consumers were becoming accustomed to color-coordinated decorating schemes, and consequently makers often gave them a choice of finishes. A label inside the drawer of the cabinet shown here indicates that it was available in different finishes, including mahogany or walnut veneer and blue or green lacquer. The style of this piece reflects a mixture of Art Nouveau (the feet and parts of the marquetry decoration) and Art Deco (the general outline), a frequent combination in American design during the 1920s and 1930s.

Hints for Collectors
Pieces combining 2 styles have attracted little collector attention. Now may be the time to buy well-made examples, such as those with handmade marquetry decoration and good design.

130 Arts and Crafts–Mission-style liquor cabinet

Description
Storage cabinet tapering outward from top to bottom. Extremely wide and overhanging top with square edge and corners supported on 2 shaped brackets at each side. 1-door cupboard with perforated oval window in center. Interior has set of revolving racks for liquor bottles. Skirt tapers slightly at each end. Shaped front feet extend from stiles. Rear bracket feet extend from side boards. Mortise-and-tenon and screwed construction.

Materials and Dimensions
Oak and quartersawed oak. Secondary wood pine. Back oak veneer over pine. Hinges: brass butt. Decorative studs: brass. Pulls: round brass knobs. Escutcheons: brass or iron keyhole surrounds. Height: 36–38″. Width: 33–34″. Depth: 14–15″.

Locality and Period
Shops and factories in the East and Midwest. c. 1900–20.

Comment
Termed a cellarette in catalogues issued by its maker, the stylistically hybrid piece shown here was produced by the Limbert Arts and Crafts Furniture Company of Holland, Michigan. The overhanging top, tapered sides, and Oriental treatment of the door relate to English Arts and Crafts prototypes. On the other hand, the use of quartersawed oak and the solid construction are typical of American Mission-style furniture.

Hints for Collectors
American furniture showing Arts and Crafts influence is rare and valuable. Look for a paper label on the backing that marks a piece as American. Such manufacturers' labels should be protected because their presence can greatly increase value.

20th-century double cabinet

Description
Long storage piece with flat, unmolded top. 2 identical 2-door cabinets mounted side by side on base. Base consists of horizontal plank joined to shaped legs. Cabinet interiors have rows of perforations to hold metal supports for 2 shelves. Rectangular splayed feet. Nailed-on plywood back. Glued, nailed, and screwed construction.

Materials and Dimensions
Maple and bleached maple, partially laminated. Hinges: brass or steel butt. Pulls: holes cut into outer layer of wood. Shelf supports: brass or steel. Height: 20–22". Width: 57–60". Depth: 12–13".

Locality and Period
Large factories throughout the East and Midwest. c. 1930–45.

Comment
Large storage cabinets of this sort were made by many different factories; the example shown here was manufactured by Ewald Holtkamp, and the design is attributed to Alvar Aalto. Very simple to manufacture and assemble, the cabinets were easily mounted singly or in a double unit. Either way, they were the epitome of modern industrial design.

Hints for Collectors
Because factory pieces of this sort go largely unnoticed and unappreciated today, they offer an appealing opportunity for the wise collector, since they are both practical and relatively inexpensive. In a sense the forerunners of Danish (or Scandinavian) Modern, they blend readily with contemporary furniture. Before you buy, make sure the laminated portions are in good condition and not separating.

Description
Cabinet with plain top mitered into plain board sides. Full-length drawer over 1-door cupboard with 1–2 adjustable shelves that rest on metal supports. Drawer and cabinet each have 1 large pull at left. Plinthlike base inset 2″ from sides and partially covered by cupboard door that extends 1″ below sides. No feet. Glued and nailed construction.

Materials and Dimensions
Maple, including bird's-eye; also mahogany veneer over maple. Secondary wood maple. Base ebonized. Hinges: steel butt. Pulls: glass disks on brass shafts. Shelf supports: steel. Height: 27–28″. Width: 16–17″. Depth: 12–13″.

Locality and Period
Better factories in the Midwest. c. 1930–40.

Comment
Also called a nightstand, the bedside cabinet is as common in the 20th century as the 1-drawer bedside stand and the commode were in the 19th. Designed by Gilbert Rohde for the Herman Miller Furniture Company of Zeeland, Michigan, this piece is part of a set that includes a matching bed, 2-piece chest, and dressing table. With its plain lines and rich, contrasting surfaces it is typical of the style favored by modern designers.

Hints for Collectors
Although originally intended for the bedroom, this piece would be useful as a storage cabinet in other rooms as well. The piece shown here has a manufacturer's label inside the drawer. This increases the value of the piece and should never be removed.

Highboys and Tall Chests of Drawers

Highboys, chest-on-chests, and tall chests of drawers are among the most spectacular and interesting types of American furniture. Size alone draws attention to these pieces. They are often more than 7' tall, and have upper drawers that can often be reached only by standing on a stool or a chair.

Highboys first appeared in England. When they were transported to America, they became immensely popular. In the hands of American cabinetmakers, they were transformed: with their fine cabinetwork and lavish carving, highboys are perhaps the pinnacle of American furniture design.

A highboy, always made in 2 pieces, consists of a base that resembles a lowboy and an upper chest of drawers. The first American examples, in the William and Mary style (133), have a flat, overhanging top; the upper section rests on a lower section that consists of 1 to 3 drawers over an elaborately scrolled skirt. Most have 5 to 6 legs, which are either trumpet- or scroll-shaped and are joined by flat, scrolled box stretchers. Queen Anne highboys (135) may be flat-topped or crowned by a high bonnet top, often ornamented with carved finials; they are mounted on elegant cabriole legs that terminate in pad or Dutch feet. They have shaped skirts, often with turned drops.

During the Chippendale period, the American highboy reached its most elaborate and exuberant stage. Although some have flat, overhanging tops, the finest examples (137) have massive bonnet tops. Carving, which had usually been confined to a limited area on Queen Anne examples, became extensive and complex. Bonnet tops incorporate elegant flame- or urn-shaped finials; corners are fluted or reeded; and cabriole legs have carved knees and bold claw-and-ball feet.

The chest-on-chest (139) was also produced in the Chippendale period. It consists of 2 chests of drawers mounted one atop the other; the finest of these pieces have decoration similar to that found on highboys. The simpler, flat-topped chest-on-chests often have short bracket legs, while the more elaborate pieces, with bonnet tops or pediments, often have cabriole legs.

Tall chests of drawers (141) were also made during the Chippendale period; these chests are made in 1 piece and typically have restrained decoration. In some cases, they are mounted on a removable frame, an innovation that had developed during the Queen Anne period and then remained popular, possibly because it facilitated moving the heavy pieces.

By the Federal period, the highboy had fallen out of fashion, but the other large chests continued to be produced. Federal tall chests of drawers, chest-on-chests, and chest-on-frames are usually flat-topped and may have either turned Sheraton-style legs or plain bracket feet. Like many Federal pieces, they are often inlaid and veneered. The few tall chests of drawers made in the Empire period are usually mounted on a base that has scrolled feet.

Victorian tall chests of drawers (143) come in a full array of revival styles and are often made of fine woods such as walnut and rosewood. Many are richly carved and embellished with gilding. Toward the end of the period, plainer pieces made of oak (145) came into vogue. This preference for oak is also evident in the simple Mission-style chests that were made in the early years of the 20th century. By the 1920s and 1930s, bold Art Deco chests (147) had replaced the plain oak pieces. Mostly factory made and usually lacquered, these striking chests bear little resemblance to the aristocratic handwrought highboys of the 17th and 18th centuries.

William and Mary trumpet-leg highboy

Description
2-piece high chest with flat, molded, slightly overhanging top. Upper section: 4 tiers of graduated drawers: a top tier of 2–3 small drawers over 3 full-length drawers, all framed by single arch molding. Lower section: shallow, rectangular center drawer flanked by 2 deeper, square drawers; or, rarely, 1 full-length drawer. Protruding molding joins 2 sections. Skirt deeply valanced. 6 trumpet-turned legs, 2 at rear and 4 across front. Flat, scrolled box stretcher. Ball or bun feet. Dovetailed, nailed, and pegged construction.

Materials and Dimensions
Walnut; drawer fronts often with walnut burl veneer; secondary wood pine. Sometimes, as shown here, japanned pine. Rarely, poplar painted and grained or maple stained red; secondary wood pine, poplar, or basswood. Pulls: brass plates with teardrop handles. Escutcheons: matching brass. Height: 64–68″. Width: 42–47″. Depth: 23–25″.

Locality and Period
New England to Pennsylvania and the Virginias. c. 1700–25.

Comment
The highboy first appeared in America during the William and Mary period. Only a few of these have survived, and most are of the trumpet-leg variety. An uncommon variation has a similar upper section, but the base is not as high and has 1 full-length drawer; there are 5 scroll-carved legs joined by a flat box stretcher.

Hints for Collectors
These highboys are easily confused with those made about the same time in England and the Low Countries. Foreign examples are usually more elaborately decorated.

Chippendale flat-top highboy

Description
2-piece high chest with flat top and overhanging, molded cornice. Top may have gallery. Front corners chamfered and reeded or with fluted columns. Upper section: 4–5 graduated, full-length drawers; top tier may have 2–3 shorter drawers or 3 short over 2 half-length drawers. Lower section: 1 full-length drawer over 3 smaller ones. Molding joins 2 sections. Scrolled skirt. Cabriole legs, sometimes with shell-carved knees. Claw-and-ball or, occasionally, drake feet. Dovetailed construction.

Materials and Dimensions
Mahogany, walnut, cherry, maple, or curly maple. Secondary wood pine or poplar. Pulls: brass willow mounts with bail handles. Escutcheons: matching brass. Height: 66–79″. Width: 40–47″. Depth: 21–24″.

Locality and Period
New England and New York. c. 1750–80.

Comment
The Chippendale flat-top highboy was never as popular as the bonnet-top highboy. Most flat-top examples have a base similar to the one on Queen Anne highboys and were made toward the beginning of the Chippendale period. The exceptions are New Hampshire examples, which date from the 1770s. In all cases, the carving is more restrained than that on bonnet-top pieces.

Hints for Collectors
This type of Chippendale highboy can be easily assembled from disparate pieces. A period chest of drawers or the upper half of a chest-on-chest mounted on a highboy base can look authentic. Check the proportions against known examples and be sure that the drawers are all made in the same way and that the upper and lower sections are constructed from the same wood.

Queen Anne flat-top highboy

Description
2-piece chest with flat, overhanging, molded top and heavily molded cornice, sometimes with secret drawer. Upper section: 4–6 tiers of drawers; top tier may have 2–3 narrower drawers; if 3, center drawer may have fan or shell carving. Lower section: 1 full-length or 2 half-length drawers over 3 smaller ones or, rarely, small central drawer flanked by 2 larger ones; central drawer may be carved. Molding joins 2 sections. Scalloped skirt, sometimes with 2 turned drops or central carved shell. Cabriole legs with pad or, rarely, trifid feet. Dovetailed construction.

Materials and Dimensions
Walnut, sometimes with burl or crotch walnut or maple veneer; also curly or tiger maple, cherry, or apple. Secondary wood pine or poplar. Pulls: brass batwing or willow mounts with bail handles. Escutcheons: matching brass. Height: 68–76″. Width: 35–46″. Depth: 17–20″.

Locality and Period
New England to Pennsylvania, south to Virginia. c. 1720–50.

Comment
Like the example shown, most highboys were not painted. However, during the William and Mary and Queen Anne periods, a few were japanned. The western version of Oriental lacquerwork, japanning required coating a piece with many layers of varnish darkened with lampblack and then applying decorations in gold and vermilion powders.

Hints for Collectors
Occasionally feet have been added to the top section of a highboy, transforming it into a chest of drawers. The clue to this change is an upper tier of 2–3 drawers that are less than full length; chests of drawers almost always had full-length drawers.

Queen Anne bonnet-top highboy

Description

2-piece high chest with bonnet top and removable, turned, and carved flame-shaped finials. Upper section: 5–7 graduated drawers; top tier may have 1 large center drawer flanked by 2 smaller ones, over 3–4 graduated drawers. Lower section: 1 full-length or 2 half-length drawers over tier of 3 taller, equally wide drawers. Molding joins 2 sections. Front may have carved shells or rosettes, particularly in upper center areas. Skirt deeply valanced. Cabriole legs with pad feet. Dovetailed construction.

Materials and Dimensions

Cherry, maple, or walnut. If walnut, drawer fronts may be burl walnut veneer. Secondary wood tulip, poplar, or pine. Finials maple or birch. Pulls: brass batwing or willow mounts with bail handles. Escutcheons: matching brass. Height: 82–94″. Width: 38–44″. Depth: 19–22″.

Locality and Period

New England west to Pennsylvania, south to Georgia. c. 1730–60.

Comment

The Queen Anne bonnet-top highboy is one of the most beautiful forms in American furniture, and frequently shows remarkable proportions and balance. Few modern cabinetmakers could put so much weight on such slim legs so gracefully.

Hints for Collectors

While bonnet-top highboys are not hard to find, strong demand has sent prices quite high. The most desirable examples have original brasses and finials that fit well and show signs of age. Knowing who made the piece increases its value.

Chippendale bonnet-top highboy

Description
2-piece high chest has bonnet top with carved rosettes and urn-
and flame-shaped finials. Upper section: shell- and floral-carved
scrollboard over 2–3 small drawers, then 2 half-length drawers
and 3 graduated full-length drawers. Drawers and scrollboard
flanked by fluted quarter-columns. Lower section: 1–2 drawers
over 3 smaller drawers; center drawer taller and usually carved.
Drawers flanked by fluted quarter-columns. Molding joins 2
sections. Valanced skirt. Cabriole legs carved at knees. Claw-
and-ball feet. Dovetailed and pegged construction.

Materials and Dimensions
Mahogany; also cherry, walnut, or maple. Secondary wood pine
or tulip poplar. Pulls: brass willow mounts with bail handles;
smaller drawers may have turned brass knobs. Escutcheons:
matching brass. Height: 86–99″. Width: 38–44″. Depth: 20–23″.

Locality and Period
Elaborate examples Philadelphia; others New England west to
Pennsylvania, south to Virginia. c. 1755–75.

Comment
This magnificent Philadelphia highboy is an example of the finest
and rarest of American furniture. A good example commands an
extremely high price. Produced by leading cabinetmakers, these
pieces were elaborately carved and perfectly proportioned. Made
in very limited numbers, they are exceedingly scarce today.

Hints for Collectors
Outstanding highboys such as the one shown here are outside the
means of most collectors. But no matter what period you are
interested in, a knowledge of the finest pieces available makes it
easier to critically evaluate the less costly and more common
examples.

Description
Massive, 2-piece storage unit with broken-pediment bonnet top and 1 screw-on finial. Upper section: 3 small drawers, the center one larger, taller, and often shell-carved, over 4 graduated, full-length drawers flanked by fluted pilasters. Lower section: 3–4 full-length block-front drawers. Plain board sides. Shaped and molded skirt with central drop. Short cabriole legs. Claw-and-ball feet. Dovetailed, nailed, and glued construction.

Materials and Dimensions
Mahogany, cherry, or pine; also maple stained to imitate mahogany. Secondary wood pine. Pulls: brass willow mounts with bail handles and brass knobs. Escutcheons: matching brass. Height: 86–90″. Width: 40–43″. Depth: 23–25″.

Locality and Period
Large factories and cabinet shops specializing in reproductions. c. 1875–1930.

Comment
The example illustrated closely resembles 18th-century pieces, is made of solid mahogany, and has hand-cut dovetails—all indications that it is an early reproduction. Because there is evidence that Colonial Revival pieces were first made around 1876, they are sometimes called Centennial furniture.

Hints for Collectors
Early, high-quality reproductions like the one shown here can be mistaken easily for original period pieces. But reproductions have thinner boards and circular saw marks. In addition, wire nails, rather than dovetails, sometimes fasten the drawers together.

Chippendale chest-on-chest

Description
Tall 2-piece chest. Top has broken pediment with 1 carved finial; may also be flat or a bonnet variation with 1–3 finials. Upper section: 5 full-length drawers or 3 small and 2 half-length over 3 full-length; top center drawer may have fan or pinwheel carving. Lower section: 4 full-length drawers or 2 half-length over 3 full-length. Front corners have reeded quarter-columns or flat, fluted pilasters topped by capitals. Sections divided by molding. Molded base. Skirt plain, scalloped, or gadrooned. Feet plain, molded bracket, or claw-and-ball. Dovetailed construction.

Materials and Dimensions
Mahogany, cherry, or walnut; rarely maple. Secondary wood pine, poplar, oak, or cedar; often used in combination. Pulls: brass willow mounts with bail handles. Escutcheons: matching brass. Height: 84–96″. Width: 42–46″. Depth: 22–26″.

Locality and Period
New England, New York, and Pennsylvania, south to the Carolinas. c. 1755–85.

Comment
The chest-on-chest was developed during the Queen Anne era and continued to be made through the Federal period. The many Chippendale variations include chests with block fronts (top and bottom or only bottom) and oxbow examples.

Hints for Collectors
High-style chest-on-chests like the one shown here are very expensive. Beware of "marriages" of pieces from different double chests or 2 chests of drawers. The molding on which the upper section rests is often a clue: if it looks new or as though it does not fit one section, the piece may be a "newly wedded" chest.

Description

2-piece double chest with overhanging, heavily molded top. Upper section: 4–5 equal or graduated drawers. Lower section: 2–4 equal or graduated drawers. Molding joins 2 sections. Skirt plain, with carved center drop, or valanced in Hepplewhite manner. Feet plain bracket or in French manner. Dovetailed construction; back nailed on.

Materials and Dimensions

Cherry, walnut, or birch. Secondary wood poplar, cedar, or pine. Sometimes stained red. Pulls: brass willow mounts, oval plates, or rosettes, all with bail handles. Escutcheons: matching brass or brass keyhole surrounds. Height: 72–80″. Width: 38–44″. Depth: 18–22″.

Locality and Period

New England west to Ohio, south to Maryland and Virginia. c. 1770–1810.

Comment

Like so many country pieces, the example illustrated shows the influence of more than one cabinetmaking period. The brasses are Chippendale and so is the heavy molding, but the wide expanses of uncarved wood, the heavier base and feet, and the drop-decorated skirt are closer to the Federal period. The mixture of styles indicates that this is a transitional piece.

Hints for Collectors

Consider country furniture as an alternative to the more expensive pieces made in Boston, New York, and Philadelphia. Examples like the one shown here, which is from a New England cabinet shop, have the grace and proportions to please even the most critical eye. In addition, they would sell for far less than documented pieces from major woodworking centers.

Chippendale tall chest of drawers

Description
Tall chest with flat, molded, overhanging top. 5–7 graduated, full-length drawers; top 2 drawers may be replaced with 3 short and 2 half-length drawers; top center drawer may have fan or shell carving. Corners chamfered or with reeded quarter-columns. Plain board sides. Molded base. Plain skirt. Feet plain or molded bracket. Dovetailed construction.

Materials and Dimensions
Maple, cherry, walnut, or birch. Secondary wood pine, poplar, or chestnut. Some country examples stained red. Pulls: brass willow mounts or brass rosettes, both with bail handles. Escutcheons: matching brass or brass keyhole surrounds. Height: 58–64". Width: 34–37". Depth: 19–22".

Locality and Period
New England and New York west to Pennsylvania, south to Maryland. c. 1755–90.

Comment
During the Queen Anne period, similar 1-piece chests were made with short cabriole legs and batwing brasses. Although handy for storage, the 1-piece chest was less practical than the chest-on-chest or highboy, both of which came in 2 sections and were consequently easier to move about. Occasionally one finds a matching set of tall and medium-size chests of drawers.

Hints for Collectors
Always check the insides of drawers; they wear down over the years and often have new backs, sides, or runners. Replacements are not objectionable if they are done well and with appropriate materials, but one should pay less for such a piece.

Description
Tall chest of drawers on low, detachable frame. Top flat, overhanging, heavily molded. 5–7 usually graduated drawers; 2 half-length drawers sometimes replace top full-length drawer. Base heavily molded, concealing juncture of chest and frame. Base of frame has plain or gently scalloped skirt. Legs and feet short, turned in late Sheraton manner. Dovetailed construction.

Materials and Dimensions
Maple, including flame and curly; also cherry, walnut, or birch. Secondary wood pine or poplar. Sometimes painted. Pulls: oval brass mounts and bail handles in the Federal manner or small, turned wooden knobs. Escutcheons: matching brass or diamond-shaped bone. Height: 57–62″. Width: 36–42″. Depth: 17–20″.

Locality and Period
New England, New York, and Pennsylvania. c. 1790–1820.

Comment
Although its popularity was greater in earlier years (c. 1770–1800), the chest-on-frame lingered on in rural areas into the 19th century. The removable base made it easier to move these chests, which was important for those examples that had small, turned legs. They were less likely to break when the lower sections could be carried separately.

Hints for Collectors
These chests are uncommon and quite desirable. Make sure that the frame belongs with the top and check the bottom of the case for nail or screw holes and for differences in wood color that might indicate that the piece once had other legs. The base should match the top in style, wood, and aging. Note that the piece illustrated lacks 2 pulls. Matching reproductions of these pulls are available.

143 Renaissance Revival side-locking tall chest of drawers

Description
Massive chest with molded top and pediment-shaped backboard. 2-drawer cabinet in front of backboard. 5–6 full-length drawers that may be locked by a vertical unit that pivots on steel rod and is hidden within front corner stile. Sides paneled. Base plinthlike. Skirt plain or, rarely, scalloped. Stiles and drawer fronts often have veneered panels. Dovetailed, glued, and nailed construction.

Materials and Dimensions
Walnut; less often oak, cherry, maple, or ash. Burl oak or bird's-eye maple veneer. Secondary wood pine or poplar. Pulls: oblong brass mounts with pendant pear-shaped pulls, or brass rosettes with pendant rings. Escutcheons: brass plates or shaped wood. Casters: iron or iron and wood. Height: 60–80″. Width: 34–43″. Depth: 18–21″.

Locality and Period
Factories in the East and Midwest. c. 1870–1900.

Comment
Similar Eastlake and Cottage-style tall chests tend to be smaller than the Renaissance Revival pieces. Although all tall chests are descended from Queen Anne examples, Empire and Victorian designers transformed the type by adding a small cabinet to the top.

Hints for Collectors
Large pieces such as the one shown can appear deceptively small in a store or at an auction. Be sure to measure the space available before you buy. Because many tall chests are nearly 7′ high, some dealers have cut off their backboards. Look for saw marks, rough spots, screw holes, and differences in wear and color that indicate such alterations.

Mission-style tall chest of drawers

Description
Chest of drawers with unmolded top. At front and sides, top
overhangs 2–3″; at rear, splashboard (3–4″ high) present. 3 tiers
of 2 half-length drawers, with wooden dividers inside, over 3 full-
length drawers of varying heights. Plain board sides. Demilune
skirt. Short, tapered legs and feet extensions of square stiles.
Pegged, dovetailed, and screwed construction.

Materials and Dimensions
Oak and quartersawed oak. Pulls: rectangular or oblong brass
plates with triangular bail handles. Height: 47–49″. Width:
35–37″. Depth: 20–21″.

Locality and Period
New York and Michigan. c. 1905–15.

Comment
Made by the shops of Gustav Stickley, this Mission-style chest of
drawers, with its characteristic demilune skirt, is distinct from
others made during the same period, not only in quality of
construction but in design. The drawer arrangement, a
combination of 6 small and 3 large drawers, is rare, as are the
different heights of the larger drawers.

Hints for Collectors
A Stickley tall chest has occasionally been mistaken for an office
filing cabinet, but filing cabinets lack the deep lower drawers and
would be made from thinner pieces of oak; they also may have
metal folder or file dividers. These chests may also be
distinguished from other oak chests of drawers of the period by
the pegs and dovetails used in their construction.

Oak tall chest of drawers

Description
Chest of drawers with flat, molded, overhanging top. 5–7 full-length drawers, equal or graduated, separated by half-round molding. Sides and back have horizontal panels in narrow, rectangular strips. Front skirt plain or demilune; side skirts plain. Square feet are extensions of stiles. Nailed and glued construction.

Materials and Dimensions
Oak and quartersawed oak with pronounced grain. Sometimes fumed or varnished. Pulls: brass plates with bail handles, pendant ring handles, or turned oak knobs. Escutcheons: brass or iron keyhole surrounds. Height: 59–65″. Width: 32–38″. Depth: 18–22″.

Locality and Period
Large factories throughout the United States. c. 1880–1920.

Comment
Mass-produced, these plain oak chests were sold through mail-order catalogues, such as Montgomery Ward's, as well as in furniture stores. Since they were manufactured by so many different companies, they vary substantially in size and decoration. The tall chest of drawers is much less common than the low chest.

Hints for Collectors
Tall chests of drawers are handy storage units, but few turn-of-the-century examples were well made. Moreover, today most chests have been "dipped" to remove the old finish, which causes separation at the joints, swelling, and even a wood deterioration marked by gray areas. Such pieces should obviously be avoided.

Description
Chest with flat, molded, overhanging top. Front corner stiles chamfered. 5–6 equal, full-length drawers have molded borders and applied, oblong decorative plates with pulls. Paneled sides. Plain skirt and molded, plinthlike base. Square, molded feet with casters. Nailed, glued, and dovetailed construction.

Materials and Dimensions
Walnut; rarely mahogany. Secondary wood pine. Pulls: turned wooden knobs inside bead-molded rosettes or leaf-carved handles. Escutcheons: wooden keyhole rosettes. Casters, when present: iron and wood. Height: 48–53″. Width: 31–34″. Depth: 18–20″.

Locality and Period
Cabinet shops and small factories in the East and Midwest. c. 1860–80.

Comment
The tall storage chest, often part of a matching suite of bedroom furniture, was popular throughout the Victorian era. Renaissance Revival examples are sometimes very ornate, with carved splashboards and ebonized accessories, but most are, like this one, rather restrained. Made of attractive and high-quality wood, few of the pieces were painted.

Hints for Collectors
This chest is, as a dealer would say, "in the rough": it needs refinishing, and the pulls on the lower drawer are missing. Because of its condition it can be purchased for perhaps 50% less than usual, and is a good example of an easy-to-restore and therefore desirable piece. Replacement pulls are not hard to find, and an application of wax will give the chest a nice finish.

Art Deco tall chest of drawers

Description
Chest of drawers with flat, molded, slightly protruding top. 6 graduated drawers divided by dust boards; interior of top 2 drawers divided by thin board. No pulls; drawer fronts slightly bowed to provide finger grips. Base inset 1–2″, resting on steel tabs. No feet. Lacquered. Glued, nailed, and screwed construction.

Materials and Dimensions
Pine and ash. Lacquered black, red, or white. Back plywood, stained to match rest of exterior. Height: 51–53″. Width: 36–37″. Depth: 20–22″.

Locality and Period
Better factories in the East and Midwest. c. 1930–45.

Comment
These well-made and appealing tall chests were often part of a bedroom suite that included bed, bureau, small tables, chairs, and possibly even a desk. The example illustrated was made by the Tri-Bond Manufacturing Company, but similar pieces were made by other manufacturers. The use of finger grips instead of drawer pulls is unusual and adds to the overall design. It is not, however, an innovation, since 17th-century chests sometimes had finger grips when pulls were not available.

Hints for Collectors
High chests similar to this one often turn up in used-furniture stores and at house sales. Both practical and attractive, and with simple lines, they blend with any decor. Extra touches, like the dust boards, always indicate a piece of better quality.

Art Deco chest of drawers and clothespress

Description
Combination of clothespress and tall chest of drawers with flat, unmolded top. Clothespress, at left, has single door. Interior with holes for removable hooks. Upper right, 2-door storage area without shelves. Below, 5 drawers, each extending across ⅔ of front. Press door and drawer pulls have characteristic Art Deco streamlining. Plain base. No feet. Glued, nailed, and screwed construction.

Materials and Dimensions
Mahogany and bleached maple with ebonized highlights; sometimes lacquer over pine. Back plywood stained ebony. Secondary wood pine or cedar. Hinges: brass or steel butt. Pulls: saw-cut, ebonized hardwood blocks. Height: 49–55″. Width: 35–38″. Depth: 20–22″.

Locality and Period
Factories in the East and Midwest. c. 1930–45.

Comment
The development of practical storage pieces like this one reflects the shrinking size of the typical 20th-century house or apartment. Combining a clothespress with a chest of drawers made it possible both to conserve space and facilitate dressing. The basic simplicity of the design meant the piece could be produced quickly and at less cost than its streamlined look would indicate.

Hints for Collectors
This is a good-looking, practical piece for the contemporary collector of Art Deco, provided the condition is good. Put together with nails, screws, and glue, the type often did not hold up well. Avoid examples that need restoration; there are enough examples available to be selective.

Lowboys, Dressing Tables, Dressers, and Shaving Stands

The first American lowboys date from the William and Mary period, and it seems probable that, like dressing tables, they were meant to provide a place where toiletries could be stored and applied. A lowboy resembles the base of a highboy; the 2 forms were often made in matching sets. William and Mary examples (149) have 1 to 4 drawers and a valanced skirt, and rest on trumpet-turned legs that are braced by flat, scrolled X-stretchers or box stretchers. By the Queen Anne period, graceful cabriole legs supported the weight of the table. Like the highboys of the period, these Queen Anne lowboys (150) have restrained decoration, typically consisting of simple carving; occasionally the skirt is embellished with drops. Chippendale examples (152) are more lavishly decorated, with intricate carving and bold claw-and-ball feet. In both the Queen Anne and the Chippendale periods, portable dressing mirrors were probably placed on top of the lowboy.

By the beginning of the Federal period, what has come to be called the dressing table took the place of the lowboy. Federal dressing tables are small and rectangular and often have a kneehole (153); on most the legs are square and tapered or thin and reeded. Like lowboys, many of these Federal dressing tables have a plain, flat top. On others, however, a small case of 2 or 3 drawers is permanently mounted at the top rear, providing additional storage space for toiletry articles. City cabinetmakers often painted or gilded their dressing tables, or hung fine fabric about their bases (155). Pieces made by rural craftsmen (154) were simpler, typically made of inexpensive wood, then grained to imitate exotic woods like mahogany.

By the late Federal period, the dressing table often included a permanently attached mirror (160). This form was immensely popular and continued throughout the Victorian period and into the 20th century. Some of the most interesting examples are in the Art Deco style. Usually made of lacquered wood, these Art Deco pieces (175) have a large round mirror between 2 boxlike sets of drawers. Other 20th-century pieces (178) are characterized by their use of industrial materials, such as tubular steel and glass.

A dresser is a high or low chest of drawers with a permanently attached mirror. Dressers first appeared in the Empire period and were perhaps most popular during the Victorian era. Early Victorian examples in mahogany, rosewood, or walnut were made in many revival styles, especially the Rococo and Renaissance. Typically these revival pieces have a large, shaped mirror, which is elaborately carved and turned, and many have marble tops.

By the turn of the century, oak was the preferred wood. Mostly factory made, these late Victorian dressers have various drawer arrangements: many have 4 or 5 full-length drawers with a mirror above, some have a deep bonnet cupboard on 1 side (164), and still others, several half-length drawers on 1 side and a mirror on the other (171). In the 20th century, Mission-style oak dressers (167) are characterized by their simple lines and sturdy construction.

Shaving stands (157) are related to dressing tables and dressers; they consist of a mirror and a boxlike storage area or a shelf for shaving necessities, both usually mounted on a turned or shaped pedestal base. Shaving stands first appeared in the Empire period and were popular throughout the Victorian era. Although their usefulness is limited today, they are unusual and appeal to many modern collectors.

William and Mary lowboy

Description
Dressing table with molded, overhanging top. Typically has 3 drawers, the center one shortest; rare early examples have 1 full-length drawer. Skirt cut in triple arch; central arch bordered by 2 turned drops. Legs turned in trumpet-and-inverted-cup or trumpet-and-vase fashion; some examples have 5 or 6 legs. Legs joined by X-shaped, scrolled stretcher, usually with 1 finial, matching or similar to drops on skirt. Ball feet. Nailed or dovetailed construction.

Materials and Dimensions
Walnut with walnut veneer; rarely solid pine. Secondary wood pine or maple. Top usually burl walnut veneer; occasionally slate. Pulls: brass square, circular, or trefoil mounts with teardrop handles. Escutcheons, when present: matching brass. Height: 29–32″. Width: 31–35″. Depth: 19–22″.

Locality and Period
New England and Pennsylvania, south to Maryland.
c. 1690–1720.

Comment
The legs of William and Mary lowboys are always joined by an X stretcher, making it possible to sit closer to the table. Because of this, many believe that lowboys were originally used as dressing tables. Lowboys were often made to match highboys and to harmonize when placed together in the same room.

Hints for Collectors
These early lowboys are rare and even harder to come by than William and Mary highboys; consequently, they are extremely costly. Most pieces have been in and out of various collections and have often been extensively restored. Check for repaired veneer and replaced finials, feet, or tops.

Queen Anne lowboy

Description
Dressing table. Top either molded and overhanging or scalloped with cutout corners. 1 full-length or 2 half-length drawers above 3 taller drawers, the middle one often sunburst- or shell-carved. Skirt valanced with triple arch; central arch has 2 turned acorn-form drops. Legs cabriole. Knees may be shell-carved. Feet pad, Spanish, or drake. Dovetailed construction.

Materials and Dimensions
Walnut, sometimes with walnut veneer; also cherry, maple, or mahogany. Secondary wood pine, cedar, poplar, or oak. Pulls: brass batwing or willow mounts with bail handles; carved middle drawer may have circular brass mount with loop handle. Escutcheons: matching brass. Height: 30–32″. Width: 31–35″. Depth: 19–21″.

Locality and Period
New England, New York, New Jersey, and Pennsylvania, south to Maryland. c. 1720–60.

Comment
The earliest Queen Anne lowboys had skirts and drawer arrangements clearly inspired by William and Mary pieces, but by the 1750s the claw-and-ball feet and reeded corners of the Chippendale era had begun to appear. Some examples were made with block fronts.

Hints for Collectors
Beware of confusing a lowboy with a highboy base. With a new overhanging, molded top, a highboy base can look much like a lowboy, although its value is considerably less. The key difference will be size. A Queen Anne lowboy is one-fifth to one-quarter smaller all the way around than a comparable highboy.

Colonial Revival lowboy

Description
Small dressing table with molded, overhanging, 2-board top. 1 full-length drawer over 3 additional drawers, the side 2 nearly square, the center one rectangular and decorated with pressed-work shell. Drawers framed by beaded molding. Plain board sides. Shaped skirt has 2 small drops. Cabriole legs leaf-carved at knees. Carved claw-and-ball feet. Pegged, dovetailed, and glued construction.

Materials and Dimensions
Mahogany or birch; also pine with mahogany veneer, or pine and maple stained to imitate mahogany. Secondary wood pine. Pulls: plain or pierced brass willow mounts with bail handles, or small brass knobs. Escutcheons: similar or matching brass. Height: 30–33″. Width: 33–35″. Depth: 19–20″.

Locality and Period
Factories in the East and Midwest. c. 1875–1930.

Comment
The approach of the nation's centennial celebration in the 1870s led to a renewed interest in early American furniture. From then until the 1930s, large numbers of pieces in what was termed the "Colonial manner" were produced. Some, like the example shown, were made by sophisticated cabinetmakers and closely followed the lines, woods, and construction methods of the 18th century. Others, however, were less exact, and sometimes several styles were combined in a single piece.

Hints for Collectors
The hand-pegging and dovetailing in this piece might suggest it is from the 18th century, but the stamped brasses, the 2-board top, and the use of pressed wood rather than carving for the shell decoration reveal its true date.

Chippendale lowboy

Description
Dressing table with molded or gadrooned overhanging top, which may have shaped corners; occasionally a band of carved fretwork below top. Front corners chamfered and reeded or with fluted columns. 1 full-length drawer over 3 narrower and taller drawers, the central one often carved with shell and streamers. Skirt scalloped and usually with shell-carved central drop. Legs cabriole. Knees carved with acanthus leaf or shell. Feet claw-and-ball or, rarely, drake. Dovetailed construction.

Materials and Dimensions
Mahogany, walnut, cherry, or curly maple. Secondary wood pine, poplar, cedar, or ash. Pulls: solid, open, or pierced brass willow mounts or, less often, rosettes with bail handles; also small brass knobs. Escutcheons: matching brass. Height: 29–32″. Width: 32–37″. Depth: 21–23″.

Locality and Period
New England, New York, Pennsylvania, and Maryland.
c. 1750–75.

Comment
Chippendale lowboys are rich in detail, with lavish carving on the legs and central drawer. The skirt, the corners, and even the underedge of the top may be embellished, which is typical of the new taste of the Chippendale period.

Hints for Collectors
With all lowboys, there is always the risk that a new top has been added to a highboy base. Examine patina and wear as well as the general style of the top to make sure it matches the base. Check also for repaired legs: look for lines made when worn legs were lengthened, and for dowels and screws used to patch legs that have cracked.

Hepplewhite dressing table

Description
Dressing table with slightly overhanging top, which may be
decorated with stringing. Long central drawer with 2 drawers on
each side, or single long drawer containing an adjustable
dressing mirror and toiletry compartments. Drawer fronts and
legs may have stringing; occasionally inlaid with oval lozenges.
Plain skirt broken by arched kneehole. Square, tapered legs.
Dovetailed construction.

Materials and Dimensions
Mahogany; also with mahogany veneer; occasionally cherry with
satinwood veneer. Secondary wood pine or poplar. Inlay
satinwood, boxwood, or holly; stringing boxwood or holly. Pulls:
round or oval brass mounts with bail handles. Escutcheons:
matching brass. Height: 29–32″. Width: 34–40″. Depth: 18–19″.

Locality and Period
New York, Pennsylvania, Massachusetts, and Maryland.
c. 1785–1815.

Comment
Hepplewhite dressing tables with 5 drawers, such as the one
shown here, are more common than those with a single drawer
and are clearly descendants of the earlier lowboy. The same case-
and-drawers form is also found in Sheraton dressing tables;
these, however, have turned and reeded legs.

Hints for Collectors
These dressing tables should not be confused with serving or side
tables, which are the same height and similar in appearance,
particularly in their drawer arrangement. What distinguishes the
dressing table is the kneehole, which is missing in the other
forms. In addition, serving and side tables are often wider than
dressing tables.

Country Sheraton cabinet-top dressing table

Description
Dressing table with slightly overhanging top and scroll-cut splashboard or gallery (4–6″ high). Mounted on dresser top is small, recessed cabinet, also with overhanging top and with 1–2 small drawers. Table base has 1–2 shallow drawers. Plain skirt. Legs turned and sometimes reeded in Sheraton manner. Usually painted or grained. Nailed or dovetailed construction.

Materials and Dimensions
Pine or poplar; sometimes figured maple. Secondary wood pine or poplar. Painted, sometimes to imitate stringing, or grained to imitate mahogany or rosewood. Pulls: turned wooden or pressed-glass knobs. Height (to top of cabinet): 36–39″. Width: 29–31″. Depth: 14–16″.

Locality and Period
New England west to the Mississippi River, south to Georgia. c. 1800–25.

Comment
The idea of a small storage cabinet above the dressing table appears to have been popular with country cabinetmakers, particularly in the Empire period. The drawers were used to store toilet items and small valuables that prosperous women in the country had acquired. Many modern dressing tables have this same basic form.

Hints for Collectors
An ordinary dressing table with a cabinet top and splashboard is not hard to locate, but an outstanding one is. Look for a piece with good lines, original paint, and finely turned legs.

155 Hepplewhite cabinet-top dressing table

Description
Dressing table with molded, slightly overhanging top. Front straight, slightly bowed, or, rarely, serpentine. Mounted on top, small, recessed cabinet, also with overhanging top and with 2–3 drawers. Table base sometimes with 1 full-length or 2 half-length drawers. Plain skirt, sometimes draped with textile material. Square, tapered Hepplewhite legs. May have stringing or be painted and have applied swag-and-tassel and/or floral decoration. Dovetailed construction.

Materials and Dimensions
Mahogany with mahogany or satinwood veneer; also pine or poplar. Secondary wood pine or poplar. If solid pine or poplar, painted, then embellished with applied decoration of brass or gilded plaster and wood. Stringing boxwood, satinwood, or holly. Pulls: brass rosettes or pressed-glass knobs. Height: 36–39″. Width: 32–38″. Depth: 14–18″.

Locality and Period
New England and New York west to Pennsylvania, south to Delaware and Maryland. c. 1800–15.

Comment
The paint, gilding, and draping on this piece suggest English influence, for few Americans worked in this manner. The finest pieces in this vein came from the Salem, Massachusetts, area.

Hints for Collectors
Intact high-style painted dressing tables are rare. Almost all have lost their original drapery, although old nail or tack holes under the skirt indicate that a piece was once draped. The applied decoration may also be gone, since it may have seemed too "foreign" for some. Look for faint outlines or ridges beneath the present paint.

Colonial Revival dressing table

Description
Delicate, thin-legged dressing table with shaped, heavily molded, overhanging top. At top rear, 2 cyma, or S-shaped, supports; between them, pivoting mirror with shaped, molded frame and openwork floral cornice. Table has 1 full-length serpentine-front drawer. Plain board sides. Front and side skirts symmetrically curved. Cabriole legs extensions of stiles. Small, cuffed feet. Dovetailed, nailed, and screwed construction.

Materials and Dimensions
Early examples mahogany or rosewood; later examples often oak. Secondary wood pine. Pulls: modified pierced brass batwing mounts with scrolled bail handles. Escutcheons, when present: matching brass. Swivels: brass. Height: 58–62″. Width: 37–40″. Depth: 19–20″.

Locality and Period
Better manufacturers in the East and Midwest. c. 1890–1915.

Comment
The cabriole-leg Colonial Revival dressing table was extremely popular at the turn of the century. Better examples, such as the one shown here, were in mahogany or rosewood; other pieces were made in oak for the mass market. Most have a large mirror and cabriole legs, but substantial variations exist, including 1-, 2-, or even 3-drawer examples as well as straight, bowfront, and double-bowfront pieces.

Hints for Collectors
Distinguish well-made dressing tables from their more common, but less desirable, cousins in oak. Better pieces are not only made of finer wood but may also have shaped fronts and high-quality brasses.

Description
Pedestal-base shaving stand with curvilinear mirror mounted in molded frame with shaped cornice. Mirror attached by swivels to U-shaped, molded support with urn-shaped finials mounted on square base. 2 storage boxes in base have lift tops and flank marble-top work area. Below, small center drawer, with molding above. Turned and shaped pedestal terminates in a drop and is mounted on 3 shaped cabriole legs with casters. Nailed and glued construction.

Materials and Dimensions
Mahogany and burled walnut; also walnut and rosewood. Secondary wood pine. Hinges: iron or brass butt. Pulls, when present: turned or shaped wooden knobs. Escutcheons: brass keyhole surrounds or plates or shaped wood. Swivels: iron or brass. Casters: iron and brass. Height: 65–69″. Width: 16–18″. Depth: 14–16″.

Locality and Period
Large factories throughout the East and Midwest. c. 1870–90.

Comment
The basic shaving stand form is that of the earlier dressing glass mounted on a pedestal and raised to a height suitable for shaving. Renaissance Revival examples bear some resemblance in form to chests of drawers in the same mode and were sometimes designed to match.

Hints for Collectors
Shaving stands are worth looking for. One of the less common Victorian forms, they often go unrecognized by both dealer and collector. In addition, with little demand for the type, current prices are usually reasonable. And, of course, they may serve today as small dressing tables.

Art Nouveau shaving stand

Description
Elongated, curvilinear, bentwood shaving stand. Oval mirror set in bead-molded frame and mounted between 2 vertical rods. 3 shelves beneath mirror, the upper one kidney-shaped and mounted on curved stiles. Lozenge-shaped central shelf cantilevered from rear legs and joined to upper shelf by decorative vase-and-flower cutout. Larger lower shelf also lozenge-shaped, and secured to all 4 legs. 2 arched rods join the 3 shelves at rear. Simple hoof feet. Screwed and glued construction.

Materials and Dimensions
Cherry, ash, or birch, steamed and bent into curving shapes; often stained to resemble mahogany. Frame and shelves sometimes pine. Height: 57–62″. Width: 20–23″. Depth: 9–11″.

Locality and Period
Austria-Hungary; made for the American market. c. 1900–05.

Comment
Art Nouveau shaving stands are fairly rare, and most of those found in this country were probably imported from Thonet or another Austro-Hungarian manufacturer. However, the Thonet firm did have outlets in this country where pieces identical to the European product were assembled. Like other Thonet pieces, these stands were so popular here that they have assumed a place in the history of American furniture.

Hints for Collectors
Bentwood is being reproduced today, although shaving stands are not among the pieces currently being made. In bentwood reproductions, the legs are usually flatter than in the turn-of-the-century pieces. And obviously, they lack signs of age and wear.

159 Cottage-style dressing table

Description
Tall dressing table with shaped splashboard. Oblong pivoting mirror in molded frame, supported on 2 shaped uprights screwed into back of splashboard. On each side of top, 1 rectangular storage box with removable top and simple, molded base. 1 full-length drawer. 2 spool-turned towel racks at sides of table, extending from splashboard to shaped brackets anchored in front stiles. Below, shelf with plain skirt. Legs turned and blocked, terminating in blunt arrow feet. Always painted. Nailed and glued construction.

Materials and Dimensions
Pine or, rarely, cedar. Painted pastel colors with darker striping and highlights. Pulls: turned wooden knobs or thin brass mounts with bail handles. Swivels: iron. Height: 48–51″. Width: 22–23″. Depth: 13–15″.

Locality and Period
Large factories throughout most of the United States.
c. 1880–1910.

Comment
This is a relatively early and uncommon form of the Cottage-style dressing table; most are combined with a chest of drawers and lack towel racks. Other unusual features are the rather elaborate mirror supports and the shaped splashboard. The presence of the shelf suggests an attempt to combine dressing table and washstand.

Hints for Collectors
This piece, with its appealing design and clean lines, represents artistic quality in Cottage furniture. Moreover, the decoration is restrained, as compared with more usual forms of the Cottage style.

Description
Dressing table with slightly overhanging top. Mounted on top of dressing table, oblong or rectangular mirror in flat or ogee frame, with lyre- or scroll-form brackets. 2 half-size drawers over single full-length drawer, or single full-length drawer over 2 square drawers that flank arched skirt. Large, flat shelf above feet. Front legs shaped like carved lyres, or turned and reeded in early Sheraton manner; rear legs plain. Feet carved and gilded wood, or cast-brass animal forms; or turned, with brass casters. Dovetailed construction.

Materials and Dimensions
Mahogany with mahogany veneer; rarely cherry or walnut. Secondary wood pine or tulipwood. Pulls: brass rosette knobs or rosette plates, plain or of lion's-head form with bail handles. Escutcheons: brass keyhole surrounds. Swivels: brass. Height: 56–60″. Width: 35–39″. Depth: 19–22″.

Locality and Period
Massachusetts, New York, and Pennsylvania, south to Maryland. c. 1810–25.

Comment
The dressing table with mirror, a forerunner of the mirrored bureau, appeared in the late Sheraton period when French Directoire taste had become influential. Such devices as the lyre-shaped legs and the animal-form feet looked forward to the coming Empire period.

Hints for Collectors
Many of these early dressing tables have lost their mirrors and pass for side or serving tables. The rear of the top sometimes has telltale marks where a mirror was once attached. Without the original mirror and brackets, the value is considerably reduced.

Country Empire dressing table

Description
2-tier dressing table. Slightly overhanging top, rounded at corners, with attached 2-drawer step-back unit. Mirror with chamfered frame hung on swivels between 2 square supports having pointed tops and chamfered, rectangular bases. Body has single full-length drawer. Plain skirt. Turned, blocked legs terminate in small ball feet. Dovetailed, nailed, and screwed construction.

Materials and Dimensions
Mahogany or pine with mahogany veneer; also walnut or walnut veneer over pine; rarely maple. Secondary wood pine. If maple, may be stained red. Pulls: turned wooden knobs. Swivels: brass. Height: 52–55″. Width: 30–34″. Depth: 18–19″.

Locality and Period
New England west to Missouri and throughout the South. c. 1820–50.

Comment
Empire dressing tables with mirrors are rare, as the form was just beginning to appear during this period. Similar pieces without attached mirrors are much more common. The blocked and turned leg on this piece is often called a New York State leg, although similarly shaped legs were used on Empire tables and servers in other eastern states as well.

Hints for Collectors
If you are fortunate enough to find one of these nice little dressers, examine the mirror attachment carefully to be sure it is original. The mirror frame and supports should match the case in wood, age, and style.

Chinese export shaving stand

Description
Blocklike shaving stand with flat, unmolded, divided lift top that opens to the sides revealing 12–14 shallow storage compartments of various shapes and sizes and forming galleried work areas. At rear center, a rectangular folding mirror that pivots in a plain frame. Below, 4 full-length drawers. Plain board sides have metal carrying handles. Plain skirt. Legs square extensions of corner stiles. Mortise-and-tenon construction.

Materials and Dimensions
Chinese hardwood. Secondary wood camphor. Hinges: iron butt. Pulls: round wooden and brass knobs. Escutcheons: oblong keyhole surrounds set vertically. Side handles: iron willow mounts with bail handles. Swivels: brass or iron. Height (closed): 33–35″. Width: 18–19″. Depth: 18–19″.

Locality and Period
China; made for export to the United States. c. 1830–40.

Comment
During the 19th century, the Chinese began to export furniture to this country. They also sold it directly to sea captains and their crews, who then brought it to the United States. Like the stand illustrated, many of these pieces were a blend of the prevailing American style (here, Empire) and traditional Chinese forms.

Hints for Collectors
It is often hard to spot a Chinese export piece. Look for an example in Chinese wood but with such additions as western hinges and locks (often furnished by the person for whom the piece was made) and pulls appropriate to American pieces of the period.

Eastlake tall chest with bonnet cupboard

Description

Tall chest of drawers with mirror and slightly overhanging, molded top. Gallery has rectangular mirror at back mounted on 2 turned supports. At left, storage cupboard for bonnets, with paneled door; at right, 2 half-length drawers with incised horizontal reeding. Below, 2–3 similarly decorated full-length drawers. Front stiles decorated with incised reeding; right stile has lock. Paneled sides. Molded, plinthlike base. Blocklike feet. Paneled, nailed, screwed, and glued construction.

Materials and Dimensions

Cherry or walnut; rarely rosewood or mahogany. Sometimes pine secondary wood. Hinges: brass butt. Pulls: dumbbell-shaped or oblong brass with bail handles. Escutcheons: oblong or rosette-shaped brass. Swivels: brass. Height: 61–64″. Width: 30–33″. Depth: 19–21″.

Locality and Period

Large furniture shops in the East and Midwest. c. 1870–90.

Comment

Chests with storage areas for bonnets appeared shortly after the Civil War and soon took the place of the cardboard bandbox. The practical addition of a mirror to the chest top made it possible both to store one's hat and put it on using the same piece of furniture.

Hints for Collectors

The bonnet chest is a practical and attractive piece of furniture particularly suited to the small home. Later examples in oak are common, but 19th-century pieces are relatively hard to find. An early cherry or walnut chest may be covered by coats of paint; to check, remove a tiny bit of paint from an inconspicuous place.

164 Late Victorian tall chest with bonnet cupboard

Description
Chest of drawers has mirror and flat, overhanging top with rounded corners. Mirror in shaped frame swivel-mounted on voluted supports above a 3–5″ splashboard. Upper serpentine-shaped section has, at left, bonnet cupboard; at right, 2 half-length drawers. Below, 2–3 straight-front, sometimes graduated full-length drawers. Paneled sides. Skirt plain or valanced. Front legs short, cabriole; rear legs plain extensions of stiles. Paneled, nailed, and glued construction.

Materials and Dimensions
Oak and quartersawed oak, later pieces sometimes oak veneer with pine or poplar secondary wood or with plywood backboard. Often varnished or shellacked. Pulls: brass rosettes or wooden knobs. Escutcheons: brass or iron keyhole surrounds. Swivels: brass. Height: 62–66″. Width: 32–36″. Depth: 15–18″.

Locality and Period
Factories throughout the United States. c. 1890–1920.

Comment
Like the earlier cherry or walnut bonnet cupboards, these oak examples were too high to be "sit-down" dressing tables and were intended as storage chests for the large bonnets favored by Victorian ladies.

Hints for Collectors
Look for oak with bowed, serpentine, or oxbow fronts. Since these pieces were harder to produce, they were made in more limited quantities. The best examples will be in solid oak rather than oak veneer over pine or poplar. Beware of warping in the curved portions of the chest, a common defect that is hard to remedy.

Late Victorian bowfront dresser

Description

Plain bowfront chest of drawers with molded, overhanging top and, at rear, low (1″) lip. Mirror in simple molded and shaped frame attached by swivels to 2 cyma, or S-curved, supports that are attached to lip. Below, 2 half-length drawers over 2–3 full-length drawers. Sides paneled. Back paneled or single piece of plywood. Plain skirt. Legs extensions of stiles; front flattened cabriole, rear square. Often mounted on casters. Paneled, nailed, glued, and screwed construction.

Materials and Dimensions

Oak or quartersawed oak, often fumed or darkened; also oak veneer with pine secondary wood. Pulls: turned wooden knobs or oblong brass mounts with bail handles. Escutcheons: brass keyhole surrounds. Casters: iron or iron and wood. Swivels: iron or brass. Height: 58–62″. Width: 39–41″. Depth: 21–22″.

Locality and Period

Large factories throughout the East and Midwest. c. 1880–1920.

Comment

Although not as common as straight-front pieces, many oak bowfront chests were produced between 1880 and 1920 and it is easy to find one today. Most were made in large factories, sold through mail-order catalogues, then shipped by rail throughout the United States.

Hints for Collectors

Note the difference between this bowfront, which was produced by steaming and bending a solid piece of oak, and Colonial Revival bowfronts, which were built up by gluing together several pieces of wood of different sizes. The most difficult and expensive technique was used in the 18th century, when some shaped fronts were carved from a single piece of wood.

Empire dresser

Description
Massive chest of drawers with molded, overhanging top. Mirror with curved upper corners, set in inlaid frame, swivel-mounted between 2 rope-turned supports with urn finials; supports attached to back. Below, 2 half-length drawers with overhanging (3–4″) bowed fronts that rest on 2 rope-turned pillars. Below, 3 bowfront full-length drawers. Unmolded base with plain skirt protrudes ½″ over carved paw feet in front; rear feet ball-turned. Paneled sides. Paneled, dovetailed, glued, and nailed construction.

Materials and Dimensions
Mahogany or mahogany veneer over pine; later examples walnut. Secondary wood pine. Pulls: brass rosettes with acanthus decoration and ring handles. Escutcheons: matching brass. Swivels: brass. Height: 70–76″. Width: 43–47″. Depth: 21–24″.

Locality and Period
New England west to Missouri, and throughout the South to Texas. c. 1820–50.

Comment
These massive Empire dressers were never common and are extremely hard to find today, for a good many were broken up and used for firewood. Like much high-style Empire furniture, they were limited by their large size to houses with very big rooms.

Hints for Collectors
Most Empire dressers have lost their large, yet fragile mirrors. Look for the telltale marks and screw holes on the back and top rear that indicate where the mirror supports were attached. Restoration is costly and rarely worth attempting.

Mission-style dresser

Description
Plain dresser with unmolded top overhanging 3–4″ at sides and front. Large, rectangular mirror in plain frame that hangs on swivels between 2 tapered, square posts joined by butterfly-shaped Dutch patches to 3″ splashboard. Below, 2 half-length drawers above 2 full-length ones, lowest one slightly shorter. Plain board sides. Demilune skirt. Legs and feet square, tapered extensions of stiles. Mortise-and-tenon construction.

Materials and Dimensions
Oak and quartersawed oak. Pulls: rectangular brass plates mounted with semicircular bail handles. Swivels: brass. Height: 62–65″. Width: 47–49″. Depth: 21–23″.

Locality and Period
New York and Michigan. c. 1905–15.

Comment
This dresser, designed by Gustav Stickley, was the prototype for the plain oak dresser of the early 20th century. Its simple lines notwithstanding, a dresser with the Gustav Stickley label or brand would command a high price today.

Hints for Collectors
Do not confuse a Stickley dresser with one of the many lesser examples turned out by large furniture companies. Even without the original mark or label, the lines and craftsmanship of this piece separate it from an ordinary example. The handsome demilune skirt, the use of hand-cut Dutch patches, and the characteristic brasses all help identify it as a piece designed by Stickley. If a piece lacks these touches, it is probably not by Stickley, even if it bears his label. Labels can be faked.

Description
Shallow dresser with removable, molded, overhanging marble top. At rear, high backboard with shaped mirror supports and fret-cut cornice. Rectangular mirror in incised frame hangs on swivels between supports. At each side of backboard, 1 oblong candle bracket with molded edge. Below, 3 graduated or equal full-length drawers with central panels in burl veneer. Top drawer interior divided into 1 large and 3 small compartments. Paneled sides and back. Plain skirt with slightly molded, plinthlike base, which conceals casters. Screwed construction.

Materials and Dimensions
Walnut with burl walnut veneer. Secondary wood pine. Pulls: circular brass rosettes with brass and ebonized turned wooden handles. Escutcheons: brass or shaped wooden rosettes. Swivels: cast and engraved brass. Casters: brass or iron. Height: 43–48″. Width: 40–44″. Depth: 16–17″.

Locality and Period
Factories throughout the East and Midwest. c. 1870–85.

Comment
Marble-top dressers were more expensive than ones with wooden surfaces, particularly since the stone was often imported from Europe. Nevertheless, they were quite popular, not only because of their appearance but also because the marble top was easy to keep clean.

Hints for Collectors
Victorian styles can be confusing. The late 19th-century piece shown here combines the rich veneer and elaborate pulls of the Renaissance mode with the angular form and fretwork typical of Eastlake pieces. In evaluating a piece, the most important consideration is how effectively the styles have been combined.

Empire dressing mirror

Description
Architectural tabletop dressing mirror with shaped and molded, overhanging top. At rear, low backboard flanked by marble pillars resting on plinthlike base. Behind pillars, rectangular mirror supports rise to a massive, molded, overhanging architectural cornice. Rectangular mirror in plain frame hangs on swivels between supports. Below, 2 graduated bowfront drawers recessed behind small flanking marble pillars. Shaped and molded base. Plain skirt. Turned acornlike feet. Dovetailed and nailed construction.

Materials and Dimensions
Mahogany or pine with mahogany veneer. Secondary wood pine. Inlay ebony; stringing boxwood. Baize-covered drawer interiors. Escutcheons: brass, mother-of-pearl, or ivory oblongs. Swivels: brass. Height: 20–22″. Width: 11–12″. Depth: 7–8″.

Locality and Period
New England west to Ohio and throughout the southern Atlantic states. c. 1815–40.

Comment
Dressing mirrors, meant to be placed on top of dressing tables, declined in popularity during the Empire period, but those that were made were often quite elaborate. Sometimes, as in the example illustrated, they resembled Greek temples. More often, they were large dressing mirrors without drawers mounted between wooden pillarlike supports.

Hints for Collectors
Regardless of period, pieces that employed mahogany, marble, mother-of-pearl, or ebony were probably made to order for wealthy customers. Only the leading cabinetmakers were likely to produce these expensive and high-quality pieces.

Eastlake oak dresser

Description
Tall dresser with lightly molded top. Removable backboard with shallow shelf mounted on 2 shaped brackets below swivel-mounted, square or rectangular mirror; frame decorated with incised lines. Above mirror, a wide frieze, set with applied, wooden rosettes and topped by similarly decorated cornice with scalloped edges. Below top, 3 full-length drawers, each with 2 bands of incised carving, similar to bands on stiles. Sides paneled. Skirt slightly curved. Plinthlike base, also with incised banding. May have casters. Paneled, glued, nailed, and screwed construction.

Materials and Dimensions
Oak; sometimes with quartersawed oak. Applied decoration maple. Originally left natural, but often enameled later. Pulls: brass rosettes with pendant loops or oblong plates with bail handles. Escutcheons: wooden rosettes. Swivels: iron or brass. Casters, when present: iron and wood. Height: 70–75″. Width: 34–38″. Depth: 16–18″.

Locality and Period
Large factories throughout the East and Midwest. c. 1880–1910.

Comment
Along with Cottage-style pieces, which were made of painted pine, these were the least expensive Victorian dressers, often selling new for $5 or less. Made in great quantity, they were shipped to all parts of the country.

Hints for Collectors
These dressers are usually a poor investment. In most cases, they are badly made from inferior and thinly cut oak, are rarely very sturdy, and have cracked frames. Despite all this, the current interest in anything oak has inflated their price.

171 Eastlake drop-side dresser

Description
Dresser with unmolded, overhanging top. On right side of top, 2-drawer case with overhanging top and paneled sides. Drawers have incised decoration. On the left, a tall, rectangular mirror set in ribbed frame, crowned by shaped and molded cornice. Mirror swivel-mounted between narrow supports; supports and cornice have incised decoration. Below, 2 equal full-length drawers, also with incised banding. Sides paneled. Plinthlike base. Plain skirt. Usually has casters. Paneled, glued, nailed, and screwed construction.

Materials and Dimensions
Early examples maple or walnut with pine secondary wood. Later, and more commonly, oak. Pulls: oblong brass plates with bail handles, or brass rosettes with pendant rings. Escutcheons: wooden squares or rosettes. Casters: iron and porcelain or wood. Swivels: brass or iron. Height: 66–70″. Width: 37–40″. Depth: 16–18″.

Locality and Period
Large factories throughout the East and Midwest. c. 1880–1910.

Comment
Although relatively easy to find, dressers with the bureau-top storage box, which appeared during the Federal era and continued into the Victorian, are less common than the usual flat-topped form. Pieces like the one shown here combine 2 necessities: a storage area and a full-length dressing mirror.

Hints for Collectors
Many oak dressers of this type are poorly made, while those in maple, like the one shown here, are usually earlier and of better quality. Look for examples in maple or walnut, which often have extensive paneling and a well-balanced design.

Cottage-style dresser

Description
Tall, mirrored dresser with elaborately scrolled back and cornice, ending in arched pediment above rectangular mirror. Turned, vertical dowels at sides of mirror above small candle shelves. Top has well-like area between 4 small drawers. 2 full-length drawers below. Sides are 2-part panels. Back of rough boards nailed vertically. Heavy, molded base and plain skirt. Flat block feet with casters. Always painted and grained. Nailed, screwed, and glued unit construction.

Materials and Dimensions
Pine; sometimes with cedar or poplar secondary wood. Painted 1–2 solid colors with contrasting striping and wood graining. Pulls: circular brass plates with ebonized hardwood drops or turned wooden knobs. Casters: porcelain and iron. Height: 82–87″. Width: 43–46″. Depth: 17–20″.

Locality and Period
Major factories throughout the East and Midwest. c. 1870–1910.

Comment
Generally made as part of bedroom sets, Cottage-style dressers are among the most visually interesting pieces of painted pine. The hand-done striping and graining might have been done in the 1820s, yet the machine-cut dovetails, screwed construction, and thin, milled boards show that the pieces are from the Industrial Age.

Hints for Collectors
Many of these dressers have been repainted, but slow, careful work with paint remover and scraper will often uncover the original paint. Occasionally the brasses have also been changed, but the originals can be replaced with accurate reproductions.

Art Deco dressing table

Description
2 sets of drawers over 1-door cupboards, joined by flat surface. Large mirror fits into slot at back; rectangular splashboard on each side of mirror. Single full-length drawer below mirror. Each side section has 4 short drawers, the fronts angled inward 15°. Below drawers, a molding and 2 1-door storage areas, each with 4 slide-out, open trays. Paneled back. Molded base. Turned feet mounted on square blocks beneath plain skirt. Glued and screwed construction.

Materials and Dimensions
Mahogany. Secondary wood pine. Inlay ebonized hardwood. Hinges: brass butt. Pulls: square German silver. Height: 48–50″. Width: 48–50″. Depth: 19–20″.

Locality and Period
Factories in the East and Midwest. c. 1925–35.

Comment
Designed by Herbert Lippman, the dressing table shown here exemplifies higher-quality Art Deco bedroom furnishings. Although such pieces were machine made, they combined quality materials with interesting design concepts. The canted construction enables someone to sit at the mirror and have all the storage areas within easy reach, and the slide-out trays provide easy access to stored items.

Hints for Collectors
Fine Art Deco pieces, such as the example shown here, are identifiable by their materials and construction: they often have paneled rather than plywood backs, German silver rather than plastic knobs, solid wood as opposed to veneers, and inlaid decoration.

Art Deco pedestal dressing table

Description

Small dressing table with molded, overhanging top that has U-shaped indentation at front. At rear, circular mirror on removable geometric support with molded base. Beneath U-shaped cutout, horizontal board mounted on shaped brackets creates impression of a drawer. Each pedestal has 2 deep drawers framed by vertical fluting. Plain board sides. Molded and fluted bases with arched skirts. Bootjack feet. Nailed, glued, and screwed construction.

Materials and Dimensions

Mahogany and bird's-eye maple veneer over pine. Pine secondary wood. Painted black to imitate ebony stringing. Pulls: long horizontal brackets of pot metal, brass, or Bakelite. Height: 60–62″. Width: 43–46″. Depth: 18–19″.

Locality and Period

Large factories throughout the East and Midwest. c. 1930–42.

Comment

Inexpensive, mass-produced pieces in the Art Deco style were usually made of pine or other inexpensive woods covered with thin coats of veneer and then painted to imitate ebony or ivory. Such pieces brought the new style to a wide audience and were instrumental in the decline of oak's popularity and in the passing of the late Victorian style.

Hints for Collectors

Mass-produced Art Deco can be found almost anywhere and may frequently be purchased for very little at secondhand shops and used-furniture stores. But, remember, it was seldom well made. There is enough available to enable one to avoid pieces with peeling veneer and warped or separating bodies—problems often seen in dressing tables.

175 Lacquered Art Deco dressing table

Description
Pedestal-base vanity with large, circular, wood-backed mirror. 2 vertical rods (1–3″ high) support back of mirror. Rectangular glass shelf resting on short dowels in front of mirror. Larger, wooden storage shelf below. 2 drawers separated by molding at bottom left; inlet for finger grips. Bottom right, 2 similar but narrower drawers adjacent to narrow cupboard with 4 small interior drawers. Slightly inset, tapered base without feet. Lacquered. Nailed, glued, and screwed construction.

Materials and Dimensions
Pine. Secondary wood pine. Support rods hickory. Solid black, green, or white lacquer finish. Hinges: steel butt. Pulls: round wooden knobs, lacquered. Height: 67–69″. Width: 52–55″. Depth: 18–19″.

Locality and Period
Better factories throughout the East and Midwest. c. 1925–40.

Comment
Low dressing tables with large, round mirrors are synonymous with the 1920s and 1930s, and many varieties are known. The design and cabinetry of the example illustrated mark it as a better-quality piece. The fingerholds for opening drawers and the small drawers inside the cupboard are details that took time and skill and are not typical.

Hints for Collectors
The large mirrors on Art Deco dressing tables were easily broken, and many pieces have replacement glass. Check for new supports and screws and for glass that looks too new to fit the period of the piece. And beware of chipped lacquer, which not only detracts from appearance but also lessens value.

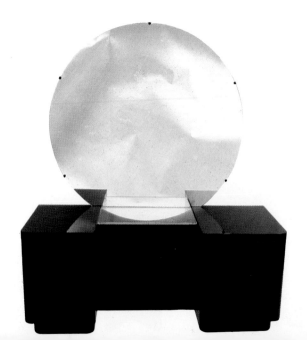

Art Deco vanity table

Description
Small, boxlike vanity table on curved, tapered legs. Square top in 2 sections divides and opens to reveal mirrored inner lid. When folded back, divided top becomes tabletop. Below mirrored lid, interior compartment with divided lift-out cosmetic tray. Table legs terminate in molded and mirrored base. Block feet. Gilded and lacquered. Screwed and glued construction.

Materials and Dimensions
Pine. Table, including outer and inner lids, lacquered and gilded. Legs and base lacquered black; base with gilded banding. Hinges: stainless-steel butt. Pulls: textile tab on inner lid. Height: 24–26″. Diameter: 12–13″.

Locality and Period
Large factories in the East and Midwest. c. 1930–40.

Comment
Diminutive dressing tables were popular in powder rooms and bedrooms in the 1930s. Small enough to be moved easily, they were essentially makeup kits on legs, and were also used in theater and nightclub dressing rooms. They were usually not part of a matching set.

Hints for Collectors
Small, unusual pieces like this one often slip unnoticed through auctions or shops. They are, however, authentic, stylish examples of the Art Deco mode and deserve to be preserved. A few will bear manufacturers' marks, but most are anonymous. Avoid those that have lost gilt or lacquer; that sort of repair can be very expensive.

Modern dressing table

Description
Dressing table with rectangular top; unmolded edge with cloth-covered, canted ends rising 2–3″. Below, 2 pedestals, each with solid-board sides and cloth-covered front. Fronts angled in toward center and divided into 6 squares. Each pedestal divided into 3 drawers of equal width and depth with protruding edge. Plain skirt. Feet square and slightly flared at front. Glued and screwed construction.

Materials and Dimensions
Maple or birch, ebonized. Partially covered with laminated white fabric. Height: 29–30″. Width: 54–55″. Depth: 18–19″.

Locality and Period
Larger factories in the East and Midwest. c. 1930–40.

Comment
Manufactured by the Herman Miller Company of Zeeland, Michigan, a major manufacturer of better-quality furniture in the 1930s, this dressing table combines an ebonized finish with laminated fabric, a new industrial material. Both the style and materials reflect the changes that were taking place in furniture design during this period.

Hints for Collectors
Pieces manufactured by Herman Miller are today attracting serious attention from collectors and dealers. Often the work of important designers, they were attractive and well made. Most examples had paper or metal labels, usually found inside drawers or on the underside of a piece. These furnishings often combine traditional Art Deco styling with the use of modern industrial materials.

Modern glass-top dressing table

Description
Dressing table with clear glass top. Glass fits into slots in back and top right, and is supported on left by metal spindle (4–5″ high) resting on 3-drawer case. Drawers mounted on plinthlike base that is inset 2″ on sides and front. On right, plain board side. No feet. Glued mortise-and-tenon and screwed construction.

Materials and Dimensions
Mahogany, maple, and bird's-eye maple. Plate-glass top. Pulls: glass disks mounted on brass shafts. Supporting spindle: stainless steel. Height: 28–29″. Width: 51–52″. Depth: 16–17″.

Locality and Period
Larger factories in the Midwest. c. 1930–40.

Comment
Created by the designer Gilbert Rohde as part of a bedroom set, this dressing table combines elements of what has come to be known as the International Style with elements of the earlier Art Deco style. Its clean lines and contrasting materials are typical of better pieces from the 1930s. As with most pieces that were originally part of a set, the dressing table shown here would be more valuable in the company of matching furnishings.

Hints for Collectors
As Rohde was a well-known designer of the period, his pieces often had factory labels that carried his name. Such labels add to the value of a piece and need to be preserved. If loose or torn, they should be reglued and covered with shellac or clear plastic. Unlabeled pieces may be identified by referring to furniture catalogues of the period, which are often available from dealers who specialize in books and paper memorabilia.

Mirrors

In Colonial America, mirrors were a luxury that few could afford. Until the late 18th century, most mirror glass was imported from England; even after that date, the English continued to export silvered glass to America. In addition, many early frames were produced in England and resemble those made in this country. English examples may even bear American labels, for some American tradesmen put their own labels on mirrors that passed through their shops. Consequently, distinguishing early American-made mirror glass and frames can baffle even experienced collectors.

The first American mirrors were tall and narrow and appeared in the Queen Anne era. Because mirror glass could be made only in relatively small sheets, most of these mirrors have 2 glass panels, with the upper panel sometimes engraved with flowers or birds. Frames either arch or are carved with scroll-cut crests (191); crested frames may have gilded floral patterns on the crest and at the sides. Like Queen Anne mirrors, those made during the Chippendale period (192) are usually tall and narrow, with elaborate fret-cut crests and aprons. There are also a few mirrors that have a broken pediment framing a gilded finial.

In the late 18th century, several distinctive Federal mirrors appeared. Some are tall and rectangular, with complex broken pediments surmounted by urn finials (193); the sides may have pendant floral sprays. Others are entirely gilded (190) and crowned by carved birds or medallions flanked by scrolled sprays. Tabernacle mirrors have an overhanging cornice beneath which hang small drops (185). Girandole mirrors (189) are circular, with convex glass and elaborately carved and gilded frames that are fitted with candleholders.

Empire mirrors are less varied. The 2 most common forms are the tabernacle mirror and the ogee-frame mirror. The former (186) is rectangular and consists of 2 sheets of glass, with a painted upper sheet; the elaborate frames are composed of turned half-round pilasters that are usually gilded. The ogee-frame type (187) is simpler; also rectangular, it consists of 1 sheet of glass enclosed in a simple ogee-molded frame.

By the Victorian period, mirror glass was inexpensive and mirrors became available to almost everyone. Large pier mirrors (184), meant to be placed between doors or windows, became popular in fashionable parlors. Smaller mirrors, in almost every shape, have frames that range from elaborately carved mahogany to simple gilded pine. By the end of the 19th century, oak was the preferred wood. The most interesting 20th-century mirrors are made of industrial materials such as chrome and steel. Bold, streamlined Art Deco examples are among the most sought-after 20th-century pieces today.

Mirrors are not always designed to hang on walls. Freestanding mirrors first appeared in the Queen Anne period, and continued to be popular throughout the Federal period. Many of these pieces consist of an adjustable looking glass mounted above a set of small drawers. Originally designed to be used on a lowboy or dressing table, they largely fell out of fashion when mirrors became attached to dressing tables. Mission-style examples (198), dating from the early years of the 20th century, are extremely plain. Other freestanding mirrors do not have a set of drawers beneath them; instead they rest on a pair of trestlelike legs (195), a tubular base (202), or other supports.

Description
Small, rectangular mirror with plain, unmolded frame. Frame mounted on T-shaped hanger; horizontal part of hanger has groove to hold bottom of mirror frame. 1–3 small wooden or brass knobs across base of hanger. Small hole at top to hang from nail or larger hole to hang over pegboard. Splined and nailed construction.

Materials and Dimensions
Pine or maple; rarely pine with maple veneer. Sometimes with dark stain. Knobs: turned wood or brass. Height: 18–20″. Width: 12–13″.

Locality and Period
Shaker communities, primarily in New England and New York. c. 1830–80.

Comment
Only Shaker mirrors are mounted on T-shaped hangers. The hangers are pierced at the top so that they can be hung from nails or, more often, pegboards. The knobs across the bottom of the hanger held combs and brushes. In many examples, a cord runs from the hanger to the back of the mirror, allowing the mirror to be adjusted to the user's needs. Most were hung quite high on the wall and, in keeping with Shaker modesty, must have reflected little more than the upper part of a person's head no matter how they were adjusted.

Hints for Collectors
Shaker mirrors of this sort are quite rare and, with their unique features, easily identified. Be wary of any mirror said to be Shaker but lacking the adjustable T-shaped hanger. The few authentic examples available are rather expensive.

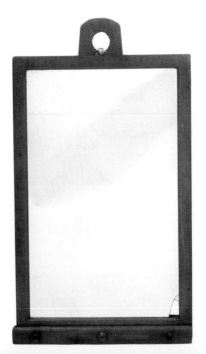

Description
Rectangular to nearly square mirror. Wide frame (2–4″) with simple interior molding. Stenciled motifs, often including eagles, stars, and flowers, on painted background. Mitered corners. Nailed and glued construction.

Materials and Dimensions
Pine or poplar; rarely maple or other fruitwood. Usually painted red or black; stenciled designs gold; occasionally gold leaf with black stenciled decoration. Height: 22–30″. Width: 14–20″.

Locality and Period
Eastern and southern United States. c. 1820–50.

Comment
Though Federal in appearance, these mirrors were often made much later, particularly in rural areas. They are similar in feeling to the stencil-decorated Hitchcock furniture from the first quarter of the 19th century and were apparently constructed by the same men. The mirrors were made in many places, but never in any quantity, and examples in good condition are relatively uncommon today. Rare examples are signed, but most agree that these signatures are those of owners rather than makers.

Hints for Collectors
Because of their rarity, these little stenciled mirrors may command a fairly high price. The more elaborate or creative the stenciling, the more expensive the mirror will be. Modern stenciling is sometimes added, so check carefully to make certain that the stenciling is old: the designs should be known 19th-century forms and show the sort of wear and blurring that comes with age.

Tramp Art mirror

Description
Square or rectangular mirror. Frame fairly thick, usually built up of several layers of thin wood, glued or nailed together, and notch-carved to form raised diamond pattern. Typically, carved rosettes at corners of frame. Often painted or gilded. Glued and nailed construction.

Materials and Dimensions
Scrap wood, most often pine, cedar, mahogany, or spruce; less often walnut or cherry; frequently from old fruit crates or cigar boxes. Often gilded or painted gold, silver, red, blue, green, or brown. Height: 10–30″. Width: 8–24″.

Locality and Period
Throughout the United States; also eastern Canada. c. 1890–1940.

Comment
Called Tramp Art in the mistaken belief that it was made by itinerants, these carved wooden pieces were actually made in great quantities by amateur craftsmen throughout the United States and eastern Canada. Patterns were often taken from magazines like *Mechanics Illustrated*. Pieces were then cut to shape with a jigsaw and notch-carved with a knife. Mirrors and picture frames are especially common.

Hints for Collectors
Tramp Art mirrors are some of the most common and least expensive of all period looking glasses. They appeal to collectors as both mirrors and folk art. Better examples are carved from solid rather than layered wood. They are also more complex in design and may have extra touches like inset colored glass or bits of ceramic. Do not buy a damaged mirror or one with missing parts; undamaged ones are fairly easy to find.

Eastlake mirror

Description
Rectangular mirror. Frame has raised squares at corners with applied, circular medallions. A strip of applied beadwork runs around center of frame. Molding around beadwork has incised decoration in Eastlake manner. Nailed and glued construction.

Materials and Dimensions
Walnut or rosewood. Sometimes gilded. Applied decoration may be maple stained to imitate walnut, or walnut or oak stained dark. Height: 20–28″. Width: 16–22″.

Locality and Period
Factories in the East and Midwest. c. 1875–90.

Comment
Machine techniques were applied to mirror construction in the Victorian era. Fifty years earlier, the medallions and beading would have been hand carved. Here they were stamped or cut out by machine and nailed or glued to the frame. The resulting uniformity of design was of less significance to the Victorians than the much greater volume of production. By the 1870s, the home of an average workingman might have had as many as 12 mirrors; in the 1820s, few working-class homes had more than one.

Hints for Collectors
Eastlake mirrors like the example illustrated are readily available and reasonably priced. They also go well with the modern interior. The best examples have well-balanced decoration and original finish. Note the resemblance between this mirror and the Tramp Art example on the preceding page. Most Tramp Art mirrors were probably based on Eastlake designs.

Description
Square mirror, hung diagonally. Frame composed of 4 molded oak slats that are mitered and joined at the corners. Beveled mirror fits into slots cut into the inner sides of the slats. Solid 1-piece backboard. Metal hooks, variously shaped, attached at 2–3 corners. Nailed and screwed construction.

Materials and Dimensions
Oak or quartersawed oak; often fumed or artificially darkened. Some examples painted white, green, or black. Hooks: brass. Iron hanger on back. Height and width: 15–18″.

Locality and Period
Large factories throughout the East and Midwest. c. 1880–1930.

Comment
Oak hall mirrors were extremely popular for half a century and many different types were manufactured. They not only added a decorative touch to the hallway, but were also very practical. The hooks provided a spot to hang hats or small articles of clothing, and in an age when appearance was important, it was convenient having a mirror available when dressing for the outdoors.

Hints for Collectors
These hall mirrors may be square, oblong, or rectangular, and the hooks plain or in plant or animal forms. Like some other types of oak furniture, they have been reproduced in the past few years. Be suspicious of pieces that have hooks that appear new, or those that have tin backs or pieces of oak joined by modern angle irons. These are all signs that a piece may be a reproduction.

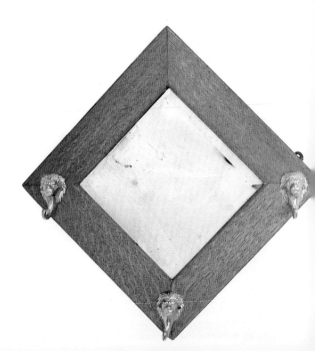

Eastlake pier glass

Description
Very tall, narrow mirror with rectangular frame and
overhanging, molded cornice in the architectural manner. Upper
edge of cornice scalloped; below, raised panel with rosettes or
foliate carving; below this, 2 carved, occasionally gilded panels.
Leaf-carved, columnar side panels terminating in square-shaped
blocks. Plain skirt. Nailed and glued construction.

Materials and Dimensions
Walnut, often with burl walnut trim; also maple or cherry. Often
gilded and/or ebonized. Iron screws and supports. Height:
52–78″. Width: 27–35″.

Locality and Period
Larger factories from the East to the Midwest. c. 1875–1900.

Comment
Often made to match a suite of Eastlake or Rococo Revival
furniture, these large mirrors flanked doors or windows in the
drawing rooms of Victorian homes. Pier glasses should not be
confused with the long mirrors that are often attached to
Victorian bureaus and dressing tables. Long mirrors, 36–44″ in
height, are smaller than pier glasses and have screw holes at the
base, or metal supports and other signs of being attached to a
piece of furniture rather than hung. Overmantel mirrors are also
similar, but they are much wider than pier glasses.

Hints for Collectors
Because of their large size and weight, few pier glasses, long
mirrors, and overmantel mirrors have survived. However, since
there is little current demand for these mirrors, they are not
particularly expensive.

185 Sheraton architectural mirror

Description
Tall, rectangular 2-part mirror with sections horizontally separated by thin muntin. Flat, molded cornice projects at corners and rests on plain or reeded architectural columns or pilasters. Row of evenly spaced decorative balls applied under cornice. Columns rest on square plinths; base of frame molded to match cornice. Smaller panel, above muntin, of carved and gilded wood or, more often, reverse-painted glass with pastoral or patriotic scenes, sailing ships, or urn with flowers or fruit. Nailed and glued construction.

Materials and Dimensions
Pine, painted and gilded; less often mahogany or pine with mahogany veneer. Applied decorative elements: carved pine or composition plaster, painted and gilded. Height: 30–52″. Width: 15–32″.

Locality and Period
New England west to Ohio, south to the Carolinas and Georgia. c. 1800–20.

Comment
These large mirrors were usually valued for their decorative effect and usefulness. The larger examples were traditionally placed between pairs of windows or doors. The upper panels or friezes often reflect the patriotic fervor of the times.

Hints for Collectors
These mirrors are relatively inexpensive and easy to find. Avoid examples that have lost their original gilding or veneer, or have had their upper panels replaced. Examples with paintings of naval battles are especially popular today. Reproductions are fairly common and can confuse even experienced collectors.

Empire tabernacle mirror

Description
Tall, rectangular 2-part mirror without cornice or apron. Upper glass decorated with reverse glass painting of landscape, figures, ships, historical events, or urn with flowers or fruit. All 4 front sides of frame decorated with applied half-round pilasters, baluster-turned or with acanthus leaf carving, or both turned and carved. Projecting corner blocks square and embellished with applied rosettes. Thin wooden muntin separates upper and lower glass. Nailed and glued construction.

Materials and Dimensions
Pine or poplar; always gilded and sometimes ebonized. Pilasters maple or walnut. Rosettes brass or composition plaster. Height: 20–48″. Width: 12–24″.

Locality and Period
New England west to the Mississippi River and throughout the South. c. 1820–50.

Comment
These extremely popular mirrors were often made in small factories. Most interesting for their reverse glass painting, they are a form of folk art, depicting either anonymous landscapes or, more often, historically important events or places.

Hints for Collectors
Empire tabernacle mirrors are fairly common, so look for intact pieces. If the top part is mirror glass—usually a replacement— rather than a reverse painting, the piece is usually not worth buying. If it has a painting, check to make sure the paint is not damaged or flaking. As a rule, never buy a mirror with a damaged painting unless the picture is historically significant or a fine piece of folk art.

Empire ogee-frame mirror

Description
Rectangular mirror without cornice or apron. Wide frame (3–5″) with 2 narrow bands of molding, sometimes gilded, flanking a wide ogee molding of figured wood or wood grain-painted to imitate figured wood. Mitered corners. Nailed and glued construction.

Materials and Dimensions
Pine, painted and gilded, with crotch mahogany, rosewood, or walnut veneer; less often pine and mahogany; also grain-painted pine. Height: 30–40″. Width: 21–23″.

Locality and Period
Eastern United States west to Missouri, and to a limited extent in the West. c. 1830–60.

Comment
Ogee mirrors vary somewhat in size and decoration, but the basic rectangular format and curve of the frame are always the same. In the 19th century, the better-quality mirrors were solid or veneered mahogany with gilded borders. The less expensive ones were often grain-painted to imitate figured wood. Used in the home from bedroom to parlor, they were hung horizontally as well as vertically.

Hints for Collectors
The ogee mirror is one of the most abundant of all antique mirrors, and is, for that reason, surprisingly inexpensive. Avoid pieces with missing veneer. Grain-painted examples, though less expensive in the 19th century, are rare today and, if the paint is original, worth considerably more than the common, veneered pieces.

Victorian oval mirror

Description
Oval mirror with convex or concave-convex molding. Frame plain or with applied, foliated scrolls at top and matching drop at bottom. May be gilded, have gilded inner molding with plain outer molding, or have no gilding at all. Nailed and glued construction.

Materials and Dimensions
Pine, ash, or walnut. Pine examples gessoed and gilded with gold leaf; ash gessoed and gilded or left plain; walnut shellacked or coated with clear lacquer. Applied decoration, when present, maple, ash, or birch. Height: 36–50″. Width: 22–30″.

Locality and Period
Factories in the East and Midwest. c. 1850–80.

Comment
Large oval mirrors of this type were designed for use in the dining and living areas of the Victorian home, and were often hung in the vertical space between doors or windows. Generally, the furniture and mirrors were of a similar style. Accordingly, oval mirrors would have been used with Rococo furnishings.

Hints for Collectors
These large mirrors have limited use in the modern home, and for that reason can often be purchased quite inexpensively. Plainer examples, like the one shown, are the most popular with modern collectors. The scrollwork pieces are less in demand, and their delicate applied decoration frequently shows damage. Original glass is most desirable and fetches high prices. However, there is nothing wrong with replacing the glass in a good-quality mirror frame if it is badly cracked or clouded. Some of these pieces may have originally served as picture frames rather than mirrors.

Federal girandole mirror

Description
Round to oval mirror with convex or, rarely, concave glass
surrounded by elaborately carved and gilded frame. Inner edge
of frame often hollow and set with balls in Sheraton manner.
Crest in form of gilded eagle, dragon, or phoenix, set on rock
forms and flanked by acanthus leaf scrolls. Floral-carved apron
terminates in floral or grape cluster drop. Semicircular
metal or gilded wood arms terminate in candleholders.
Nailed and glued construction.

Materials and Dimensions
Carved and gilded pine. Applied decoration carved and gilded
pine or composition plaster. When present, candle arms and
sockets brass. Height: 48–57″. Width: 24–35″.

Locality and Period
Boston, New York, Philadelphia, and Baltimore. c. 1790–1815.

Comment
Because their convex glass allowed one to see at a glance all of a
crowded ball- or dining room, these mirrors were supposedly a
favorite with hostesses. They are Sheraton in feeling, especially
in the small balls on the inner part of the frame. Never made in
large numbers, they are not readily available today, and when
they do appear, they are expensive. English examples can be
confused with American pieces, and reproductions have been
made, so be sure to get a guarantee that the mirror is original
and American before you buy.

Hints for Collectors
Few early mirrors retain their original glass, so those that do are
especially valuable. No matter what its condition, the original
glass, or even a very early replacement, enhances the value of a
mirror.

Federal gilded mirror

Description
Tall, rectangular mirror with frame of carved and gilded wood
and gesso. Scrolled and pierced pediment with a spread-wing
eagle atop an oval shield. On shield, sheaf of wheat against a blue
painted ground bordered by 13 stars. At each side of eagle,
curling bellflower wreaths. At each side of frame, pendant husks;
frame interior beaded and molded. Symmetrically draped skirt
with a central fruit-carved drop. Nailed and screwed
construction.

Materials and Dimensions
Pine or poplar. Applied decorative elements carved pine or
hardwood. Gesso-covered, then gilded and painted. Height:
34–42″. Width: 16–18″.

Locality and Period
New England west to Ohio, south to the Carolinas. c. 1790–1810.

Comment
Gilded mirrors featuring eagles, cornucopia, and patriotic
symbols were popular in America following the Revolutionary
War. Originally classical symbols associated with ancient Greece
and Rome, these motifs were adopted eagerly by the young
Republic. The sheaf-of-wheat device stands for prosperity; the 13
stars, of course, represent the original states.

Hints for Collectors
Carved and gilded mirrors like this one are highly desirable
collector's items. However, they are quite fragile, and in most
cases will have been damaged and repaired. While extensive
restoration is never desirable, do not pass up such a mirror just
because some areas have been replaced or regilded. Very few
examples exist today in perfect condition.

Queen Anne fret-carved mirror

Description
Tall, relatively narrow mirror, usually with 2 pieces of glass. In early examples, upper glass may have engraved or cut floral or geometric decoration. Thin, saw-cut frame has scalloped crest, often with matching apron; crest and sometimes apron decorated with applied, carved, and gilded floral motifs. Sides of frame decorated with applied, carved, and gilded pendant fruits and flowers. Glued and nailed construction.

Materials and Dimensions
Earliest examples walnut or pine with walnut veneer; rarely stained pine or maple. Later examples solid mahogany or pine with mahogany veneer. Applied decoration gilded pine, poplar, or maple; rarely japanned. Height: 36–58″. Width: 16–25″.

Locality and Period
New England west to Pennsylvania, south to Maryland and Virginia. c. 1725–55.

Comment
By the Queen Anne period, American cabinetmakers were producing their own frames, but continued to import mirror glass from England and the Continent. Framed English mirrors were also imported and, though somewhat more elaborate, are often difficult to distinguish from American-made examples.

Hints for Collectors
Early mirrors are rarely found in mint condition. Though glued and supported on the back with wooden blocks, the delicate fretwork is often cracked and chipped. Many mirrors may lack ornamentation or supporting blocks. Others will show replacement parts readily identified by an examination of the unfinished back. These mirrors are rare and command extremely high prices.

Chippendale fret-carved mirror

Description
Rectangular mirror with 1 piece of glass. Frame with simple inner molding, either flat or rounded. Saw-cut fretwork crest and matching apron in complex scroll pattern. Crest may have applied, carved, and gilded central medallion in form of phoenix or eagle. Apron may have applied shell or floral device, also carved and gilded. Nailed and glued construction.

Materials and Dimensions
Usually pine with mahogany veneer; also solid mahogany, walnut, or pine with walnut veneer. Applied decoration pine or maple, sometimes gilded; holly or boxwood stringing rare. Height: 34–37″. Width: 21–23″.

Locality and Period
New England west to Pennsylvania, south to the Carolinas. c. 1750–80.

Comment
Chippendale mirrors of this sort are fairly common. The fretwork varies somewhat from piece to piece: floral in inspiration, though very abstract, it is a simplified version of the Rococo outline popular on French furnishings of a slightly earlier period. As with Queen Anne looking glasses, it can be difficult to distinguish between domestic and imported mirrors. Many examples bear the labels of American craftsmen or merchants, but often the labels indicate only where the piece was bought.

Hints for Collectors
Condition and decoration are important in choosing a Chippendale fret-carved mirror. Look for pieces with the original gilding and applied decoration, particularly those with a phoenix or eagle, and those with a minimum of repair to the fretwork and veneer.

Hepplewhite fret-carved mirror

Description
Rectangular mirror with carved crest in broken pediment form, terminating in gilded rosettes. Crest may have inlaid central medallion in urn or shell form. Above, carved and gilded urn filled with wooden and gilded plaster flowers on wire stems. Saw-cut, fretwork apron may have inlaid central medallion. Sides of frame embellished with pendant floral sprays hung on wire. Nailed and glued construction.

Materials and Dimensions
Mahogany or pine with mahogany veneer; rarely walnut or pine with walnut veneer. Applied decoration carved pine or composition plaster that is gilded and mounted on wire framework. Inlay satinwood; stringing holly or boxwood. Height: 50–60″. Width: 20–23″.

Locality and Period
New York, Boston, Philadelphia, and Baltimore. c. 1780–95.

Comment
The pedimented crests of these mirrors closely resemble the broken pediments found on Chippendale highboys. On somewhat later Hepplewhite mirrors (the so-called filigree type), the pediment is replaced with a complex openwork floral arrangement of carved wood and composition plaster on wire.

Hints for Collectors
The applied decorations are very fragile, and few pieces are intact. Good, accurate restoration is therefore quite acceptable. Check mirrors carefully for manufacturers' labels or stamps. Any American label of the period increases a mirror's value, even if the mirror was made abroad and sold here. Labels were glued on the outside of the backboard, on the inside, or even on the back of the glass itself.

Art Deco mirror

Description
Square or rectangular metal-frame mirror with molded, slightly overhanging top surmounted by metal urn with stylized floral decoration. Turned rods at sides join top to molded, slightly protruding base. Rods have small, stylized urn finials and shaped drops. Welded and screwed construction.

Materials and Dimensions
Stainless steel; also aluminum and brass. Tin backboard. Brass decorative inlay. Hanger supports: iron. Rods: brass. Height: 20–23″. Width: 17–19″.

Locality and Period
Large factories throughout the United States. c. 1920–40.

Comment
The use of industrial materials such as aluminum, steel, and plastic in mirrors is a 20th-century phenomenon. Although this piece shows Federal characteristics such as the urn finials and centerpiece, in overall feeling it is most closely related to the Art Deco style.

Hints for Collectors
Mirrors with metal frames from the 1930s and early 1940s are relatively common, so look for the most interesting examples: those with original mirrors and sophisticated touches, such as this combination of stainless steel and brass. While these mirrors can sometimes be found in antiques shops, the best places to look for them are used-furniture stores, attics, or house sales. Inexpensive today, these mirrors are sure to increase in value, especially since Art Deco furnishings are becoming so popular with collectors.

195 Victorian cast-iron cheval glass

Description
Rectangular to nearly square dressing table mirror enclosed in metal frame of complex form—with drapery, curvilinear motifs, and a griffinlike figure at each side. Attached by swivels to A-shaped side supports topped by elaborate finial, matched by interior drop. Supports joined by shaped horizontal stretcher. Hoof-shaped feet. Welded and screwed construction.

Materials and Dimensions
Frame cast iron; swivels cast iron or brass. Typically painted white, but also other colors. Height: 20–24″. Width: 18–20″.

Locality and Period
Factories in the East and Midwest. c. 1865–85.

Comment
Cheval mirrors were square or rectangular and mounted on adjustable swivels. They were developed in the 18th century and were soon modified in size and form to serve as dressing mirrors. The use of cast iron for such pieces was, however, a late Victorian innovation and part of the contemporary interest in other cast-iron furniture. The complexity of this example reflects highly developed factory casting techniques.

Hints for Collectors
Always check cast-iron pieces carefully for cracks and repaired breaks. Although these pieces were often damaged and repaired by soldering, a coat of paint may obscure the solder marks. So examine backs and undersides, which were usually not painted, to determine if repairs have been made. Cracks or repairs in a piece should be reflected in the purchase price.

Queen Anne dressing glass

Description
Small, rectangular tabletop mirror. Vertical frame plain, slightly molded, with saw-cut, scalloped crest; no apron. Swivel-mounted, with metal pins secured to frame. Frame has plain stretcher and shaped bracket feet. Nailed and glued construction.

Materials and Dimensions
Pine with mahogany veneer; occasionally solid mahogany, walnut, or cherry. Sometimes painted or japanned. Swivels: iron. Height: 13–42″. Width: 6–22″.

Locality and Period
New England, New York, west to Pennsylvania. c. 1730–50.

Comment
Dressing glasses appear to have been developed in the early 18th century. Customarily set on a lowboy or other small table, they were the forerunners of bureau mirrors. The swivel device, an early innovation, was popular because it gave views from different angles. While most Queen Anne dressing glasses lack the supporting set of small drawers common in later types, a few are known, including a rare block-front piece.

Hints for Collectors
Queen Anne dressing mirrors are not common, but can be found. Though they vary in height from 1′ to 3′ or more, they are rather plain and might be overlooked by those unfamiliar with the type. Since authentic pieces are not very popular or expensive, a Queen Anne mirror is worth considering by anyone who wants to own a piece of 18th-century American furniture.

197 Colonial Revival dressing mirror

Description
Small dressing-table or bureau-top portable mirror set in frame with straight bottom and curved top corners. Molded frame crowned by a simple fret-cut scallop with central turned finial. Mirror supports are baluster-turned uprights fixed in a stepped and molded rectangular base with rounded corners. Nailed, glued, and screwed construction.

Materials and Dimensions
Pine, maple, or birch; stained dark brown or black. Swivels: brass or iron. Height: 18–22". Width: 17–19". Depth: 4–5".

Locality and Period
Large factories throughout the Midwest and the East. c. 1900–35.

Comment
Dressing mirrors continued to be made through the mid-1930s, though they were considered somewhat unfashionable by the time of World War I. Since most people preferred dressing tables or dressers, or even wall-hung mirrors, a very limited number of dressing mirrors were produced. Examples in the Colonial Revival style are somewhat uncommon. Most such pieces are vaguely Federal in feeling, though it is evident that the designers had no particular 18th-century style in mind.

Hints for Collectors
If in doubt as to whether you have a dressing mirror or a mirror that has been removed from the back of a dresser or dressing table, examine the bottom and lower front. Screw holes indicate that the piece was once attached to another piece of furniture.

Mission-style dressing mirror

Description
Low, rectangular dressing-table or bureau-top mirror set in plain, unmolded frame. Mounted between 2 square supports with rounded tops. Unmolded, overhanging top of storage box forms work surface. Below, 2 half-length drawers separated by square-cut stile. Square stiles taper sharply at base to form short legs. Paneled sides and back. Paneled and glued mortise-and-tenon construction.

Materials and Dimensions
Oak and quartersawed oak. Pulls: small, turned wooden knobs. Swivels: brass. Height: 21–23″. Width: 30–32″. Depth: 10–11″.

Locality and Period
Factories in the East and Midwest. c. 1905–20.

Comment
Though dressing mirrors are shown in Gustav Stickley catalogues, it seems that few were made. No doubt they were unnecessary, since mirrored dressing tables and dressers were extremely popular by the early 20th century and found in almost every American home.

Hints for Collectors
Of little practical value, the dressing mirror is still an interesting piece of miniature furniture, reflecting the style of its period. For the collector looking for a reasonably priced, authentic, and possibly signed piece of Mission-style furniture, a dressing mirror can be a good choice. The best examples will have exposed pegs and tenons, and will be made of solid oak rather than veneer.

199 Federal-style mirrored dressing box

Description
Small, rectangular box with hinged lift top. Hinged mirror inside top swings up and rests at angle against top. Below mirror, storage well. 1 pull-out drawer at base of box. Dovetailed construction.

Materials and Dimensions
Mahogany and mahogany veneer or pine with mahogany veneer; sometimes cherry or walnut. Secondary wood pine. Stenciled gilding at corners and edges. Hinges: brass or iron butt. Pulls: brass knobs. Escutcheons: carved bone or ivory. Height: 5–7″. Width: 14–16″. Depth: 6–7″.

Locality and Period
New England west to Ohio, south to Georgia. c. 1800–60.

Comment
At a time when few dressing tables were furnished with mirrors, least of all in public houses, it was customary for travelers to carry a mirrored dressing box. In addition to the mirror, the dressing box provided storage for cosmetics or shaving materials.

Hints for Collectors
This dressing box is a good example of how earlier styles may linger on long after they have been superseded by newer ones, and how a piece may be of later date than its style would suggest. Although clearly in the Federal mode of the early 1800s, the example shown here bears the paper label of Charles A. Baudouine, a New York City cabinetmaker active in the mid-1800s.

Hepplewhite dressing glass

Description
Oval or shield-shaped tabletop mirror. Swivel-mounted to 2 cabriole uprights, which terminate in metal rosettes. Uprights mounted on low cabinet base. Cabinet may have serpentine, oxbow, bow-shaped, or demilune front. 2–3 drawers—usually 1 long center drawer flanked by 2 square ones. Drawers often decorated with inlay, reeding, or stringing. Feet stump or plain or ogee bracket. Nailed and glued construction.

Materials and Dimensions
Usually pine with mahogany veneer; occasionally mahogany or cherry. Secondary wood pine or poplar. Inlay satinwood; stringing holly or boxwood. Pulls: small brass, ivory, or turned wooden knobs; rarely, oval brass mounts with bail handles. Escutcheons: brass or diamond-shaped carved bone. Brass swivels and rosettes. Height: 21–25″. Width: 18–28″. Depth: 10–12″.

Locality and Period
New England west to Ohio, south to the Carolinas. c. 1785–1815.

Comment
Also known as shaving or toilet glasses, these pieces are among the most interesting examples of smaller cabinetry. The curving frontal forms imitate those of period chests of drawers, possibly so that the dressing glass could be placed on a matching chest.

Hints for Collectors
One can find a variety of dressing glasses, from the Queen Anne through the Empire periods; Federal examples alone are sufficiently varied to make up a sizable collection. Because dressing glasses are small, a collector may accumulate a representative group in a relatively small space.

Art Deco vanity mirror

Description
Circular tabletop mirror in stainless-steel frame, mounted on swivels inside a metal hood. Concealed bulb lights mirror. Round metal tube connects mirror hood and curvilinear, machine-decorated base; base has small storage drawer. Stainless-steel back. Welded and screwed construction.

Materials and Dimensions
Anodized aluminum and stainless steel. Pulls: tablike aluminum knob cast as part of drawer front. Attached electric cord cloth over rubber. Height: 13–15″. Width: 7–8″.

Locality and Period
Factories and light-fixture shops throughout the East and Midwest. c. 1925–45.

Comment
Small mirrors mounted on metal bases were very popular during the 1930s and 1940s. This example is very Art Deco in feeling; the curvilinear, "streamlined" effect of the hood and base is similar in design to contemporary architecture, trains, and automobiles. The idea of indirect lighting utilized here was another innovation of the period. Most of these mirrors are made of extremely durable materials and are usually found in good condition.

Hints for Collectors
Small Art Deco accessories like this are good examples of what the period has to interest collectors. Good-looking and compatible with modern décor, they combine attractive design and an elegant style. Unfortunately, these pieces must often be rewired before they can be used.

Description
Small, rectangular tabletop mirror in steel frame. Glass supported by U-shaped tubular-steel framework and attached with screws and washers. Flat steel support rod bisects back horizontally. Fiberboard backing. Screwed and soldered construction.

Materials and Dimensions
Stainless steel and tubular steel. Steel screws and washers. Height: 16–19″. Width: 10–12″.

Locality and Period
Large factories in the East and Midwest. c. 1925–60.

Comment
Extremely simple, yet fashionable, tabletop mirrors like this one remained popular for a long time, and even today variations are being produced. For many years, they were widely used in shoe stores. The basic form—a swivel-mounted mirror-on-frame—dates to the early 19th century. What is new are the materials used and the industrial design typical of this century.

Hints for Collectors
Among the least expensive of the mirrors made in the first half of the 20th century, these pieces would make a nice addition to an Art Deco bedroom or bath. They have the streamlined look and bold lines particularly characteristic of the era. As investments, though, they are of doubtful value, being both too plain and too plentiful. The exceptions are those pieces made by well-known designers or those that are made of unusual materials or in an unusual fashion.

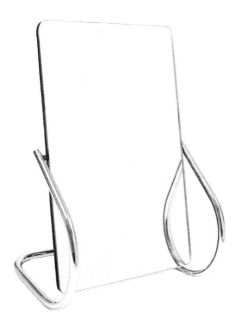

Chests of Drawers

The chest of drawers is as basic a household item today as it was when it first appeared in America some 300 years ago. Its origins can be traced to the early, boxlike 6-board chest with a hinged lift top that was made by the first settlers. By the 1650s, carpenters had added 1 or 2 drawers beneath the storage well, creating the blanket chest. Eventually additional drawers were also added to replace the well, and the lid became a fixed top, creating the chest of drawers. The blanket chest continued to be popular into the 19th century, but it was often disguised behind a set of false drawer fronts (226) so that it resembled the chest of drawers, which had become far more fashionable.

Early chests of drawers have 3 to 4 full-length drawers that are equally tall; these pieces are often made of panels that fit within stiles and rails. In William and Mary pieces (203), the 4 drawers are often graduated, and the chests are typically constructed of plain boards that are nailed or dovetailed together. This basic form did not change until the Chippendale period. At that time, cabinetmakers began to create shaped chests, which might have bowed, serpentine (209), oxbow (204), block (206), or bombé (208) fronts. These pieces all required more skill, time, and materials than plain chests; needless to say, they were more expensive. Shaped fronts continued to be made by Federal craftsmen, who sometimes crowned their chests of drawers with a splashboard or a low set of small drawers, or a combination of both (227).

Although chests of drawers made in the 18th and early 19th centuries are structurally similar, their hardware and feet reflect the periods in which they were made. For example, a William and Mary chest typically has teardrop pulls and ball feet, while a Queen Anne example has batwing mounts and plain bracket feet. Some Chippendale pieces have plain or molded bracket feet, and others claw-and-ball feet; most have willow mounts. Federal chests of drawers often have French feet or turned Sheraton-style legs; most have rectangular or oval mounts with bail handles. An Empire chest of drawers might have scroll-cut or paw feet and animal-form mounts.

Victorian chests of drawers, reflecting the diversity of the period, were made in all the popular revival styles, including Rococo, Renaissance, and Gothic. Some Victorian chests rest on a plinthlike base (217), which often conceals an innovation of the period—metal casters.

Chests of drawers made in the 20th century (230) usually resemble those made earlier, yet some are distinguished by their use of new materials. Modular chests are perhaps the most interesting 20th-century form; these pieces can be used either by themselves or in groups of 2 or more.

William and Mary plain chest of drawers

Description
Plain chest of drawers has top usually decorated with thumbnail molding. 3–5 full-length drawers. Single- or double-arch molding frames drawers. Molded base. 4 turned ball feet, 2 ball and 2 peg feet, or 4 peg feet. Peg feet, when present, extensions of side boards. Nailed or, later, dovetailed construction.

Materials and Dimensions
Pine; rarely maple with pine secondary wood. Often stained red; rarely with painted floral or pictorial designs. Ball feet, when present: typically maple. Pulls: brass teardrops or bail handles. Escutcheons: matching brass. Height: 36–38″. Width: 38–44″. Depth: 18–22″.

Locality and Period
New England west to Pennsylvania. c. 1690–1720.

Comment
This is the simplest chest of drawers and a direct descendant of the 6-board chest. It is closely related to the lift-top blanket chest, which has a large storage space reached through a hinged top and often concealed behind 2–3 false drawer fronts. The chest of drawers, however, is a later development and reflects the need for more convenient storage space.

Hints for Collectors
These chests are among the most available and least expensive William and Mary pieces. Check that the feet are not replacements or, even worse, additions to a chest that never had ball feet. Chests with painted floral or pictorial designs are rare and valuable, but should be inspected carefully to ensure that the decoration was not added later.

Chippendale oxbow-front chest of drawers

Description
Oxbow-front chest of drawers with overhanging, molded top. 3–4 equal or graduated full-length drawers. Plain board sides and back. Protruding, molded base with skirt. Molded or ogee bracket feet. Dovetailed, pegged, and nailed construction.

Materials and Dimensions
Mahogany; also walnut, cherry, or maple. Secondary wood pine or poplar. Pulls: plain brass rosettes with bail handles, or plain or pierced brass willow mounts with bail handles. Escutcheons: shaped brass ovals with scrolled tops and bottoms or plain vertical ovals. Height: 30–33″. Width: 36–39″. Depth: 19–21″.

Locality and Period
New England west to Pennsylvania, south to Virginia. c. 1760–80.

Comment
Oxbow drawer fronts are found almost exclusively on Chippendale and early Federal chests, and are less common than the serpentine front. The piece illustrated here has a damaged drawer front, which will require expert restoration. This type of damage may lower value 10% to 15%.

Hints for Collectors
Always make sure an oxbow-front chest of drawers is a period piece and not a reproduction. The style was quite popular among the makers of Colonial Revival furniture from 1876 until well into the 20th century. Clues to look for in reproductions are thin, stamped, rather than cast, brasses, oxbow fronts made from several pieces of wood glued together rather than a single carved board, and the use of wire nails.

205 Hepplewhite oxbow-front chest of drawers

Description
Oxbow-front chest of drawers with overhanging, molded top. 4 equal or graduated full-length drawers, sometimes with veneered fronts and/or stringing and inlay. Front corners, top, and feet may be chamfered. Molded base. Plain skirt. Feet plain molded brackets or in French fashion. Dovetailed construction.

Materials and Dimensions
Mahogany, cherry, or maple; drawer fronts sometimes with curly maple or satinwood veneer. Secondary wood pine or poplar. Stringing and inlay, usually in checkered form, holly or boxwood. Pulls: oval Hepplewhite brass mounts with bail handles. Escutcheons: oblong brass plates or ivory diamonds. Height: 33–38″. Width: 38–43″. Depth: 26–28″.

Locality and Period
New England west to Ohio, south to Maryland. c. 1780–1810.

Comment
Compared with other Federal pieces, such as sideboards, these chests are rather conservative in design and decoration. Veneer is rare, as is stringing, and in most cases the cabinetmakers relied for effect on the finely grained mahogany.

Hints for Collectors
Check whether a piece has the original hardware. Plugged holes indicate other fittings. Any replacement should be stylistically correct. As tastes changed, chests of drawers often acquired inappropriate pulls and escutcheons, such as pressed-glass Empire pulls and, later, the carved fruitwood pulls popular in the Victorian period.

Colonial Revival block-front chest of drawers

Description
Small block-front chest of drawers with overhanging, molded top. 3–4 graduated drawers separated by molded dividers. Plain board sides. Heavily molded base. Plain skirt. Plain bracket feet. Glued and nailed construction.

Materials and Dimensions
Cherry, pine, birch, or maple, stained to imitate mahogany. Secondary wood pine. Pulls: brass willow mounts, plain or pierced, with bail handles. Escutcheons: matching brass. Height: 28–30″. Width: 32–34″. Depth: 18–20″.

Locality and Period
Large factories in the East and Midwest. c. 1890–1930.

Comment
This piece is a good example of Colonial Revival style and more faithful than most to the 18th-century prototype. In general, such pieces differ from the original in materials, proportions, and styling. This chest, for example, is of less expensive woods, but is stained to imitate the mahogany of the original. Further, it is not as high or wide as the model on which it was based and has plain bracket feet rather than molded ones.

Hints for Collectors
Colonial Revival pieces are just beginning to attract buyer attention, and well-made examples like the one shown here are ideal for those who appreciate 18th-century styling but never expect to own a period piece. The more closely a revival piece imitates the original, the more desirable it is. In general, the most faithful Colonial Revival reproductions were made in the late 19th century.

Description
Block-front chest of drawers with overhanging, molded top. 3–5 equal or graduated full-length drawers. Top or, in rare cases, all drawers may bear shell carving. Base has heavy molding. Skirt plain, scalloped, or gadrooned; if plain, may have shell-carved central drop. Claw-and-ball, plain, or molded bracket feet. Dovetailed construction.

Materials and Dimensions
Mahogany; also cherry, walnut, or curly maple. Secondary wood pine or poplar. Pulls: brass willow mounts or rosettes, both with bail handles. Escutcheons: matching brass. Height: 30–36″. Width: 34–37″. Depth: 20–22″.

Locality and Period
New England, primarily Rhode Island, Connecticut, and Massachusetts. c. 1760–80.

Comment
These rare chests were made by only a few sophisticated cabinetmakers in a limited area, but their distinctive design is generally regarded as a genuine American innovation. The most unusual feature of the block-front form is the shaped front, a taxing chore for the craftsman for it was often carved from a single thick board. Examples with shell carving are mostly from the Newport, Rhode Island, area. These also required great skill, whether the shells were carved directly on the drawer fronts or were done separately and then glued on.

Hints for Collectors
These chests are rare and extremely expensive. A substantial number of reproductions were made around the turn of the century. Proportions, construction, and decoration for the existing examples are well known; your example should conform.

Chippendale bombé chest of drawers

Description
Kettle-shaped chest of drawers with sharply overhanging, molded top. Front and sides curve sharply outward, then curve in again at base. 4 equal or graduated full-length drawers; bottom 3 conform to curved shape. Base protruding and heavily molded, often with a scrolled central drop that may be shell-carved. Short cabriole brackets with plain or leaf-carved knees. Carved claw-and-ball feet. Dovetailed and pegged construction.

Materials and Dimensions
Mahogany. Secondary wood pine. Pulls: brass willow mounts with bail handles. Escutcheons: matching brass. Height: 35–38″. Width: 36–38″. Depth: 21–22″.

Locality and Period
In and around Boston, Massachusetts. c. 1760–75.

Comment
In America, the bombé form was used on only 3 types of furniture—the chest of drawers, the slant-front desk, and the slant-front secretary—and for only a brief period of time. English examples are slightly more numerous; they can be distinguished by their more ornate form and decoration.

Hints for Collectors
Period bombé chests are extremely expensive and seldom appear on the market. To distinguish Colonial Revival reproductions from 18th-century pieces, examine the sides and drawer fronts carefully. If seams are present, the piece is a reproduction. Colonial Revival examples used smaller pieces of wood glued together to build up the sides and drawer fronts, whereas in 18th-century examples these parts were often carved from single pieces of wood.

209 Chippendale serpentine-front chest of drawers

Description
Serpentine-front chest of drawers with molded, overhanging top. 4–5 full-length graduated drawers, or 2 half-length drawers over 3 full-length ones. Corners may be chamfered and reeded or decorated with geometric patterns or reeded quarter-columns. Base heavily molded, often with carved central drop. Claw-and-ball, plain, or molded bracket feet; rarely front feet claw-and-ball and rear feet bracket. Dovetailed construction.

Materials and Dimensions
Mahogany; also cherry or walnut; rarely curly or tiger maple. Secondary wood pine or poplar. Pulls: brass willow mounts or brass rosettes, both with bail handles. Escutcheons: matching brass or brass keyhole surrounds. Height: 32–37″. Width: 37–42″. Depth: 20–23″.

Locality and Period
New England west to Pennsylvania, south to Georgia. c. 1750–80.

Comment
Like other elaborately shaped pieces, those with serpentine fronts reflected the European Rococo style. These furnishings were made almost exclusively by cabinetmakers in major urban centers and were always expensive.

Hints for Collectors
Serpentine fronts are bowed at the center and hollowed out on each side. Oxbow fronts have a hollow center and swell on each side. The serpentine front is perhaps a bit more common than th oxbow and may be slightly less expensive; however, both types command extremely high prices.

Hepplewhite serpentine-front chest of drawers

Description
Serpentine-front chest of drawers with overhanging, molded top. Front corners plain and square or slightly chamfered, rarely with fluting. 4 graduated drawers with cock-beaded edges. Drawer fronts frequently veneered or outlined with stringing. Solid board sides and back. Skirt plain or valanced, sometimes with inlaid central drop. French or scrolled bracket feet. Dovetailed construction.

Materials and Dimensions
Cherry, mahogany, or maple. Bird's-eye maple or satinwood veneer. Stringing and inlay boxwood. Pulls: oval brass mounts or rosettes, both with bail handles. Escutcheons: oval or oblong brass, or diamond-shaped carved bone. Height: 35–37″. Width: 40–44″. Depth: 21–23″.

Locality and Period
New England west to Ohio, south to Georgia. c. 1785–1805.

Comment
Chests with shaped fronts were most common during the Federal period. After 1820, they fell out of fashion and were infrequently manufactured. Examples from the Chippendale and Federal periods represent one of the high points in American cabinetmaking.

Hints for Collectors
Whatever its period, a serpentine-front chest of drawers is always more expensive than one with a straight front. The work involved in shaping the front and doing the chamfering made it difficult to produce more than a small number of pieces, particularly since these were usually elaborately veneered and inlaid. Expensive when made, these Hepplewhite examples are even more so today.

Hepplewhite bowfront chest of drawers

Description
Chest of drawers with moderately bowed front and unmolded, slightly overhanging top with stringing around edge. 4–5 equal or graduated full-length drawers. Fronts plain or veneered, usually banded with inlay; base may also be inlaid. Plain board sides. Skirt shaped, scroll-cut, or with center drop. Outswept French feet. Dovetailed construction.

Materials and Dimensions
Mahogany or cherry; rarely birch. Secondary wood pine. Contrasting veneer and stringing. Veneer crotch grain mahogany (as seen here), satinwood, or bird's-eye maple. Stringing and inlay boxwood. Pulls: oval or oblong brass mounts with bail handles. Escutcheons: brass or ivory, shield- or diamond-shaped or oval plates. Height: 36–38″. Width: 40–43″. Depth: 21–22″.

Locality and Period
New England west to Ohio, south to Georgia. c. 1785–1810.

Comment
Easier to find than serpentine-front chests of the same period and style, Hepplewhite bowfront chests of drawers were made in fairly large numbers. The characteristic combination of swelling front and sweeping French feet is one of the most sophisticated and appealing of forms.

Hints for Collectors
Note the spots on this chest where veneer is missing or has lifted away from the surface. Be wary about buying a piece with extensive damage to the veneer because restoration is expensive. However, on an especially fine piece, like the one shown here, the cost of restoration may be justified.

Hepplewhite straight-front chest of drawers

Description
Chest of drawers with unmolded, overhanging top. 3–4 graduated full-length drawers, or 2–3 smaller drawers over 3 full-length ones. If 2 smaller drawers, each half-length; if 3, center one very narrow. Plain board sides. Valanced skirt. Plain French feet, formed from extensions of skirt and side boards. Often with elaborate inlay and stringing. Dovetailed or nailed construction.

Materials and Dimensions
Mahogany, cherry, or maple. Secondary wood pine. Inlay boxwood, bird's-eye maple, or birch; stringing boxwood. Pulls: oval brass mounts with bail handles or plain brass rosettes with circular handles. Escutcheons, when present: brass ovals applied vertically, diamond-shaped ivory, or brass keyhole surrounds. Height: 35–41″. Width: 42–45″. Depth: 20–22″.

Locality and Period
New England west to Ohio, south to the Carolinas. c. 1785–1815.

Comment
The straight-front Hepplewhite chest of drawers shown here is attributed to the New York City cabinetmaker Michael Allison. In general, many more high-style, straight-front chests were made than chests with bowed or serpentine fronts. This piece is distinguished because it has 3 small upper drawers; usually there is only 1 full-length drawer.

Hints for Collectors
Always look for the touches that make a piece special. Many of the better Hepplewhite chests, for example, are inlaid, although very few have the eagle-and-stars inlay seen in the example illustrated. A chest with this sort of decoration is of much greater value than a plain Hepplewhite example.

Description
Chest of drawers with slightly overhanging, shaped and reeded top. 4 equal or graduated full-length drawers or a tall top drawer over 3 shorter, graduated ones. Front ends have carved or reeded, ¾-round corner posts or flat, reeded stiles. Plain board or, more often, paneled sides. Skirt plain or slightly shaped with central drop. Turned and slightly tapered Sheraton feet with cuff. Usually veneered and may be inlaid as well. Dovetailed and paneled construction.

Materials and Dimensions
Mahogany with crotch mahogany or satinwood veneer; also cherry with figured maple veneer. Secondary wood pine or poplar. Inlay satinwood, holly, or boxwood. Pulls: oblong, oval, or round brass mounts with bail handles or brass rosette knobs. Escutcheons: brass keyhole surrounds. Height: 37–45″. Width: 42–46″. Depth: 21–24″.

Locality and Period
New England west to Ohio and throughout the South. c. 1800–20.

Comment
Although these chests closely resemble Hepplewhite examples, the carving and turning of the legs and feet mark them as Sheraton. While most Sheraton chests of drawers have straight fronts, some have serpentine or bowed fronts.

Hints for Collectors
Sheraton chests of drawers are often underpriced at auction compared with costly Hepplewhite pieces of the same period. Look for the finest examples—those with excellent workmanship, carved and reeded corner posts, or good wood graining. They are most likely to increase in value.

Sheraton bowfront chest of drawers

Description
Bowfront chest of drawers with overhanging top. Corners cut to conform to shape of reeded stiles, which are ¾-round with turned capitals. 4–5 equal or graduated full-length drawers. Drawer fronts plain or veneered, usually with stringing. Plain board sides. Shallow skirt plain or elaborately valanced. Legs are ring-turned extensions of stiles. Round or ball feet. Dovetailed construction.

Materials and Dimensions
Mahogany; rarely cherry. Secondary wood pine. Drawer fronts satinwood or flame or curly maple veneer. Stringing boxwood. Pulls: oval brass mounts with bail handles. Escutcheons: brass keyhole surrounds. Height: 41–44″. Width: 44–47″. Depth: 23–25″.

Locality and Period
New England west to Ohio, south to Georgia. c. 1790–1815.

Comment
Sheraton chests of drawers are usually plainer than Hepplewhite chests of the same period, and tend to lack the veneering and inlay so characteristic of the latter. The example shown here, though typical of the Sheraton bowfront form, is unusual in having such fine veneered drawer fronts.

Hints for Collectors
Sheraton bowfront chests of drawers are not hard to find. The example illustrated, however, with its cutout areas at the top, its reeding and graceful skirt, is particularly well made. Details like these set a piece apart and make clear the difference between the ordinary and the exceptional example.

215 Sheraton transitional bowfront chest of drawers

Description
Bowfront chest of drawers with overhanging, plain or molded top. 4–5 slightly bowed, equal or graduated full-length drawers. Stringing present on drawer fronts and along end posts. Base slightly molded. Carved feet shaped like lion's paws, sometimes set on small casters. Dovetailed construction.

Materials and Dimensions
Mahogany, walnut, or cherry. May be partly veneered in mahogany or maple. Secondary wood pine or poplar. Stringing boxwood or holly. Pulls: brass lion's-head mounts with ring handles or rosettes; also oblong plates with bail handles, or pressed Sandwich-glass knobs. Escutcheons: brass rosettes. Casters: brass. Height: 34–38″. Width: 30–36″. Depth: 19–21″.

Locality and Period
New York, Massachusetts, and Pennsylvania. c. 1805–20.

Comment
These late Sheraton pieces were influenced by the French Directoire style, which dominated Continental design prior to the Napoleonic era. In America, it chiefly affected cabinetmakers working in major centers. The use of carved animal-paw feet and ornate pulls heralded the Empire period. Late in the Federal period, brass casters became popular because they helped to move large pieces of furniture.

Hints for Collectors
The rather ornate pulls are original, as can be seen by examining the marks they have made on the chest front and the holes drilled for them. If the holes and the wear marks do not match the current pulls on a chest of drawers, you can be sure they are replacements. Use the marks as a guide in obtaining the correct replacement brasses.

William and Mary paneled chest of drawers

Description
1- or 2-piece 4-drawer chest with several sunken panels set within applied molding arranged in geometric patterns. Molded, slightly overhanging top. Band of molding encircling waist conceals small, flat dowels that hold 2 sections together. Sides undecorated panels. Base molded. Feet typically of turned ball variety, but may be peglike extensions of stiles or, rarely, a variation of bootjack. Paneled stile-and-rail construction.

Materials and Dimensions
Oak; occasionally pine. Feet turned walnut or maple; sometimes ebonized. Secondary wood pine or cedar. Sometimes painted black to imitate ebony. Pulls: brass teardrops, small brass bail handles, or turned wooden knobs. Escutcheons: matching iron plates or iron squares, set at an angle. Height: 35–48″. Width: 38–43″. Depth: 20–23″.

Locality and Period
New England, particularly Massachusetts. c. 1680–1710.

Comment
These pieces are the last development of the Pilgrim-century chest. Some came in 2 parts, probably to make them easier to transport. Such chests are, in a sense, the forerunners of the chest-on-chests of the Chippendale period. Needless to say, paneled chests of drawers are uncommon and high-priced. Better examples are found primarily in museum collections.

Hints for Collectors
As with all 2-unit pieces, be sure that the sections were originally joined to each other. They should match in wood type, style, and signs of wear and finish. Also see if the applied molding around the panels is original. Like spindles and bosses, molding often fell off and was later replaced.

Eastlake marble-top chest of drawers

Description
Chest of drawers with separate, slightly overhanging marble top without molding. 2 half-length drawers protruding 1–2″ over 2–3 full-length drawers. Drawer fronts have central, horizontal panels or grain painting. Paneled sides and back. Stiles decorated with incised floral devices and reeding. Plinthlike base also protrudes 1–2″ and has horizontal channels. Rear feet plain, block-shaped extensions of stiles, sometimes with casters. Glued, screwed, and nailed construction.

Materials and Dimensions
Oak or walnut; also cherry or butternut. Secondary wood pine. Drawer fronts with burl panels or grain painting to imitate burl. Top: marble. Pulls: brass mounts with bail handles or pendant ring handles. Escutcheons: iron keyhole surrounds. Casters: brass or iron. Height: 28–33″. Width: 38–40″. Depth: 18–20″.

Locality and Period
Large factories throughout the East and Midwest. c. 1860–1910.

Comment
Like much other Victorian furniture, these chests of drawers were often part of a bedroom set and some incorporated a mirror. A more complete (and more expensive) assemblage would have included a high chest of drawers as well as the more common low version. The finest examples will feature inlay in lighter-colored woods or brass.

Hints for Collectors
Not as popular today as Rococo or Gothic Revival, Victorian Eastlake furniture is a good choice for those interested in assembling complete parlor or bedroom sets. It is both abundant and reasonably priced.

Cottage-style chest of drawers

Description
Low, painted or decorated chest of drawers. Top has straight, rounded, or molded edges and square or rounded corners. 3–5 full-length drawers. Front edges of chest may be chamfered. Sides either paneled or solid board. Back composed of several overlapping boards nailed vertically. Skirt plain or slightly valanced; usually made of 1 separately applied piece of wood. Plain bracket feet, sometimes with casters. Always painted. Nailed and glued construction.

Materials and Dimensions
Pine; rarely cedar. Originally painted in pastel shades and decorated with painted striping in constrasting color; painted floral medallions on drawer fronts. Pulls: brass rosettes with loop handles, turned wooden knobs, or carved wooden fruit- and foliage-shaped handles. Escutcheons: carved wood or iron or brass keyhole surrounds. Casters: iron or wood and iron. Height: 32–37″. Width: 34–40″. Depth: 17–20″.

Locality and Period
Large factories throughout the East and Midwest. c. 1860–1910.

Comment
Victorian Cottage funishings were inexpensive and customarily made in bedroom sets that included a chest of drawers, mirrored bureau, bed, several chairs, and a washstand-commode.

Hints for Collectors
Cottage furnishings represent an excellent buy today: at auction a complete bedroom set may cost less than you might expect to pay for a single piece in another style. Look for these pieces in rural areas and only consider examples that are well painted and in good condition.

Description
Chest of drawers with paneled sides and overhanging top. 4 graduated full-length drawers. Skirt plain. Feet short, turned, and shaped in late Sheraton manner. Usually elaborately decorated with painted designs. Dovetailed and paneled stile-and-rail construction; top and drawer bottoms may be attached with nails.

Materials and Dimensions
Pine, tulipwood, or poplar; occasionally mixed. Originally painted in green or brown, then decorated with various motifs—such as birds, flowers, fans, shells—in red, white, yellow, and blue. Pulls: turned wooden knobs or, less commonly, brass rosette knobs. Escutcheons: oval brass plates. Height: 47–52″. Width: 42–46″. Depth: 21–23″.

Locality and Period
The Mahantango Valley area of Pennsylvania. c. 1820–40.

Comment
An interesting example of regional design currently popular with collectors, these chests of drawers and a few similar desks were produced in a small rural area of Pennsylvania during the first half of the 1800s. In form they resemble other late Sheraton country chests of the same period, but like dower chests they have distinctive decoration. Traditional Pennsylvania German motifs, such as the bird and the flower basket, are blended with Federal devices, such as the fan and simulated dentil molding, in a most appealing composition.

Hints for Collectors
Because only a few of these chests are available, they bring high prices. Some may rest unrecognized in attics or barns in the area where they were produced.

Description
Painted chest of drawers with slightly overhanging, unmolded top. 4 graduated drawers, the fronts often with beaded molding and painted to imitate inlay. Paneled sides. Symmetrically valanced skirt. Square stiles turned at base to form short legs. Small ball feet. Painted and grained. Paneled, dovetailed, and nailed construction.

Materials and Dimensions
Pine, painted and grained to imitate mahogany, with drawer and side panels painted to look like flame mahogany, satinwood, or bird's-eye maple. Pulls: brass rosette knobs or oblong mounts with bail handles. Escutcheons: brass keyhole surrounds or small brass rosettes. Height: 40–44″. Width: 39–41″. Depth: 21–22″.

Locality and Period
New England west to Ohio and throughout most of the South. c. 1800–30.

Comment
The sophisticated country chest of drawers shown here is quite similar to a high-style Sheraton example. The rural artisan imitated the more expensive materials and sophisticated carving of the city piece. Such imitation is common among 19th-century country furnishings.

Hints for Collectors
Painted country Sheraton chests of drawers are among the more reasonably priced early 19th-century pieces, and cost substantially less than Hepplewhite examples. Look for chests with well-shaped skirts and legs and well-preserved paint. Refinished or stripped pieces are of relatively little value.

Victorian bowfront chest of drawers

Description
Bowfront chest of drawers with rectangular, removable, slightly overhanging marble top that conceals H-shaped wooden framework above upper drawer. 3–4 equal or graduated full-length drawers. Paneled drawer fronts slightly bowed. Paneled sides. Back is 1 large panel. Skirt elaborately valanced on front and sides. Legs and stumplike feet, usually with casters, extensions of half-round stiles. Paneled, nailed, glued, and dovetailed construction.

Materials and Dimensions
Walnut; also cherry or rosewood. Secondary wood pine. Pulls: carved wooden fruit-shaped handles or brass mounts with bail handles. Escutcheons: applied, carved wood or brass plates or keyhole surrounds. Casters: iron or iron and wood. Height: 34–44″. Width: 34–37″. Depth: 17–19″.

Locality and Period
Better factories in the East and Midwest. c. 1845–75.

Comment
Few Victorian serpentine and bowfront chests of drawers were made. Most examples were produced in the early part of the period before mass production became common.

Hints for Collectors
A good early Victorian bowfront or serpentine-front chest of drawers is relatively rare and should not be confused with later, mass-produced examples, which were marked by a lack of handcrafting. Look for evidence of handwork in rough-planed backboards, carved pulls, and hand-cut rather than machine-cut dovetails.

Federal miniature chest of drawers

Description
Miniature chest of drawers with plain, overhanging top. 3 full-length drawers. Plain board sides terminating in bootjacks. Valanced skirt and plain bracket feet at sides. Dovetailed and nailed construction.

Materials and Dimensions
Mixed woods; often combinations of walnut and maple, mahogany and satinwood, or all maple. Example shown, cherry with solid tiger maple drawer fronts. Pulls: brass rosette knobs. Escutcheons: brass keyhole surrounds. Height: 14–17″. Width: 13–15″. Depth: 12–14″.

Locality and Period
New England west to Missouri, south to the Carolinas. c. 1810–50.

Comment
Small and carefully made chests of this sort appear frequently in shops. Each example differs slightly from the next, and experts disagree about what they were originally used for. They are seldom true miniatures, for rarely are the proportions those of full-size pieces. Most likely, they were simply trinket boxes made as novelties, salesmen's samples, or possibly test pieces made by apprentices.

Hints for Collectors
Whatever their original purpose, small, well-made sets of drawers are highly collectible and bring substantial prices. Look for examples with good lines, balanced proportions, and appealing combinations of wood. Figured maple is especially desirable. Occasionally these pieces bear a coat of original paint, but natural finishes are more common.

Country Hepplewhite chest of drawers

Description
Chest of drawers with overhanging, unmolded top. 4 graduated
full-length drawers typically present; rarely, large top drawer
over 3 equally tall drawers. Skirt plain or with deeply cut
valance, often with cyma curves framing small central drop. Feet
plain, tapered brackets or a slightly outcurved, simplified version
of French foot. Dovetailed or, rarely, nailed construction.

Materials and Dimensions
Maple, including flame and curly maple; also cherry or birch.
Secondary wood pine, cedar, or poplar. Rarely inlaid or veneered
with apple or birch. May be grained or painted red, blue, brown,
or gray; sometimes painted to imitate inlay and veneer. Pulls:
brass rosettes with bail handles or turned wooden knobs.
Escutcheons: oval brass plates or diamond-shaped bone. Height:
30–35″. Width: 38–42″. Depth: 16–18″.

Locality and Period
New England west to the Mississippi River, south to Georgia.
c. 1790–1820.

Comment
These simple and appealing pieces were largely the prototype
used by Shaker and other traditional cabinetmakers during the
19th century. The rarest and most interesting of these chests
were painted with medallions and ovals to imitate the inlaid and
veneered surfaces of their city cousins.

Hints for Collectors
These chests of drawers are relatively easy to find and
inexpensive. Look for nice proportions, minimum restoration, a
good coat of paint, or finely figured wood. An example in flame or
curly maple is a real find, as are good grained imitations.

Description
Plain chest of drawers with overhanging, unmolded top. 4
drawers, sometimes with top and bottom drawers taller than
middle 2. 2–3 drawers have locks. Plain skirt. Legs are square,
tapered extensions of stiles or, in South and Midwest, turned in
late Sheraton manner. Dovetailed construction.

Materials and Dimensions
Pine, cherry, maple, butternut, or walnut. Often stained with
light, transparent coat of red, blue, or yellow. Pulls: turned
wooden knobs. Escutcheons, when present: brass keyhole
surrounds. Height: 37–44″. Width: 34–38″. Depth: 20–26″.

Locality and Period
New England, New York, Kentucky, and parts of the Midwest.
c. 1810–70.

Comment
Like much Shaker furniture, the chest shown here was
influenced by the Federal style, particularly in the construction
of the square, tapered legs. However, Shaker examples are far
less elaborate in construction and decoration than most Federal
pieces. A few may have a scalloped skirt, but most are very
plain. Indeed, severity and lack of decoration, as well as perfect
proportions, characterize the best Shaker pieces.

Hints for Collectors
Anyone offered a supposed Shaker piece should check it for form,
methods of construction, and materials. Shaker pieces may be
confused with country Federal-style pieces. Generally, Shaker
examples will be dovetailed, not nailed, will have only wooden
pulls, and will be made of better-quality boards of a uniform size.
If the boards had knots, the Shakers removed the knots and
replaced them with wooden patches.

Miniature chest of drawers

Description
Miniature chest of drawers with overhanging, slightly molded top. 3–5 sometimes graduated full-length drawers. Skirt plain or slightly valanced. Feet typically tapered extensions of end boards, but may be ball or turned Sheraton type. Nailed or, occasionally, dovetailed construction.

Materials and Dimensions
Pine, poplar, cherry, maple, walnut, or butternut. Secondary wood pine or poplar. Some examples with drawer fronts inlaid or veneered in contrasting wood such as boxwood or holly. Pine and poplar chests often painted in solid color; graining or sponging rare. Pulls: small turned wooden buttons; also pressed Sandwich-glass or brass rosettes. Escutcheons, when present: iron or brass keyhole surrounds. Height: 12–23″. Width: 16–26″. Depth: 9–12″.

Locality and Period
New England west to Missouri, south to the Carolinas and Georgia. c. 1810–60.

Comment
A miniature chest of drawers only 12″ high was probably meant to be a true miniature or perhaps a salesman's sample. Larger examples were most likely built as toys or even as children's chests. The best examples were in hardwood.

Hints for Collectors
In Europe, particularly in the British Isles, miniature chests of drawers were made in large quantities, and it is often difficult to distinguish them from American examples. Being relatively uncommon today, both domestic and foreign chests bring relatively high prices.

Federal false-drawer blanket chest

Description
Lift-top blanket chest with 2 real full-length drawers and 2 false ones. Slightly overhanging, hinged top lacks molding and is often battened. Top covers storage well, camouflaged behind false drawer fronts. Skirt plain or slightly valanced. Feet tapered, in simplified French style, extending from end boards. Often painted. Dovetailed or nailed construction.

Materials and Dimensions
Pine, cherry, birch, or maple. Secondary wood pine or poplar. Pine chests may be painted red, blue, or green; or sponged or grained to imitate mahogany, rosewood, or curly maple. Hinges: iron butt. Pulls: turned wooden knobs or small brass knobs; rarely, brass rosettes with bail handles. Height: 41–46″. Width: 40–44″. Depth: 17–19″.

Locality and Period
New England west to Indiana, south to Virginia. c. 1800–20.

Comment
Like most painted blanket chests, the overall style of this piece is Federal. Blanket chests with false drawer fronts are relatively common and appear to reconcile the need for a practical area in which to store bedding with a style that dictated drawers rather than a plain front. When well executed, these pieces look like true chests of drawers.

Hints for Collectors
Note the high quality of grain painting on the piece shown here: not only are the drawer fronts carefully tinted to imitate wood grain, but they are also surrounded by a checkered light-and-dark pattern to simulate the inlay common on Federal pieces. Examples such as this are, of course, more desirable than plainer blanket chests.

Federal-Empire splashboard chest of drawers

Description
Country-made chest of drawers with overhanging top surmounted by case of 2–3 small drawers backed by shaped splashboard (4–6″ high) that may have voluted ends. Below, 3–4 sometimes graduated full-length drawers. Skirt plain or simply shaped. Feet turned Sheraton type, peg, or plain bracket. Often painted or grained. Dovetailed or nailed construction.

Materials and Dimensions
Pine, cherry, or walnut. Drawer fronts occasionally veneered in bird's-eye maple or curly maple. Secondary wood pine. If pine, often painted or grained, particularly in imitation of crotch mahogany. Pulls: turned wooden knobs or, less often, brass rosette or pressed-glass knobs. Escutcheons: brass or iron keyhole surrounds. Height: 34–40″. Width: 38–48″. Depth: 18–20″.

Locality and Period
New England to Missouri and throughout the South. c. 1820–50. Also the Southwest. c. 1870.

Comment
The splashboard chest of drawers is related to the somewhat earlier Federal dressing table with a splashboard. Earlier examples have Sheraton characteristics, particularly the turned foot, while later chests show the broad surfaces and lines of Empire pieces.

Hints for Collectors
Be sure that the small case of drawers atop the chest is original; some have been added to enhance the value of an ordinary chest of drawers. An inspection of the back of the piece will usually be sufficient.

Empire chest of drawers

Description
Heavy chest of drawers with slightly overhanging top. Typically with large, slightly overhanging top drawer supported on pillars; pillars may be square, turned, carved with a pineapple-and-acanthus pattern, or in spiral twist. 3 smaller, graduated full-length drawers under large drawer. Alternatively, tiers of 2–3 smaller drawers above 3–4 full-length ones. Plain board or paneled sides. Skirt plain or slightly shaped. Turned ball or carved animal feet. Dovetailed or nailed construction.

Materials and Dimensions
Mahogany; drawer fronts veneered in crotch grain mahogany or figured maple. Sometimes cherry or maple with curly or tiger maple drawer fronts. Secondary wood pine or poplar. Pulls: brass lion's-head plates with pendant rings, brass rosette knobs, oval Hepplewhite mounts with bail handles, or turned wooden or pressed-glass knobs. Escutcheons: brass keyhole surrounds. Height: 44–49″. Width: 39–47″. Depth: 20–22″.

Locality and Period
New England west to the Mississippi River and throughout the South. c. 1815–50.

Comment
Empire chests of drawers are more massive than their Federal predecessors. The overhanging drawer and the plain or carved flanking pillars are distinctive. Although veneer is common, inlay and stringing are rarely seen.

Hints for Collectors
Look for early Empire chests of drawers with good proportions, nice use of veneer, and subtle carving. Although these pieces are often very attractive, they are still not fully appreciated and may be bargains.

Art Deco chest of drawers

Description
Chest of drawers with molded top rounded at corners. Narrow band of checkering in ebonized wood and lighter inlay just below top. 4 full-length drawers, with top one slightly shorter than others. Vertical band of ebonized wood on stiles and extending across base. Plain skirt. Small block feet slightly recessed. Back is nailed board, but sides have glued-on veneer. Glued and nailed construction.

Materials and Dimensions
Pine or cedar with flame-grained mahogany veneer. Inlay satinwood; ebonized wood details. Plywood back. Pulls: rectangular blocks of ebonized wood. Height: 42–46″. Width: 33–36″. Depth: 19–21″.

Locality and Period
Large factories throughout the East and Midwest. c. 1925–35.

Comment
American Art Deco designs are less elaborate than those made in Europe. Made by factories in large quantities, they were usually part of a bedroom set, which might also have included a dressing table, bed, and several chairs. The use of veneers with grains running at right angles for contrast and the checkered design beneath the top are characteristic of many Art Deco pieces here and abroad.

Hints for Collectors
Note the damaged veneer at the base of the piece shown here. In the 20th century, sophisticated equipment makes it possible to saw very thin pieces of veneer, and in many modern pieces, this veneer may peel off. Since repair is expensive, collectors should look for pieces that are relatively intact.

Modern chest of drawers

Description
Low chest of drawers with unmolded top. At right, a solid block, recessed 1–2″ from drawer fronts, forms a terminus in contrasting wood and color. 4 equal full-length drawers with veneered fronts. Right side veneered; left side plain board. Plinthlike base also inset 1–2″. No feet. Glued and screwed construction.

Materials and Dimensions
Pine with maple or bird's-eye maple veneer on top and drawer fronts and mahogany veneer on base and right side of case. Secondary wood pine. Pulls: circular glass disks mounted on brass shafts. Height: 35–36″. Width: 45–46″. Depth: 17–18″.

Locality and Period
Larger factories in the Midwest. c. 1930–44.

Comment
The chest shown here was designed to be either used by itself or placed end to end with an almost identical piece. When they are used together, the mahogany panels on the outside ends of the chests enclose the pieces and make them look like a long 8-drawer chest. Gilbert Rohde, the designer of this piece, was a pioneer in the field of modern furniture and created many outstanding forms between 1930 and 1944, while working for Herman Miller.

Hints for Collectors
Examine pieces of this sort in antiques stores and look at catalogues from the period in order to familiarize yourself with the basic forms. This will enable you to know if you are buying a piece that may be part of a larger unit. In this case, the stepback on the right side is a clue to look for pieces with a matching left-side stepback.

Chests and Blanket Chests

6-board chests were among the first pieces of furniture made by settlers in America. These long, low pieces (237) were formed from 6 boards (top, bottom, front, back, and 2 sides), which were roughed out with an axe or saw and then fastened together with wrought nails. The top was hinged to the back. This basic form is practical and easy to construct, and consequently endured throughout the 19th century. Many examples are plain and purely functional, but some have simple moldings across the front or are decorated with paint or carving.

In the last quarter of the 17th century, cabinetmakers in the Northeast began to construct paneled chests (249). Panels were fastened between horizontal boards, called rails, and vertical boards, called stiles. Unlike 6-board chests, which were mostly made of pine, these chests were often of oak, usually with pine tops. Most have 1 or 2 drawers beneath the storage well, and the best pieces have elaborate carving, applied geometric moldings, turned, split spindles, and bosses. The carving may include names or dates, or motifs particular to one cabinetmaker, and the spindles and bosses are often painted black to imitate ebony. Some paneled chests are mounted on 4 legs (252).

In the 18th and 19th centuries, several variations of the 6-board chest became common. The sea chest (232) first appeared around 1775. Its sides slope outward from the top to the bottom, to provide stability in rough weather. Sea chests typically have rope handles or beckets, and often are decorated with painted nautical scenes, either on the front or inside the lid. Another variation, the dome-top chest (231), became popular around 1800.

The chest was often combined with 1 or more drawers in the 18th and 19th centuries. In the chest-over-drawers (243), the chest is wide and low, with a single tier of 1 to 3 low drawers across the bottom. Blanket chests (244) are taller; they have 2 or more full-length drawers usually forming at least half of the chest.

Miniature chests (234), small storage boxes (233), and children's chests (235) have always been popular in America. They are constructed in the same fashion as full-size pieces, but are often lavishly decorated because many were intended as gifts.

Because chests changed little over the years, it can be difficult to determine when a particular example was made. The best clues are hardware and feet. The earliest chests have wooden pin or iron snipe or cotter-pin hinges; the strap hinge was introduced after 1700, and most pieces made after 1800 have butt hinges. Differences in the style of feet also can help determine age. For example, plain or molded bracket feet signal that a piece is probably Chippendale, dating from about 1750 to 1775. Similarly, French feet indicate that a chest was made after 1785, in the Federal period.

Chests are abundant, and appealing examples often appear on the market. Look for good original grain- or sponge-painting, or for other touches, such as fine dovetailing, that separate exceptional pieces from the ordinary.

Painted dome-top chest

Description
Low chest with dome-shaped lift top. Sides and bottom composed of 5 boards joined together at right angles. Interior may have boxlike till at 1 end, sometimes with lift top and molded edge. Handles sometimes present. Usually painted. Dovetailed or nailed 6-board construction.

Materials and Dimensions
Pine. Usually painted red, blue, gray, green, or brown; also sponged or grained in 2 contrasting colors, typically red and black or brown and yellow. Hinges: iron butt. Escutcheons, when present: brass plates or keyhole surrounds. Handles, when present: iron. Height: 14–18″. Width: 36–44″. Depth: 15–18″.

Locality and Period
New England west to Ohio, south to the Carolinas. c. 1800–50.

Comment
Widely used by 19th-century travelers, dome-top chests may have been designed to prevent stacking and consequent damage to the chest and its contents. To form the top, 1 or more boards were steamed until they became flexible, then fastened to curved end boards. Almost all were originally painted. The chest shown here is vinegar grained, a technique involving the dilution of pigment with vinegar.

Hints for Collectors
Dome-top chests are common and easy to locate, so look for the better examples. Good original paint, especially graining or sponging, is an asset, as are dovetailing, an interior till, or an attractive escutcheon. Hardware that has been replaced can decrease the value by 10% to 30%.

Sea chest

Description
6-board chest with front and back sloping outward from top to bottom. Simple thumbnail-molded lift top often has end battens to prevent warping. Interior storage till often present. Small casters sometimes added to late 19th-century examples. Woven rope handles or beckets frequently present. Originally painted; often decorated with painted or carved nautical scenes, slogans, seamen's names, and dates, usually on front of chest or inside lid. Nailed or dovetailed 6-board construction.

Materials and Dimensions
Pine; rarely cedar. Battens ash or maple. Originally painted red, blue, green, gray, or black. Hinges: iron strap or butt. Escutcheons, when present: oval brass plates or iron or brass keyhole surrounds. Casters: brass. Height: 15–19″. Width: 44–48″. Depth: 15–18″.

Locality and Period
Atlantic seaboard from Maine to the Carolinas; rarely the Great Lakes region. c. 1780–1900.

Comment
Sea chests are a variation of the common 6-board chest. Their shape gave them stability and may also have made it easier to stack and open them in the narrow storage areas of sailing ships.

Hints for Collectors
Sea chest prices are dependent upon the presence and quality of decoration. A well-painted example is a piece of folk art and may command a very high price, while a plain, refinished chest is usually inexpensive. As a result, many examples have recently been retouched. Look for paint crazing and signs of wear to assure yourself that you are getting an early composition. And remember, not all seamen were good artists.

Pennsylvania-type decorated box

Description
Deep box with overhanging, slightly molded, hinged lid. Lid has flat cleat or batten at each end; front ends of battens chamfered. Sides, lid, and ends painted and decorated with incised carvings of compass-drawn, starlike figures (patera). Dovetailed or nailed 6-board construction.

Materials and Dimensions
Pine or poplar; early and rare examples oak or walnut. Incised carving combined with painted decoration in red, yellow, black, green, and brown. Hinges: iron snipe or butt. Height: 8–12″. Width: 12–16″. Depth: 8–10″.

Locality and Period
Pennsylvania and parts of western New Jersey. c. 1760–1800.

Comment
These early boxes are decorated with devices that resemble the hex signs often seen on Pennsylvania barns and were probably made in that state. Certainly, the shape and decorative motifs are similar to those of boxes made by the German-speaking immigrants who settled much of Pennsylvania and neighboring states.

Hints for Collectors
Do not confuse authentic old Pennsylvania-type boxes with the popular hex-painted containers that are available at every crafts store and some antiques shops. Old Pennsylvania-type boxes have age-darkened wood, worn surfaces, and rusted hinges. In addition, they are made of much thicker wood than the new hex-painted boxes, and authentic examples never bear the marks of the modern circular saw.

234 Miniature chest

Description
Small storage chest. Domed or flat lift top has molded edge. Early examples may have sheathed, or linenfold, molding on front. Plain or molded base. Feet, when present, plain bracket, peg, or William and Mary ball type. Often painted; also painted and decorated with pictorial scenes or abstract designs. Inlay and veneer sometimes present. Dovetailed or nailed construction.

Materials and Dimensions
Pine, maple, poplar, cherry, walnut, or mahogany. Secondary wood pine. Often painted, especially pine examples. Hinges: iron snipe or butt; also brass butt. Escutcheons: brass or iron plates or keyhole surrounds. Height: 5–8″. Width: 8–12″. Depth: 5–7″.

Locality and Period
New England, New York, and Pennsylvania south to Maryland. c. 1700–1850.

Comment
Chests are perhaps the most popular type of miniature furniture and reflect a long European tradition. The earliest American examples date from the William and Mary period. Most were probably made to order and then decorated by men and women who gave them to loved ones as gifts.

Hints for Collectors
Inspect miniatures closely. Because they are so popular, many are still being made in the old style and manner. Most makers do not intend to deceive, but once a piece leaves their hands it may be artificially distressed and aged. Examine the wood for signs of warping and shrinkage, and look for tiny rust spots on the iron fixtures. These are characteristic of older, authentic examples. Signed and dated examples are particularly desirable.

Child's chest

Description
Small storage chest with lift top. Lid has applied, slightly overhanging, molded edge. Well may have till with lift top. Applied molding at base. 4 shaped bracket feet are either applied or extensions of front, back, and sides. Often painted or grained. Nailed or dovetailed construction.

Materials and Dimensions
Pine, poplar, maple, birch, or walnut. Pine and poplar examples often painted red, blue, white, or green, or grained in contrasting hues. Hinges: iron or brass butt. Escutcheons, when present: brass keyhole surrounds. Height: 16–18″. Width: 17–20″. Depth: 11–13″.

Locality and Period
New England west to the Pacific coast and throughout the South. c. 1800–75.

Comment
Small chests for the storage of children's clothing and playthings were made in large numbers during the 19th century. Examples with feet, like the one illustrated, were intended to be used in the home, while others were trunks for traveling. A few had locks, but more commonly these chests had small holes through which a string might be drawn to join the lid and the front.

Hints for Collectors
Although children's chests are usually larger than miniature 6-board chests, the 2 types can be confused. Children's chests usually have a bulky, almost boxlike silhouette. Also, they lack the elaborate inlay and paint decoration customarily found on miniatures.

Painted panel chest

Description
Low chest has overhanging lift top with applied molding.
Interior may have small till with molded lift top. Front and sides
have scalloped skirts. Plain bracket feet may be extensions of
front and end boards. Painted panels on top, front, and sides.
Paneled and dovetailed or nailed construction.

Materials and Dimensions
Pine; rarely poplar or cedar. Pine till. Panels painted red, green,
or blue; rest of piece sponge- or grain-painted in shades of
brown, red, or yellow. Hinges: iron snipe, strap, or butt.
Escutcheons: iron keyhole surrounds. Height: 24–26″. Width:
36–39″. Depth: 18–20″.

Locality and Period
Primarily New York and New Jersey. c. 1800–40.

Comment
A number of paneled chests like this one have been found,
especially in central New York State and the Hudson River
Valley. Unlike those on dower chests, the panels on chests from
this region are rarely decorated, although they are painted.
Better examples, like the one shown, have valanced skirts and
well-shaped feet.

Hints for Collectors
In rare instances, this kind of chest originally had decoration and
motifs that are associated with the German settlers in
Pennsylvania. Later, the original decoration may have been
concealed with a solid color. To test for such underpainting,
remove only a very small area of paint from an inconspicuous
place. If decoration is present, have the overpainting removed by
a professional restorer.

Early 6-board chest

Description
Lift-top chest made of 6 boards: top, bottom, front, back, and
2 sides. Battens sometimes present at ends of top. 1–3 strips of
horizontal sheathed, or linenfold, molding on front. Gouge or
notch carving at front corners. Feet, when present, extensions of
side boards cut in bootjack fashion. Nailed or dovetailed 6-board
construction.

Materials and Dimensions
Pine; rarely oak with pine top. Probably originally painted red,
brown, green, or black. Hinges: iron snipe. Escutcheons: brass
or iron oval plates or keyhole surrounds. Height: 23–25″. Width:
52–55″. Depth: 17–19″.

Locality and Period
New England, especially Massachusetts and Connecticut.
c. 1680–1710.

Comment
The piece shown here is an example of the earliest form of the
6-board chest. The decorative molding is called sheathed because
it resembles the molding or sheathing on the walls of some of the
oldest Colonial homes. The piece illustrated here has traces of
reddish-brown stain, suggesting that it was originally painted.

Hints for Collectors
Most of the many 6-board chests available today were made after
1800. To spot an early example, look for sheathed molding,
wrought- rather than cut-iron nails, and gouge carving. As with
all chests, make sure the top and hinges have not been altered or
replaced. However, even with replaced tops or hinges, chests of
this sort from the 17th century are uncommon enough to bring a
good price.

Pilgrim-century carved and painted chest-over-drawer

Description
Low chest-over-drawer has slightly molded, overhanging lift top with a cleat or batten at each end. Top opens to reveal well with narrow, open till at upper left. Applied molding at base of well. Front of chest covered with floral and geometric carving, accentuated by punch work, including a frieze directly below lid. Below, a narrow full-length drawer with carved, geometric frieze that matches carving just below lid. Solid board back. Plain skirt. Bootjack feet extensions of plain side boards. Originally painted. Nailed and pegged construction.

Materials and Dimensions
Pine, carved, punch-decorated, and painted, often in red, black, or green. Hinges: long hardwood pins fixed through end cleats. Lock: iron. Height: 30–33″. Width: 46–49″. Depth: 18–19″.

Locality and Period
Connecticut and Massachusetts, primarily the Connecticut River Valley from Deerfield to Wethersfield. c. 1680–1710.

Comment
The carving on late 17th-century chests is often so distinctive that it is possible to identify certain groups of related pieces and the area in which they were made and used. A fair number of these chests have survived, indicating that they were probably made in some quantity. However, today they command a very high price.

Hints for Collectors
Old records and traces of color on existing pieces indicate that almost all Pilgrim-century chests were originally painted in strong colors, including red, black, and green. If a chest has traces of paint, they should never be removed. Chests with their original paint are far more valuable than those without.

239 Storage chest

Description
Very long, low chest with slightly overhanging lift top that has molded edge. Underside of top has 3 battens running front to back. No till. Molded and protruding (1–2″) base. Metal handles at each end. Applied, turned ball feet. Dovetailed and nailed 6-board construction.

Materials and Dimensions
Pine. Feet maple, ash, or other hardwood. May be stained red, blue, green, or brown; sometimes grain-painted; also sponged in 2 colors. Hinges: iron butt. Escutcheons: brass or iron keyhole surrounds or plates. Handles: iron. Height: 22–25″. Width: 60–66″. Depth: 16–19″.

Locality and Period
New England west to Ohio, south to the Carolinas. c. 1800–70.

Comment
These long chests were designed to store clothing, blankets, and other bulky objects. Despite the handles, they usually stayed in one place and served the same function as a clothespress. Similar but more roughly made pieces were used to store grain and produce. Many of these chests were broken up when they were no longer needed, possibly because they were so large and took up so much space. In any case, few examples are found today.

Hints for Collectors
Determining the age of a 6-board chest can be difficult, since they were made for hundreds of years and varied little. Examine the hinges and nails and look for saw marks and dovetails. These and the type of decoration, can help date a piece. For instance, carved examples are typically from the 17th or very early 18th century.

Empire 6-board chest

Description
Low chest with overhanging, molded lift top. Well sometimes has small till, which may have lift top. Base molding matches molding on top. Plain skirt. Feet turned in Empire style and doweled or nailed on. Always painted. Nailed or dovetailed 6-board construction.

Materials and Dimensions
Pine or poplar; rarely walnut or maple. Secondary wood pine or poplar. Painted red, blue, green, or gray, or elaborately sponged in earth tones with circular designs; some examples grained to imitate mahogany or other expensive woods. Hinges: iron butt or strap. Escutcheons: brass or iron keyhole surrounds. Height: 23–26″. Width: 44–49″. Depth: 19–21″.

Locality and Period
New England west to Missouri, south to the Carolinas. c. 1820–50.

Comment
A variation of the common 6-board chest, these turned-foot chests were particularly popular in Pennsylvania, where they replaced the earlier bracket-foot dower chests. The turned foot is generally bulky and adds little to the appearance of the piece.

Hints for Collectors
Chests that originally had feet may have lost them over the years. In addition, they may have been replaced if they broke or became worn. Look for lines where new sections may have been glued or doweled on and check for uniform wear. The better the condition of the graining or sponging on the chest, the higher the price it will bring.

Dower chest

Description
Lift-top chest, sometimes over 1–3 drawers. Top has nailed-on molding, which often matches base molding. Top or front and ends painted with motifs such as birds, unicorns, hex signs, hearts, flowers, names, and dates. Decoration usually restricted to 2–3 panels, but may cover entire surface. Chest mounted on massive molding over bracket or shoe feet. Dovetailed or nailed construction.

Materials and Dimensions
Pine, tulipwood, or poplar; occasionally walnut. Panels rarely decorated with white wood inlay or wax intarsia. Chest typically painted: usually blue or green ground with white panels decorated in red, yellow, black, and brown. Hinges: iron butt or strap. Pulls: iron or brass rosettes with bail handles. Escutcheons: brass plates or keyhole surrounds. Height: 34–39″. Width: 40–50″. Depth: 18–24″.

Locality and Period
Pennsylvania, western New Jersey, and Virginia. c. 1770–1830.

Comment
Traditionally this chest was made for a young woman's dowry and used to store textiles such as quilts and show towels. The initials and names on the chest are usually those of the bride. These chests are modeled on and closely resemble Middle European examples, particularly those from Germany.

Hints for Collectors
Learn the differences between American and European pieces. The latter tend to be more elaborately decorated, with heavier and more ornate hardware. Many dower chests have been stripped and repainted. Authentic examples should display wear, age crazing, and faded paint.

Chippendale chest-over-drawers

Description
Lift-top chest-over-drawers. Top has molded, slightly
overhanging edge. Well has small lift-top till at upper left.
Protruding molding present at base of well. Below, 2 half-length
drawers with thumbnail-molded edges. Protruding, molded base
with plain skirt. Plain or shaped bracket feet. Dovetailed or
nailed construction.

Materials and Dimensions
Walnut; also maple, birch, and pine. Secondary wood pine. Pine
examples usually painted red or blue. Hinges: iron strap or butt.
Pulls: brass rosette, oval, or willow mounts, all with bail handles.
Escutcheons, when present: matching brass. Height: 29–32″.
Width: 49–52″. Depth: 22–24″.

Locality and Period
New England west to Pennsylvania, south to the Virginias.
c. 1760–90.

Comment
Low chests were not as popular in cities as were chests of
drawers and chest-on-chests. However, they were favored by
rural carpenters because they were easier to make than the
taller pieces. Well-made low chests like the example illustrated
were the high-style version of the country storage chest.

Hints for Collectors
The better-quality chests are distinguished by the molding just
above the drawers and well-detailed bracket feet, elements
seldom found on typical country chests. Chippendale chests are
still fairly common, and can be bought at country shops,
especially in the area between New York and western
Pennsylvania.

Hepplewhite chest-over-drawers

Description
Low chest-over-drawers. Lift top has applied, molded, and overhanging edge. Well has narrow lift-top till at upper left. Below well, applied and protruding molding. 2 half-length drawers with molded edges. Protruding molded base with plain skirt. Shaped French feet. Nailed or dovetailed construction.

Materials and Dimensions
Walnut, mahogany, or pine. Secondary wood pine. Pine examples often stained red or blue. Hinges: iron strap or butt. Pulls: plain brass rosette mounts with bail handles or oval Hepplewhite mounts with bail handles. Escutcheons: brass ovals or oblongs, mounted vertically. Height: 24–28″. Width: 47–52″. Depth: 21–23″.

Locality and Period
New England west to Ohio, south to Maryland. c. 1790–1815.

Comment
The stylish French feet and graceful brasses mark this as a Federal chest, a type somewhat less common than the similar Chippendale chest. Although the piece here is of pine, most were made of the richer mahogany or walnut and were rarely painted or decorated; the wood was considered decoration enough. Unlike most Federal pieces, these chests rarely had inlaid decoration.

Hints for Collectors
A chest of this quality would be a fine addition to any collection, provided that it was in good condition with minimal restoration. Ideally the brasses should be original. Examine the inside of the drawers to see if the posts for the brasses go through the right holes. Filled holes, whether new or old, mean there were once pulls of a different type.

Hepplewhite blanket chest

Description
Lift-top blanket chest. Overhanging top has plain or molded edge and may have battens at ends. Well sometimes concealed by 1–3 false drawer fronts. Below well, 1–2 full-length drawers. Skirt plain or deeply valanced. French feet. Nailed or dovetailed construction.

Materials and Dimensions
Walnut, cherry, or maple; also pine. Secondary wood pine. Constrasting inlay sometimes present. Pine examples usually painted or grained in red, yellow, brown, black, or green, often in combination. Hinges: iron butt or snipe. Pulls: oval brass mounts with bail handles. Escutcheons: oval brass plates or brass keyhole surrounds. Height: 35–44″. Width: 36–45″. Depth: 17–20″.

Locality and Period
New England west to Ohio, south to Maryland. c. 1790–1815.

Comment
The grain painting on the chest shown here is quite sophisticated. The red and black background imitates flame mahogany and the sponged yellow border represents inlay, probably in satinwood. Note the warped top. It could have been prevented had battens been applied at right angles to the grain.

Hints for Collectors
The skirt of this chest is very close to the floor, indicating that the feet have worn down considerably. Although this kind of wear does indicate age, it usually diminishes value. And even though experienced collectors may find it worthwhile to have the feet lengthened, this too will reduce worth. To determine whether the feet have been lengthened, look for saw lines, differences in wood grain and age, and new paint.

Shaker blanket chest

Description
Blanket chest with molded, overhanging lift top battened at each end. Well may have till with lift top. 1, 2, or, very rarely, 3 equal or graduated full-length drawers below well, sometimes divided on exterior by thin wooden strips. Solid board sides. Base protruding, molded, with plain skirt. Feet extensions of base cut in half-moon, simplified French, or ogee form; rarely, turned Sheraton feet. Dovetailed or nailed construction.

Materials and Dimensions
Pine, maple, poplar, or cherry, alone or in combination. Secondary wood, when present, pine. Natural wax finish, or frequently stained green, yellow, red, or blue. Hinges: iron strap. Pulls: small turned wooden knobs. Escutcheons: iron keyhole surrounds or applied, diamond-shaped bone. Height: 40–44″. Width: 40–42″. Depth: 18–20″.

Locality and Period
Shaker communities from Maine to Indiana and Kentucky. c. 1800–60.

Comment
The Shaker blanket chest is a simplified version of the country Federal piece. Northern examples have a Hepplewhite look, while Kentucky pieces often have stubby Sheraton-style legs.

Hints for Collectors
Shaker blanket chests are easily confused with those made by others. A coat of "Shaker red" paint is not enough to mark a piece Shaker, nor is general similarity in form. Superior workmanship, excellent lines and balance and, most of all, a history of use in a Shaker community are the most reliable criteria.

3-drawer blanket chest

Description
Tall blanket chest has lift top edged with applied molding. Well has small till, also with molded lift top. Front of well molded and paneled to imitate 3 drawers. Below, 3 equal or graduated, full-length drawers. Plain board sides. Valanced skirt. Applied molding at base of chest. Plain bracket feet. Paneled, dovetailed, and nailed construction.

Materials and Dimensions
Pine, usually stained red, blue, green, or brown; also stained to look like maple or cherry. Hinges: iron snipe or butt. Pulls: turned wooden knobs or brass willow mounts with bail handles. Height: 44–48″. Width: 36–39″. Depth: 18–21″.

Locality and Period
Primarily New England and New York. c. 1780–1810.

Comment
3-drawer blanket chests with lift tops are relatively early and rare. The paneled upper area is an early feature much like the so-called linenfold molding on some low chests.

Hints for Collectors
There are many blanket chests available, so look for the better examples, like the one shown here. The combination of paneling, original red stain, and 3 graduated drawers (most have drawers of equal height) mark this piece as better than average. Although the pulls fit into original holes, they are not original, being too heavy and machine turned. Such replacements devalue a piece by 10% to 20% and should be considered when arriving at a purchase price.

Description
Paneled chest-over-drawers with molded, overhanging lift top.
Well concealed behind 2 panels, which have molded borders.
Molding around waist of piece divides well from 2 graduated full-length drawers. Plain skirt has slight molding. Shaped or plain
bracket feet. Dovetailed and paneled stile-and-rail construction.

Materials and Dimensions
Cherry, mahogany, or walnut. Secondary wood pine or poplar.
Sometimes originally stained red. Hinges: iron butt. Pulls: brass
willow mounts or brass rosettes, both with bail handles.
Escutcheons: brass keyhole surrounds or oval plates set
vertically. Height: 37–40″. Width: 41–44″. Depth: 18–19″.

Locality and Period
Long Island, New York. c. 1770–90.

Comment
The manufacture of these unusual and attractive blanket chests
appears to have been confined to Long Island. The paneled fronts
are an interesting anachronism, as paneled construction was
rarely used as a primary construction method after the Queen
Anne period. Unlike most blanket chests, which by the 1770s
were mostly country pieces, the example illustrated is in the
high-style tradition.

Hints for Collectors
Prices for the same piece may vary considerably from place to
place. Because this chest is a local type, it has greater value in
the Long Island area than other regions, where it may not be
appreciated. These chests are relatively rare.

Hadley-type chest

Description
Paneled chest-over-drawers with overhanging, molded lift top battened at ends. Well concealed behind 3 sunken panels. Below, 1–2 full-length drawers. Stiles, rails, face of well, and drawers decorated with incised motifs, including tuliplike flowers, trailing stems, and leaves. Each side 2 or 4 panels. Solid board back. Plain skirt. Legs and feet square extensions of corner stiles. Paneled and pegged stile-and-rail construction.

Materials and Dimensions
Oak with pine top. Originally stained black, or black and red. Hinges: iron snipe. Pulls: turned wooden, spindlelike knobs. Escutcheons, when present: iron keyhole surrounds. Height: 40–43″. Width: 46–49″. Depth: 16–20″.

Locality and Period
Connecticut River Valley area of western Massachusetts, particularly near Hadley. c. 1675–1710.

Comment
Called Hadley chests because they first appeared in the Hadley-Hatfield area of western Massachusetts, these elaborately decorated, late 17th-century pieces were apparently made as dower chests. Many have carved initials on the center panels, and of those, some have been identified as belonging to women who lived in the Hadley-Hatfield area.

Hints for Collectors
The few Hadley chests that appear on the market are rarely ever intact, yet always expensive. It is common for legs and even lower drawers to have been restored, and most tops are replacements for originals that long ago cracked and were discarded. Anyone buying such a chest should have it examined by a furniture expert.

Spindle-decorated chest

Description
Paneled chest-over-drawers with overhanging, molded lift top.
Front usually entirely carved with shallow abstract floral and
leaflike designs; hearts, initials, full names, and dates may also
be present. Front also embellished with applied split spindles
and bosses. 3 inset panels with more fully developed floral
design; panels above and below usually have matching designs.
Applied, turned spindles between panels and on stiles. Below
well, 1–3 drawers. Sides paneled, undecorated. Legs, when
present, square extensions of stiles. Paneled and pegged stile-
and-rail construction.

Materials and Dimensions
Oak; top pine or, rarely, oak. Many originally stained in
combinations of red, brown, and black. Turned and split spindles
and bosses: ebonized maple. Hinges: oak pins or iron snipe. Pulls:
turned wooden knobs. Escutcheons, when present: iron keyhole
surrounds. Height: 46–48″. Width: 42–47″. Depth: 18–22″.

Locality and Period
Connecticut River Valley area of western Massachusetts.
c. 1675–1715.

Comment
Similar carved oak chests were made in other parts of
Massachusetts, in Connecticut, and elsewhere. Regional types
can often be recognized because of their distinctive carving. All
of these early oak chests are rare.

Hints for Collectors
The application of split spindles and bosses reflects the growing
influence of English William and Mary design elements at the
end of the 17th century. On many of these pieces, the spindles
and bosses have been lost.

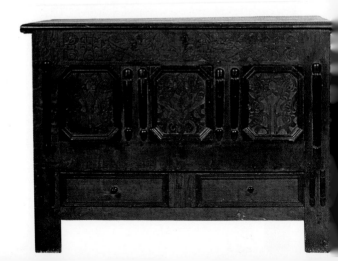

Colonial Revival paneled chest-over-drawers

Description
Massive chest-over-drawers with molded, overhanging lift top battened at each end. 3 sunken panels on upper chest decorated with incised sunflower design and separated by applied split spindles. Molding present between chest and 2 full-length drawers. Drawer panels decorated with applied bosses flanked by small applied split spindles. Upper side panels have split bosses. Molding present at base. Legs rectangular extensions of stiles. Paneled and pegged construction.

Materials and Dimensions
Oak, sometimes with pine top. Secondary wood pine. Spindles and bosses: ebonized maple. Hinges: iron snipe or cotter pin. Pulls: small turned wooden knobs. Height: 39–41″. Width: 47–49″. Depth: 20–22″.

Locality and Period
New England. c. 1920–30.

Comment
This extremely high-quality reproduction of the 17th-century Connecticut sunflower chest was produced in the shops of Wallace Nutting, a collector of Pilgrim-century furnishings. Unlike most Colonial Revival furniture, many of Nutting's pieces were handmade from appropriate woods and closely imitate the original pieces.

Hints for Collectors
Because they may be mistaken for the 17th-century originals, Nutting chests present a challenge to the collector. Modern circular saw marks, thinner wood, and an absence of early tool marks characterize later chests. Once frowned on by collectors, these chests are now much sought after. Look for pieces with Nutting's brand or paper label.

Description
Massive storage and display piece with molded, slightly overhanging top over frieze of carved tendrils. 2 large cupboards present; doors carved with tulip and sunflower motifs and divided by solid carved panel. Below, 1 full-length drawer carved to match upper frieze. Sides carved and paneled. Below, broad open shelf, made of 5 boards, with elaborately carved skirt. Front stiles square, leaf carved above, then bulb turned between cupboard and shelf; at shelf level, stiles square-shaped, plain, terminating in turnip feet. Pegged mortise-and-tenon and paneled construction.

Materials and Dimensions
Oak with pine top. Secondary wood pine. Some pieces with baluster-turned columns and applied spindles of ebonized maple. Hinges: wooden pins or iron snipe. Pulls: turned wooden knobs. Height: 56–60″. Width: 46–52″. Depth: 20–24″.

Locality and Period
Massachusetts, Connecticut, and Virginia. c. 1640–80.

Comment
Some court cupboards had 1 central, recessed upper cupboard with sharply canted sides that left a triangular space at each corner. All were luxury items made only for the wealthy, who used them to display pewter, silver, and other precious items. Only a few dozen remain today.

Hints for Collectors
Like many other early American furnishings, court cupboards can be confused with similar European pieces. Although a more elaborate style may distinguish the imports, the best test is often the wood type. The piece shown here is partially made of American yellow pine, indicating it was made in this country.

Pilgrim-century chest-on-frame

Description
Paneled lift-top chest permanently mounted, typically on turned base. Well concealed behind 2 or more panels varying in size and design, sometimes with applied, split spindles and bosses. Rarely, notch carving at corners. Below, 1 full-length drawer sometimes present. Legs extensions of stiles turned in vase-and-disk or spool manner; in earliest examples legs may not be turned. Paneled stile-and-rail construction.

Materials and Dimensions
Oak; top pine; base oak or maple. Sometimes painted red, with black floral spray design. Spindles and bosses: usually ebonized. Hinges: wooden pin, or iron snipe or staple. Pulls: turned wooden knobs. Height: 35–38″. Width: 25–28″. Depth: 16–18″.

Locality and Period
Massachusetts. c. 1670–1700.

Comment
Similar in appearance and construction to larger chests of the period, these small chest-on-frames were perhaps intended to accommodate small valuables. Fewer than 100 are known to exist, and thus they rarely appear on the market.

Hints for Collectors
Be sure that the chest is not just an early box to which a set of legs has been added. If there are signs of wear under the box, it was not originally on a frame. Very similar, though somewhat more elaborately decorated chest-on-frames were made in Europe at about the same time. Be sure that the dealer guarantees American origin.

Small Storage Units

Small cupboards, cabinets, shelves, and other storage units have long been part of the American domestic scene. Those produced before 1860 were mostly handmade by country craftsmen; few came from the sophisticated urban cabinetmakers who fashioned high-style furnishings. After 1860, when mass-production became common, the majority were factory made. Most were of pine or other softwoods and were nailed or dovetailed together. Typically, the smaller of these pieces were designed to hang on walls, and the larger ones to stand on tables. Some were shaped to fit into corners.

Decoration varies from simple to complex. 18th-century pieces and those made by the Shakers often have a plain coat of red, blue, or yellow paint. Some candle boxes and spoon racks have painted or carved designs that elevate these simple country pieces to the realm of folk art. Although most Victorian examples were factory made, many have elaborate decoration, including applied wooden devices, fret carving, and ornate hinges and escutcheons.

Like their larger relatives, small cupboards and cabinets may be unadorned and strictly utilitarian (271) or richly decorated and intended as much for show as for function (265). The finest Victorian examples, made of walnut or ebonized hardwood, may often be found in the Anglo-Japanese, Eastlake, and Renaissance Revival styles. Still others incorporate mirrors (262) and are, in a sense, forerunners of the mirrored oak bathroom cupboards that became popular in the early 1900s.

Shelving units, which were mostly designed for the display of knickknacks, also come in a variety of styles. The early country-made pieces may incorporate a set of small drawers below several shelves (253). Later examples often have 4 or 5 shelves that become gradually deeper toward the bottom. Some of these (259) have scalloped side boards or other embellishments. Hanging pewter shelves (254) often have low galleries or interior slots, designed to hold plates and other treasured objects in place.

Miscellaneous storage units include spoon racks (256), candle boxes (255), pipe racks (258), and spice cabinets (272). Many of these pieces were specially made for loved ones, and are richly decorated with carving or painting. Consequently they are among the most desirable of all small collectibles.

Hanging shelf-and-drawer unit

Description
Shallow hanging wall unit with flat top terminating in applied, shaped cornice. Sides taper back from base at 15–20° angle. 2–3 shelves over 2–4 half-length or 2 full-length drawers. Shelves vary in depth, with narrowest at top. Shallow, rectangular drawers separated by narrow molding. Usually painted. Dovetailed or nailed construction.

Materials and Dimensions
Pine, poplar, maple, walnut, birch, or combinations of hardwoods and softwoods. Usually painted red, blue, green, or white; occasionally grained or sponged. Pulls: brass or turned wooden knobs; later, iron Victorian handles. Height: 32–35″. Width: 21–24″. Depth: 5–9″.

Locality and Period
New England west to the Missouri River and throughout the South. c. 1800–70.

Comment
Hanging shelf-and-drawer units were secured to the wall by nails or screws driven through the backboard, or with wire hangers like those used on picture frames. Originally, such pieces were used to store spices and other kitchen items, but later they became whatnot shelves for the living room.

Hints for Collectors
These shelf-and-drawer units are very popular with collectors and often bring relatively high prices. Look for them at yard and garage sales and in junk shops. Often relegated to the garage or barn when they went out of fashion, they sometimes pass unnoticed in a load of discarded furnishings. Dovetailing and the use of cut nails are signs of an early example.

Pewter shelf

Description
Hanging or freestanding storage unit with plain top. 2 shelves: higher shelf same depth as top; bottom shelf 1–2″ deeper. Plain board sides scallop-cut and carved in a shallow, beadlike pattern. Similarly carved gallery (1–2″ high) at front of bottom shelf. Often painted. Nailed or dovetailed construction.

Materials and Dimensions
Usually pine or poplar; also cherry, maple, walnut, or birch. Pine and poplar examples typically painted red, green, blue, gray, or yellow. Height: 24–27″. Width: 20–23″. Depth: 8–9″.

Locality and Period
New England west to Pennsylvania, south to Virginia. c. 1770–1830.

Comment
When owning pewter was fashionable, a family's collection was always prominently displayed, usually in a large pewter cupboard. A small pewter shelf like the example illustrated might have been used to display special pieces. Plates would have gone on the lower, galleried shelf, while saltcellars, creamers, and other smaller pieces would have been kept on the higher one. Somewhat similar shelves were made during the Victorian era and used to display porcelain.

Hints for Collectors
There are many sets of shelves available to collectors, but one like this is unusual and, for that reason, very desirable. The scalloped and carved design and the good, old paint distinguish it from an ordinary piece, making it more expensive as well as an excellent example of the form.

Hanging double candle box

Description
Hanging candleholder with 1–2 shallow, open compartments attached to backboard that has plain or shaped top. Sides of compartments may be shaped. Hole for hanging in upper part of backboard. Base molded or plain. Frequently painted or decorated, usually simply, rarely elaborately. Dovetailed or, more often, nailed construction.

Materials and Dimensions
Usually pine or poplar; rarely walnut or cherry. Pine and poplar examples painted blue, gray, green, red, or brown, or grained or sponged. Height: 10–16″. Width: 10–13″. Depth: 4–6″.

Locality and Period
New England west to Ohio, south to the Carolinas. c. 1790–1850.

Comment
There are 2 types of candle boxes: covered, slide-top true boxes and wall-hanging examples, which are rarely covered. Both were designed to hold the tallow candles routinely used in country homes until after the Civil War. Double-compartment examples, such as the one shown here, are fairly rare; the decoration on this piece greatly enhances an otherwise simple form.

Hints for Collectors
Look for hanging candle boxes. They have often been overlooked, even by those familiar with the more common covered candle boxes. Traces of wax in the compartments reveal that a piece has actually been used to store candles. Painted or decorated candle boxes are most desirable. Reproductions are often sold in gift stores; these usually have 1 compartment and are held together with wire nails.

Hanging spoon rack

Description
Elaborately constructed hanging set of shelves. Backboard
scroll-cut at shoulders to form low splashboard (3–4″ high), then
extended above in round, lollypop-shaped form with narrow,
perforated shelf for spoons. Sides have shaped tops. 2 or, more
often,'3 narrow shelves across front, with scallop-cut galleries
and spoon holes. Iron ring on back for hanging. No molding.
Often painted. Nailed or dovetailed construction.

Materials and Dimensions
Usually pine or poplar; also maple, walnut, or birch. Most
originally painted blue, red, or green; decoration and grain-
painting less common. Height: 25–28″. Width: 10–14″.
Depth: 4–5″.

Locality and Period
New England west to Ohio, south to Maryland. c. 1780–1830.

Comment
Racks for silver or pewter teaspoons were once common in
American homes, but few were decorated as elaborately as the
one shown here. The repeated star and tulip design appears to
have been made with a stencil and is related to traditional cookie-
cutter patterns.

Hints for Collectors
As with pipe racks, candle boxes, and other desirable small
pieces, spoon racks are still being reproduced. To determine
authenticity, look for crazing and signs of wear, especially on the
perforated shelf, where the storage and removal of spoons may
have damaged the paint, and at the corners, where impact may
have caused chipping. Backs should not be painted or show fresh
paint stains.

Decorated hanging candle box

Description
Hanging candleholder with 1 boxlike compartment attached to backboard. High backboard elaborately saw-cut in symmetrical scallops, swirls, or wavelike patterns. Backboard and exterior walls of compartment richly decorated with compass-drawn geometric motifs such as stars, circles, hexagons, and octagons; interiors of motifs further divided with scratch carving. Plain skirt. Usually painted. Dovetailed or nailed construction.

Materials and Dimensions
Usually pine; sometimes poplar, cedar, or walnut. Painted in combinations of red, black, yellow, green, and brown. Height: 22–27″. Width: 11–14″. Depth: 4–6″.

Locality and Period
New England to Ohio, south to Virginia. c. 1770–1840.

Comment
Although most often associated with Pennsylvania and other areas settled by German immigrants, elaborately decorated wall boxes such as this one were produced in many areas of the eastern United States. Because of the great amount of time such decoration required, it seems likely that most such pieces were intended as gifts or were made as special orders rather than for general sale.

Hints for Collectors
Although the candle box shown here is genuine, be wary of elaborately decorated pieces. Because this type of box is quite desirable, reproductions involving the decoration of old but plain containers are appearing on the market. Look for signs of paint crazing, wear, and aging of wood. If the incised patterns are sharply etched, be suspicious; the edges should be rounded and softened with age.

Description
Tall hanging container with shaped back and deep, open compartment. Shallow full-length drawer across front. Front and sides plain or elaborately cut and shaped. Hole in back for hanging, often piercing finial. Base molded or, more often, plain. Usually painted. Dovetailed or nailed construction.

Materials and Dimensions
Typically pine, poplar, birch, walnut, or maple. Secondary wood pine. Usually grain-painted, as in example illustrated; also sponged or painted solid red, blue, gray, green, or dark brown. Pulls: brass or turned wooden knobs. Height: 15–19″. Width: 8–9″. Depth: 3–4″.

Locality and Period
New England west to Pennsylvania, south to Virginia and the Carolinas. c. 1700–1830.

Comment
Pipe racks or boxes, as they are also called, are often very old, some of the earliest having been made by Dutch settlers in what is now New York State. The long-stemmed, clay "churchwarden" pipes favored by early smokers were stored in the upper, open area. Tobacco or flint and tinder used to light the pipe might be kept in the drawer below. The better examples, like the one shown, are dovetailed and elaborately scrolled.

Hints for Collectors
Many of these racks have been stripped of their original paint and refinished, which substantially lessens their value. Early and well-decorated examples usually command a high price. Consequently, excellent reproductions are not uncommon. The best of these defy most tests for age and authenticity, so buy only from a reputable dealer.

Description

Hanging set of 2–5 narrow shelves. Backboard usually with rounded or scallop-cut crest. Sides plain or scalloped. Shelves with plain or, rarely, bowed fronts. Usually has hole in back for hanging. Molded base. Usually painted. Nailed or, less often, dovetailed construction.

Materials and Dimensions

Pine or poplar; occasionally walnut, oak, or other hardwoods, or combinations of hardwoods and softwoods. Painted red, blue, gray, green, or brown; may also be grain-painted or decorated; oak examples usually unpainted. Height: 24–30″. Width: 12–18″. Depth: 5–7″.

Locality and Period

New England west to California and throughout the South. c. 1800–1900.

Comment

Sets of open wall shelves are among the most common hanging storage pieces. Made in great variety, usually at home rather than by trained cabinetmakers, most examples are plain and some are even crude. The best have elaborately shaped sides and backboards or original paint or decoration. The sophisticated grain-painting on the piece shown (probably intended to imitate oak) marks it as a fine example.

Hints for Collectors

Wall shelves are just as practical today as they were a hundred years ago. Ideal for the display of miniatures and other small collectibles, they are usually inexpensive. Exceptions are decorated pieces and those with their sides cut in the shape of a whale's back. Other desirable examples are dovetailed pieces and those with 4 or more shelves.

Victorian whatnot shelf

Description
Multipurpose shelf unit for tabletop or wall. 3 molded shelves
increasing in depth from top to bottom, with scroll-cut
backboards. Screw holes in top of backboard for hanging. Side
boards scroll-cut and decorated with applied fret-cut and incised
oak leaves. Short hooflike feet. Screwed construction.

Materials and Dimensions
Walnut, cherry, or pine. Usually varnished; pine examples
sometimes painted and gilded. Applied decoration walnut, maple,
or cherry; sometimes stained. Height: 26–28″. Width: 20–23″.
Depth: 6–8″.

Locality and Period
Large manufacturers in the East and Midwest. c. 1870–1910.

Comment
Dual-purpose shelves like the example shown here were widely
used throughout the Victorian era. Some held pictures and
personal objects, but most were used to display the knickknacks,
porcelain figures, and odd bits of glass that Victorians were so
fond of. Since many of these objects were quite small, the
backboards kept them from falling off the shelves.

Hints for Collectors
The applied oak leaves on this piece suggest that it may be
Canadian. Like the beaver, the oak leaf is a Canadian symbol,
and its appearance on a rug or piece of furniture is often a clue to
origin. All such clues, however, must be evaluated in
combination with other evidence, including the history of the
piece, the woods employed, the construction methods, and so
forth.

Fret-carved hanging corner cabinet

Description
5-sided hanging corner cabinet. Slightly overhanging top. Angled, 2-piece back extends above cabinet to form backboard with scalloped top and intricately fret-cut surface. Narrow, angled sides flank plain, paneled door; interior shelfless. Base extension of backboard. Nailed and paneled construction.

Materials and Dimensions
Pine, walnut, or maple. Often varnished; also grained, sponged, or painted, often in red, blue, or gray. Hinges: brass butt. Escutcheons: iron or brass keyhole surrounds. Height: 20–24″. Width: 14–16″. Depth: 8–10″.

Locality and Period
New England west to Ohio, south to the Carolinas. c. 1860–90.

Comment
A cabinet like this one is an interesting blend of rural cabinetwork and Victorian taste. The form is old (similar examples were made in the 18th century), but the addition of the complex carving on the backboard identifies this as a late 19th-century piece.

Hints for Collectors
While its form alone might indicate that the piece illustrated is quite early, the astute collector would recognize several signs that point to a later date. The hinges, which are original, are factory-made brass from the late 19th century. The lack of pegs in the door frame and the signs of a circular saw on the boards also mark the piece as late Victorian. Do not be misled by form; always check details.

Victorian mirrored hanging corner cabinet

Description
5-sided corner cabinet with mirror. Flat, slightly overhanging top. Back rises to form shaped gallery or backboard, with applied strip of decorative molding across top. Single door has mirror mounted with applied, beaded molding; interior with single shelf. Base with applied molding. Nailed construction.

Materials and Dimensions
Walnut with applied oak decoration; also all pine. May be stained dark and varnished, or painted white or black. Hinges: brass butt. Escutcheons: brass or iron keyhole surrounds. Height: 19–22″. Width: 14–16″. Depth: 10–11″.

Locality and Period
Large factories throughout the East and Midwest. c. 1860–1900.

Comment
Simply constructed mirrored cabinets like this one were normally used in bathrooms and bedrooms rather than the more public areas of the house. Intended for the storage of toilet articles and medicines, similar cabinets in modern designs are still popular in the American home.

Hints for Collectors
Corner cabinets were more difficult to construct than flat wall cabinets and are correspondingly more difficult to find. Almost any hanging corner cabinet in good condition is a good investment, especially if it is well proportioned and nicely decorated. Those pieces made in the first half of the 19th century are usually more valuable than those made in the second half; earlier examples are usually dovetailed rather than nailed together.

Eastlake mirrored hanging shelves

Description
Hanging unit with mirror, shelves, and single full-length drawer. Fret-cut backboard rises to shaped cornice, with full-length shelf (4–6″ deep) supported on cutout brackets. Below shelf, mirror with rounded corners flanked by turned hairpin holders. Top of drawer forms additional full-length shelf. Cutout skirt on front, back, and sides. Incised and turned decoration in Eastlake manner. Nailed construction.

Materials and Dimensions
Chestnut, pine, walnut, or oak. Shellac finish. Pulls: turned hardwood knobs. Height: 26–30″. Width: 19–21″. Depth: 8–9″.

Locality and Period
Large factories in the East and Midwest. c. 1880–1910.

Comment
Mirrored shelves like this were a form of portable dressing table. Toilet articles could be kept in the drawer and on the shelf above the mirror. Hairpins and small objects went in the barrel-like storage units, while the broad shelf formed by the top of the drawer provided a work surface. The whole thing could be hung on a wall or moved from place to place.

Hints for Collectors
The Victorians were good at making the most of limited space, as this compact unit illustrates. While not easy to find, particularly with a drawer, a mirror-and-shelf combination is useful in a small city apartment and also makes a nice display shelf. The earlier examples will be in walnut, while most turn-of-the-century pieces are oak. The earlier pieces usually have superior decoration.

Description

Ornate set of wall shelves with fret-cut decoration. Upper shelf surrounded by gallery (4–6″ high) cut in openwork pattern of bars and stylized flowers. Wavelike fretwork finial. Below upper shelf, backboard decorated with incised lines, geometric devices, and applied disk. Lower shelf has shallow semicircular gallery with incised dots and dashes. Molded, slightly overhanging base. Elaborately valanced skirt has 3 lobes decorated with incised dots and dashes and hung with pendant balls; center lobe also has applied, decorative disk. Screwed construction.

Materials and Dimensions

Early examples walnut or oak; later ones oak. Sometimes stained or fumed. Height: 24–28″. Width: 16–19″. Depth: 5–7″.

Locality and Period

Large factories throughout the East and Midwest. c. 1875–1900.

Comment

American Eastlake-style furniture was usually decorated with saw-cut fretwork and incised geometric patterns. This sort of decoration, easily done with the development of automatic fret-saws and gouging devices, was ideal for cheap, mass-produced furnishings. As a consequence, pieces in the Eastlake mode are still abundant and generally inexpensive, as compared with other Victorian styles.

Hints for Collectors

The most desirable Eastlake pieces are made of walnut, like the shelves illustrated here. Earlier than most oak examples, they are usually better made and may be less expensive as well, since the current demand for oak has raised the price of all oak furniture.

Anglo-Japanese hanging cabinet

Description

Ornate hanging cabinet with shaped and decorated backboard. Flat, molded top has 2 turned urn finials. Backboard has incised Oriental-style patterns and rises 8–10″ at center, 2–3″ on each side. Central cabinet has elaborately hinged glass door; 1 shelf inside. On each side of cabinet, shallow, shaped shelf. Below cabinet, 1 full-length, shaped and molded shelf. Deep skirt sharply valanced and with incised designs. Nailed and screwed construction.

Materials and Dimensions

Maple or birch. Often painted to imitate ebony. Hinges: scroll-shaped brass. Pulls: small brass knobs. Escutcheons: brass ovals. Height: 33–36″. Width: 24–26″. Depth: 7–8″.

Locality and Period

Better factories in the East. c. 1885–1900.

Comment

The Anglo-Japanese manner is an important Victorian substyle. It was prompted, no doubt, by the importation of Japanese woodblock prints and other objects in the second half of the 19th century and by the display of Japanese art objects at the Philadelphia Centennial Exhibition in 1876. Prior to that time, few Americans had been exposed to Japanese decoration.

Hints for Collectors

Anglo-Japanese pieces are often not recognized as such, or are confused with those executed in the more common Eastlake style. While the use of fretwork and incised decoration is common to both, Anglo-Japanese pieces are embellished with clearly Oriental motifs such as bamboo, plum blossoms, and pagodas. In addition, the overall ebonizing seen in this example was rare in Eastlake pieces.

Glazed hanging wall cabinet

Description
Hanging cabinet with flat or pedimented top; top with or without molding. May have cutout decorative crest, as shown here. 1–2 glass doors with simple square or rectangular panes. 2–3 interior shelves. 1–3 small drawers sometimes present below doors. Usually painted. Nailed or dovetailed construction.

Materials and Dimensions
Pine, cedar, or poplar; occasionally maple, birch, or mixed softwoods or hardwoods. Usually painted plain red, blue, or brown, or grained or sponged in earth tones. Hinges: iron butt. Pulls: brass, turned wood, or porcelain knobs; also brass or iron hooks with eyes. Escutcheons, when present: brass or iron butt. Height: 30–36″. Width: 32–36″. Depth: 10–16″.

Locality and Period
New England west to the Mississippi River and throughout the South. c. 1780–1880.

Comment
Glazed wall cabinets provided the householder with both storage and display space for family porcelain and silver. Some examples are quite large and heavy, considering that they had to be suspended. Most were painted to harmonize with walls and ceiling.

Hints for Collectors
Wall cabinets are easy to confuse with tabletop pieces. The latter were made to sit on tables but then often converted to hanging units by the addition of holes. Because they were seen from below, hanging units usually have more elaborate bases than tabletop pieces, so if the bottom is painted or if it has a molding, the cabinet was probably meant to hang on a wall.

Anglo-Japanese mirrored cabinet

Description
2-door cabinet for wall or tabletop use. Top has 3-sided gallery of turned spindles. Each molded door frames oval, beveled glass mirror. Interior has 2–3 fixed narrow shelves. Side boards have incised decoration. Elaborate bentwood skirt and turned spindles. Sides and back of base galleried to match top. Turned ball feet. Glued, nailed, and screwed construction.

Materials and Dimensions
Oak or oak veneer over pine; often fumed, as here. Shelves and back sometimes pine or plywood. Hinges: brass butt. Pulls, when present: brass pendant ring handles or rosette knobs. Escutcheons: round, ebonized hardwood. Height: 25–28″. Width: 17–20″. Depth: 7–9″.

Locality and Period
Factories throughout the East and Midwest. c. 1860–90.

Comment
The use of beveled glass and the sophisticated gallery and skirt mark the piece shown here as a better than average factory product. Such cabinets were often found in Victorian parlors or drawing rooms, where they were used for curios and small pieces of glass or pottery.

Hints for Collectors
Victorian cabinets of this type are very common. The more desirable examples will have solid wood rather than plywood backs, and will be solid oak, not veneered. Better-quality pieces, like the one shown here, will also have a careful, balanced design and not the prefabricated and "nailed-on" decoration common in examples made toward the end of the 19th century.

Architectural tabletop cupboard

Description
Tabletop cupboard with top forming a triangular pediment. 2 long, narrow, battened doors; interior with 2–3 simple shelves. No molding on doors or base. No skirt or feet. Usually painted. Dovetailed or nailed construction.

Materials and Dimensions
Pine or poplar; rarely maple or birch. Commonly painted solid red, blue, green, or white, sometimes 2 colors; graining or sponging relatively rare. Hinges: iron or brass butt. Pulls: brass, porcelain, or turned wooden knobs. Escutcheons: brass keyhole surrounds. Height: 28–34″. Width: 22–26″. Depth: 12–15″.

Locality and Period
New England and New York. c. 1790–1840.

Comment
The finest architectural cupboards are usually the late 18th-century corner and side cupboards, many of which were built in. Tabletop cupboards of the sort shown here are rare, especially in this form, a miniature Federal-style doorway complete with grained wood, paneling, and stringing, all mimicked in paint. The fine workmanship and superb condition make this an outstanding piece.

Hints for Collectors
Tabletop cupboards are usually larger than the hanging variety and more difficult to find. Since most are simple country pieces designed for the kitchen or workshop, their paint will often be the deciding factor in evaluating them. Look for good, old finish —note age, wear, and suitability to the piece. Graining or sponging is an asset. Pieces as well decorated as the one shown here are rare.

Victorian hanging file cabinet

Description
Shallow cabinet with flat top and elaborate, scrolled backboard
(5–8″ high). Center of backboard embellished with stamped metal
tag that bears patent date. 2 paneled, grain-painted doors open
to reveal several tin sheets with iron clips for recipes,
correspondence, etc. Sides paneled in 2 oval units. Paneled and
mortise-and-tenon construction; back nailed on.

Materials and Dimensions
Cherry, walnut, or oak; grained panels typically pine. Secondary
wood pine. Hinges: iron butt. White metal escutcheon and
swivel-type latch. Height: 36–39″. Width: 22–25″. Depth: 11–13″.

Locality and Period
Throughout the East and Midwest, usually in large factories.
c. 1880–1910.

Comment
The Victorians excelled in orderliness, and hanging cabinets such
as the one shown here were used in the kitchen to store recipes
and in the study to file accounts. Although most were patented
and factory made in large quantities at low prices, a few of the
more desirable homemade examples may be found.

Hints for Collectors
Do not mistake a factory-made cabinet of this sort for a
handcrafted example. The patent date, the narrow machine-cut
boards, and the elaborate jigsaw-cut backboard all indicate a
factory origin. Even if the interior file sheets have been removed
to make the piece more appealing to collectors, it should still be
possible to determine the purpose of the piece from the holes
that remain.

Shaker tabletop cupboard

Description
Large tabletop cupboard with slightly overhanging, molded top.
1 narrow central door, paneled and pegged. Interior with 3–4
shelves. Dovetailed and paneled construction.

Materials and Dimensions
Pine; maple and chestnut less common. Sometimes stained red,
yellow, or green. Hinges: iron butt. Pulls: brass or turned
wooden knobs. Escutcheons: brass or iron keyhole surrounds.
Height: 28–31″. Width: 21–23″. Depth: 11–12″.

Locality and Period
Shaker communities from New England to Indiana, south to
Kentucky. c. 1800–70.

Comment
The Shakers produced a variety of tabletop and hanging
cupboards. Usually they were intended to contain small kitchen,
work, or personal items, and were therefore relatively shallow.
On a hanging cupboard, the backboard is often extended and has
a slot so that the cupboard can be hung on a nail or pegboard.

Hints for Collectors
Shaker cupboards may easily be confused with similar non-
Shaker storage pieces. Look for evenly spaced, well-cut
dovetails, relatively tall, narrow proportions, and extreme
simplicity of design, all of which usually indicate Shaker
workmanship. In addition, beware of reproductions. Shaker
furniture has become extremely popular and is often duplicated
by modern cabinetmakers. Once a piece has passed from their
hands, it may be misrepresented to an unsuspecting buyer. Look
for the usual signs of age or, better yet, only buy examples with
established histories within Shaker communities.

Tabletop cupboard and drawers

Description
Small tabletop or shelf-size storage piece, with plain, overhanging top above full-length drawer. Below left, 1-door cupboard without interior shelves. Below right, 2 small, square drawers. Plain board sides. Lightly molded edge around base. Nailed construction.

Materials and Dimensions
Pine or poplar; rarely cherry, maple, or birch. Secondary wood pine. Natural or stained red, brown, or green; rarely sponge- or grain-painted. Hinges: brass or iron butt. Pulls: porcelain, brass, or turned wooden knobs. Escutcheons: brass or iron keyhole surrounds. Height: 17–20″. Width: 15–17″. Depth: 10–12″.

Locality and Period
New England west to Texas and throughout the South. c. 1820–70.

Comment
Small storage pieces like this were often made either in a cabinetmaker's shop or by a local carpenter and used in the kitchen or pantry to store spices, food, and utensils. Few had feet, and even the addition of a simple base molding, like that on this piece, would have been thought fancy. Holes in the back indicate that a cupboard was hung, but most were too heavy and were kept on a tabletop.

Hints for Collectors
Small cupboards of this sort are quite popular and have been reproduced or retouched. Be wary of pieces that are elaborately sponged or grained. Most were not highly decorated originally, and examples with faked decoration have been appearing on the market. To determine age, look for paint wear, dirt, and crazing.

Spice cabinet

Description
Small cabinet with a flat, overhanging top that has plain or molded edge. Back may extend upward to form curved backboard, often pierced for hanging. 6–20 small square drawers of equal size. Plain board sides. Base plain or molded to match top. Feet, when present, ball type or bootjack extensions of side boards. Often painted. Dovetailed or nailed construction.

Materials and Dimensions
Pine or poplar; sometimes oak, maple, cherry, walnut, or fruitwoods. Pine and poplar examples often painted red, blue, yellow, white, or gray; sometimes sponge- or grain-painted. Pulls: turned wooden pins or brass or porcelain knobs. Height: 16–32″. Width: 14–28″. Depth: 8–10″.

Locality and Period
New England west to the Mississippi River and throughout the South. c. 1780–1880.

Comment
Rare early 17th-century spice cabinets were similar to miniature highboys or chest-on-chests. Later and more common pieces like the one shown here are less elaborate, consisting of a series of small drawers, usually of the same size. Some of these pieces may have been used as jewelry cabinets.

Hints for Collectors
Spice cabinets are extremely popular, and many have been reproduced. Beware of 20th-century examples. To identify earlier pieces, check the nails, which should be square-headed. Smell the drawers; they should have rich odors from having stored herbs and spices for many years. Look at the drawer linings and slides and around the pulls. Since these pieces were used constantly, they should show signs of wear.

Miscellaneous Furnishings

The furnishings included in this section are largely types that became common in the Victorian period but continue to be found in the American home. Some, such as bookcases, smoking stands, and plant holders, are familiar to almost everyone. Others, such as display easels, room dividers, and portable bars, are less well known but equally part of the American decorative scene. The selection presented here illustrates the stylistic and functional diversity available to the collector.

Reflecting this diversity are the racks that were found in almost every Victorian household, and were intended to hold items ranging from hats to pipes and guns. Hall racks (319) are perhaps the best known; although most are factory made of oak, some rare handcrafted examples are today valued as pieces of folk art rather than as utilitarian objects. Gun racks (274) appeared in lodges and men's clubs as the western plains were opened and a hunting craze swept across America. And by the 20th century, magazine racks (275) were found in almost every living room and library.

Stands are as varied as racks. Planters and plant stands (292), for instance, first became well known in America in the mid-19th century and have remained popular ever since. Although the most typical examples are made of wicker, today some collectors seek out fiberglass pieces made as recently as 1960. Smoking stands (283) are equally diverse. As cigarette and cigar smoking became widespread, smoking stands became a necessity in parlors, restaurants, trains, and ships. Available examples range from simple rustic pieces to sophisticated ones made of steel and aluminum. Still other stands displayed paintings (322) or held music, especially during the home recitals that were popular around the turn of the century.

By the 1800s, most Americans could afford books, and when they had acquired a number of them, they began to buy bookcases (302). In Victorian homes, these were usually built in, but freestanding examples were manufactured as well. Those made in the 20th century run the gamut of modern styles, including Art Deco and Mission.

A few early country pieces, such as the dough box (297) and bucket bench found in rural kitchens, are also included here, as well as a Federal knife box (326).

The specialized objects in this section are generally smaller than most of the other pieces covered in this book, and many of them are especially appealing to a collector with a sense of humor and an eye for bargains.

Hanging cattle-horn hat rack

Description
Wall-hung hat rack with 4 cattle horns, mounted on a shieldlike
wooden plaque. Eyelet at center top for hanging. Lower set of
horns 14–16″ long, curving forward and up. Upper set 8–9″ long,
turning sharply up. A block of wood, padded and velvet-
wrapped, joins lower pair and encloses bases of upper ones.
Screwed and nailed construction.

Materials and Dimensions
Typically longhorn cattle horns mounted on oak, ash, or pine
board. Sometimes deer or antelope horns similarly mounted.
Eyelet: iron. Brass-headed tacks sometimes secure velvet.
Height: 12–16″. Width: 22–26″. Depth: 11–14″.

Locality and Period
Large specialized factories in the East and Midwest. Rare
examples handmade, especially in the Far West. c. 1880–1910.

Comment
The hunting craze that accompanied the opening of the western
plains, and the legend of the cattle-driving cowboy, contributed
to the turn-of-the-century vogue for horn furniture. While
unusual forms like sofas and even desks can be found, the most
common pieces are chairs and hat or hall racks such as the
example illustrated. Most were originally used in hunting lodges,
although they were also found in metropolitan men's clubs.

Hints for Collectors
Although horn furniture is rapidly increasing in price, the
market is still small and confined primarily to a few large cities,
including New York. Consequently, a hat rack like this can
usually be found at a reasonable price in a small city or rural
area. Before you buy, make sure that a piece is in good condition
and not infested with vermin.

Rustic gun rack

Description
Folding wall rack with nearly square framework of rough
branches, cut so that shorter, Y-shaped twigs at front form
notches to hold long guns. Frame decorated with thinner
branches bent into horseshoe shapes. Metal loops on back for
hanging. Often painted. Nailed construction.

Materials and Dimensions
Hickory, ash, or birch; also other supple hardwoods. Typically
banded or dotted with paint—usually red, brown, silver, or gold.
Hangers: tin or sheet iron. Height: 30–36″. Width: 16–22″.
Depth: 6–8″.

Locality and Period
Throughout the Northeast, primarily New York State, and parts
of the northern Midwest. c. 1900–40.

Comment
These decorative wall racks were used in mountain hunting
camps as storage racks for rifles, shotguns, or fishing rods. Most
were made locally and sold at country stores or roadside stands.
Since they were small and attractive, they were sold as
souvenirs and carried throughout the country.

Hints for Collectors
The so-called rustic, twig, or Adirondack furnishings are not to
everyone's taste. They are, however, increasing in popularity,
particularly among city collectors, so this is a good time to buy.
Look for twig furniture at yard and church sales and in small
antiques shops in the mountains where they were originally
made and used. The more desirable examples will have unusually
shaped frames with interesting paint decoration. Rare signed
and dated pieces are always a find.

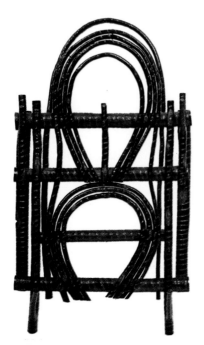

Bamboo magazine rack

Description
Low magazine rack. Openwork bamboo walls with stiles rising 2″ above top of rack. Front and back walls each have 2 horizontal rails and 2 vertical stiles that terminate in outswept legs and small hooflike feet. 3 additional bamboo rods in outer walls intersect to form a triangle, usually inset with a painted leather panel. Central divider: 2 vertical bamboo end stiles and 2 rods crossing diagonally to form an X. Bottom solid wood, usually covered with leather. Nailed and glued construction.

Materials and Dimensions
Bamboo; bottom pine. Leather, when present, glued on, machine-embossed, and stained, and with brown and yellow floral design. Decorative leather side panels painted 2 contrasting colors. Height: 16–20″. Width: 15–19″. Depth: 11–13″.

Locality and Period
Factories primarily in the East. c. 1880–1910.

Comment
The interest in Oriental objects at the turn of the century led to the production of all sorts of furnishings that were vaguely eastern in style. Bamboo was extremely popular and used in openwork screens, sets of shelves, bars, and magazine racks. Many examples, like the one shown here, were quite sophisticated and elaborately decorated.

Hints for Collectors
Similar magazine racks are now being imported from Hong Kong and elsewhere in Asia. A new rack would not, however, have the Art Nouveau embossed leather bottom or the triangular leather insets seen here. The age and wear evident in this piece would also be missing on a new piece.

Corner umbrella rack

Description
Small, 3-sided umbrella and cane holder with curved front and 2 straight sides. Turned stiles topped with ball finials, above double gallery of reeded horizontal rods and short, turned spindles. Wedge-shaped lower shelf with molded front edge supported on 4 turned feet, 3 of them extensions of stiles, the 4th screwed into bottom of shelf. Circular cutout on shelf holds stamped metal drip pan. Glued and screwed construction.

Materials and Dimensions
Oak. Shelf oak, stained ash, or hickory. Drip pan: brass, tin, or copper. Height: 29–33″. Width: 15–17″. Depth: 11–12″.

Locality and Period
Large factories throughout the East and Midwest. c. 1880–1920.

Comment
Small and practical, these elaborate, galleried Victorian racks fit easily into a corner. They were constructed entirely of machine turned and cut elements and could be assembled either in the plant or wherever they were sold. They held not only umbrellas but also the canes and walking sticks favored by gentlemen around the turn of the century.

Hints for Collectors
Umbrella racks similar to this are being reproduced today. However, they are made of oak that is lighter in color and weight, and the pieces are turned from wood ¼–½″ smaller in diameter than that of the originals, which are usually 1½–1¾″ thick. A rack that is old will show wear on the base of the feet and around the hole where the drip pan fits. A new drip pan does not necessarily mean a piece is new; many pans were lost and replaced over the years.

Mission-style umbrella stand

Description
Tall umbrella or cane holder. 4 square stiles taper inward 4–5″
from top and terminate in blunt ends. Stiles joined 4–5″ from top
by rectangular stretchers. Second group of stretchers (2–3″
above floor) forms a box with solid board bottom, set into slots on
insides of stretchers. Legs and blunt feet slightly chamfered
extensions of stiles. May have metal drip pan. Pegged mortise-
and-tenon construction.

Materials and Dimensions
Oak and quartersawed oak. Drip pan, when present: tin or
copper. Height: 33–36″. Diameter: 11–12″.

Locality and Period
Factories in the East and northern Midwest. c. 1900–20.

Comment
Although the example shown here is from the shop of Gustav
Stickley, similar umbrella stands were produced by many larger
manufacturers. Few of these, however, would have had the
careful attention to detail, pegged construction, and balanced
design seen here. Mass-produced stands were usually joined with
screws or angle irons set on the inside of the frame where they
would not show. Despite its excellent workmanship, such a piece
would have sold for only a few dollars when new.

Hints for Collectors
Makers' marks are important, even on minor examples like this
one. The presence of the Gustav Stickley brand name on the base
of this piece justifies a high price, whereas an almost identical
unmarked piece from a mass manufacturer would fetch
significantly less.

Mission-style solid board umbrella stand

Description
Umbrella holder made from 6 oak slats, each with a bootjack cutout at the bottom. Slats fitted around a square wooden block at base and joined at top and bottom by metal angle irons and screws. Screw heads concealed on exterior by round wooden bosses. Slats do not fit flush but are separated by ¼″ space. Brass inner tray or drip pan covers bottom of stand. Screwed construction.

Materials and Dimensions
Oak or quartersawed oak. Angle irons: brass or iron. Drip pan: brass. Height: 33–35″. Diameter: 10–11″.

Locality and Period
Factories in the East and northern Midwest. c. 1905–20.

Comment
Umbrella stands similar to this one appear in the catalogues of several early 20th-century producers of Mission-style furnishings. Wastebaskets are closely related in appearance and structure, but they taper outward from bottom to top. The construction is extremely simple and was well suited for large shops that wanted to create the appearance of Stickley-type Mission furniture while not actually doing the handwork for which he and comparable designers were known.

Hints for Collectors
Don't confuse pieces by Stickley, Roycroft, and others with mass-produced Mission-style examples like that shown here. Unlike this piece, put together with screws whose heads are concealed under wooden bosses (a common mass producers' trick), a Stickley-type stand would have pegged mortise-and-tenon construction.

Victorian cast-iron umbrella stand

Description
Metal stand in form of partially opened umbrella. Stand has 6 perforated pieces of arched metal that interlock with fingerlike tabs and are secured with wire (possibly a later addition). Umbrella shaft terminates in a handle in the form of a gloved hand that grips a short rod. 6 spokes 8–10″ below handle divide interior of rack. Separately cast base with molded edge, decorated with long slots, terminates in 12 short, flaring feet. Usually painted. Cast and wired construction.

Materials and Dimensions
Cast iron, painted green and white or other contrasting colors. Brass tubing and iron wire. Height: 27–29″. Diameter at base: 15–17″.

Locality and Period
Iron foundries and novelty metal shops in the East and Midwest. c. 1880–1910.

Comment
Victorian whimsy in furniture was often expressed in umbrella stands and hat racks. Some pieces were homemade, but many more were manufactured commercially and widely sold. The casting of this piece, particularly the central portion, indicates a high degree of technical skill.

Hints for Collectors
Umbrella stands like this are not easy to find, but are worth the search. Although factory made, this piece might be considered folk art and would, in that case, bring a higher price on the market. Look for these novelties at house and church sales, and in small-town or rural shops. As with any metal piece, missing or damaged parts can be a problem.

Rococo Revival cast-iron umbrella rack

Description
Curvilinear 3-piece stand with vertical back that separates into 2 curving sections at base. At top, horizontal eyeglasslike loops for umbrellas and canes. Base heavy, indented, sometimes with drip pan. Decorative handle at top for carrying. Overall floral motif. Bolted and soldered construction.

Materials and Dimensions
Cast iron. Drip pan, when present: tin or brass. Height: 27–30″. Width: 18–21″. Depth: 8–10″.

Locality and Period
Large foundries and factories throughout the East and Midwest. c. 1890–1920.

Comment
Umbrella and cane racks were common in the Victorian era, and few entrance halls were without one. They were made in various materials and styles, sometimes in combination with a coat rack or mirror. Because of its weight, cast iron was seldom used for anything but small pieces like this one. It was obviously a good material for umbrella racks since it helped prevent heavily loaded racks from toppling over.

Hints for Collectors
Umbrella and cane racks are as handy today as they were 100 years ago, especially in a hall or foyer. Examples are numerous enough for a buyer to be selective, and pieces with any damage to the cast iron are better left alone. Once the metal has aged and become brittle, repair work is almost impossible without doing further damage, and replacements for missing parts are expensive and hard to find.

Match holder and ashtray on stand

Description
Slim circular ashtray. Bowl-shaped disposal area has rolled lip. Above, match holder made from piece of rectangular metal folded over to form 3-sided pocket and supported on 2 stamped metal arms with flat, oval areas on which to rest cigarettes. Long, circular, fluted stem terminates in molded half-round base. Always painted. Soldered and screwed construction.

Materials and Dimensions
Copper and thin sheet metal. Painted red, black, green, or in various combinations. Height: 25–28″. Diameter at widest point: 5–6″.

Locality and Period
Factories and metalworking shops throughout the United States. c. 1920–40.

Comment
Ashtrays and stands were common furnishings throughout the late 19th century; however, until World War I smoking was generally confined to men's studies, clubs, and barrooms. As increasing numbers of women began to smoke in the 1920s and 1930s, many ashtrays on stands were made; these were often smaller and lighter so that they could be moved about easily. By the 1930s, new industrial materials had replaced the bronze and cast iron used earlier.

Hints for Collectors
Ashtrays like the one shown here go well with furnishings from the 1920s and 1930s. Indeed, they were sometimes made to match a living room or parlor set. They are quite inexpensive at present and can often be found in secondhand shops or at house and yard sales.

Wicker smoking stand

Description
Small, portable smoking stand with horseshoe-shaped handle of wicker-wrapped wood. Round top shelf with low, braided wicker gallery and indentation for ashtray. Round bottom shelf, 6–8″ above floor, also with woven wicker gallery. 3 legs of wicker-wrapped wood support shelves and taper sharply outward at level of lower shelf. Feet plain extensions of legs. Usually painted. Woven and wrapped wicker; nailed construction.

Materials and Dimensions
Wicker-wrapped birch, ash, or oak; shelves pine. Often painted white, green, brown, black, or red. Height: 32–36″. Diameter at base: 8–10″.

Locality and Period
Throughout the United States. c. 1900–40.

Comment
Small smoking stands like this were often made to match sets of wicker porch or parlor furniture. Most were round, although a few square or rectangular examples were also made. They were almost always painted.

Hints for Collectors
Wicker smoking stands are easily distinguished from somewhat similar small plant stands: smoking stands have much smaller shelves, a carrying handle that makes the top shelf too shallow for plants, and an indentation for an ashtray. These smoking stands are common and can be purchased for very little. However, they are also fragile and damaged examples should be avoided. Be sure to check the slim legs; if they are cracked or broken, reject the stand.

Art Deco smoking stand

Description
Ashtray on stand has doughnut-shaped receptacle with recesses for cigarettes, mounted on flat, circular tray with curved edge. Above this, an arched, tubular handle pierced in center for knobbed plunger that opens disklike trap, so ashes fall into hollow shaft (15–18″ deep). Shaft terminates in round, molded base. Welded and screwed construction.

Materials and Dimensions
Stainless steel or stainless steel and aluminum. Steel may be enameled black, red, or white. Spring steel plunger device. Height: 25–27″. Diameter at top: 16–17″.

Locality and Period
Large factories in the East and Midwest. c. 1930–45.

Comment
The stand seen here was designed by Henry Dreyfuss and manufactured for use on the famous train, the *20th Century Limited*, but the type was widely made during the 1930s. The spring-loaded device for clearing the ashtray is an interesting 20th-century development, and the use of so-called industrial materials (steel and aluminum) is characteristic of design concepts emerging at the time.

Hints for Collectors
Ashtrays of this type are plentiful and can often be purchased for practically nothing at yard or church sales, or from secondhand-furniture dealers, although they may command much more at shops specializing in Art Deco furniture. If not damaged, they can usually be cleaned up quickly with a commercial metal cleaner and polisher. Damages to avoid include dents, corrosion, and scratched enamel.

Rustic smoking stand

Description
Stand with cabin-shaped box on square top that rests on tripod base. Top has slightly chamfered corners. At front of top, bent twigs shaped to hold 2 glasses or ashtrays; at rear, small, log-cabin-shaped box has peaked roof that lifts off, revealing storage well for cigarettes. Legs rough branches with bark, reinforced by stick stretchers in triangular pattern. Coils of twig rise from stretchers, forming decorative loops below top. Other twigs secured to corners of top and joined together to form carrying handle. Nailed construction.

Materials and Dimensions
Ash, hickory, or other strong, flexible wood. Pine top and box. May be painted silver, gold, or other colors. Height: 25–28″. Width: 13–15″. Depth: 12–14″.

Locality and Period
Small shops and hobbyists, primarily in New England, upstate New York, and northern Michigan. c. 1910–40.

Comment
Rustic, twig, or Adirondack furniture was intended primarily for use in mountain lodges and summer homes. It was made and sold locally in resort areas, although some pieces, like the smoking stands, were also sold through chain stores like Woolworth's.

Hints for Collectors
Although many people find rustic furnishings crude and unappealing, they are inexpensive and fairly easy to find. Some pieces are relatively plain and uninteresting, but others, like the one shown here, with its log-cabin cigarette box and bent twig decoration, are fine examples of 20th-century folk art.

Mission-style plant stand

Description
Small plant holder with square, unmolded 1-board top that overhangs 2–3″ at sides. A 3″ gouge or finger grip cut into wood under each side of top. Skirts on 4 sides cut in shallow arc. Square legs and plain feet tapered extensions of stiles that flare out near floor. Glued mortise-and-tenon construction, with screwed-on top.

Materials and Dimensions
Oak or quartersawed oak. Height: 17–20″. Width: 12–13″. Depth: 12–13″.

Locality and Period
Factories in the East and Midwest. c. 1905–20.

Comment
Although similar plant stands in several sizes have been found with the labels or marks of either Gustav Stickley or L. and J. G. Stickley, most examples are by unidentified makers. Frequently they are mistaken for small tables, but an examination of period catalogues makes clear that these pieces were sold as plant stands.

Hints for Collectors
Attractive and useful, these stands make good bed- or chair-side tables. As a general rule, the better ones are pegged or dovetailed. Mass-produced pieces such as the one shown here are usually held together with screws, nails, or glue. Even factory-made pieces can be attractive additions to a room; look for little touches like the under-the-top handholds and the flaring, tapered legs seen here. Plant stands are among the more affordable pieces in the Mission style.

Victorian double-shelf plant stand

Description
Tall plant stand with square, unmolded top overhanging 1–2″. Below top, gallery (5–7″ high) of wooden rods wrapped in split wicker, set vertically between top and horizontal stretchers. Gallery supported at corners by short pieces of wicker set at 45° angles. Square shelf of woven wicker 4–5″ above floor, similarly supported. Wicker-wrapped stiles slightly canted. Legs and feet simple extensions of stiles. Often painted. Wrapped and nailed construction.

Materials and Dimensions
Hardwood rods, usually birch or maple, wrapped in split wicker. Pine top. Often painted white, green, or red. Height: 30–36″. Width and depth at top: 11–12″; at bottom: 12–14″.

Locality and Period
Small shops and individual craftsmen throughout the United States. c. 1880–1935.

Comment
Simple plant stands like this were made in great quantities over a long period of time, mostly for sun porches and patios. They are seldom of any discernible style, although the gallery work and wicker support brackets seen in the example illustrated reflect an Anglo-Japanese influence. Similar pieces with curvilinear supports and decoration have an Art Nouveau look.

Hints for Collectors
Although more expensive than they once were, old plant stands are still reasonably priced and plentiful. Interesting, well-proportioned examples can be used as small tables or as display stands. Make sure the wicker is not fraying or split. Repairing wicker is more difficult than it looks.

Description
3-legged, octagonal stand with sides of top composed of 6–8″ lengths of unpeeled branch laid one on the other in log-cabin fashion. Bottom solid board, cut in 8-sided shape. Legs joined in tripod form, with Y-shaped branch for support below juncture. Nailed construction.

Materials and Dimensions
Ash, hickory, birch, or similar flexible hardwood. Bottom pine or ash. May be painted or paint-decorated. Height: 28–32″. Diameter at top: 12–15″.

Locality and Period
Hobbyists or small manufacturers in parts of New England, upstate New York, and the northern Midwest. c. 1900–40.

Comment
Plant stands were made in various shapes and sizes, although most were round or rectangular. Large numbers were produced in rural shops and bought for use in summer homes. A large house might have as many as 2 dozen planters. Most of the stands are similar, suggesting that there may have been a single design source, possibly a 1930s magazine like *Popular Mechanics*, which frequently published blueprints for such pieces.

Hints for Collectors
Compare this plant stand with similar wicker pieces. Although both types have the same basic outline, the rustic craftsmen who made pieces like the one shown here used fewer materials and simpler methods. A fine-quality rustic piece can be distinguished from an ordinary one by good lines, well-chosen materials, and interesting decoration.

Bamboo planter

Description
Planter on tripod frame. Container made of split bamboo strips
resting on a round wooden bottom. Strips bound together with 2
bands of woven rattan. U-shaped bamboo side handles. Base 3
canted bamboo legs supported by U-shaped brackets and bamboo
stretchers, bound together with sections of split cane. Feet
simple extensions of legs. Nailed and wrapped-rattan
construction.

Materials and Dimensions
Bamboo, pine, and rattan. Sections may be stained green or
brown. Height: 23–27″. Diameter at top: 14–16″.

Locality and Period
Shops specializing in bamboo and rattan work throughout the
United States. Similar examples imported from Southeast Asia.
c. 1925–40.

Comment
Simple bamboo planters like this were sometimes included in sets
of porch or parlor furniture, but for the most part they were sold
inexpensively in department stores and florist shops. Examples
made before 1925 are usually more ornate and better built than
pieces from the 1930s.

Hints for Collectors
Bamboo planters tend to be rather fragile, and many have some
damage. The example illustrated has lost part of its rattan
wrapping and would need to be repaired before it could be used.
In general, since these planters are both common and
inexpensive, avoid damaged ones. However, a piece with an
unusual shape or out-of-the-ordinary weaving may be worth the
cost of repair.

Modern abstract planter

Description
Simple planter with cone-shaped, removable bowl in a tripod base. Legs are 3 rope-twisted metal rods that form tripod directly below bowl, and flare up and out to form flat supports that hold it. Feet plain extensions of legs. Welded construction.

Materials and Dimensions
Base wrought iron, painted black. Bowl Filon, a type of fiberglass; usually red, blue, green, or yellow. Height: 30–34″. Diameter at top: 13–14″; at bottom: 11–12″.

Locality and Period
Many factories throughout the East and Midwest. c. 1945–60.

Comment
The use of synthetics for planters was a natural result of the Industrial Age and the modern movement in furniture design. Man-made materials like Filon are not affected by moisture, and therefore, unlike wood or metal, are especially suited for holding soil. Planters like the one shown here are still common in public areas, where they are often accompanied by 1950s-style plastic and metal chairs, tables, and sofas. Although furniture like this was not manufactured in sets, the pieces often closely resemble one another, both in lines and materials.

Hints for Collectors
Still very easy to find, especially in secondhand stores and at yard or house sales, these planters are inexpensive, colorful accessories that accent modern furnishings. However, because they are both fragile and top-heavy, they should be handled with care.

Victorian wicker tripod planter

Description
Tripod-based plant stand with wicker body woven on framework
of vertical wooden rods. Body decorated with ropework and
tapers in from shoulder. Bottom wrapped with ropework and has
central drainage hole. 3 slender, turned legs taper out from body
and are set into bottom of body at an angle. Legs supported at
midpoint by turned stretchers, rope-bound at corners. Feet plain
extensions of legs. Woven and glued construction.

Materials and Dimensions
Ash, hickory, or oak rods with wicker body and pine bottom.
May be painted, usually white, green, or brown. Height: 32–34″.
Diameter at top: 14–16″.

Locality and Period
Large factories and smaller shops throughout the East and
Midwest. c. 1860–1920.

Comment
These pieces are more complex and somewhat less common than
their rectangular counterparts, but are nevertheless easy to find.
Most were used for the ferns and large, flowering plants with
drooping leaves that were so popular during the Victorian era.

Hints for Collectors
These wicker planters are inevitably weakened when stripped by
one of the commercial dipping processes. To change the color of a
piece, repaint over the current finish. It will not seriously affect
the value and, indeed, may actually enhance the worth of the
piece. And before you buy any piece of wicker, make sure that it
is in good condition and that it is still strong enough to support
weight.

Art Nouveau cast-iron fish tank

Description
Large, round, watertight tank with circular, plinthlike iron base and molded central supporting column in form of bulrushes and 4 pelicans. Tank is circular tray with pierced and scalloped edge, from which rise 8 floral-form columns (2–3″ wide) topped with lily-pad and tulip devices. Between columns, plates of glass. In center of tank, a large column (4–6″) with lily-form capital. Hinged door in base conceals interior pipes. Cast, soldered, and bolted construction.

Materials and Dimensions
Cast iron and glass. Iron usually painted silver, white, or green. Hinges: iron butt. Height: 42–47″. Diameter at top: 30–34″.

Locality and Period
Foundries and larger factories throughout the East and Midwest. c. 1900–10.

Comment
Cast-iron fish tanks were found in formal gardens, sun-rooms, and on porches during the Victorian era. Interior pipes, reached by the door in the base, allowed water to flow through the pedestal to the small fountain inside the tank.

Hints for Collectors
Fish tanks of this size and weight were never common, and would have been fairly expensive even when they were new. Pieces like the one shown here are hard to find; a junkyard or salvage company that sells objects from demolished houses is a more likely source than an antiques shop. And a tank such as this, in the popular Art Nouveau style, may have more value in today's market.

Victorian wicker planter

Description
Rectangular plant stand with woven wicker compartment on
framework of turned wooden rods. Wicker compartment fitted
with waterproof liner. On sides above compartment, handlelike
rods; below, decorative wickerwork. Legs, supported by 4
turned stretchers, terminate in blunt knobs. Woven and glued
construction.

Materials and Dimensions
Usually turned ash, hickory, or birch, with woven wicker body.
Compartment bottom, when present, pine. Frequently painted
white, green, or brown. Waterproof liner: tin. Height: 28–32″.
Width: 29–33″. Depth: 12–14″.

Locality and Period
Factories and shops, primarily in the East and Midwest.
c. 1860–1920.

Comment
One of the most popular forms of plant stands, these rectangular
pieces were used for a number of years all over the country.
They often held ferns, the special favorite of Victorian
housewives, and might be found on the porch, in the solarium, or
even in the parlor. In general, higher-quality pieces had more
elaborately woven designs.

Hints for Collectors
Most Victorians repainted their wicker pieces almost every year,
so don't be put off by old wicker that has been recently
repainted. If an example has a deteriorating finish, go ahead and
repaint it; this will not significantly lessen the value. But if
you're lucky enough to find an unpainted wicker planter,
preserve the natural condition; these pieces are especially
desirable.

Description
Rectangular plant stand with open well lined in welded metal sheets; well has slightly molded edge. Legs, inset at corners of box, are chamfered at box level, and taper sharply outward from floor, forming small, hooflike feet. Horizontal gallery of square-cut wooden rods form box stretcher 6–8″ above floor level. Glued and nailed construction.

Materials and Dimensions
Maple and pine with maple veneer, or all pine with maple veneer. Waterproof liner: copper or galvanized tin. Height: 30–33″. Width: 36–39″. Depth: 10–14″.

Locality and Period
Large factories in the East and Midwest. c. 1925–35.

Comment
Planters first became popular during the Victorian era, and by the early 20th century were being made in every material from wicker to metal. This Art Deco example was designed by Antonin Raymond and produced by several furniture factories. Despite the somewhat unusual horizontal gallery, it is a more or less typical Art Deco planter.

Hints for Collectors
Plant stands are most effective when their form relates to that of the other funishings. If a room is decorated in the Art Deco style, attractive matching plant stands can be easily found, and for less money than the more popular Victorian examples in wicker. Art Deco pieces like the one shown here are sometimes available at used-furniture stores.

Description
Book or storage rack mounted on sticklike frame. V-shaped trough of 2 boards joined at right angle. 5-sided, caned ends extend 2″ above sides. Thin legs canted outward, extending to plain shoe feet; front and rear feet joined by stretchers. Horizontal stretchers 10–12″ above floor, 1 on each side and 1 lengthwise parallel to trough. Wide, decorative stile with rectangular cutout, flanked by 2 narrow stiles, joins lengthwise stretcher to book trough. Screwed construction.

Materials and Dimensions
Oak, ash, or maple, ebonized. Ebonized cane trim. Height: 29–32″. Width: 25–27″. Depth: 11–12″.

Locality and Period
New York. c. 1903–12.

Comment
Attributed to Roycroft Industries of East Aurora, New York, this piece is a close copy of an English Arts and Crafts book trough, showing how influential the English style was in America. Elbert Hubbard, owner of Roycroft, visited the Arts and Crafts designers in England shortly before 1900. He brought back many of their design concepts and began using them in Roycroft pieces.

Hints for Collectors
Book troughs were never very popular, possibly because the number and types of books they could hold was very limited. Consequently few examples remain today, and those are frequently mistaken for planters. The black paint, or ebonizing, is original and appropriate to the piece and should never be stripped off. Though their usefulness is limited, book troughs are worth buying for their interesting form.

Art Deco liquor cabinet

Description
Cabinet with molded lift top concealing shallow well. Inside of top mirrored. Below well, small 2-door storage area without shelves. Body mounted on bentwood legs, attached to solid base with slightly molded edge. Lacquered. Glued and screwed construction.

Materials and Dimensions
Pine. Lacquered inside and out. Hinges: steel butt. Height: 32–34″. Width: 24–26″. Depth: 15–16″.

Locality and Period
Better factories in the East and Midwest. c. 1925–40.

Comment
Liquor cabinets are a relatively recent phenomenon, having evolved from the sideboard, or, more accurately, the part of the sideboard used for wine storage. The first liquor cabinets appeared in the late 19th century, but the majority date from the 20th.

Hints for Collectors
These Art Deco pieces have a distinctly modern look and fit easily into the contemporary home. Their relatively small size makes them good for apartments, too. Examples with the original finish can often be bought quite reasonably at flea markets and small antiques shops, although pieces in pristine condition will cost considerably more. Many examples found in antiques shops have been relacquered, often in different colors than those they bore originally. Most 1930s pieces were lacquered gray, white, or black, but restored lacquer finishes may be in green, red, or other vibrant colors.

Art Deco humidor

Description
Boxlike humidor with flat top molded at sides. 1-door cupboard, veneered in radiating diamond-shaped motif in light and dark wood, opens to reveal a copper-lined storage area. Cupboard supported at each side by 3 grooved stiles with chamfered ends, attached 2–3″ below top. Stiles joined at base by stretchers resting on 2 shaped, grooved shoe feet. Glued and nailed construction.

Materials and Dimensions
Walnut and walnut veneer over pine. Stile grooves and feet painted black to simulate ebony. Hinges: steel butt. Pulls: circular Bakelite disks on rectangular chrome or steel bases with chamfered ends, mounted vertically. Liner: copper. Height: 21–24″. Width: 13–16″. Depth: 10–11″.

Locality and Period
Larger factories throughout the East and Midwest. c. 1928–40.

Comment
Humidors are designed to keep pipe tobacco moist and fresh. A few 19th-century examples are known, but the great majority date from this century. Like the example illustrated, they were often designed to be part of a matching parlor or living room set that would include a sofa, occasional tables, and various chairs.

Hints for Collectors
Although these humidors often resemble small Art Deco bedside or liquor cabinets, they can be distinguished because they were always originally lined in metal. Even if the lining has been removed, tack holes will show where it was once attached. Although they can be used to store tobacco, these humidors are useful for storing other small items as well.

Dough box on stand

Description
Long box with removable lid on stand. Top of box often battened at each end to prevent warping. Box has tapered sides that are recessed into front and back. Interior well without dividers. Stand is dovetailed into box and has horizontal frame with valanced front skirt. Rectangular legs tapered toward bottom. Usually painted. Dovetailed, pegged, nailed, and screwed construction.

Materials and Dimensions
Pine, poplar, walnut, cherry, maple, or mixed woods. Often painted red, blue, green, brown, or gray; sometimes grain- or sponge-painted. Height: 26–32″. Width: 34–39″. Depth: 21–24″.

Locality and Period
New Jersey, Pennsylvania, Ohio, and parts of Virginia. c. 1750–1850.

Comment
The dough box on a stand or frame is also known as a kneading table. Its production was confined primarily to those areas where German immigrants settled. Rising bread dough was stored in the box, then kneaded on the top, which was also used as a general work surface. Tabletop dough boxes are more common than those on a frame.

Hints for Collectors
The dough box on a stand is very popular with collectors—so much so that in the past 50 years many plain boxes have been fitted with legs to supply the demand. To make sure a stand is original, turn the box over and look for signs of wear on the bottom. Scratches and other marks indicate that a box was slid on and off a work table and did not originally have a stand.

Colonial Revival tea cart

Description
2-part tea cart. Top has removable glass tray in molded frame with 2 demilune handles; 2 symmetrically shaped drop leaves at sides. At one end, baize-lined drawer for silver. Baluster-turned stiles support an unmolded, rectangular shelf with shaped corner brackets. Oblong battens on underside of shelf at each end. 2 sets of wheels, the larger pair wood with turned spokes and rubber tires; the smaller pair brass, also with rubber tires. Nailed, screwed, glued, and dovetailed construction.

Materials and Dimensions
Walnut; sometimes maple stained to resemble mahogany. Secondary wood pine. Hinges: brass or iron butt. Pulls: brass or turned wooden knobs. Height: 27–29″. Width: 26–28″. Depth: 16–17″.

Locality and Period
Large factories in the East and Midwest. c. 1910–40.

Comment
Though found in late Victorian and Art Deco styles, most tea carts are in the Colonial Revival mode. They were made both with and without removable glass trays.

Hints for Collectors
Not often used today for their original purpose, tea carts are suitable as television or stereo carriers. They are easy to locate in used-furniture stores and secondhand shops and are usually reasonably priced. The earlier examples have handcrafted details and are most desirable. Some carts that originally had glass trays have lost them over the years. Replacing the glass is perfectly acceptable and does not substantially lessen the value of a piece.

Modern tea cart

Description
3-tiered serving cart with glass shelves. Upper 2 shelves rest in rectangular metal frames and are removable. Bottom shelf traylike, with low gallery at each end. Rectangular metal stiles flare out at top and are joined by glass panels to form handles. Lower ends of stiles curve in and are joined by rectangular metal rails on which lower shelf rests; stiles mounted on swiveling casters. Welded and screwed construction.

Materials and Dimensions
Stainless or tubular steel; shelf frames sometimes aluminum. Shelves shatterproof glass, sometimes frosted. Casters: steel and hard rubber. Height: 28–30″. Width: 29–33″. Depth: 16–18″.

Locality and Period
Better manufacturers in the East and Midwest. c. 1930–50.

Comment
Tea carts first appeared in the 19th century; early Victorian examples were made of wood, and later ones, of wood, rattan, and glass. In the late 1920s, the use of industrial materials like stainless steel led to sleek, modern-looking carts that went with the late Art Deco or Art Moderne furnishings of the period.

Hints for Collectors
Though these tea carts were manufactured relatively recently, they are still not very common. For the most part, collectors have little interest in them, and often confuse them with examples made in the past 20 years, which frequently have plastic shelves and thin steel or aluminum tubing. Authentic period pieces can be found in secondhand-furniture shops and similar outlets and blend well with the industrial furnishings that are so popular today.

Description
Set of storage or display shelves with overhanging top above 4 shelves. Top and 3 highest shelves decorated with applied, sausage-turned molding; lowest shelf with plain molded edge. Shelves supported by rope-turned corner stiles that flare out sharply below lowest shelf to terminate in carved paw feet, sometimes with casters. Glued, screwed, and nailed construction.

Materials and Dimensions
Oak; also walnut or hardwood, such as ash or maple, with pine shelves. Casters, when present: iron and wood. Height: 34–38″. Width: 21–24″. Depth: 17–19″.

Locality and Period
Factories throughout the East and Midwest. c. 1880–1910.

Comment
Sets of shelves served various purposes in the Victorian home. They were used to display the knickknacks so popular at the time or to store magazines. Since most were mass-produced, they were inexpensive and could be owned by nearly everyone. Similar pieces listed in manufacturers' catalogues of the time were generally listed simply as "sets of shelves."

Hints for Collectors
The workmanship and quality of Victorian shelves varied greatly. Some are plain or poorly constructed, while others are sturdy and well decorated. The carved feet and applied decorative molding of the piece shown here mark it as one of the better examples and, for that reason, desirable. Always be sure to examine both applied molding and carved feet; replacing parts of either is difficult and expensive.

Revolving book and magazine rack

Description
Cagelike set of revolving shelves, mounted on a separate, X-shaped base. Overhanging, molded top. 1–2 thin board shelves. Sides of shelves have slatlike boards mounted vertically and supported by horizontal crosspieces. Each side has 3–4 slats and an open area through which books are inserted. Heavy unmolded base consists of 2 thick pieces of wood joined at right angles, mounted on 4 casters. Unit revolves on vertical metal rod running through center. Nailed, glued, and screwed construction.

Materials and Dimensions
Walnut or oak; also pine and ash or hickory, stained to imitate walnut or cherry. Rod: iron. Casters: iron or brass. Height: 32–40″. Diameter: 19–22″.

Locality and Period
Shops and factories throughout the East and Midwest. c. 1890–1935.

Comment
Revolving book and magazine racks were a Victorian invention, and typical of the era in their practicality. Early examples were of walnut or mixed woods stained to look like walnut or cherry, but by 1910 most were made of oak in the simple, rectilinear Mission style.

Hints for Collectors
Practical and attractive, revolving book racks may be used today for their original purpose or for anything from plant stand to serving table. They are relatively inexpensive and often found at auctions. Better examples are of sturdier and more complex construction. Avoid pieces in which the revolving mechanism is damaged; it can be expensive to repair.

Mission-style bookshelves

Description
Small set of 3–4 unmolded shelves. Each shelf mounted inside and fastened to 4 corner stiles that rise 2–3″ above top shelf and terminate in tapered, blunt ends. 1–2 smaller slats on sides of shelves between front and back stiles. Plain legs and feet extensions of stiles. Screwed and nailed construction.

Materials and Dimensions
Typically oak, sometimes quartersawed. Occasionally ash, maple, or hickory stiles and pine shelves, all stained to imitate walnut or cherry. Height: 34–38″. Width: 18–23″. Depth: 10–12″.

Locality and Period
Large factories throughout the East and Midwest; also hobbyists. c. 1900–35.

Comment
Small sets of shelves like these were made in great numbers and sold in shops as well as by mail. When shipped, they arrived in sections ready to be screwed together. Because they had no cross bracing and were made of relatively light materials, the shelves were easily broken and often repaired. Consequently right-angle metal supports were frequently added under the shelves. Until World War II, shelving units like the one shown here were a popular manual arts project in high schools throughout the United States.

Hints for Collectors
Among the least expensive of the popular Mission-style pieces, these shelves make good plant or display stands. Look for the more solidly made examples and the relatively small number with the label or mark of an important maker, such as Stickley, Roycroft, or Limbert.

Victorian bamboo shelves

Description
Etagèrelike set of 3–4 solid shelves, with lightly molded edges, in decorative bamboo framework. At rear, 3–4 bamboo stretchers are topped by a gallerylike unit of horizontal, vertical, and angled spindles arranged in geometric form. 4 stiles decorated with painted or burned designs, and topped by turned, ball-shaped finials. Between stiles at sides, short pieces of bamboo set gallery fashion to simulate turned spindles. Plain legs and slightly knobbed feet extensions of stiles. Screwed construction.

Materials and Dimensions
Bamboo, or hardwood turned and stained to simulate bamboo. Shelves pine or oak. May have brass finials. Height: 46–55″. Width: 24–32″. Depth: 10–13″.

Locality and Period
Large factories in the East and Midwest. Some made in the Orient for the American market. c. 1875–90.

Comment
Bamboo display shelves were popular with the Victorians, who were interested in anything Oriental. Because bamboo was both strong and light, it was a practical material for furniture. The geometric patterns seen here were meant to resemble the shoji screens used as room dividers in Japan.

Hints for Collectors
Once abundant, Victorian bamboo shelves are not easy to find, although similar sets of shelves are being imported today from Hong Kong and Taiwan. The new ones are much lighter than 19th-century examples and most are poorly made. They are easily recognized by their lack of finials and decoration, as well a by their lack of wear.

Description
Tall, triangular set of graduated shelves, with largest at bottom.
4–6 shelves with bowed or serpentine fronts, supported by
baluster- or spool-turned spindles, each one terminating in a
steeple or ball-turned finial. Sides have pierced galleries 2–3″
high, with uppermost ones the tallest and most elaborately
scrolled. Ball-turned legs and feet attached through lowest shelf,
usually about 3–4″ above floor. Nailed, screwed, and glued
construction.

Materials and Dimensions
Walnut, ash, or maple; ash and maple sometimes stained to
resemble walnut or cherry. Sometimes with stained pine shelves.
Height: 55–60″. Width: 12–21″. Depth: 10–18″.

Locality and Period
Large factories throughout the East and Midwest. c. 1860–80.

Comment
Known as whatnots, elaborately shaped corner shelves were
very common in Victorian parlors and sitting rooms. The shelves
were usually filled with small Staffordshire figures, Sandwich
glass, and other decorative objects. They are closely related to
the larger and more elaborate Victorian étagères, which are
usually more expensive.

Hints for Collectors
Whatnots are being reproduced in various sizes today; some are
as short as 3′ and others as tall as 5′. To determine if a piece is
new, check for a new finish, lack of wear, and a general
skimpiness of material. Among older examples, the choicer ones
are well-made pieces in walnut, with elaborate turnings and
molding. Avoid pieces in which the galleries are broken; they are
expensive to repair.

Mission-style magazine pedestal

Description
Tall, narrow storage unit with thick, unmolded, overhanging top. Square case tapers out from top to bottom. 4–5 graduated shelves widen and deepen toward bottom. Exposed, wedged tenons both 3–4″ below top and as part of lowest shelf. Roycroft trademark and stylized floral decoration incised into 1 side. Feet simple, cutout extensions of side boards. Pegged and wedged mortise-and-tenon construction.

Materials and Dimensions
Oak and quartersawed oak, fumed or darkened. Height: 62–66″. Top: 14–15″ square. Base: 17–18″ square.

Locality and Period
The Roycroft factory, East Aurora, New York. c. 1908–15.

Comment
The Roycroft community near Buffalo, New York, founded in 1895, began to manufacture furniture in 1900. Each piece was entirely handcrafted, its style influenced by the English Arts and Crafts movement. Roycroft Industries, as it was known, produced neither the quantity nor variety of furnishings turned out by Stickley and other Mission-style makers, and today examples from its shop are relatively uncommon.

Hints for Collectors
While smaller pieces are fairly easy to find, a large, signed example of Roycroft furniture is not. Most pieces were signed or marked with a brand, so be sure to look for it. Mission-style pieces were sometimes painted later, so it may be necessary to remove a coat or two of paint to find the mark. Unlike the Stickley marks, the Roycroft one is usually in a conspicuous place, often on the side or top of a piece.

Semicircular stepped shelves

Description
Set of curved display shelves. 3 flat boards cut in scalloped steps and mounted vertically. Across these, 3 semicircular boards (6–8″ wide) create horizontal shelves. At top, smaller, half-moon shelf resting on finial-like ends of 3 vertical supports, which taper down to flat feet. Usually painted. Nailed or, rarely, nailed and dovetailed construction.

Materials and Dimensions
Pine, cedar, or poplar. Usually painted green, red, blue, or white. Height: 36–40″. Width: 48–52″ at widest point. Depth: 24–32″ at deepest point.

Locality and Period
Throughout the United States. c. 1880–1940.

Comment
Carpenters and handymen made semicircular, or demilune, stepped shelves like these for florists' shops or plant nurseries, where they were used to display potted plants and vases with bouquets. Many were also used in late Victorian homes, on porches and in solariums. Since most were made by carpenters, not cabinetmakers, they are apt to be rather crudely constructed.

Hints for Collectors
Neither scarce nor, in many cases, particularly well made, demilune steps are still in demand among collectors and dealers —but not for their original use. In shops today, they most often display antiques, especially country objects like stoneware pots. In homes, they are likely to be found in the kitchen, filled with cooking utensils.

Art Deco wall shelves

Description
Set of 4 shelves that are progressively wider and deeper from top to bottom; front of shelves veneered. Backboard rectangular. Top shelves have molded, downcurved ends. 2 square stainless-steel columns near front extend downward to lowest shelf. Ends of lowest shelf curve upward and are joined to shelf above it by 2 square wooden blocks. Lacquered. Screwed and glued construction.

Materials and Dimensions
Various hardwoods: maple, birch, or ash. Also pine. Rosewood veneer. Lacquered gray, pale green, white, or brown. Columns: steel or chrome. Height: 31–33″. Width: 42–45″. Depth: 12–13″.

Locality and Period
A few quality factories in the East and Midwest. c. 1930–40.

Comment
The creation of Paul T. Frankl, a well-known furniture designer of the 1930s, these shelves were designed to be hung, but can also be put on a flat surface. Originally, they were part of a bedroom set and, like most designer furniture, represented the top of the line. Similar pieces in greater quantity were also made by mass producers, and these constitute most of what is available to today's collector.

Hints for Collectors
Furniture identifiable as the work of an important designer like Paul Frankl is always more valuable than an almost identical, mass-produced piece. Even without identifying marks, the origin of a piece can still be traced by using period furniture makers' catalogues.

20th-century mirror-back shelves

Description
Heavy set of shelves with central mirror at back. Mirror frame wider at sides than at top, mitered at upper corners, and mounted on a rectangular base 9–10″ deep. 2 flaring, rectangular shelves, with molded edges, ⅔ of way up each side of frame; shelves covered with imitation lizard skin. Glued, screwed, and nailed construction.

Materials and Dimensions
Maple or birch, lacquered and covered with imitation lizard skin made of laminated textile. Plywood back. Shelves and base black glass; mirror clear glass. Height: 31–32″. Width: 44–45″. Depth: 9–10″.

Locality and Period
Factories in the East and Midwest. c. 1935–55.

Comment
This set of mirrored shelves was designed to be hung on a wall or mounted on a flat, tablelike top. Relatively narrow and made of glass, the shelves were unsuitable for displaying anything other than knickknacks. Bold pieces such as this were popular during the 1950s, when imitation animal skins and raised or embossed surfaces were in style.

Hints for Collectors
Though barely 30 years old, pieces like the one shown here are already attracting enthusiastic collectors. While a few shops in big cities sell them, the best places to look are secondhand stores and rummage sales, where they still cost very little. These shelving units are relatively common, so avoid pieces that need repair.

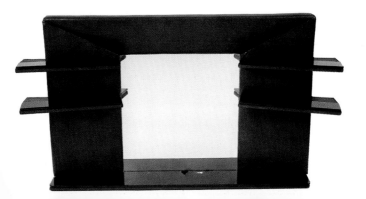

Description
Set of low book or storage shelves. Rectangular, unmolded top protrudes beyond base at front, back, and sides. Unmolded shelf below also protrudes and has 2 battens with chamfered ends attached to its underside. 2 wide boardlike stiles have chamfered upper edges joining top. Stiles curve in to meet nearly square, unmolded base that is, in addition, a shelf. Base rests on 2 rectangular block feet. Usually painted. Glued and screwed construction.

Materials and Dimensions
Ash, oak, maple, or pine. Usually painted or lacquered in a pastel shade, most often an off-white or blond tone. Height: 21–23″. Width: 26–29″. Depth: 11–13″.

Locality and Period
Larger factories throughout the East and Midwest. c. 1930–45.

Comment
The "blond look" in furnishings was especially popular during the 1930s. Many pieces, including chests of drawers, tables, and sets of shelves, were either made from maple and given a clear finish, or made from some other wood and then painted to resemble maple. This color preference cut across the price spectrum from the finest to the least expensive furnishings.

Hints for Collectors
1930s blond furniture is staging a comeback, and as a result prices are increasing. Still, inexpensive pieces can be found, particularly in secondhand stores and at yard sales in the Midwest.

Art Deco sofa-side shelves

Description
Set of 3 low, molded shelves extending from single board.
Slightly overhanging top shelf is approximately ½ length of
lower 2 shelves. Short, rectangular wall extends out between
center and upper shelves. Bottom shelf supports rectangular wall
placed at right angle to wall above. Plain board back extends
from top shelf to floor. 2 short stump feet at front of shelves.
Screwed construction.

Materials and Dimensions
Maple; also ash, oak, or pine stained to resemble maple. Height:
22–24". Width: 29–31". Depth: 15–16".

Locality and Period
Large factories throughout the East and Midwest. c. 1935–45.

Comment
This piece was produced by the well-known firm of Heywood-
Wakefield, but similar sets of shelves were made by many other
contemporary furniture factories. They were intended to be
placed at the end of a sofa, with the open area of the shelves
pointing into the room. Typically, a lamp might occupy the top
shelf, with books, magazines, or knickknacks on the lower ones.
Such units were often used in pairs.

Hints for Collectors
These shelves are in the blond wood so favored by designers in
the 1920s and 1930s and are essentially Art Deco in feeling,
though they have some elements of the Modern style. The blond
look is once again gaining popularity, so buy now before prices
rise further. Heywood-Wakefield examples are particularly
desirable. Look for the firm label under the shelves.

Mission-style sectional bookcase

Description
Set of bookshelves assembled from 4–5 separate units. Separate,
flat top with unmolded edge grooved to fit into lower sections.
Each unit has hinged glass front in wooden frame, also grooved
for stacking, and supported on X-shaped metal supports.
Separate, grooved base with slightly tapered, square legs.
Nailed, screwed, and glued construction.

Materials and Dimensions
Usually oak with plywood back; sometimes pine with oak veneer
or cherry stained to imitate walnut, also with plywood back.
Hinges: brass or steel butt. Pulls: brass knobs. Shelf supports:
steel. Height: 48–55″. Width: 44–48″. Depth: 12–15″.

Locality and Period
Large factories throughout the East and Midwest. c. 1905–35.

Comment
Developed in the late 19th century, the sectional bookcase was
popular for both home and office. The separate bookshelves could
be stacked to the desired height and completed with a matching
top and bottom. Most such pieces were made in quantity by large
furniture factories and sold to libraries and businesses. Many still
have their original labels.

Hints for Collectors
Though not as inexpensive as they once were, sectional
bookcases are still fairly good buys. Sturdy and attractive, they
are a practical addition to any home library. In choosing
individual units, be sure to avoid any that are damaged, as they
will weaken the entire structure.

Art Deco skyscraper bookcase

Description
Asymmetrically shaped bookcase with plain, unmolded top, ornamented with rectangular wooden slab 1–2″ high. 8–10 cubbyholes of varying shapes and sizes, above 3–4 long, narrow drawers, increasing in length toward base, to a full-length drawer at bottom. Plain, plinthlike base. Plain board sides, decorated with square blocks at floor level. No feet. Nailed and glued construction.

Materials and Dimensions
Pine; also birch or maple, usually darkened with stain. Pulls: rectangular wooden slats applied horizontally. Height: 44–47″. Width: 34–37″. Depth: 12–14″.

Locality and Period
Shops in the East and Midwest. c. 1928–40.

Comment
The "skyscraper" look in furniture was a reflection of the architecture that began to develop in New York City and elsewhere soon after World War I. Tall, angular skyscrapers, like the majestic Empire State Building, symbolized the bold, new style of the modern age. Skyscraper bookcases, chests of drawers, and even desks were a mark of sophisticated taste throughout the 1930s.

Hints for Collectors
Typical skyscraper furniture is rarely recognized for what it is, except by a few avid collectors. Look for it in used-furniture stores, or at bazaars and yard sales. Though the maker of this piece is not known, designers like Paul Frankl developed a "skyscraper" style; marked pieces by them are increasing in value.

313 Country bucket bench

Description
Simple utility piece with plain board sides that curve at top to
form base for a narrow, molded shelf. Below, 2 deeper shelves;
upper 1 has surface carved in 2 squares. 2 lower shelves have
back between them, forming boxlike storage area. Plain bootjack
feet extensions of side boards. Nailed or dovetailed construction.

Materials and Dimensions
Pine or poplar. Natural or stained red, blue, yellow, white, or
brown. Height: 27–32″. Width: 25–28″. Depth: 12–14″.

Locality and Period
New England west to Texas and throughout the South.
c. 1820–80.

Comment
When water came from a well or hand pump, every kitchen,
washroom, or porch had a bucket bench. Two wooden or metal
buckets sat on the central shelf, while washing materials, bowls,
and pitchers were stored below. The narrow upper shelf was a
handy place to put a soap dish, razor, or towel.

Hints for Collectors
Most bucket benches are rather crude, and an example with
appealing lines and original stain, like the one shown here, is
rare. Even a unique example, however, must be checked for dry
rot. Since these benches often got soaked with water, many show
the brown, powdery rot, which weakens and destroys wood
fibers. Look for it particularly around the feet and on the bucket
shelf. If there are signs of dry rot, no matter how charming the
piece is, it is not worth buying.

Oak mirrored hall rack

Description
Tall, shallow clothing stand, with mirror above and seat below.
Large mirror has 1–6 metal hooks on each side, and an arched
top set in a molded frame with valanced base. Back wraps
around to form 5–7″ side boards curved at top and a yoke-shaped
cornice. At seat level, side boards shaped to form armlike
gallery, surrounding slightly overhanging lift top that opens to
reveal storage chest. Plain skirt. French feet cutout extensions
of side boards. Nailed and glued construction.

Materials and Dimensions
Oak; sometimes quartersawed oak. Applied molding and
decorative details maple, stained to match. Hinges: brass or iron
butt. Hooks: brass or iron. Height: 68–73″. Width: 39–45″.
Depth: 15–19″.

Locality and Period
Large factories throughout the East and Midwest. c. 1880–1930.

Comment
At one time, every respectable house or apartment had an
entrance hall, and every entrance hall had a hall rack or tree.
Racks generally combined clothing hooks, a large mirror, and a
storage chest for bulky items like overshoes. Although the
example shown here is curvilinear in form and somewhat Art
Nouveau in style, it is still one of the plainer hall racks. They
were often much more ornate.

Hints for Collectors
Hall racks remain popular and practical today, and are in some
demand. Examples in antiques shops may command a high price.
To find a more reasonably priced piece, check yard sales or
country auctions, or, better yet, put an ad in a rural newspaper.
There are still lots of racks in old homes.

Description

Combination clothes rack and umbrella stand. Carved central column mounted with 2 sets of deer horns, the higher set fitted with carved wooden head, and oval mirror in gilded pineapple-shaped frame resting on plinth. At each side of shaped and gilded central column, elaborate, leaf-shaped supports with clothes hooks, bound to column with flexible metal rods. Heavy, shaped base mounted on short, scroll-shaped feet. 2 depressions in base for metal umbrella stands, with eyeglass-shaped metal supports above. Carved, nailed, and glued construction.

Materials and Dimensions

Pine; painted, stenciled, and gilded. Hooks and supports: iron. Rods: steel. Height: 80–86″. Width: 36–42″. Depth: 12–15″.

Locality and Period

Throughout the United States. c. 1880–1940.

Comment

The Victorian love for hall trees expressed itself not only in the purchase of factory-made examples, but also, if less frequently, in the creation at home of some remarkable pieces of folk art. The piece shown here is unique, as no 2 pieces of folk art are ever quite alike. Nevertheless, it reflects the originality, flamboyance, and love of detail that characterize the best of such work.

Hints for Collectors

Pieces like this one are seldom available and should be bought when they are seen. In addition, since they are one of a kind, they make an exception to the rule against buying damaged objects. Even if such a piece needs extensive restoration, it is still probably worth buying.

Victorian cast-iron hall tree

Description
Elaborate floral-form coat rack. Top narrows to columnar shaft, supporting delicate curvilinear arms, mounted with 6 S-shaped coat hooks. Looplike finial topped with foliate motif. Heavy, vase-shaped base with triangular front feet, and cutout rectangular area to hold drip pan. Welded and screwed construction.

Materials and Dimensions
Cast iron. Often painted black, white, or brown. Drip pan: tin, brass, or copper. Height: 70–76″. Width: 30–36″. Depth: 10–14″.

Locality and Period
Foundries and large factories throughout the East and Midwest. c. 1860–90.

Comment
Because of the weight and relative fragility of cast iron, it was generally used only for smaller umbrella racks; a large hall tree like this was relatively uncommon. The lush floral forms so appealing to Victorians were especially suited to cast iron, as the many Victorian tables, chairs, and hall trees made of cast iron illustrate.

Hints for Collectors
The large size of this cast-iron hall tree makes it especially desirable. A small amount of rust on such a piece is not a problem; it can be removed readily and is seldom structurally damaging. Breaks and missing elements are more serious, however, and may require costly restoration. Where major repairs are required, it is advisable to get an estimate on the needed work before buying the piece.

Bamboo hall rack

Description
Tall hat, coat, and umbrella rack. Rear stiles rise to form framework for 6 bamboo clothes hooks. 2 horizontal rods near top form base for 2 square mirrors in bamboo frames, set on the diagonal. Below mirrors, 2 decorative forms of straight and curving rods. Boxlike lower section of 8 joined rods, the upper 2 divided by shorter rods into slots for umbrellas or canes, the lower 2 housing rectangular drip pan. Plain feet extensions of stiles. Screwed construction.

Materials and Dimensions
Bamboo, sometimes decorated with bands of paint or burned (pyrographic) areas. Drip pan: tin, brass, or copper. Height: 80–84″. Width: 30–34″. Depth: 10–13″.

Locality and Period
Larger factories in the East and Midwest. c. 1890–1920.

Comment
Bamboo has long appealed to both eastern and western cabinetmakers because of its strength and durability. It was not until the Victorian era, however, that the material was widely used in this country. The objects most commonly seen are hall trees, sets of shelves, and planters. It was also the framework for wicker furniture.

Hints for Collectors
Do not confuse old bamboo furniture with modern examples. New pieces lack the dark, aged look of the earlier ones, as well as the usual wear and damage. Earlier pieces also have handwork like wicker-wound joints, chamfered corners, and brass finials, while mass-produced, modern examples do not.

Anglo-Japanese hall rack

Description
Tall clothes and umbrella stand. Upper part has small, herringbone-pattern plaque and angled, open cornice. Below, narrow stiles and rails forming geometric patterns, within which are openwork areas, a fan-shaped device, and a rectangular mirror. 6 metal coat hooks on stiles and rails. Square stiles support narrow drawer with incised line decoration and shaped brackets. Rectangular base with tapered bracket feet and 2 cutouts for drip pans. Rear feet plain extensions of stiles. Nailed, glued, and screwed construction.

Materials and Dimensions
Cherry, maple, or other hardwood; sometimes stained to imitate ebony or mahogany. Pulls: brass rosette mounts with bail handles or brass knobs. Drip pans: tin, brass, or copper. Hooks: brass or iron. Height: 79–82″. Width: 23–26″. Depth: 10–12″.

Locality and Period
A few of the larger factories in the East and Midwest. c. 1880–1910.

Comment
The Anglo-Japanese version of the Victorian style, while popular abroad, arrived late in the United States and had little impact. Its effect is seen primarily in the galleried tables and stands, folding chairs, and screenlike hall racks of the late 19th and early 20th centuries.

Hints for Collectors
Pieces in the Anglo-Japanese style are often overlooked and can be bought quite reasonably. Their lines usually blend well with the most modern interior. Smaller auctions and antiques shops are good sources for these unusual Victorian pieces. The example shown here is missing 1 foot, which slightly decreases its value.

319 Oak hall rack

Description
Tall hall rack with slatlike rear stiles joined by a horizontal yoke back decorated with incised lines and circular devices. Below, short gallery of 3 spindles. Within this framework, vertical and horizontal slats support long, rectangular mirror. Below, incised side stretchers extend to front stiles and are joined by incised front board with scalloped skirt. Central square shelf creates 2 rectangular openings for umbrellas or canes. Directly below, 2 metal drip pans set into lower full-length shelf at base. Plain lower skirt. Front stiles turned and ⅓ length of back ones; turned ball feet. Rear feet plain extensions of stiles. 6–10 metal clothes hooks arranged at various places on frame. Glued mortise-and-tenon and screwed construction.

Materials and Dimensions
Oak and quartersawed oak. Applied decoration, when present, maple or other hardwoods. Clothes hooks: brass. Drip pans: tin, usually painted white. Height: 77–81″. Width: 29–34″. Depth: 14–16″.

Locality and Period
Large factories throughout the East and Midwest. c. 1880–1930.

Comment
Oak was by far the most popular material for the Victorian hall tree or rack. The openwork form is most common, although examples with solid backs and lift-top storage wells were also made.

Hints for Collectors
Oak hall trees similar to this are being reproduced. Be wary of pieces that show little wear or age and have complete sets of shiny, new brass clothes hooks.

Oak hall tree

Description
Tall storage piece with turned central rod terminating in ball-like finial, below which are attached 6–8 short dowels (5–7″ long) from which to hang hats or clothing. Bottom of rod plain or terminating in round drop. Rod may also have turned decoration at center. 4 shaped feet, sometimes with metal caps, attached to central rod with screws. Screwed construction.

Materials and Dimensions
Oak; also oak with ash or hickory clothing rods stained to match oak. Caps: brass or tin. Height: 65–70″. Diameter at base: 28–36″.

Locality and Period
Manufacturers throughout the United States. c. 1880–1930.

Comment
Simple hall trees or clothes racks like this were made in large numbers and are still easy to find. When new, they sold for as little as $1.25 and could be ordered through the mail. They arrived knocked down and were assembled at home. Most turn-of-the-century houses had 3 or 4, primarily in outer hallways or entrance foyers. They were also used in bedrooms.

Hints for Collectors
These practical hall trees are still in demand, so much so that they are frequently reproduced. An early example, such as the piece shown here, will be bent from the weight of the clothing that was hung on it over the years. A new piece will be straight, and its feet will lack the wear on the bottom that comes from being moved around on the floor. Many early pieces have new dowels, since they often broke off and had to be replaced.

Modern music stand

Description
Tripod-shaped music stand. Music platform composed of 4 slightly curved wooden slats; bottom slat has a raised 2″ gallery. Slats fastened horizontally across fishhook-shaped vertical member that divides into 3 curvilinear legs or supports near floor level. Glued and laminated construction.

Materials and Dimensions
Oak; rosewood slats. Height: 54–55″. Width: 23–24″. Depth: 17–18″.

Locality and Period
Produced in limited quantities in the East. c. 1950–60.

Comment
Music stands appeared in quantity as early as the Empire period. However, most were made during the Victorian era, when every middle-class home had a piano and amateur recitals were held often, requiring several music stands for the participants. Some of these stands were of brass and iron, but most were made of wood, often in a style contemporary to the period, such as Eastlake or Rococo Revival.

Hints for Collectors
This music stand was created by the well-known American furniture designer, Wendell Castle. Lyrical in form, it reflects the sophisticated modern look developed after World War II. Designer pieces such as this are often extremely collectible as soon as they are produced and thus violate the traditional requirement that an object acquire some age for value. Become familiar with the work of contemporary designers in order to recognize pieces that will continue to increase in value and desirability.

Description
Triangular folding metal stand. 2 long tubular rods with turned
acornlike finials are joined 4–5″ below their apex by a 5–6″ rod
with turned pieces at each end; second joining rod (17–19″ long)
near base. Slightly above longer rod, 2 applied knobs. Long
tubular back support extends from short rod and attaches to
main unit by a metal chain. 2 turned, acorn-shaped feet; back rod
plain. Welded and screwed construction.

Materials and Dimensions
Tubular brass or brass and cast iron. Iron examples always
painted solid colors. Chain: brass or iron. Height: 56–62″. Width:
23–26″. Depth: 24–28″ (open).

Locality and Period
Metal shops throughout the East and Midwest. c. 1870–1915.

Comment
Triangular stands for the display of oil paintings or large prints
were once common in Victorian homes. Some were of brass, such
as the example illustrated, or painted iron. Others were of wood
in the Gothic Revival or Eastlake styles and might be elaborately
painted, fret-cut, and even inlaid with mother-of-pearl and
semiprecious stones.

Hints for Collectors
Brass stands for the display of paintings have been reproduced
over the past few years. Be wary of examples that show little
wear on the bottom of the metal feet and few scratches at points
of contact, such as the large knobs on which the paintings rested.
In most cases, early brass was thicker than that used for
reproductions. Examine a period piece in a museum collection to
learn what to look for.

Modern room divider

Description
Openwork trapezoidal space divider with 4 solid wood sides, each 4–5″ wide. Inside wooden framework, a diagonal grid of wooden slats, forming squares. Cone-shaped, turned legs slant out. Feet square blocks with rounded corners. Glued and screwed construction.

Materials and Dimensions
Oak, cherry, or mahogany. Sometimes painted a solid color, commonly black or white. Height: 46–48″. Width: 53–56″. Depth: 6–8″.

Locality and Period
Large factories in the East and Midwest. c. 1945–55.

Comment
Dividers of various sorts have been used for years. In the Victorian era, for example, fabric screens or dividers of openwork bamboo were popular. Designed to suggest different areas of a room rather than actually screen off one part, this modern example has a lyrical feeling in its overall shape and almost resembles a musical scale.

Hints for Collectors
Though of no great age, this kind of quality piece appeals to sophisticated buyers looking for 1950s collectibles. Well made and unique in form, it is more like a sculpture than a piece of furniture. While not a one-of-a-kind item, manufacturers made only a limited number of these pieces and, for that reason, they should increase in value. The most desirable pieces still have their original finish, but refinished examples are more in demand than those that are badly worn.

Bamboo bar

Description
Kidney-shaped portable serving bar of upright bamboo trunks
mounted on a wooden base. Slightly overhanging, molded top
edged with split bamboo. Bamboo bar rail, steamed and bent to
shape, around front and sides, 5–7″ below top. Plain skirt
covered with shaped bamboo. Back open to interior, which has
1-shelf storage area. Stumplike feet with arched supports.
Nailed, screwed, and wrapped-rattan construction.

Materials and Dimensions
Bamboo and rattan, with pine shelf and base. Bar top: formica
over pine. Height: 41–44″. Width: 34–40″. Depth: 23–25″.

Locality and Period
Large factories throughout the United States. c. 1930–50.

Comment
Small home bars are a 20th-century creation that first appeared
in the late 1920s. Bamboo examples were often made to match
sets of bamboo porch or parlor furniture. Both fashionable and
light enough to be portable, they were very popular. Formica
tops are the most common, but glass and stainless steel were also
used.

Hints for Collectors
A good place to look for bamboo bars and related furnishings is in
Florida and California, where they were, and still are, popular.
New bamboo bars are imported today from Asia, but they are
not as sturdy or well built as those from the 1930s and 1940s.
Signs of age and a patina, or darkening of the wood, help identify
older pieces.

Description
Heavy sheet-metal trunk bound with wooden slats reinforced with brass. Lift top has 3–4 wooden slats and brass corner supports. Boxlike compartment (4–6″ deep) with snap-on lid is divided into 7–10 large and small storage units and fits across interior top. Compartment lifts out to allow access to rest of interior. Base of trunk reinforced like top, and may have small built-in wheels on bottom. 2 leather straps encircle entire trunk. Leather carrying handles on each side. Nailed and welded construction.

Materials and Dimensions
Sheet steel painted black, blue, or brown. Hardwood slats. Interior compartment thin wood covered with wallpaper or cloth. Bindings, locks, snaps, and hinges: brass. Height: 21–24″. Width: 33–36″. Depth: 19–21″.

Locality and Period
Larger factories throughout the United States. c. 1900–40.

Comment
Though commonly associated with oceanic travel, most so-called steamer trunks never got near salt water. They were, on the other hand, the successors to the 19th-century wooden flat- and dome-topped storage chests and traveling boxes. Earlier examples were smaller and of dome-topped tin, while later ones, such as the example illustrated, were of sturdier sheet metal.

Hints for Collectors
Metal trunks are popular collectibles. They can be used for storage or even travel, but most end up as coffee tables or display pieces. Avoid badly rusted trunks, for they will prove difficult to restore or repair. If they have been repainted, they can be stripped just like a piece of wooden furniture.

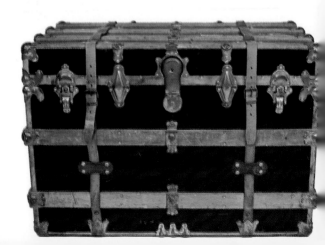

Federal knife box

Description
Lift-top container with sloping lid and serpentine front. Inlaid with pilasters in contrasting wood. Interior contains piece of wood cut out to hold knives of various sizes. Interior lid decorated with line-and-star inlay. Base molded to match top. Dovetailed or glued construction.

Materials and Dimensions
Mahogany, walnut, cherry, or birch; usually 2 or more hardwoods together. Secondary wood pine or maple. Inlay maple, satinwood, or boxwood. Hinges: iron or brass butt. Pulls: silver or silver-plated, round or oval mount with tiny ring. Escutcheons: silver or silver-plated oval. Height: 14–16″. Width: 9–11″. Depth: 7–8″.

Locality and Period
Southern New England west to Pennsylvania, south to Maryland; also made in England. c. 1780–1810.

Comment
Knife boxes are the most sophisticated of all household containers. Made from a variety of precious woods, they were used to hold the silver-handled table knives found only in the homes of the very wealthy. Typically made in pairs, they occupied a place of honor on top of the family sideboard.

Hints for Collectors
Many knife boxes were made in England for export and sale here, and were often decorated with symbols familiar to Americans, such as the eagle and Federal shield. For that reason the origins of a piece can be hard to determine. The use of native woods, like birch, maple, and pine, is helpful in identifying American examples, but one should always get a written guarantee of provenance.

Fire Screens

Before the introduction of central heating, fire screens were common in many homes, where they were placed near the occupants of the room to shield them from the heat and glare of fires. These devices date as far back as the Middle Ages, when people needed protection from the blazing fires that burned in massive fireplaces. The earliest American examples date from the 18th century. The most common American type is the pole screen—usually fitted into a pedestal atop a tripod base—adapted from English Queen Anne and Chippendale models. In construction, these resemble tilt-top tables, but their lines are more delicate.

Because they were luxury items, few 18th-century screens remain today; those that do can be difficult to date. It is tempting to consider the simplest screens with cabriole legs to be Queen Anne in style, dating from about the 1740s, but evidence proves that they were made after the Revolution, at the end of the Chippendale era. Although most Chippendale examples (330) have fairly large panels and elaborately carved pedestals and legs, the bases of others are more restrained, suggesting that the panels themselves were meant to provide most of their decoration. The panels displayed fine needlework or, later, paintings, often made by the women of the house, as well as prints or various fabrics.

In the Federal era, simplified screens were based on the earlier Colonial examples. A new type (328), with a smaller panel, a delicately turned pedestal, and curving, tapered legs, also became common. Like most Empire pieces, fire screens in that style (331) have heavier proportions. Their pedestals are simpler and often set on tripod platforms with scroll or ball feet. On later Empire examples, the frames are thicker. In the early 19th century, the cheval screen—a large rectangular screen mounted on 2 pairs of trestlelike legs—became popular in America.

Cheval screens (332) were common in elegant Victorian interiors and were made in all the fashionable Victorian styles. The form was particularly well suited to the eclectic 1880s, when Eastlake and Oriental-inspired examples were produced in brass, gilded wood, and various other materials. Colonial Revival fire screens (327), made several decades later, are relatively uncommon since fireplaces had been largely replaced by modern heating in the early 20th century.

Most fire screens have mortise-and-tenon construction. If a tripod base is present, it may be dovetailed into the central pole. Victorian and 20th-century examples may be glued or screwed together.

Fire screens have great decorative appeal for the modern collector. Few pieces have original needlework, but an appropriate period replacement does not substantially lower value.

Description
Fire screen with octagonal, oval, or rectangular gilt-edged panel consisting of woodblock-printed cloth or, less often, paper picture. Panel fastened onto long wooden pole by brass mount, allowing it to be raised and lowered. Pole fits into turned pillar set on round molded base or, more often, on tripod base.

Materials and Dimensions
Walnut and pine, usually with gilded details. Panel: printed paper or cloth. Fixtures: brass. Height: 61–65″. Diameter at base: 9–11″.

Locality and Period
Throughout the United States. c. 1900–30.

Comment
Since most Colonial Revival pieces were functional as well as decorative, and since fire screens were for the most part unnecessary by the early 20th century, fire screens in this style are uncommon. The screen shown here does not really resemble any American example. It is likely that the designer mistook an English design for an American design, a fairly common error made by Colonial Revival manufacturers.

Hints for Collectors
Colonial Revival pieces were made at every level of quality, and are not in great demand. Look for the best examples available, which you should be able to find at reasonable prices. Fire screens often came in pairs, and a matching set is always more valuable than a single example. Although fire screens are one of the more uncommon types of Colonial Revival furniture, their relative scarcity does not necessarily increase their price.

Description
Fire screen with rectangular leather panel set into and framed
by wooden backing. Panel fastened onto long wooden pole by
brass loop, allowing it to be raised and lowered. Pole topped by
urn-shaped finial and set into vase-shaped pedestal resting on
cylindrical base. 3 low, curved legs molded on top; rings separate
plain feet from legs. Legs sometimes square or rectangular, with
spade feet. Inlay sometimes present on legs and frame.

Materials and Dimensions
Mahogany. Inlay, when present, fruitwood. Panel: leather. Loop:
brass. Height: 57–61″. Width of panel: 12–14″.

Locality and Period
Better shops in the East. c. 1785–1820.

Comment
Fire screens were luxuries probably found only in upper-class
homes, where they added an accent of fashionable decoration.
Although it is difficult to identify the cities in which simple pieces
like the one shown here were made, this example is clearly
American. The combination of conservative elements, such as the
molded detail on the pedestal, and high-style elements, such as
the fashionably curved legs, is typical of American work early in
the Federal era.

Hints for Collectors
Look for fire screens with elaborately detailed pedestals or
panels. The most desirable still have their original panels; if they
are missing, replacements should be from the correct period. It
seems likely that the panels were originally protected with glass,
but examples with unbroken original glass are rarely found
today.

Chippendale fire screen

Description
Fire screen with square or rectangular needlework panel in molded wooden frame. Panel mounted by brass loop on simple wooden pole, allowing panel height to be adjusted. Pole set into vase-shaped pedestal with ring turnings; turned parts of pedestal occasionally have carved decoration. Tripod base has low cabriole legs and snake feet.

Materials and Dimensions
Mahogany. Panel: needlework or printed cotton fabric. Loop: brass. Height: 60–64″. Width of panel: 21–23″.

Locality and Period
Better shops in the East. c. 1760–80.

Comment
Early American cabinetmakers produced elegant Chippendale pieces; some were plain and others had elaborate carving. The fire screen illustrated here has a superbly turned pedestal and resembles examples made in Newport, Rhode Island. Fine carved decoration is typical of pieces made in Philadelphia.

Hints for Collectors
Chippendale fire screens are rare, especially fine examples like the one shown here. Since reproductions do exist, be sure to check for patina and subtle signs of wear on the feet and adjusting pole to make sure you are getting a period piece. Because many of the Chippendale fire screens that appear on the market are British, it is wise to have proof of American origin before you buy. A history of American ownership is also helpful. Look for a native American secondary wood behind the panel, or for the distinctive carving that is associated with some of the American centers.

Chippendale fire screen

Description
Fire screen with square or rectangular panel of printed cotton or
needlework set in molded wooden frame. Panel mounted by
brass loop to a plain cylindrical pole topped by a turned, pointed
finial; panel height adjustable. Pole set into vase-shaped pedestal
with rounded, reeded rim above plain ring-turned baluster on
spiral-fluted ball; pedestals are often plainer. Tripod base has 3
cabriole legs with carved scrolls on knees and sides. Paw feet
have carved claws clutching flattened balls.

Materials and Dimensions
Mahogany. Panel: needlework or printed cotton. Loop: brass.
Height: 54–58″. Width of panel: 21–23″.

Locality and Period
Better shops in the East. c. 1750–81.

Comment
Fire screens, made to shield people sitting in front of fireplaces,
appeared in America about 1750, but were used much earlier in
England. They often have fine needlework panels like the one
shown here, although printed cotton was also used. The 5-toed
feet and spiral flutings on the pedestal base of this screen are
unusual. Most Chippendale screens have plainer pedestals than
the example illustrated.

Hints for Collectors
Fire screens with tripod bases resemble small tripod-based
tables. Over the years, some fire screens have been converted to
tables, and some tables to fire screens. To make sure you are
getting an original fire screen, examine the base and the frame;
they should be made from the same wood and be in a similar
state of repair.

Empire fire screen

Description
Fire screen with rectangular needlework panel framed by scalloped wooden strips. Panel attached to rod by circular iron clamps, allowing it to be raised or lowered. Rod has urn-and-ball finial. Pedestal columnar or octagonal, tapering outward from top to bottom, with ring molding at top and bottom. Low, flat tripod or square base has scroll feet.

Materials and Dimensions
Mahogany and mahogany veneer over pine. Panel: wool needlework. Clamps: iron. Height: 60–64″. Width of panel: 17–19″.

Locality and Period
Throughout the United States. c. 1830–50.

Comment
Several American books on furniture design that were published about 1840 present pieces similar to the one shown here. Although the Gothic-style panel may be a replacement of the original, the subject matter would have been popular around 1840, when Gothic elements were often mixed with classical Empire ones.

Hints for Collectors
The simple, heavy lines of the piece shown here indicate that it probably dates from the latter part of the Empire era. Earlier examples from around 1820 have elaborate touches, such as exuberant molding. Although not common, Empire fire screens sometimes appear on the market and are usually reasonably priced. They are much easier to find than fire screens from the 18th century.

Description
Rectangular wooden fire screen with pictorial tapestry. Frame gilded wood, with Western and Oriental motifs. Top rail crowned by scalloped projection enclosing a fleur-de-lis flanked by Oriental motifs. Straight stiles have inscribed decoration. Top of frame consists of pierced 3-part panel carved in Oriental foliate pattern. Sides and bottom of frame outlined with applied decoration of angular Oriental motifs. Trestle base terminates in lion's-paw feet.

Materials and Dimensions
Pine, gilded. Panel: woolen tapestry. Height: 42–46″. Width of panel: 29–31″.

Locality and Period
New York, Boston, and other major eastern centers. c. 1875–90.

Comment
Trestle-supported rectangular fire screens, also called cheval screens, were 19th-century holdovers of an 18th-century form. Fire screens became more decorative than functional after 1850, and gilded examples were popular after 1870. The screen shown here has an interesting mixture of gilding, trestle legs, and Oriental-inspired ornament. Because of its overall angular, nonclassical design, this screen seems most closely tied to the Eastlake style, although it also has Renaissance Revival elements.

Hints for Collectors
Fire screens were still luxuries in the 19th century, so they are fairly rare. Because the fabric was often replaced, make sure the design is appropriate. Avoid pieces with damaged gilding. Regilding is difficult and expensive, and if there is substantial damage, a piece may not be worth restoring.

333 Eastlake brass fire screen

Description
Rectangular fire screen with embroidered, woven, or paper panel under glass, framed in brass. Top has straight rail resting on gallery of 7 vase-shaped spindles, each with a finial. Frame consists of stamped-brass strips with floral motifs, corner rosettes, and linear borders. Below frame, gallery of 9 double-vase-shaped spindles set into plain lower stretcher. 2 pairs of cabriole legs. Claw-and-ball feet.

Materials and Dimensions
Brass. Panel: silk embroidery, wool, or paper, enclosed by glass. Height: 44–48″. Width of panel: 27–29″.

Locality and Period
Throughout the United States. c. 1875–90.

Comment
The screen shown here, with its large rectangular panel and its galleries of spindles above and below, is Eastlake. However, claw-and-ball feet are uncommon on Eastlake pieces, and the floral-embroidered pattern on the panel is more closely linked to the Rococo Revival style. Similar pieces sometimes incorporate motifs inspired by Oriental design.

Hints for Collectors
A fire screen such as the one shown here, made of brass, glass, and fabric, is surprisingly fragile. Although brass is a durable material, make sure the spindles and finials are sturdy, since they can snap off after years of wear and are difficult and expensive to replace. Few pieces have original glass, but replacement glass does not lessen value.

Anglo-Japanese fire screen

Description
Rectangular fire screen with stiles and rails turned to imitate
bamboo. Double glass panel encloses dried leaves and flowers or
needlework. Wooden frame has 1 bamboo-turned panel above
and 2 below. Trestles at base have 3 stiles reinforced by 2 rails;
outer stiles flare out to form hooflike feet.

Materials and Dimensions
Maple. Glass. Panel: dried leaves and flowers or needlework.
Height: 42–46". Width of panel 24–26".

Locality and Period
Major shops in the East. c. 1875–85.

Comment
Large rectangular fire screens like the one shown here were
popular around 1880 in elegant rooms furnished in a variety of
styles. The term "Anglo-Japanese" is used to describe Oriental-
influenced objects of the period because English cabinetmakers
pioneered in the use of Oriental motifs on Western furniture
forms. Some American shops, especially those in New York,
produced work in the same spirit. This design is simple enough
to be taken for a piece made in the Orient. The Victorians were
fond of collecting botanical specimens; the use of dried leaves and
flowers is as much Western as Oriental in inspiration. Much more
often, the panels were of needlework.

Hints for Collectors
In the 1880s, designers often placed furniture of various styles in
the same room, although consistency in style was favored for
small rooms. A screen like this may have been part of a bedroom
set or used in an elegant parlor.

Checklist for Identifying Styles

Pilgrim Style: 1630–1690
Appearance: Massive.
Essential elements: Heavy square or turned stiles. Detailed floral and geometric carving. Applied moldings, bosses, and split spindles. Some painted decoration.
Primary woods: Oak; sometimes with turned parts of maple or hickory. *Secondary woods:* Pine, ash, maple, or hickory.
Major construction methods: Nailed and paneled construction; also large dovetails.
Notable forms: Bible boxes, low chests, court and press cupboards.

William and Mary Style: 1690–1725
Appearance: Tall and slender.
Essential elements: Crisp, narrow turnings. Legs often vase- or trumpet-shaped, frequently joined with stretchers. Ball, bun, turnip, or scroll (Spanish) feet. Elaborate carving in low relief. Elegantly grained surfaces; also veneer, painted decoration, and japanning. Teardrop or bail handles or wooden knobs.
Primary woods: Walnut or maple. *Secondary woods:* Pine or poplar.
Major construction methods: Dovetailed, nailed, paneled, and pegged mortise-and-tenon construction.
Notable forms: Highboys, lowboys, slant-front desks.

Queen Anne Style: 1725–1750
Appearance: Slim and delicate.
Essential elements: Curving lines. Subtly carved decoration. Cabriole legs. Bracket, pad, slipper, trifid, and, toward the end of the period, claw-and-ball feet. Valanced skirts. Well-formed cornices. Turned drops and finials. Batwing brasses.
Primary woods: Walnut; also maple, cherry, or, later, mahogany. *Secondary woods:* Maple, cherry, ash, or pine.
Major construction methods: Dovetailed, pegged mortise-and-tenon, and nailed construction.
Notable forms: Slant-front desks, secretaries, desk-on-frames, chests of drawers, lowboys, highboys.

Chippendale Style: 1750–1780
Appearance: Broad and curvilinear.
Essential elements: Curving, elaborately carved parts, particularly cornices, pediments, and finials on highboys, chest-on-chests, and secretaries. Block, serpentine, oxbow, and bombé fronts. Carved motifs such as scrolls, shells, and acanthus leaves. Cabriole legs with claw-and-ball feet; also bracket feet. Fretwork decoration. Reeded quarter-columns on chests and other case pieces. Willow brasses.
Primary woods: Mahogany; sometimes walnut, maple, or cherry. *Secondary woods:* Cedar, pine, beech, holly, birch, or tulip.
Major construction methods: Dovetailed, pegged mortise-and-tenon, and nailed construction.
Notable forms: Lowboys, bonnet-top highboys, secretaries, kneehole desks, chest-on-chests, linen presses, corner cupboards.

Federal Style (Hepplewhite and Sheraton): 1780–1820

Appearance: Slender and delicate.

Essential elements: Geometric shapes. Simplified classical ornamentation and patriotic American symbols, executed in low relief, inlay, veneer, or paint. Round or square tapered legs, sometimes reeded; also turned legs. Spade, arrow, French, or bracket feet. Tambour doors. Stamped round, rectangular, or oval brasses.

Primary woods: Mahogany; satinwood and other contrasting woods for inlay and veneer. *Secondary woods:* Pine, cedar, or poplar.

Major construction methods: Dovetailed, pegged mortise-and-tenon, and nailed construction.

Notable forms: Sideboards, servers, and serving tables; dressing tables, chests of drawers, dressing mirrors.

Empire Style: 1815–1840

Appearance: Massive and bulky.

Essential elements: Heavy geometric shapes. Bold carving in high relief, emphasizing outline rather than detail. Oversize classical motifs. Stenciling or gilded brass or bronze decoration. Veneer usually present. Scroll-shaped legs. Large scroll, ball, or carved animal feet, sometimes in gilded brass. Marble tops. Brass, glass, or wooden knobs.

Primary woods: Walnut, cherry, mahogany, rosewood, or grained maple; pine, birch, or other local woods for country pieces. Various mahogany and walnut veneers. *Secondary woods:* Usually pine.

Major construction methods: Dovetailed, pegged mortise-and-tenon, and nailed construction.

Notable forms: Sideboards, dressing tables, pedestal desks, chests of drawers with splashboard.

Country and Shaker Furniture: 1690-1900

Appearance: Varies with period and style, but generally rectilinear.

Essential elements: Simplified shapes, traditional construction, and minimal decoration, all derived from fashionable designs of the 17th to 19th centuries. Turned or cutout parts. Often painted.

Primary woods: Pine, maple, or various local fruit- and softwoods. *Secondary woods:* Pine or poplar.

Major construction methods: Mortise-and-tenon construction, often pegged, nailed, or dovetailed.

Notable forms: Cupboards, dry sinks, chests, hanging racks.

Victorian Revival Styles: 1840–1880

Appearance: Medium-size to massive.

Essential elements: In Rococo Revival style, curving shapes, floral, foliate, and fruit carving, cabriole and scrolled legs (often with casters), marble tops. In Gothic Revival style, Gothic motifs such as arches, tracery, and quatrefoils, boldly turned and cutout parts, spiral- or spool-turned legs (often with casters), and plinthlike bases. In Renaissance Revival style, rectilinear shapes, Neoclassical motifs such as columns, pediments, and cartouches, veneered panels, applied moldings, turned and

cutout parts on factory pieces, elaborate inlay on better
examples.
Primary woods: Walnut, mahogany, or rosewood; also cherry,
oak, ash, or pine. *Secondary woods:* Pine.
Major construction methods: Machine-dovetailed, nailed, glued,
and mortise-and-tenon construction; also lamination and soldered
cast iron.
Notable forms: All types.

Cottage Style: 1860–1910

Appearance: Generally blocky.
Essential elements: Broad, flat surfaces. Applied moldings.
Surfaces always painted and sometimes gilded or stenciled with
floral motifs and landscapes.
Primary woods: Pine. *Secondary woods:* Pine.
Major construction methods: Machine-dovetailed, mortise-and-
tenon, nailed, and glued construction.
Notable forms: All types of bedroom furnishings.

Eastlake Style: 1870–1890

Appearance: Medium-size and delicate.
Essential elements: Simple rectilinear shapes. Geometric or
floral ornamentation, often carved in low relief, and inscribed
linear decoration. Turned spindles and stiles. Inset panels.
Scroll-cut brackets. Middle or Far Eastern motifs. Some
ebonizing.
Primary woods: Oak, walnut, cherry, or maple. *Secondary
woods:* Oak or pine.
Major construction methods: Machine-dovetailed, nailed, glued,
and mortise-and-tenon construction.
Notable forms: Drop-side dressers, cylinder-front secretaries.

Anglo-Japanese Style: 1880–1910

Appearance: Delicate and angular.
Essential elements: Asymmetrical designs. Fret carving
combined with slender, turned elements. Incised decoration.
Often ebonized.
Primary woods: Maple, birch, ash, cherry, or other hardwoods.
Secondary woods: Pine, ash, and oak.
Major construction methods: Nailed, glued, and screwed
construction; also machine-dovetailed construction.
Notable forms: Etagères, shelving units, small cabinets.

Art Nouveau Style: 1895–1910

Appearance: Elongated and flowing.
Essential elements: Sinuous, attenuated forms. Elaborate
carving or inlay. Floral, curving, and organic motifs.
Primary woods: Oak for mass-produced pieces; mahogany,
walnut, or rosewood for elegant examples. *Secondary woods:*
Pine or oak.
Major construction methods: Machine-dovetailed, nailed, glued,
and mortise-and-tenon construction.
Notable forms: Glass-front china cabinets, étagères.

Colonial Revival Style: 1890–1925

Appearance: Narrower and more slender than 18th-century originals.

Essential elements: Traditional 18th-century motifs and shapes rendered more schematically and sometimes combined in new ways.

Primary woods: Oak, or traditional high-style woods such as mahogany and walnut. *Secondary woods:* Pine or oak; plywood backs.

Major construction methods: Some modern construction techniques such as machine-cut dovetails; also mortise-and-tenon and dovetailed construction.

Notable forms: Most Colonial types, such as lowboys and chest-on-chests.

Arts and Crafts and Mission Styles: 1900–1920

Appearance: Medium and boxy.

Essential elements: Simple rectilinear forms. Exposed tenons and pegs. Mission-style pieces unpainted and undecorated. Examples in the Arts and Crafts tradition have more decoration, including some ebonizing, applied elements, and painting. Brass triangular and oblong pulls. Wooden knobs.

Primary woods: Oak. *Secondary woods:* Pine or oak.

Major construction methods: Dovetailed, and pegged and wedged mortise-and-tenon construction; also glued construction for mass-produced examples.

Notable forms: All types.

Art Deco Style: 1925–1945

Appearance: Small to medium-size.

Essential elements: Bold geometric shapes on traditional forms. Simplified geometric ornamentation. Lacquerwork common.

Primary woods: Pine or maple, often lacquered; also mahogany, cherry, rosewood, or ebony for finer examples. *Secondary woods:* Pine, oak, or plywood. *Other materials:* Sometimes metal, plastic, or glass.

Major construction methods: Soldered, laminated, molded, glued, and screwed construction.

Notable forms: All types.

Modern Style: 1925–1950

Appearance: Small to medium-size.

Essential elements: Innovative forms. Industrial materials. Minimal decoration.

Primary woods: Pine or maple, lacquered and painted; also teak, mahogany, or rosewood for elaborate pieces. *Secondary woods:* Plywood, pine, or oak. *Other materials:* Tubular steel and other metals, plastic, or glass.

Major construction methods: Soldered, laminated, molded, glued, and screwed construction.

Notable forms: Modular and built-in furniture.

List of Plates by Style

Anglo-Japanese
Cabinets: 265, 267. Etagère: 122. Fire screen: 334. Hall rack: 318.

Art Deco
Cabinets: 120, 129, 295. Chests of drawers: 147, 148, 229. Desks: 62, 75. Dressing tables: 173–176. Mirrors: 194, 201.
Miscellaneous furnishings: 283, 296. Planter: 293. Secretary: 61. Serving table: 36. Shelves: 307, 309, 310, 312. Sideboard: 37.

Art Nouveau
Cabinet: 129. Desk-over-bookcase: 87. Etagère: 121. Fish tank: 291. Shaving stand: 158.

Arts and Crafts
Book trough: 294. Cabinet: 130. Desk: 50. Secretary: 86. Sideboard: 35.

Chippendale
Chests: 139, 141, 204, 207–209, 242, 247. Cupboards: 104, 112. Desks: 47, 53, 54, 66. Fire screens: 329, 330. Highboys: 134, 137. Lowboy: 152. Mirror: 192. Secretary: 81.

Colonial Revival
Bookcase: 115. Cabinet: 119. Chests: 138, 206, 250. Desk: 58. Dressing mirror: 197. Dressing table: 156. Fire screen: 327. Lowboy: 151. Sideboard: 31. Tea cart: 298.

Cottage
Chest of drawers: 218. Commodes: 6, 10, 12. Dresser: 172. Dressing table: 159.

Country
Boxes: 39, 233. Blanket chests: 226, 246. Cabinets: 266, 272. Candle boxes: 255, 257. Chests: 140, 235, 236, 239, 240. Chests of drawers: 219, 220, 223, 225. Commode: 11. Cupboards: 91, 99–102, 107, 268, 271. Desks: 43, 45, 47. Dressing tables: 154, 161. Dry sinks: 1–3. Miscellaneous furnishings: 256, 258, 297, 313. Secretaries: 83, 85. Servers: 24, 26. Shelves: 253, 254, 259, 306. Sideboard: 23. Wardrobes: 95, 96, 98. Washstand: 16.

Eastlake
Bookcase: 113. Chests: 163, 217. Commode: 5. Desk: 65. Dressers: 170, 171. Fire screens: 332, 333. Mirrors: 182, 184. Shelves: 263, 264.

Empire
Chests: 227, 228, 240. Commode: 13. Cupboards: 109, 110. Desk: 67. Dresser: 166. Dressing table: 161. Fire screen: 331. Mirrors: 169, 186, 187. Secretaries: 79, 85. Servers: 24, 25. Sideboards: 20, 23.

Federal (*see also* Hepplewhite and Sheraton)
Chests: 222, 226, 227. Commode: 18. Cupboards: 111, 268. Dressing box: 199. Knife box: 326. Mirrors: 189, 190. Server: 26. Washstand: 15.

Gothic Revival
Vitrine: 117.

Hepplewhite
Chests: 205, 210–212, 223, 243, 244. Desks: 68, 69. Dressing tables: 153, 155. Fire screen: 328. Mirrors: 193, 200. Secretaries: 59, 78. Serving table: 28. Sideboards: 32, 33.

Mission
Bookshelves: 302, 311. Cabinets: 114, 130. Chest of drawers: 144. Desks: 48, 49, 70, 73, 74. Dresser: 167. Magazine pedestal: 305. Mirror: 198. Plant stand: 285. Server: 27. Umbrella stands: 277, 278.

Modern (*see also* 20th century)
Chest of drawers: 230. Desk: 76. Dressing mirror: 202. Dressing tables: 177, 178. Miscellaneous furnishings: 299, 321, 323. Planter: 289. Sideboard: 38.

Pilgrim
Chests: 238, 252. Pipe rack: 258.

Queen Anne
Desks: 51, 52, 57. Highboys: 135, 136. Lowboy: 150. Mirrors: 191, 196. Secretary: 82.

Renaissance Revival
Cabinets: 127, 128. Chests of drawers: 143, 146. Cupboard: 116. Etagère: 123. Fire screen: 332. Shaving stand: 157. Sideboard: 19. Wardrobe: 125.

Rococo Revival
Sideboard: 22. Umbrella rack: 280.

Rustic
Gun rack: 274. Plant stand: 287. Smoking stand: 284.

Shaker
Chests: 224, 245. Commode-washstand: 14. Cupboards: 105, 270. Desks: 44, 60. Mirror: 179. Secretary: 84. Washstand: 4.

Sheraton
Chests: 142, 213–215, 220. Dressing tables: 154, 160. Mirror: 185. Secretaries: 77, 83. Server: 30. Serving table: 29. Sideboard: 34. Washstands: 16, 17.

20th century (*see also* Art Deco, Mission, and Modern)
Cabinets: 131, 132. Shelves: 308.

Victorian (*see also* Anglo-Japanese, Art Nouveau, Cottage, Eastlake, Gothic Revival, Renaissance Revival, and Rococo Revival)
Cabinets: 126, 261, 262, 269. Chests of drawers: 164, 221. China closet: 118. Commodes: 7–9. Desks: 56, 72, 80, 88–90. Dressers: 165, 168. Hall tree: 316. Mirrors: 183, 188, 195. Plant stand: 286. Planters: 290, 292. Shelves: 260, 300, 303, 304. Umbrella stand: 279. Wardrobes: 94, 95.

William and Mary
Box: 40. Chests of drawers: 203, 216. Desks: 46, 55. Highboy: 133. Lowboy: 149.

Construction and Connoisseurship

The most difficult problem facing the collector is determining if a piece is, as dealers say, "right," which means that it is in its original condition, without major restoration. Learning how to decide that a piece is indeed "right" requires a combination of knowledge and instinct. The former involves the study of how furniture has been made and designed over the years, as well as the ability to apply this knowledge to a particular piece. For many collectors the latter develops only after years of looking at and handling antique furniture. Each piece has a fascinating story to tell, and only an experienced collector can unravel the details by inspecting its exterior, interior, and hardware, as well as the way in which the piece is constructed.

The seasoned collector realizes that it takes many related skills to evaluate furniture successfully. In addition to a knowledge of specific styles, an understanding of construction methods is vital. With some experience, it is relatively easy to tell if a piece has appropriate hardware, correct proportions, authentic carving and turnings, and period tool marks. Condition is equally important. Even a novice can learn to spot the damage done as wood shrinks, but a degree of sophistication is needed to discover the more subtle signs of wear. Detecting when 2 pieces have been "married," or inappropriately combined, is not difficult, once the basic types of furniture are known. It takes more experience to spot reproductions and outright fakes, but, using the information provided in the following pages, beginning collectors can approach a piece intelligently.

How an Expert Evaluates Furniture

"Seeing" a piece of furniture rather than merely "glancing" at it is the key to recognizing antique pieces. Experts use all the tools available to them, including touch and smell, as they evaluate furniture. The information provided here will help you understand how an expert might approach a piece. Once you have acquired the skills outlined in this essay you would probably proceed like this:

Appraising the Overall Appearance
Begin by observing the piece from a distance. If possible (and in small, cramped shops it usually isn't) walk around it slowly, and determine whether its proportions are correct. Most early pieces have standard specifications. For example, an 18th-century lowboy is about 20 percent smaller all around than the base of a highboy, which it resembles. From a distance this difference in proportion is obvious to a trained eye. Other disproportionate elements, such as legs that are too long or too short, or an upper section of drawers that seems too heavy, are also noticeable when viewed from afar. Studying the overall piece helps you spot those elements that seem somehow wrong; this instinctive feeling is usually based on fact. For example, the legs may look awkward, because they are inappropriate to the period in which the piece was made, or the carcass too heavy, because the piece may have been built out of several pieces. Even though an examination from a distance is necessary, the most important clues about the piece will be discovered by a thorough inspection of the exterior and interior.

Examining the Exterior
First, evaluate the outside of the piece under consideration. Is the finish original, or has it been applied at a later date? Touch the surface. It should feel smooth and worn from years of use. Assess the fittings, such as pulls and escutcheons. Are they

original or reproductions? On a chest of drawers or a related piece, look at the back to see if the backboard is original or whether, as is often the case, it has fallen off and been replaced, sometimes with plywood. This will also give you the opportunity to inspect the nails, for backboards were almost always nailed on. Are the nails appropriate to the time the piece was made? If possible, turn the carcass upside down and look closely at the feet. Do they show enough wear for a piece that has been slid across the floor for a century or 2? Do the feet display any thin lines that indicate splices—where new wood has been applied to portions of the foot that have worn away? The bottom of the chest should have an even, dark brown stain that comes with age; lighter areas may reveal that the wood has not had constant exposure to air and light, indicating that the bottom is not original, or that the piece had a different arrangement of legs or perhaps none at all. This would be the case if the top of a highboy had been converted into a tall chest.

Examining the Interior

After the exterior has been thoroughly examined, turn your attention to the interior of the piece. For pieces such as blanket chests that have lift tops, see if the hinges are original, and if the top is intact. Often hinges break off or pull out and are reset in different spots; this is indicated by filled holes in the lid and in the edges of the carcass. If the lid has been pushed back too far, it may split along the edge of the hinges. These considerations apply to cupboard doors and other hinged elements.

Drawers usually show the effects of constant use over the years; they have often been replaced or repaired. To check their condition, remove them and see if the runners have been replaced. The bottom of the drawer should show wear identical to the runners; if the 2 don't match, the drawer may be a replacement. Next, smell the inside of the drawers; clothing, herbs, or food have a faint aroma that clings to old furnishings and is unmistakable once you have smelled it. The inside of the drawer front should also be inspected for any plugged holes, indicating that the pulls have been changed. If a drawer front is veneered, look for signs that the veneer is original; it has sometimes been added to enhance the value of an otherwise plain piece.

Judging a Piece

A general examination like the one outlined here varies, of course, for each type of furniture. Only after the process has been completed will an expert comment on authenticity. The judgment will reflect a thorough knowledge of furniture types, construction methods, period hardware, patina, proportions, tool marks, wood types, and all the other elements that go into the history of a piece of furniture.

Such is the knowledge of a lifetime, and it cannot be acquired simply by reading this or any other book. However, by studying the following section and the examples illustrated in this guide, is possible to acquire a solid background that will enable you to spot most fakes and major restoration jobs, as well as to begin a more sophisticated study of furniture.

Decorative Styles

Understanding American furniture depends upon a thorough knowledge of decorative history styles. To acquire this background, a novice should begin by studying the pieces illustrated in this guide, as well as those in museums. In their basic lines, proportions, and decoration, furnishings have changed substantially over the years. These topics are discussed in the essay on American Furniture Styles and in the Checklist for Identifying Styles.

Every furniture style, from Pilgrim to Art Deco, has its merits and devotees. The type of furniture you collect is less important than the quality of the pieces you own. There are fine, ordinary, and mediocre examples in every category. For knowledgeable collectors, the List of Plates by Style (pp. 408–409) divides the entries in this book into categories. Once acquainted with the best examples of the style, you should use them as models when you purchase furniture.

Proportions

In each stylistic period, even though they produced unique pieces, cabinetmakers also adhered to certain general proportions. Chairs, for example, usually have seats about 17–18″ above the floor, and low chests of drawers have 3–4 drawers and are 34–40″ high. Moreover, large case pieces, such as highboys and secretaries, have a distinct balance between the top and bottom sections and between the top unit and the cornice or bonnet top. Such relationships are more a matter of the craftsman's eye than of exact mathematical measurements, but they are evident to anyone who frequently observes period furnishings.

The departure from normal proportions often marks a piece as a reproduction. Colonial Revival furniture makers were especially fond of adding their own little "touches" to standard Queen Anne and Chippendale forms for both aesthetic and economical reasons. Questionable pieces should be compared with known period examples.

Hardware

Hardware is one of the elements in furniture that, to a large extent, is determined by period and style. Becoming familiar with the types of pulls, hinges, and escutcheons used during different stylistic periods will make it easier for you to date the pieces you encounter. The Glossary and Hardware section contain illustrations of the major types of hardware.

As a general rule, the earliest hardware was hand-wrought or cast, either in iron or brass. By the mid-19th century, it was usually made by stamping, either by hand or, in the 20th century, by machine presses. Stamped hardware is much lighter than cast or wrought hardware.

In recent years, several factories have specialized in producing excellent duplicates of 18th- and 19th-century cast-brass pulls and wrought-iron hinges. These reproductions are very convincing, and may be invaluable when you have to match missing or damaged pulls or hinges. Only their lack of wear and patina reveal that they are not really old.

Nails and Screws

Like pulls, escutcheons, and hinges, particular types of nails and screws were manufactured during specific periods. They are good clues to use in dating the pieces of furniture you find.

Nails

Three major types of nails—wrought-iron, machine-cut, and wire —have been used in the construction of American furniture. Since almost all case pieces have some nailed elements, knowing how to recognize these types can help you date pieces.

The earliest nails are made of wrought iron. They were widely used from the time of the first settlers until about 1815. They are sharply pointed, with round or rectangular heads. If the head is round, it should bear the facets made from hammer strokes. Machine-cut, or square, nails became common by 1815 and continued to be used until around 1890. These nails have more or less square-shaped heads and bodies tapering to blunt ends. By 1890, the modern wire nail, with its familiar round head and body, had replaced the earlier types.

Some pieces of furniture dating from the 17th and 18th centuries may have 19th-century nails because they were repaired over the years. However, as a general rule, a piece of furniture is roughly the same age as its earliest nail. No rule is without exceptions, however: fakers occasionally use early wrought-iron nails.

Screws

Pulls and hinges are almost always attached by screws. If it is possible to remove a screw from a piece of furniture, it may provide clues to age and authenticity. Until about 1815 screws were hand-shaped and cut with blunt ends. They had horizontal grooves, or worming, and off-center slots on their heads. Each hand-shaped screw may be a slightly different length. Factory screws, which appeared in the middle of the 19th century, look much like those made today. They have centered slots in their heads, pointed ends, and angled grooves, or worming. If modern screws are present in a piece supposedly made before 1850, it may mean that the parts they affix are replacements or that perhaps the entire piece is a reproduction. Since screws made before 1840 have not been copied, reproduction hardware will almost always be secured with modern screws.

Another point to keep in mind is that in the 18th century, screws and nails were concealed by colored beeswax, and in the 19th century, by wooden plugs.

Construction Methods

The techniques employed in making furniture have changed substantially over the years with the introduction of new tools, new methods, and new materials. An understanding of these developments will make it easier not only to date pieces but also to recognize restorations and reproductions. Although the simplest construction methods are usually the ones employed during the earliest years of American furniture production, country cabinetmakers continued to use many of these methods even after more advanced forms had become common in urban centers. Thus it is important to consider the method of construction as just one of several clues as you attempt to date a piece of furniture.

The types of construction discussed here—6-board, paneled, mortise-and-tenon, and dovetailed—are those you will most frequently encounter.

Six-board Construction

One of the most basic methods of construction consists of fastening 6 boards together to form a chest. One board serves as bottom, and the others as top, sides, front, and back. Most often the boards are simply nailed together, although in finer pieces dovetails may be employed. Typically the lid of a 6-board chest is hinged, allowing access to a storage well.

Six-board construction was most common in the early Colonial 414 years, although it lingered in rural areas well into the 19th century. Even today, craftsmen occasionally utilize this simple method for sturdy, everyday pieces.

Paneled Construction
In the late 17th, early 18th, and late 19th centuries, paneled construction was common. In this method, horizontal boards, called rails, are fastened to vertical elements, called stiles. These stiles and rails are grooved, so that panels can be inserted into the grooves. Frequently the panels are slightly recessed, and in the finest early pieces, they are elaborately carved. Paneled construction was the primary method used for chests made during the Pilgrim century. Even today it is employed for portions of furniture, such as doors and sides, though it is rarely used for an entire piece.

Mortise-and-Tenon Construction

The mortise-and-tenon joint was introduced to America with the first settlers. It is the primary method for constructing chairs, tables, and related pieces, and in addition is often utilized for case pieces.
Like paneled construction, the method uses horizontal rails and vertical stiles. The end of one piece is cut into the shape of a thin rectangular projection, or tenon, that fits into a corresponding hole, or mortise, chiseled into the other piece. In the Colonial period, mortise-and-tenon joints were most often pinned together with wooden pegs for added strength; both the mortise and the tenon had holes drilled into them, and a peg or pin was inserted into the holes, locking the 2 pieces together. Nails or glue became more common in the 19th and 20th centuries for the reinforcement of joints.

Dovetailed Construction

Another way to interlock parts of furniture is with dovetails. They are triangular projections on one piece of wood that fit into similarly shaped slots on a second piece. Dovetails made in the 17th century are very large; most drawers required only one. However, by 1720 they had become smaller (1–1½″) and several were used for each drawer. Dovetails were also used to join tops and sides of chests, chests of drawers, and other case pieces. Until the 1860s, dovetails were laboriously hand cut, but after the Civil War several types of dovetail-cutting machines appeared. Machine-cut dovetails are still used today. They may be recognized by their small size (½–¾″), their regularity, and their less sharply angled shape. Another type of machine-made dovetail, used only during the Victorian period, looks like a series of half moons with a dot in the center of each.
Dovetails help date furniture. Earlier examples are larger and hand-cut; later ones, smaller and factory-made. The presence of factory-made dovetails in an 18th-century-style piece is a clear indication that it is a Colonial Revival reproduction.

Turnings and Carving
Turned wood is formed on a lathe, which is a device for rotating a piece of wood while various cutting tools are applied to it. Lathes may be powered by hand or by machine. In the 17th and 18th centuries, turned wood varied subtly in detail, and no 2 hand-turned elements are exactly alike. Later examples, made on machine-powered lathes, are crisper, often smaller in scale, and more uniform in pattern.
Carving is sometimes added later to otherwise plain pieces in an attempt to make them more desirable. On 17th- and 18th-century

furniture, carving should be deep since thick wood was employed and large cuts were made in it. Flat carving on a Chippendale piece may indicate that carving was added at a later date. Recent carving on an older piece tends to be either too simplified or else too complex in detail.

The differences between authentic and reproduced or faked carving are evident on the claw-and-ball feet that are common on Chippendale furniture. Genuine 18th-century American feet are modeled on a bird's or a dragon's claw, but imaginatively simplified, whereas Colonial Revival examples from the early 20th century are more stiffly schematic, lacking the vitality of the originals.

The carving on claw-and-ball feet also conveys the difference between American and English work; the English carved claw is rendered more faithfully and realistically.

Moldings, reeding, and fluting were also executed both by hand and by machine. If done by hand, these elements will appear slightly uneven, especially when viewed down the length of the ridges. In contrast, machine-produced elements are regular and smooth.

Tool Marks

Since the tools used in furniture making have changed through the years, an inspection of tool marks provides helpful clues for dating pieces. Especially before 1900, cabinetmakers commonly left tool marks on unfinished areas of furnishings, such as the undersides of tabletops, the backs of case pieces, and the bottoms of drawers.

The most common marks are saw cuts and hand-tool scars. Operated by hand or waterpower, the earliest saws moved up and down in a straight line leaving a series of straight parallel lines on the wood's surface. The circular saw, which came into general use after about 1840 and is still used in furniture making, leaves a series of concentric, arclike marks. As a general rule, furniture containing boards with these semicircular scratches dates from after the Empire period. Thus a Chippendale-style highboy whose backboards show such scars is quite likely to be a reproduction.

Early boards often vary slightly in width or thickness. Since wood was plentiful during the Colonial period, chest tops and other large flat surfaces were often made of a single plank, sometimes as much as a yard wide. Tops made from narrower boards (under 20″) may indicate later work.

Hand-tool marks can also prove helpful in identification. A small pointed tool called a scribing awl was used to outline the form of hand-cut dovetails and mortises. The indentations left by the awl are called scribe marks. If in doubt about whether a set of dovetails is hand- or machine-cut, look for the thin scribe marks. If they are absent, the dovetails were machine-made.

Several different planes were used to smooth boards in handmade furnishings. Wide ridges with raised centers left by the jack plane will often appear on the backboards and undersides of case pieces. Narrower planes lacking the raised center were used for finishing work, and their tracks may appear on drawer bottoms. These planes were gradually eliminated with the introduction of power-driven belt sanders and other mechanical devices, although they may have been used on country pieces made as late as 1900. The absence of appropriate tool marks on a supposed 18th-century piece should be cause for alarm.

Cabinetmaker's Marks

Regrettably most cabinetmakers did not mark their pieces, and not all the existing marks can be trusted. Manufacturers' marks are found on perhaps one percent of all pre-Civil War furnishings. After that the percentage begins to rise, reaching perhaps 60 percent in 20th-century furniture. Early marks were brands burned into the surface of the wood, a simple chalk or penciled notation, or a paper label glued to the surface. All would have been placed in an inconspicuous spot, such as the back of a drawer or the inside of the case. As the value of identified pieces has risen, so has the incidence of forgery. Fake brands and signatures may be applied, or a manufacturer's advertisement from a newspaper of the period may be used as a facsimile. Anyone offered an allegedly marked example, particularly an early or desirable one, should verify this with an expert. Moreover, since so few pieces of furniture were marked, collectors should be familiar with the other ways a piece may be identified. Particularly after 1870, many furniture manufacturers' annual catalogues contained pictures of the pieces they made. Some catalogues (such as the early 20th-century Stickley catalogues) have been reproduced and can be purchased. Others may be found in specialized libraries. By referring to such booklets, one may be able to identify a specific piece. Many pieces have been traced either through their history or through a maker's mark to a specific manufacturer. It may be possible to establish the identity of similar but unmarked examples through reference to these. Also, certain design characteristics, such as the laminated backs of Belter pieces, are associated with an individual or small group of workshops. Such characteristics are often helpful in dating a piece or establishing its country or region of origin.

Patina and Wear

Perhaps the most subtle distinctions among pieces of furniture are those relating to patina and wear. Simply stated, patina is the aged condition of a painted or unpainted surface resulting from years of exposure to light and air, abrasions, polishing, and normal handling. In this sense, patina also encompasses wear, including the chipping away of corner areas, the loss of veneer, and the warping and cracking common to wood as it dries out. Although these conditions are acquired with time and use, they can also be faked to some degree. The patina of an unpainted piece of furniture will vary with its exposure to light and air. Exposed areas will turn a mellow nut-brown and acquire a dry dusty surface. If the surface is handled often, it will become smooth, almost velvety, from friction and the natural oils of the skin. Areas that are touched most often will be darkest. Unexposed areas such as drawer bottoms and interiors will have a lighter complexion and will feel dry. Painted surfaces will become darker and more subdued with age. Our ancestors were much fonder of bright colors than is commonly thought today; in fact, some of these colors might be considered too bright for current tastes. However, over the years this paint has faded and the colors have mellowed.

Shrinkage

For unpainted and painted pieces, normal wear manifests itself in many ways. With age, wood shrinks across the grain. This causes tabletops to warp. Sides of chests shrink so much that their drawers become too long for their compartments (since long sides cut with the grain do not shrink). Shrinkage and attempts to force drawers closed may split off backboards from chests of drawers.

Veneer was in most cases applied with glue. As the glue becomes brittle and the veneer and the surrounding areas of solid wood shrink and draw apart, some veneer may fall off. Wooden pegs, when present, protrude from the shrinking wood or drop out; dovetails may separate. In the 19th century the common, though unfortunate, practice of nailing them back together usually resulted in cracked dovetails.

Feet wear down from contact with the floor. As a result, the once sharply cut edges of bracket feet become rounded and even chipped away—a process that takes place to a lesser extent with the sides, tops, and skirts of case pieces. Areas that are constantly used, such as those next to keyholes, pulls, and latches, gradually become worn or slightly concave.

These are a few examples of how a piece of furniture normally ages, and taken together they are signs of authenticity.

However, evidence of patina and wear alone is not enough to confirm a piece's proper age. Both can occur naturally in just 2 to 3 decades. Unseasoned wood (often used in Colonial Revival pieces) will warp and shrink more rapidly. Recent abuse and unusual weather conditions may hasten the aging process and possibly mislead collectors.

Artificially Produced Signs of Age

Disreputable sellers may try to fake both patina and wear. For instance, some pieces of painted country furniture, stripped of paint or not originally painted, have been given a coat of blue or red milk-base paint, or even sponged or grained. It is not as difficult as one might imagine to age this new finish even in a few days' time. Smaller pieces may be placed in an oven before the paint is completely dry to create a rough, blistered appearance associated with the passage of time. With larger furnishings the application of a coat of weak paint remover achieves the same result.

Furthermore, the judicious application of sandpaper and steel wool in areas likely to be worn, plus the addition of some dirt to darken the surface, will rather effectively mimic natural paint loss and wear.

Practical Tests for Determining Age

Aside from acquiring a feel for the authentic, the careful observer may choose to apply several practical tests.

Repainters often neglect to distress and age all the paint on a piece. New and obviously unaged paint may sometimes be found in such out-of-the-way places as sides and bottoms of drawers and under the skirt. These are areas that would not originally have been painted, and the careful oldtime craftsman would not have left drippings there either. Look also in these areas for signs of paint remover used in taking off a previous finish. The abraded areas where wear has been simulated are visible with a magnifying glass. If the wear consists of sharp, often parallel lines instead of smooth weblike crazing, it is an indication that the wear was artificially induced. Be particularly suspicious of paint that covers cracks and of chips where wood is missing. An piece of furniture that shows extensive wear at pulls and around doors but practically no wear or paint loss elsewhere should be treated with suspicion.

However, one should weigh all factors carefully. Remember tha
some old pieces may have very little wear or loss of paint but w

still have faded paint or other signs of age, either because they were handled with great care, or because they went out of style soon after they were made and were carefully retired to the attic. The only thing worse than getting stuck with a repainted piece is to miss a good buy on an authentic painted example because you thought the paint wasn't right.

Wormholes
Although undesirable, wormholes are usually interpreted as a sign of old age. However, they may have been made recently, either by worms or with a drill. Fake holes are generally straighter than the meandering pathways created naturally by worms. Wormholes are rarer on American pieces than on European furniture. In some humid areas of New England, however, worm damage was more common.

Reproduction, Fakes, and Alterations
The greatest problem facing the novice collector is learning to distinguish genuine antiques from reproductions, fakes, and pieces that have been altered. Although working with an honest and well-informed dealer minimizes this problem, every collector should be able to make his or her own judgments. Familiarity with the basic forms, construction techniques, and materials of genuine pieces should make it easier to spot examples that are not what they seem to be. Caution should be balanced with openmindedness; the latter is vital, since an unusual, though authentic, variation may put off the overly cautious collector. There are exceptions to every general rule in judging furniture, and an unusual detail may be acceptable if it is not anachronistic and if the other elements of the piece are consistent with the basic style.

Reproductions
The manufacture of reproductions has been a legitimate business for about a century. They are generally easy to recognize. The authentic lines and proportions characteristic of each period have rarely been duplicated convincingly. Modern construction techniques and inaccurate or poorly executed details also reveal a reproduction. A handsome lowboy, for instance, may look impressive until you notice that its legs are a bit too thin, the edges of its top too plain, and the feet insufficiently worn, telling you that it is actually a 1920s reproduction rather than the early 18th-century piece it appeared to be. On the other hand, many reproductions, particularly Colonial Revival pieces from about the turn of the century, have a charm of their own once they are recognized as reproductions.

Fakes
Most fakes are harder to detect as they are intended to deceive through feigned signs of age and concealed evidence of their recent manufacture. Rare and valuable pieces are most often faked; 19th- and 20th-century designs attract fakers much less frequently. Except for some extremely well-made examples, most fakes display a telltale inconsistency or other indication of recent manufacture. Even a maker's label can be faked by using an advertisement cut out from an old newspaper (the signs of this trick are the printing on the back of the paper and the small-size type), while other "old labels" have been fabricated in other ways.

Altered Pieces
Pieces of furniture that have been altered are far more common

than outright fakes and range from those that have been honestly repaired or restored to those deliberately altered to enhance their value. Restoration can be so extensive that a piece may hardly qualify as an antique anymore. If repairs are minor and well done, an object need not be rejected, but its value will probably be lower. Pieces may also have been altered to suit contemporary tastes: for instance, a commode may have been converted to a dry sink. Since carving, painting, inlay, or other decoration tend to increase the value of a piece, these have sometimes been added later. Such decoration is generally less well done than original work, but it may be difficult to detect if the additions were made just shortly after the piece was produced.

Other examples of altered pieces are those that have been "married"—that is, assembled with genuine antique parts salvaged from other pieces—to make them more desirable or to replace missing sections. Since all the parts, in such cases, will have the plausible signs of age, the indications of reassembly will be inconsistencies in woods, construction techniques, and decorative details.

Reproductions, fakes, and altered pieces are among the serious pitfalls in collecting antique furniture, but with experience a collector should be able to detect the deficiencies in such pieces.

General Types of Woods

American furniture has been made of many different woods and combinations of woods. Recognizing the wood from which a piece is made is often helpful in determining origin and approximate date of manufacture. However, woods, particularly when aged or painted, are often difficult to identify. Verbal descriptions of wood grain, color, and the like are seldom sufficient. Even so, every collector should have a general awareness of the types of woods used in American furniture.

Primary and Secondary Woods

Primary woods are those used for the main body or carcass of a piece of furniture, especially for exposed areas. Such woods are often of an attractive color and/or grain. Good examples are mahogany, walnut, oak, and maple.

Secondary woods are those used for concealed areas of a piece. They are frequently inexpensive and readily available local timbers such as poplar or pine. They may be employed for the backs and undersides of chests of drawers and other case pieces, and for the sides, backs, and bottoms of drawers. They are usually lighter in weight than primary woods and hence their use reduces the overall weight of a piece—an important structural consideration.

Fancy Grains

Some woods have a particularly attractive grain or can be cut to produce such a grain, and cabinetmakers have long employed these timbers to create decorative furnishings. Often called fancy grains, these woods may either be used solid or as a veneer, that is, cut in thin layers and then applied over plainer wood.

Figured Maple

Maple trees produce several types of fancy or figured woods, including bird's-eye and curly maple. The former is characterized by irregularly spaced brownish-gold dots against a lighter background, the latter by dark irregular wavy or curling lines against the lighter ground.

Burl

Used only as veneer, burl comes from irregular growths on the trunks of various trees and is characterized by a convoluted brown grain against a lighter background. Burls occur most often on walnut, ash, and oak trees, though the latter was used more frequently in Europe than in America.

Crotch Wood

This is the wood cut from the area where the tree trunk forks into 2 large branches. It has an unusual plumelike figure with curling branches flowing out on each side of a central shaft. Most often used are crotch-grain mahogany and walnut.

Quartersawed Wood

In this rather complex technique, several diagonal cuts are made to produce wood with an attractive and strong grain. Oak is most often sawed in this way.

Oyster Wood

This wood is produced by cutting straight across the concentric annual growth rings of a tree so as to produce thin sheets of veneer that resemble bulls' eyes.

American and European Woods

421 While it is appealing to think that American furnishings can be

distinguished from similar English and European examples merely on the basis of the woods from which they were made, it is seldom so simple. In the first place, the same or very similar trees grow in both areas. For example, oak, birch, and walnut are common to North America and Europe. Secondly, North American woods such as pine were often imported for use by European furniture makers. However, a few general guidelines may be applied. Oak was seldom used in the United States from the late 17th to the late 19th centuries, while it was widely employed in Europe during that period. Pine as a secondary wood is characteristically American; its use in Europe was limited. Poplar is a typical North American secondary wood. American furnishings are more likely to be composed of several woods than their European counterparts. Fruitwoods, such as apple and cherry, were more often employed in this country. Although English Queen Anne furniture was usually mahogany, that wood was not used here until late in the Queen Anne period, and only became common for fine American furniture in the Chippendale period.

Woods by Stylistic Periods

While it is doubtful that there was any time at which a given wood was completely ignored by American craftsmen, there is no doubt that, like their European counterparts, they have at various times favored certain woods. As a consequence, the wood of which a piece is made can provide guidelines in determining the period in which the piece was constructed. The following are the woods most commonly used during the major stylistic periods in America.

Pilgrim: 1630–1690
Primary woods: oak; occasionally maple or hickory.
Secondary woods: pine, ash, maple, or hickory.

William and Mary: 1690–1725
Primary woods: walnut or maple.
Secondary woods: pine or poplar.

Queen Anne: 1725–1750
Primary woods: maple; also cherry or mahogany; some birch.
Secondary woods: pine, poplar, maple, cherry, or ash.

Chippendale: 1750–1780
Primary woods: mahogany, walnut, cherry, or maple.
Secondary woods: pine, cedar, beech, holly, birch, or poplar.

Federal: 1780–1820
Primary woods: mahogany, maple, cherry; inlay and veneer in figured maple, birch, box, or satinwood.
Secondary woods: pine, cedar, or poplar.

Empire: 1815–1840
Primary woods: walnut, cherry, mahogany, rosewood, or grained maple.
Secondary woods: pine, birch, or other local woods.

Victorian: 1840–1900
Primary woods: mahogany or rosewood; later walnut, oak, ash, cherry, pine, or various exotic woods; also laminated wood, bentwood.
Secondary woods: pine or oak.

Modern: 1900–1960
Primary woods: mahogany, maple, ash, fruitwoods, ebony, pine; various exotic woods; pressed or laminated wood; bentwood.
Secondary woods: pine, ash, or plywood.

Glossary

Illustrated entries are indicated by dots.

- **Acanthus-leaf decoration**
  Decoration resembling the thick, scalloped leaves of the acanthus plant; often carved on knees of Chippendale cabriole legs.

  Applied
  Shaped or carved separately and then nailed, pegged, or glued to a surface.

  Architectural furniture
  Pieces, such as corner cupboards, built into rooms when the rooms are designed; also furniture with decorative elements, such as pilasters, derived from architecture (*see* plate 104).

- **Arrow foot**
  A cylinder-shaped foot that is tapered and separated from the leg by a turned ring.

  Backboard
  The board or boards that make up the back of a piece of case furniture and sometimes extend above the top.

- **Bail handle**
  A half loop that when attached to posts on a back plate forms a drawer pull; usually made of brass or iron.

- **Ball foot**
  A round, turned foot most popular in the William and Mary period; also used on some Empire and Victorian pieces.

  Banding
  A narrow border of contrasting inlay or veneer, often framing a drawer front.

  Base
  The lowest structural element of a case piece, directly above the feet; in 2-part pieces, also the lowest part of the upper section.

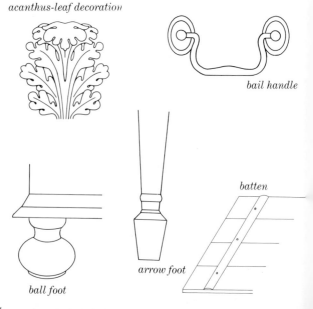

acanthus-leaf decoration

bail handle

batten

arrow foot

ball foot

- **Batten**
  A strip of wood attached at right angles to the grain of a lid or other element to prevent warping.

- **Batwing brass**
  A mount or escutcheon that resembles the outspread wings of a bat; most common on Queen Anne furniture.

  Beading
  A series of adjacent beadlike balls used as decorative molding.

- **Bellflower**
  A classical floral motif consisting of a series of 3- or 5-point petals in bell shape; carved or inlaid.

  Bentwood
  Strips of wood that are steamed and bent into curving forms; perfected by Michael Thonet in the 19th century.

- **Beveled**
  Having a flat area made by cutting away a corner or edge formed by 2 surfaces at right angles to each other; chamfered.

  Block front
  A type of shaped front on a piece of case furniture, characterized by 2 projecting ends that flank a recessed center (*see* plate 207).

  Bombé
  Having a front and sides that swell outward (*see* plate 208).

- **Bonnet top**
  A broken pediment, with the open central area resembling a bonnet in shape; typically found on 18th-century highboys and chest-on-chests.

- **Bootjack foot**
  A foot formed by cutting a triangular section from a side board.

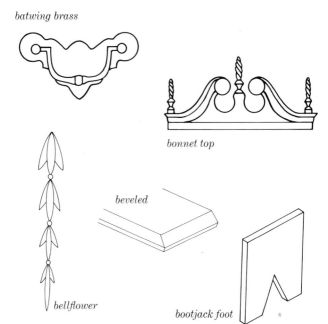

batwing brass

bonnet top

beveled

bellflower

bootjack foot

Boss
A small, round or oval, applied wooden ornament; often ebonized.

Bowfront
Curving outward continuously from ends to center (*see* plate 21).

• **Box stretcher**
A stretcher with flat or turned units forming a square or rectangular enclosure.

Bracket
A shaped wooden or metal support, usually in the form of a right angle.

• **Bracket foot**
A shaped foot that extends from a mitered corner to the front and side; may be plain, scrolled, or molded.

• **Broken pediment**
A pediment in which the curved or straight elements do not meet at the apex.

• **Bun foot**
A squat version of a ball foot, flattened slightly at the top and bottom.

Burl
A hard, woody growth on a tree, characterized by a highly mottled grain; often used for veneer.

• **Butt hinge**
A hinge with flat, rectangular leaves joined by a circular rod; a thin metal pin runs through the rod.

• **Butterfly hinge**
A hinge with flat, flaring leaves; named because of its resemblance to the wings of a butterfly.

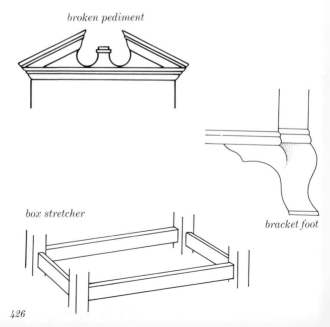

broken pediment

box stretcher

bracket foot

• Cabriole leg
An S-shaped leg, with outcurving knee and incurving ankle, based on the shape of an animal's leg; usually terminating in a pad foot in the Queen Anne period, and in a claw-and-ball foot in the Chippendale period.

Candle bracket
A small, shaped bracket, usually scroll cut, intended as the resting place for a candleholder or oil lamp; typically found on secretaries and dressers.

Candle slide
A small, square or rectangular wooden surface that pulls out from a secretary or desk to support a candleholder.

Cane
Tightly woven split rattan or other fibrous material.

Canted
Having a sloping or angled surface.

• Capital
The enlarged top of a column; often carved.

Carcass
The main body of a piece of case furniture.

Cartouche
An ornate Rococo decorative motif with scrolled edges; used on Chippendale and various 19th-century revival-style pieces.

Case furniture
Furniture that encloses a space and is generally boxlike in structure, such as chests, cabinets, secretaries, and related pieces.

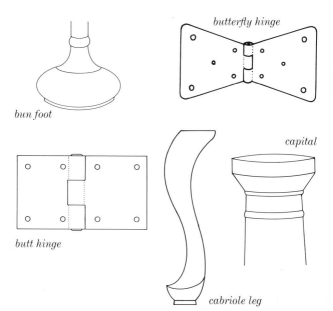

butterfly hinge

bun foot

capital

butt hinge

cabriole leg

- **Caster**
  A small wheel attached to the feet or base of furniture by a cuplike device or a long rod that fits into a hole; used to facilitate moving furniture.

- **Chamfered**
  Having a flat area made by cutting away a corner or edge formed by 2 surfaces at right angles to each other; beveled.

  Chip carving
  Carving in low relief with a chisel or gouge; also known as gouge or notch carving and usually done in geometric patterns.

  Chrome
  Metal, usually steel, coated with an alloy of chromium and having a shiny silverlike appearance; used frequently in 20th-century furniture.

- **Claw-and-ball foot**
  A foot characterized by a carved claw grasping a ball; usually wooden, but also ormolu or brass with a glass ball; usually the termination of a Chippendale or Colonial Revival cabriole leg.

  Column
  A classical pillar consisting of a capital, cylindrical shaft, and base; often used on Federal, Empire, and Renaissance Revival furniture.

- **Cornice**
  The horizontal molding or group of moldings at the top of a piece of case furniture.

- **Cotter-pin hinge**
  A hinge consisting of 2 pieces of interlocking wirelike iron; also called a snipe hinge.

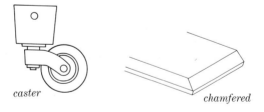

caster

chamfered

cornice

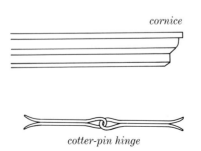

cotter-pin hinge

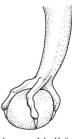

claw-and-ball foot

Country furniture
Simple pieces made between the late 17th and late 19th
centuries; usually constructed by rural craftsmen.

Crazing
Minute cracks in a painted or varnished surface caused by age.

Crotch grain
Veneer cut from the intersection of the trunk and a major branch
of a tree, usually mahogany.

Cylinder front
A quarter-round front that pivots open from front to back; found
primarily on Victorian desks and secretaries (*see* plate 88).

Cyma curve
A continuous double curve, roughly S-shaped, with one part
convex and the other concave.

Demilune
Crescent-shaped, half-round.

• **Dentil molding**
Geometric molding consisting of a series of projecting
rectangular blocks resembling teeth.

• **Dovetail**
A roughly triangular tenon or mortise used in the joining of 2
elements; named because its shape resembles the tail of a dove.

Dovetailed construction
A form of joining using interlocking, dovetail-shaped tenons and
mortises.

Dowel
A wooden rod or pin used to join 2 pieces of wood; usually
machine-cut.

dentil molding

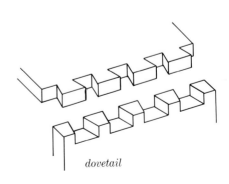

dovetail

Drop
A turned wooden decorative element, often urn- or bell-shaped, attached to the underside of a surface.

Drop front
A front hinged at the bottom to fall forward.

Dust board
A piece of flat, thin wood used to separate a drawer space from the ones above and below it.

Dutch patch
A roughly bow tie-shaped piece of wood used to hold 2 other wooden pieces together; often used in repairs.

Ebonized
Stained or painted black to resemble ebony.

Escutcheon
A decorative plate that covers a keyhole; usually brass, but also bone, wood, and other metals.

Fall front
The upright lid or writing flap of a desk or secretary, hinged at the bottom to fall forward and form a writing surface; supported by brackets beneath the opened front.

Fiberglass
Glass in a fibrous form; often used in 20th-century furniture design.

Finial
A small wooden or metal decorative element, usually affixed to the top of a pediment; turned, carved, or cast, most frequently in the form of a flame or urn.

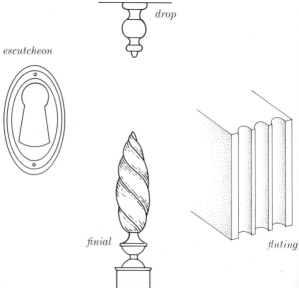

escutcheon

drop

finial

fluting

Flush
Even with an adjacent surface.

- **Fluting**
A series of narrow grooves or channels cut parallel to each other in a surface; derived from ancient architecture and often used on Chippendale and Federal furniture.

- **French foot**
A simple outswept bracket foot; often found on case furniture in combination with a valanced skirt.

- **Fretwork**
Decorative cutting executed with a fret saw, typically in balancing scrolls that create a floral-like appearance.

Frieze
The flat band directly beneath the cornice; often decorated.

Fume
To artificially darken wood, typically oak.

- **Gadrooning**
Carved ornamental edging consisting of a series of convex sections resembling curved, oval fluting or reeding.

- **Gallery**
A decorative raised border of wood or metal extending around the back and sides of a shelf or the top of a piece of furniture.

Gesso
A thick mixture of plaster of Paris, glue, and water, which is applied as a base coat to cover rough spots on wood and provide a surface for gilding or painting.

Gilded
Decorated with a thin application of gold or gold paint.

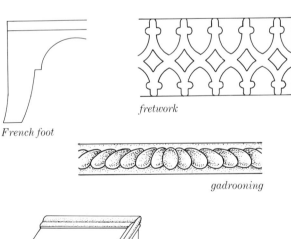

fretwork

French foot

gadrooning

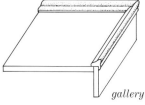

gallery

Glazed
Set with panes of glass.

• **Gothic arch**
A narrow, pointed arch or archlike decorative element; common on Victorian furniture of the Gothic Revival.

Graduated
Becoming progressively smaller or larger.

Half-column
A turned, split column mounted against a flat surface as a decorative device; sometimes ebonized.

• **H hinge**
A decorative hinge consisting of 2 tall leaves that together resemble the letter H.

Incised
Cut into a surface.

Inlay
Small pieces of contrasting colored wood or other materials set into recesses carved out of a solid surface.

Japanned
Decorated with layers of colored varnish and gilt on a solid black or red background in imitation of Oriental lacquerwork.

Joint
The point where 2 units in a piece of furniture meet and are structurally connected.

• **Keyhole surround**
A type of escutcheon, consisting of a piece of keyhole-shaped ivory, brass, or iron inset into wood.

Gothic arch

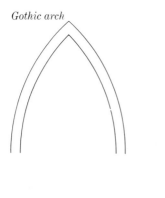

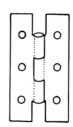

H hinge

keyhole surround

- **Knee**
  The upper, convex curve of a cabriole leg.

  Kneehole
  The open space in the center front of a desk, sometimes extending through to the back, and usually flanked on each side by a set of drawers.

  Lacquered
  Decorated with several coats of natural varnish; an ancient Oriental technique introduced to the West in the 17th century.

  Laminated wood
  Thin sheets of wood glued together with their grains perpendicular to each other; strong and highly suited to complex decorative carving; first used extensively by the furniture maker John Henry Belter in the 19th century.

  Linenfold molding
  Molding that resembles folded linen; also called sheathed molding.

  Locker
  A small central cupboard in the wells of many 18th-century desks and secretaries.

  Low relief
  Shallow carving, with the design raised only slightly from the background.

- **Marlborough leg**
  A straight-sided square leg, introduced by Thomas Chippendale and widely used during the period.

  Marquetry
  A technique in which elaborate patterns are formed by the

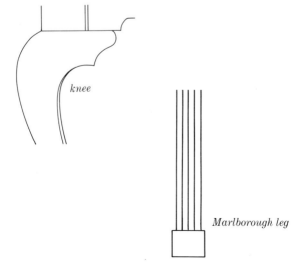

knee

Marlborough leg

insertion of shaped pieces of wood or other materials into a layer
of veneer; this in turn is applied to another surface.

• Mitered
Cut at an angle.

Molding
A continuous, rounded strip of wood applied to furniture as a
decorative element.

Mortise
A square, round, triangular, or most often rectangular slot cut
into a piece of wood to hold a projecting tenon of matching shape.

• Mortise-and-tenon construction
A technique for joining 2 pieces of wood in which a tenon, or
shaped projection, is inserted into a mortise, or cavity; wooden
pegs may further strengthen the bond.

Mount
A pull, escutcheon, or other decorative element applied to
furniture; may be metal, glass, bone, wood, or another material.

Muntin
A wooden or lead strip that divides the panes of glass in a
window or glazed door.

Ogee molding
Molding characterized by a single or double cyma curve.

Ormolu
Gilded bronze or brass; used on mounts, feet, and decorative
details and common in late Federal and Empire furnishings.

Oxbow
Curved inward between outcurved ends and center; also called
reverse serpentine (*see* plate 204).

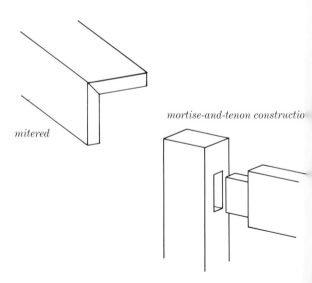

mortise-and-tenon construction

mitered

- **Pad foot**
  A simple, curving foot, sometimes set on a cushionlike disk; customarily the termination of a Queen Anne cabriole leg; also called a Dutch foot.

Panel
A thin rectangular or square board held in place by grooves cut into the inner sides of stiles and rails.

Paneled construction
A technique for constructing case furniture, in which flat wooden panels are fitted into grooves cut in thicker pieces of wood, termed stiles and rails, and often secured with pins.

Patent furniture
19th-century furniture characterized by innovative design, improved construction techniques, or inventive mechanisms; not always legally patented.

Patina
The mellow and worn quality that a surface acquires through age and use; highly prized on most antique furniture.

- **Paw foot**
  A stylized foot carved to resemble an animal's paw, usually that of a lion.

Pedestal desk
A flat-top desk supported on each side of a kneehole by a bank of drawers.

- **Pediment**
  The triangular or curved cresting above a piece of furniture, doorway, or building; called a broken pediment when the sides do not meet at a point.

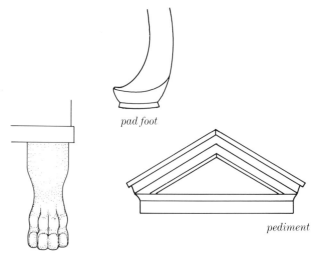

pad foot

pediment

paw foot

Peg
A carved or turned wooden pin that passes through both units of a mortise-and-tenon joint to bind them together; early pegs are hand carved and usually square or octagonal; later examples are typically turned, round dowels.

Pierced decoration
Decoration created by cutting openwork designs into a piece of wood with a jigsaw.

Pigeonhole
An open-fronted storage unit in the well of a desk or secretary.

Pilaster
A rectangular column that projects slightly from a surface; used as an ornamental detail on furniture.

Plinth
The base of a column or pedestal or the heavily molded base of a piece of case furniture that lacks feet.

Plywood
Thin sheets of wood glued together with their grains at right angles to create a strong material.

Primary wood
The wood from which the bulk of a piece, particularly its visible portion, is made.

• **Pull**
A handle or knob used to open a drawer or door.

Quarter-round pilaster
One quarter of a turned circular column.

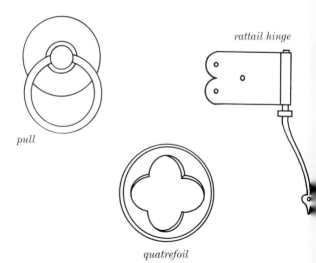

rattail hinge

pull

quatrefoil

Quartersawed
Sawed from 1 of the 4 sections of a quartered log; often oak, producing wood with an attractive grain.

• **Quatrefoil**
A decorative motif consisting of 4 lobes or sections in an abstract floral design.

Rail
A horizontal structural element, usually connecting 2 vertical elements, called stiles.

• **Rattail hinge**
A decorative hinge that resembles a rat's tail.

Rattan
Palm stems, usually split, used in making wicker furniture.

• **Reeding**
A series of parallel, carved, rounded, and closely set ridges or beads.

Relief carving
Projecting decoration formed by carving away the background from a flat surface; called high relief when deeply cut, and low relief when shallowly cut.

• **Rosette**
A circular floral decoration; may be carved wood or cast or stamped metal.

Scratch carving
Simple shallow carving, usually geometric, executed with a V-shaped chisel.

Scroll
A spiral form resembling a partially rolled scroll of paper.

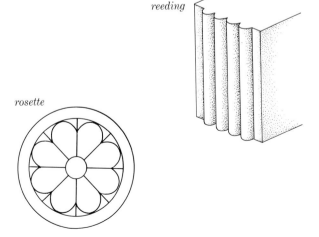

reeding

rosette

Secondary wood
Wood used for unexposed areas, such as drawer interiors,
concealed shelves, and backs; usually an inexpensive softwood
such as pine or poplar.

Serpentine
Convex in the center, flanked by concave ends (*see* plate 210).

Sheathed molding
Molding resembling the folds of linen or other cloth; also called
linenfold molding.

• **Skirt**
The bottom, independent element of a case piece, plain or shaped
and running between 2 vertical members; also called an apron.

Slant front
A lid or front hinged at the bottom that when upright rests
against the well top at an angle and falls forward to form a
writing surface; the writing surface is supported beneath by
slides or brackets.

Slide
A small square or rectangular piece of wood, often with a brass
knob, that pulls out to form a support for the lid of a slant-front
desk.

• **Slipper foot**
A pointed and elongated variation of the pad foot; most often
used on Queen Anne furniture.

• **Snake foot**
A narrow, elongated foot with a pointed end; found on Queen
Anne furniture.

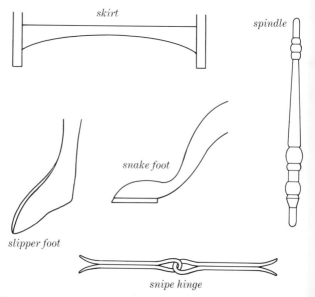

skirt

spindle

snake foot

slipper foot

snipe hinge

- **Snipe hinge**
  A hinge consisting of 2 pieces of interlocking wirelike iron; also called a cotter-pin hinge.

- **Spade foot**
  A tapered, rectangular foot; commonly found on Hepplewhite furniture.

- **Spanish foot**
  A scrolled foot with curving vertical ribs; used on turned legs in the William and Mary and Queen Anne periods.

- **Spindle**
  A slender turned rod set vertically in rows to make up a gallery; common on Victorian furniture.

- **Splashboard**
  A shaped extension of a backboard.

  Stenciling
  Painted decoration applied through a cutout pattern; common on country and late 19th-century mass-produced furniture.

  Stile
  A vertical structural unit.

  Stile-and-rail construction
  Construction characterized by the use of horizontal elements, called rails, and vertical elements, called stiles, usually joined by mortises and tenons.

- **Strap hinge**
  A decorative hinge consisting of 2 plates: a small rectangular leaf and, at a right angle, a long thin leaf.

  Stretcher
  The turned rods or flat boards used to reinforce furniture legs.

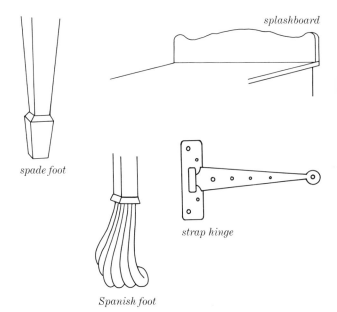

splashboard

spade foot

strap hinge

Spanish foot

Stringing
Narrow strip or strips of decorative inlay; frequently used to outline drawers and usually in light-colored wood.

• **Swag**
A decorative detail that is curved between 2 points; common on Federal and Victorian furniture, where it is often accompanied by carved floral or fruit forms.

Tambour door
A flexible sliding door composed of thin, vertical strips of wood glued to a heavy cloth; common on Federal furniture (*see* plate 68).

• **Teardrop brass**
A diamond-shaped or round mount or escutcheon; named for its pendant handle, which resembles a teardrop.

Tenon
A square, round, triangular, or rectangular wooden tongue that fits into a corresponding cavity, or mortise.

Till
A small box, with a hinged or sliding lid, attached to the inside of a low chest or blanket chest.

Transitional
Combining elements of 2 different stylistic periods in a single piece.

• **Trefoil**
A 3-lobed decorative motif.

• **Trifid foot**
A 3-lobed foot; found on Queen Anne cabriole legs; also called a Drake foot.

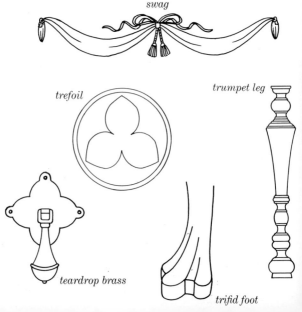

swag

trefoil

trumpet leg

teardrop brass

trifid foot

- **Trumpet leg**
  A turned leg that resembles a trumpet standing on end; characteristic of William and Mary furniture.

  Turned
  Shaped on a lathe; the wood rotates around a horizontal axis and is shaped by fixed chisels.

- **Turnip foot**
  A ball foot with a small collar at the base.

- **Valance**
  A balanced scroll on the lower edge of a cross member, typically the skirt.

  Veneer
  A thin layer of wood that is glued or nailed to the surface of a thicker piece for decoration and contrast; typically an expensive, attractive wood is applied to a common wood, such as pine.

  Well
  The hollow storage area within a desk or chest.

  Wicker
  Woven rattan, willow, bamboo, or other imported grasses.

- **Willow brass**
  A mount or escutcheon with a scrolled outline; common on Chippendale pieces.

- **X stretcher**
  A stretcher in the form of an X running diagonally between the legs; also called a cross stretcher.

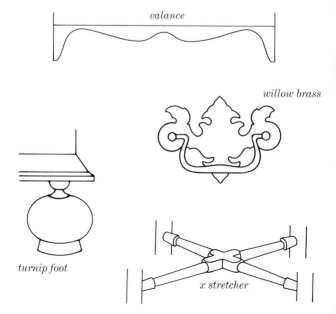

valance

willow brass

turnip foot

x stretcher

Bibliography

Andersen, Timothy J., *et al.*
California Design 1910
Pasadena, California: California Design Publications, 1974
Reprinted Santa Barbara, California: Peregrine Smith, Inc.,
1980.

Andrews, Edward Deming and Faith
Religion in Wood: A Book of Shaker Furniture
Bloomington, Indiana, and London: Indiana University Press,
1966.

Bishop, Robert
How to Know American Antique Furniture
New York: E. P. Dutton, Inc., 1973.

Bjerkoe, Ethel Hall
The Cabinetmakers of America
Garden City, New York: Doubleday & Co., Inc., 1957
Reprinted Exton, Pennsylvania: Schiffer Publishing, Ltd., 1981.

Butler, Joseph T.
American Antiques, 1800–1900: A Collector's History and Guide
New York: The Odyssey Press, 1965.

Cathers, David M.
*Furniture of the American Arts and Crafts Movement, Stickley
and Roycroft Mission Oak*
New York: New American Library, 1981.

Clark, Robert Judson, ed.
The Arts and Crafts Movement in America
Princeton, New Jersey: Princeton University Press, 1972.

Comstock, Helen
*American Furniture: Seventeenth, Eighteenth, and Nineteenth
Century Styles*
New York: The Viking Press, 1962
The Looking Glass in America 1700–1825
New York: The Viking Press, 1964, 1968.

Corbin, Patricia
All About Wicker
New York: E. P. Dutton, Inc., 1978.

Downs, Joseph
*American Furniture: Queen Anne and Chippendale Periods in
the Henry Francis du Pont Winterthur Museum*
New York: The Macmillan Co., 1952.

Elder, William Voss
*Maryland Queen Anne and Chippendale Furniture of the
Eighteenth Century*
Baltimore: The Baltimore Museum of Art, 1968.

Fairbanks, Jonathan, and Bates, Elizabeth Bidwell
American Furniture 1620 to the Present
New York: Richard Marek Publishers, 1981.

Fales, Dean A., Jr.
American Painted Furniture 1660–1880
New York: E. P. Dutton, Inc., 1979.

Fitzgerald, Oscar P.
Three Centuries of American Furniture
Englewood Cliffs, New Jersey: Prentice-Hall, Inc., 1981.

Garvin, Donnabelle and James, and Paige, John F.
Documented New Hampshire Furniture, 1750–1850
Hanover, New Hampshire: University Press Service of New England, 1979.

Gusler, Wallace B.
Furniture of Williamsburg and Eastern Virginia, 1710–1790
Richmond, Virginia: Virginia Museum of Fine Arts, n.d.

Handberg, Ejner
Shop Drawings of Shaker Furniture and Woodenware. 3 vols.
Stockbridge, Massachusetts: Berkshire Traveller Press, 1973, 1975, 1977.

Hanks, David
Innovative Furniture in America: From 1800 to the Present
New York: Horizon Press Publishers, 1981.

Hillier, Bevis
The World of Art Deco
New York: E. P. Dutton, Inc., 1981.

Horner, William Macpherson, Jr.
Blue Book, Philadelphia Furniture, William Penn to George Washington
Philadelphia: privately printed, 1935.

Hummel, Charles F.
A Winterthur Guide to American Chippendale Furniture: Middle Atlantic and Southern Colonies
New York: Rutledge Books/Crown Publishers, Inc., 1976.

Kassay, John
The Book of Shaker Furniture
Amherst, Massachusetts: University of Massachusetts Press, 1980.

Ketchum, William C., Jr.
The Catalog of American Antiques
New York: Rutledge Books, 1977; revised 1980.

Kettell, Russell Hawes
The Pine Furniture of Early New England
New York: Doubleday, Doran & Co., Inc., 1929
Reprinted New York: Dover Publications, Inc., n.d.

Kirk, John T.
Early American Furniture: How To Recognize, Buy and Care For the Most Beautiful Pieces—High Style, Country, Primitive, and Rustic
New York: Alfred A. Knopf, 1970
The Impecunious Collector's Guide to American Antiques
New York: Alfred A. Knopf, 1975.

Kovel, Ralph and Terry
American Country Furniture: 1780–1875
New York: Crown Publishers, Inc., 1965.

Lockwood, Luke Vincent
Colonial Furniture in America. 2 vols.
New York: Charles Scribner's Sons, 1926.

Madigan, Mary Jean Smith
Eastlake-Influenced American Furniture, 1870–1890
Yonkers, New York: The Hudson River Museum, 1973.

Makinson, Randell L.
Greene & Greene: Furniture and Related Designs
Santa Barbara, California: Peregrine Smith, Inc., 1978.

McClelland, Nancy
Duncan Phyfe and the English Regency
New York: Dover Publications, Inc., 1980.

McClinton, Katherine Morrison
Collecting American Victorian Antiques
New York: Charles Scribner's Sons, 1966
Reprinted Des Moines, Iowa: Wallace-Homestead Book
Company, 1978.

Meader, Robert F. W.
Illustrated Guide to Shaker Furniture
New York: The Greystone Press, 1950
Reprinted New York: Dover Publications, Inc., 1972.

Metropolitan Museum of Art
Nineteenth Century America: Furniture and Other Decorative Arts
New York: New York Graphic Society, 1971.

Miller, Edgar G., Jr.
American Antique Furniture. 2 vols.
1937; reprinted New York: Dover Publications, Inc., 1966.

Montgomery, Charles F.
American Furniture: The Federal Period 1785–1825
New York: The Viking Press, 1966.

Morse, John D., ed.
Country Cabinetwork and Simple City Furniture
Charlottesville, Virginia: University of Virginia Press, 1970.

Nagel, Charles
American Furniture 1650–1850
New York: Chanticleer Press, 1949.

Nutting, Wallace
Furniture of the Pilgrim Century. 2 vols.
Framingham, Massachusetts: Old America Company, 1921, 1924
Reprinted New York: Dover Publications, Inc., 1965
Furniture Treasury. 3 vols.
Framingham, Massachusetts: Old America Company, 1928–1933
Reprinted New York: The Macmillan Co., 1948, 1954.

Ormsbee, Thomas Hamilton
Field Guide to Early American Furniture
Boston: Little, Brown & Co., 1951
Field Guide to American Victorian Furniture
Boston: Little, Brown & Co., 1952.

Otto, Celia Jackson
American Furniture of the Nineteenth Century
New York: The Viking Press, 1965.

Page, Marian
Furniture Designed by Architects
New York: Whitney Library of Design, Watson-Guptill
Publications, 1980.

Pain, Howard
The Heritage of Country Furniture
New York: Van Nostrand Reinhold Co., 1978.

Rice, Norman S.
New York Furniture Before 1840
Albany, New York: Albany Institute of History and Art, 1962.

Schiffer, Herbert F. and Nancy
Woods We Live With
Exton, Pennsylvania: Schiffer Publishing, Ltd., 1977.

Schiffer, Herbert F. and Peter B.
Miniature Antique Furniture
Wynnewood, Pennsylvania: Livingston Publishing Co., 1972.

Schwartz, Marvin D.
American Furniture of the Colonial Period
New York: The Metropolitan Museum of Art, 1976
Country Style
Brooklyn, New York: The Brooklyn Museum, 1956.

Schwartz, Marvin D.; Stanek, Edward J.; and True, Douglas K.
The Furniture of John Henry Belter and the Rococo Revival
New York: E. P. Dutton, Inc., 1981.

Shea, John G.
Antique Country Furniture of North America, and Details of Its Construction
New York: Van Nostrand Reinhold Co., 1975, 1980.

Stickley, Gustav
Craftsman Homes: Architecture and Furnishings of the American Arts and Crafts Movement
1909; reprinted New York: Dover Publications, Inc., 1979.

Tracy, Berry B.; Johnson, Marilynn; Schwartz, Marvin D.; and Boorsch, Suzanne
Nineteenth-Century America: Furniture and Other Decorative Arts
New York: The Metropolitan Museum of Art, 1973.

Warren, David B.
Bayou Bend: American Furniture, Paintings and Silver from the Bayou Bend Collection
Houston: Museum of Fine Arts, 1975.

Watson, Aldren A.
Country Furniture
New York: Harper & Row Publishers, Inc., 1974.

White, Marshall S.
Wood Identification Handbook
New York: Charles Scribner's Sons, 1981.

Williams, H. Lionel
Country Furniture of Early America
New York: A. S. Barnes, 1963, 1978.

Antiques Publications

Antique Monthly
P. O. Drawer 2
Tuscaloosa, Alabama 35401
(800) 633-5957

Art & Antiques
Billboard Publications
1515 Broadway
New York, New York 10036
(212) 764-7300

Connoisseur
Hearst Publications
224 West 57th Street
New York, New York 10019
(800) 247-5470

Hobbies, The Magazine for Collectors
Lightner Publishing Corporation
1006 S. Michigan Avenue
Chicago, Illinois 60605
(312) 939-4767

The Magazine Antiques
Straight Enterprises, Inc.
551 Fifth Avenue
New York, New York 10017
(212) 922-1818

Maine Antique Digest
Box 358
Waldoboro, Maine 04572
(207) 832-7534

Newtown Bee
5 Church Hill Road
Newtown, Connecticut 06470
(203) 426-3141

Ohio Antiques Review
Box 538
Worthington, Ohio 43085
(614) 885-9757

Spinning Wheel Magazine
1981 Moreland Parkway
Annapolis, Maryland 21401
(301) 269-0681

Tri-State Trader
P. O. Box 90
Knightstown, Indiana 46148
(317) 345-5134

Public Collections

Most large art museums contain American furniture. In addition, many of the historic houses and buildings that are open to the public have fine examples. The sources listed below indicate significant permanent collections.

New England
Connecticut. Hartford: Wadsworth Atheneum. New Haven: Yale University Art Gallery.
Maine. Columbia Falls: Ruggles House. Ellsworth: Colonel Black Mansion. New Gloucester: The Shaker Museum.
Massachusetts. Andover: Addison Gallery of American Art, Phillips Academy. Boston: Museum of Fine Arts; The Society for the Preservation of New England Antiquities. Deerfield: Historic Deerfield. Hancock: Hancock Shaker Village, Shaker Community. Milton: China Trade Museum. Sturbridge: Old Sturbridge Village.
New Hampshire. Manchester: The Currier Gallery of Art.
Rhode Island. Providence: Museum of Art, Rhode Island School of Design.
Vermont. Shelburne: Shelburne Museum.

Mid-Atlantic Region
Delaware. Winterthur: Henry Francis du Pont Winterthur Museum.
Washington, D.C. Department of State Diplomatic Reception Rooms; National Museum of American History, Smithsonian Institution; The Octagon House; Renwick Gallery of the National Museum of American Art, Smithsonian Institution; The White House.
Maryland. Baltimore: Baltimore Museum of Art.
New Jersey. Newark: Newark Museum and the Ballantine House.
New York City. The Brooklyn Museum; Cooper-Hewitt Museum, Smithsonian Institution's National Museum of Design; Dyckman House and Museum; The Metropolitan Museum of Art; Morris-Jumel Mansion; Museum of American Folk Art; Museum of the City of New York; Museum of Modern Art; The New-York Historical Society; Old Merchant's House; Abigail Adams Smith Museum.
New York. Albany: Albany Institute of History and Art. Cooperstown: New York State Historical Association. Long Island: Old Bethpage Village, Old Bethpage. Old Chatham: The Shaker Museum. Rochester: The Margaret Woodbury Strong Museum. Utica: Munson-Williams-Proctor Institute.
Pennsylvania. Philadelphia: Historical Society of Pennsylvania; Independence Hall; Philadelphia Museum of Art.

South
Florida. Winter Park: The Morse Gallery of Art.
Georgia. Atlanta: The High Museum of Art.
Louisiana. New Orleans: Longue Vue Center for Decorative Arts.
Missouri. Kansas City: William Rockhill Nelson Gallery and Atkins Museum of Fine Arts. St. Louis: St. Louis Art Museum.
North Carolina. Winston-Salem: Museum of Early Southern Decorative Arts.
Virginia. Norfolk: Chrysler Museum at Norfolk. Richmond: Virginia Museum of Fine Arts. Williamsburg: Colonial Williamsburg; The Abby Aldrich Rockefeller Collection of American Folk Art.

Midwest
Illinois. Chicago: Art Institute of Chicago; Chicago Historical Society.
Indiana. Indianapolis: Indianapolis Museum of Art.
Kansas. Lawrence: Helen Foresman Spencer Museum of Art, the University of Kansas.
Michigan. Dearborn: Greenfield Village and Henry Ford Museum. Detroit: Detroit Historical Museum; Detroit Institute of Arts.
Minnesota. Minneapolis: Minneapolis Institute of Arts.
Ohio. Cincinnati: Cincinnati Art Museum. Cleveland: Cleveland Museum of Art; Western Reserve Historical Society. Toledo: Toledo Museum of Art.
Wisconsin. Milwaukee: Milwaukee Public Museum; Villa-Terrace Museum of the Decorative Arts.

Rockies, Southwest, and West Coast
Arizona. Tucson: Arizona Historical Society.
California. Los Angeles: Hollyhock House; Los Angeles County Museum of Art. Oakland: The Oakland Museum. Pasadena: Gamble House. San Diego: San Diego Museum of Art, Balboa Park. San Francisco: M. H. de Young Memorial Museum, Fine Arts Museums.
Colorado. Denver: The Denver Art Museum.
Texas. Dallas: Dallas Museum of Fine Arts. Houston: The Bayou Bend Collection, The Museum of Fine Arts.
Washington. Seattle: Seattle Art Museum.

Where to Buy Antique Furniture

Throughout America, antique furniture is available at thousands of shops, shows, flea markets, house sales, and auctions. Each source has its advantages and disadvantages.

Shops
Many, if not most, antiques are sold by dealers. These professionals are usually glad to share their knowledge with customers. In an antiques shop or a dealer's home, you have time to examine a piece thoroughly, and you rarely need to make an immediate decision to buy. Since there are dealers specializing in virtually every field and in every price range, you are sure to find one who suits your taste and budget.

Shows
Antiques shows take place regularly in most cities and give collectors a chance to meet a number of dealers at one time. Because many collectors come to these shows, dealers usually exhibit their finest wares there, making it somewhat easier for collectors to find objects that are hard to locate. But antiques shows last only a few days, and since several collectors are often interested in the same item, decisions must be made rather quickly.

Flea Markets and House Sales
At flea markets, the sellers are rarely professionals. Most of the merchandise is inexpensive, undocumented or unidentified, or sometimes even new. Here you must depend totally on your own knowledge. The same is true of house sales: whether it is a tag, garage, or private sale, buyers must be able to distinguish between true bargains and overpriced knickknacks.

Auctions
Whether they are held in the city or in the country, auctions are exciting. Buyers have only moments to place a bid, and the bids determine the eventual selling price. But buying at auction requires self-restraint. A particular auction may not have the specific object you are seeking, and it may be best to wait until you find exactly what you want.

Advice for Buyers
No matter where you buy, be cautious. Although dishonest practices are rare, anyone may occasionally be guilty of poor judgment; deliberate deceptions are far less common than honest mistakes. Deal with the most reputable people you can find and if you suspect that an object is not what it is said to be, don't buy.

Buying at Auction

Most collectors eventually try buying at auctions. The lure is understandable, for tales abound of detecting rare pieces concealed by coats of paint and dirt, or sought-after objects that fetch half their predicted price. Most of these tales date from the 1920s to 1940s, when bargains were commonplace. Auctions today are attended by an army of sophisticated collectors and dealers, well-schooled in what to look for and how much to pay. The best tool in buying—no matter where—is a knowledge of furniture styles, construction methods, and current market prices. And at auction, knowing the rules of the game can help prevent costly mistakes.

How an Auction Works
An auction is a sale of objects to the highest bidders. The seller, or the consignor, offers goods to prospective buyers through his agent, the auctioneer. The bidder offering the most money for a given item buys the "lot" (one piece or a group of pieces sold together). The auctioneer always tries to stimulate bidding and to get the highest price, since he (or his firm) generally receives a percentage of the sale as payment or commission.

The Viewing and Other Preliminaries
The first step toward informed bidding is to attend the viewing before the auction, an advertised period of a few hours or days during which the objects offered may be examined by the public. Never bid on something unless you have checked it thoroughly at the viewing. Compare what you see with the information given in the catalogue, if one is available. If you have any question about an object, its attribution, or its condition, talk to the auctioneer or the firm's specialist in that field. If a catalogue is not available, carry a small notebook to jot down the lot number and other information about the object, particularly its condition. If you feel uncertain about the auctioneer's or your own judgment about a piece, especially an expensive one, you may wish to hire a consultant—often a dealer who, for a fee, will advise you or sometimes even bid for you.
The viewing is also a good time to find out what form of payment the auctioneer requires. Some will take only cash or certified checks; others will accept personal checks with proper identification, or credit cards.

The Sale
At most larger auctions, the auctioneer will provide estimated price ranges for the pieces in the sale. These are usually printed in the auction catalogue or on a separate list. Though pieces quite often sell for more or less than the estimates, these should give you some idea of what the auctioneer expects a piece to fetch. Also, many large auction houses allow a seller to set a "reserve" on a lot—the price below which it will not be sold, frequently close to the low estimate. If bidding does not reach this minimum, the lot will be withdrawn and returned to the consignor for a small handling fee.
Decide in advance the price you are willing to pay for a particular lot. The Price Guide section of this book provides general guidelines and prevailing market price ranges to help you set your own bidding limit.
The best place to sit at an auction is toward the rear, where you can best see what is going on. There are two customary ways to bid—by raising a hand or by using the numbered paddle sometimes furnished by the auctioneer. Listen closely because the bidding is often extremely rapid. When your pre-established

price limit has been reached, stop. This is the key to wise auction bidding.

Patience and persistence are required, since at every auction some pieces may sell for more or for less than most people anticipate. There is almost always a "sleeper" or two, particularly just after or even just before a high-priced lot has captured the attention of the audience.

At many auction houses, someone who has attended the viewing but cannot be present at the auction itself can leave a bid with the personnel. Such bids will be treated as the maximum the absentee bidder is willing to spend, so that if there is little competition when the auction house bids for you, the final price you pay may be far less than your top bid. An out-of-town collector who has seen an auction catalogue but cannot attend the viewing and auction may sometimes be allowed to place a bid by telephone, but such blind bidding is not recommended unless the bidder delegates someone to examine the object for him prior to the sale.

Collecting Your Purchases

The fall of the gavel and the cry "sold" mark a successful bid. Now the buyer must pay for the purchase and remove it from the auction premises. Large auction houses will ship items for a fee; most auctioneers do not have such services, however, and the buyer is responsible for transporting a purchase within a stated time limit.

Price Guide

Sooner or later every experienced collector will buy a piece of furniture for much less than its true market value. More often, however, novices pay far more than they should because they are unfamiliar with contemporary prices. To appreciate bargains when they occur and protect against buying foolishly, it is vital to understand today's marketplace. In the past 20 years, interest in antiques and collectibles has grown tremendously, making it increasingly difficult to keep abreast of current values. As certain types of furniture become popular, their prices may double or triple, while other less popular pieces may decrease in value or simply keep pace with inflation. To follow these trends, collectors keep informed about auction reports and talk to dealers about price variations.

Many beginners regard auctions as the ultimate price determinant, for they do offer the most dramatic evidence of the market in action. A piece is presented; all bidders compete as equals; the highest bidder purchases the piece. Were it only so easy. Anyone who has observed 2 bidders competing for the same object knows that this type of warfare can drive prices well above a reasonable figure. And because some collectors seek out objects that were once owned by the famous, prestige can warp auction records as well. On the other hand, auction prices can be unrealistically low if, for some reason, attendance at the sale is poor or doubt has been cast on the authenticity of the lot. Yet in spite of the fact that auction results must be dealt with cautiously, they do reflect long-term market trends.

Dealers' prices are often the most accurate guide to what is happening on the market. Their retail prices are based on the wholesale price plus a reasonable amount for overhead and profit. Because dealers must remain competitive, their prices tend to become uniform over a period of time.

This price guide is based on auction records and consultations with dealers and knowledgeable collectors. Remember that experienced collectors understand, and we agree, that a price guide is just that, a guide. No 2 objects are identical, and no 2 buying situations are the same. The prices listed here are national averages. Some types of furniture are more popular in certain parts of the country. For example, oak generally brings more on the West Coast than it does on the East, and Victorian items are more in demand in the South than they are in the North. An even more important variable is the presence or absence of a maker's mark. A good piece of Federal furniture may bring $3000, but if it bears the mark of a famous cabinet shop, it may fetch as much as $30,000. Similarly, a plain Mission-style chest of drawers may cost as little as $250, but if it has the label of Gustav Stickley's firm, the price may soar to as much as $3000. The prices given here assume that each piece is in good condition, with no major restoration, even if the illustrated example clearly shows some damage. Before you buy a repaired, altered, or damaged piece, be sure to adjust the prices given here accordingly. On the other hand, if a piece has exceptional veneer or outstanding decoration, such as fine carving, it will of course command a higher price than an average example. Scarcity also affects prices. Some rare period pieces are almost impossible to price accurately. For example, there are so few 17th-century court and press cupboards in existence that they seldom appear on the market; when they do, competition is stiff and prices may leap from one sale to the next. Some pieces made in the past century are handcrafted and one of a kind; if they have never changed hands, no auction record exists for them.

Furniture from the 1940s and 1950s also rarely appears at auction; the prices given for these modern pieces are based on dealers' estimates.

Sometimes a particular type of object will capture the public fancy, and prices will rise accordingly. When interest diminishes, prices usually fall. These trends are hard to predict. Currently Art Deco and 20th-century modern pieces are becoming increasingly popular, especially in metropolitan areas. Although many of these pieces were mass-produced and are still abundant, in city stores they may command hundreds of dollars. For finer pieces, some collectors are willing to pay thousands of dollars. The ranges given here reflect urban prices as well as what you may expect to pay in a country or secondhand shop. Finally, and most important, the objects featured here stand for a class of similar objects. Consequently, the prices given refer to that class, as the very wide range (e.g., $1500–10,000) for some suggests, and not to the specific pieces shown.

Dry Sinks, Washstands, and Commodes

These pieces are extremely popular with collectors, and, luckily, numerous examples are available. Simple dry sinks often cost only $200 to $500, while elaborate examples can fetch as much as $2500. Washstands come in almost every price range. Some late Federal and Empire stands can be had for $350, but the rarer Shaker pieces may command as much as $8500. Most commodes cost between $300 and $500. Oak pieces are usually good buys, selling for less than $300, and Cottage-style pieces seem underpriced, sometimes bringing as little as $150 or $200. More costly are marble-top commodes, those made of fine woods, and pieces with good grain- or sponge-painting, but even these are often priced at less than $500. The rarest and most expensive commodes are the early Federal examples.

1 Primitive dry sink $150–275
2 Single-door dry sink $400–650
3 Double-door dry sink $1500–2500
4 Shaker washstand $7500–8500
5 Eastlake commode $275–375
6 Cottage-style commode $250–550
7 Victorian marble-top commode $400–500
8 Victorian single-door commode $350–450
9 Victorian commode $125–275
10 Cottage-style "necessary" $150–600
11 Decorated lift-top commode $300–850
12 Cottage-style lift-top commode $200–550
13 Empire lift-top commode $250–450
14 Shaker child's commode-washstand $3500–5000
15 Late Federal transitional washstand $350–650
16 Country Sheraton washstand $1000–1500
17 Sheraton washstand $1500–3000
18 Federal marble-top commode $30,000–50,000

Servers, Serving Tables, and Sideboards

These pieces are available in many forms and in almost every price range, from simple servers that may fetch only $125 to Federal sideboards that often command more than $20,000. In general, Empire, Victorian, and Colonial Revival examples are the best buys. Well-made Empire sideboards and servers in mahogany or walnut sometimes cost as little as $300, and many Victorian pieces are only slightly more expensive. Elaborate Federal sideboards are out of the reach of most collectors, and even the smaller Federal serving tables and servers may cost $1000 to $3000 or more. But because they are so scarce, they make good investments. For those who want a piece that looks like a Federal sideboard, but not at a 4- or 5-figure price, Colonial Revival pieces are good alternatives. Most retail in antiques stores for $300 to $700, and sell for even less at country sales and in secondhand stores. These are also good places to look for factory-made 20th-century pieces. Often overpriced in city stores at $500 or more, they are plentiful and can be tracked down in secondhand stores or stored in attics. On the other hand, some hand-crafted 20th-century examples are one of a kind and justifiably expensive.

19 Renaissance Revival sideboard $700–900
20 Empire sideboard $550–750

21 Oak bowfront sideboard $300–450
22 Rococo Revival sideboard $650–850
23 Painted country Empire sideboard $450–750
24 Country Empire server $400–600
25 Empire square-leg server $500–700
26 Painted country Federal server $1500–10,000
27 Mission-style server $125–650
28 Hepplewhite serving table $3000–5000
29 Sheraton serving table $2500–4500
30 Sheraton server $1500–2500
31 Colonial Revival sideboard $150–600
32 Hepplewhite tambour sideboard $8000–12,000
33 Hepplewhite serpentine and bowfront sideboard
   $15,000–25,000
34 Sheraton bowfront sideboard $9000–13,000
35 Arts and Crafts sideboard $12,000–18,000
36 Art Deco serving table $600–1000
37 Art Deco sideboard $1500–6000
38 Modern molded-plywood sideboard $250–500

Desks and Low Secretaries

The desks featured here range from as little as $150 to more than
$80,000. Most expensive are the early period pieces. Although
many 19th- and 20th-century desks bring only a few hundred
dollars, certain styles have attracted much attention from
collectors and consequently are relatively high-priced. For
example, oak kneehole and rolltop desks, which were mostly
mass-produced, can fetch as much as $3000; and in large cities,
Art Deco pieces are also costly. However, bargains may still be
found. Look for Empire and Victorian desks made of walnut or
mahogany. Relatively unpopular now, these quality pieces can
often be had for less than $1000. Late Victorian oak and Colonial
Revival slant-front desks usually range from $300 to $600, as do
Mission-style pieces that lack the mark of a major manufacturer.
Finally, some Victorian wicker pieces and country schoolmasters'
desks may cost only $300 and can sometimes be found for even
less in rural shops.

39 Desk or Bible box $400–700
40 William and Mary inlaid desk box $7000–10,000
41 Carved desk or Bible box $2750–4500
42 Slope-lid desk box $3000–5000
43 Countinghouse desk $150–350
44 Shaker child's desk $4500–6500
45 Schoolmaster's desk $500–900
46 William and Mary desk-on-frame $12,000–18,000
47 Country Chippendale desk-on-frame $2900–3800
48 Mission-style slant-front desk $250–500
49 Mission-style slant-front desk $250–1000
50 Arts and Crafts slant-front desk $9000–15,000
51 Queen Anne slant-front desk $7000–16,000
52 Queen Anne miniature slant-front desk $10,000–15,000
53 Chippendale slant-front desk $4000–6000
54 Chippendale oxbow slant-front desk $8000–12,000
55 William and Mary slant-front desk $25,000–35,000
56 Late Victorian slant-front desk $350–550
57 Queen Anne desk-on-frame $10,000–20,000
58 Colonial Revival desk-on-frame $400–900
59 Hepplewhite bowfront tambour secretary $5500–9500

60 Shaker sewing desk $8500–12,000
61 Art Deco secretary $400–2000
62 Art Deco kneehole desk $250–750
63 Pedestal desk $400–700
64 Rolltop desk $1500–3000
65 Eastlake rotary cylinder desk $2500–6500
66 Chippendale kneehole desk $55,000–85,000
67 Empire kneehole desk $1000–2800
68 Hepplewhite tambour desk $4000–6500
69 Hepplewhite fold-out writing desk $4000–6000
70 Mission-style kneehole desk $250–700
71 Child's rolltop desk-on-frame $155–225
72 Victorian wicker desk $350–850
73 Mission-style writing table $150–550
74 Mission-style desk with writing boxes $200–400
75 Art Deco pedestal-base desk $300–600
76 Modern free-form desk $600–850

Secretaries and Tall Desks

The best buys here are pieces in the Empire, Victorian, and Colonial Revival styles. Largely ignored by collectors, Empire secretaries can often be had for less than $2000; Federal examples made only 2 or 3 decades earlier may bring 7 or 8 times as much. Sturdy Victorian fall-front and cylinder pieces are often overlooked, and are good values at less than $1500. In contrast, because the Art Nouveau desk-over-bookcase and the late Victorian side-by-side are usually poorly made, they seem overpriced at even $1000. Unlike most Victorian pieces, the Wooton desk is expensive. Because few are available, collectors compete actively for them when they appear on the market. Further, few are alike, so they vary greatly in price. Most Colonial Revival secretaries are well made and offer a collector a chance to own what looks like an 18th-century piece for as little as $1500. The attractive and small Arts and Crafts and Mission-style pieces are now favorably priced at $600 to $900. But, as always, if a Mission piece bears the mark of a well-known designer, such as Gustav Stickley, it can cost 2 or 3 times as much as an unmarked example. Although William and Mary, Queen Anne, and Chippendale secretaries command extremely high prices, they continue to increase in value, making them attractive investments for those who can afford them.

77 Sheraton secretary $3000–5000
78 Hepplewhite secretary $8000–15,000
79 Empire secretary $1500–2500
80 Victorian fall-front desk-over-cupboard $600–1500
81 Chippendale block-front secretary $100,000–150,000
82 Queen Anne flat-top secretary $16,000–28,000
83 Country Sheraton secretary $4000–10,000
84 Shaker built-in secretary $5000–7500
85 Country Empire secretary $1500–3500
86 Arts and Crafts secretary $600–900
87 Art Nouveau desk-over-bookcase $250–450
88 Victorian cylinder desk $800–1200
89 Side-by-side $800–1000
90 Wooton desk $7000–35,000

Cupboards, Cabinets, and Other Large Storage Pieces

The prices here are as varied as the objects themselves. Because cupboards and cabinets are extremely popular with collectors, most are fairly expensive. The exceptions are rough, undecorated country pieces and some cabinets made in the 20th century, which often sell for a few hundred dollars. Most cost considerably more. For example, no matter how simple they appear, well-made side cupboards usually range between $1000 and $2000, corner cupboards often fetch between $2000 and $3000, and glazed pieces may cost as much as $8000. For fine period pieces, prices can soar to $10,000.

Wardrobes usually bring less, in part because they are so large, making them impractical for many homes. Some late Victorian examples sell for as little as $450, although the oak pieces made around 1890 are currently quite popular and may command prices of more than $1000. Less common forms, such as linen presses and étagères, are priced according to age, scarcity, workmanship, and condition. Early period pieces are the most expensive, followed by a few exceptionally well-crafted Victorian examples.

Colonial Revival cabinets generally remain good buys, with many selling for less than $500. Furniture made in the 1950s is attracting increasing collector attention. Although most pieces are now priced from $250 to $500, prices seem to go up every year, making this a good time to invest.

91 Jelly cupboard $350–750
92 Hudson Valley kas $4000–9000
93 Linen press $3000–6000
94 Victorian wardrobe $400–750
95 Country wardrobe $500–2500
96 Paneled wardrobe $1400–1850
97 Icebox $400–900
98 Built-in country wardrobe $750–2000
99 Built-in side cupboard $1200–1600
100 Solid-door corner cupboard $2000–3000
101 Open cupboard $1800–2400
102 Scalloped open cupboard $2000–3000
103 Low scalloped corner cupboard $2000–3000
104 Chippendale architectural built-in corner cupboard $3000–8000
105 Shaker cupboard-over-drawers $2500–3500
106 Hoosier cabinet $300–650
107 Glazed setback cupboard $1300–1700
108 Glazed corner cupboard $3000–4000
109 Empire glass-front cupboard $2500–3250
110 Empire corner cupboard $3000–4000
111 Federal corner cupboard $4000–8000
112 Chippendale glazed cupboard $5000–10,000
113 Eastlake bookcase and cabinet $4000–6000
114 Mission-style glass-front cabinet $600–1000
115 Colonial Revival glass-front bookcase $200–550
116 Renaissance Revival corner cupboard $900–1600
117 Gothic Revival vitrine $1500–4500
118 Victorian china cabinet $450–950
119 Colonial Revival china cabinet $250–450
120 Art Deco china cabinet $500–1000
121 Art Nouveau étagère $750–1500
122 Anglo-Japanese étagère $1500–3500
123 Renaissance Revival cupboard-base étagère $4000–12,000
124 Neo-Grec cabinet $6500–12,000

125 Renaissance Revival wardrobe $750–1250
126 Victorian transitional bedside cabinet $350–550
127 Renaissance Revival bedside cabinet $400–700
128 Renaissance Revival music cabinet $550–750
129 Art Nouveau–Art Deco cabinet $150–250
130 Arts and Crafts–Mission-style liquor cabinet $150–450
131 20th-century double cabinet $400–650
132 20th-century bedside cabinet $175–400

Highboys and Tall Chests of Drawers

This group contains some of the rarest and most costly pieces of American furniture as well as some of the least expensive. At one extreme, highboys from the William and Mary, Queen Anne, and Chippendale periods typically cost from $15,000 to more than $150,000. At the other extreme, plain oak factory-made chests of drawers from the turn of the century may sell for as little as $125. Highboys are expensive because they were made during a relatively short period and because many are extraordinarily well crafted. Colonial Revival pieces, which often fetch as little as $1200, are realistic alternatives for most collectors.

Tall chests of drawers remained popular for a much longer period of time and consequently offer a much wider stylistic and price range. As usual, early period pieces are the most costly, and Victorian and 20th-century examples the best buys. Victorian oak chests, many of them in the Eastlake style, often sell for $300 to $800, but occasionally bring as little as $125. Walnut and mahogany revival pieces usually cost more.

In general, pieces made in the 20th century are unevenly priced. Those bearing the mark of a well-known manufacturer bring hundreds of dollars more than their unmarked counterparts. Unless you are interested in the work of a particular designer, look for quality of design and construction, rather than an important name, in these modern pieces.

133 William and Mary trumpet-leg highboy $40,000–100,000
134 Chippendale flat-top highboy $15,000–30,000
135 Queen Anne flat-top highboy $15,000–20,000
136 Queen Anne bonnet-top highboy $30,000–60,000
137 Chippendale bonnet-top highboy $85,000–155,000
138 Colonial Revival chest-on-chest $1500–3000
139 Chippendale chest-on-chest $40,000–60,000
140 Federal flat-top chest-on-chest $12,000–20,000
141 Chippendale tall chest of drawers $5500–8500
142 Sheraton tall chest-on-frame $3500–6500
143 Renaissance Revival tall chest of drawers $950–2500
144 Mission-style tall chest of drawers $300–3000
145 Oak tall chest of drawers $125–250
146 Renaissance Revival tall chest of drawers $500–1000
147 Art Deco tall chest of drawers $300–800
148 Art Deco chest of drawers and clothespress $300–1000

Lowboys, Dressing Tables, Dressers, and Shaving Stands

The pieces in this group vary considerably in price, from rare lowboys that may command as much as $60,000 to some 19th- and 20th-century dressing tables and dressers that sell for a few hundred dollars. Next to lowboys, Federal and Empire pieces with fine woods and decoration are the most expensive, selling for at least $1000 and often for as much as $10,000. Collectors interested in these periods should consider the country and painted pieces that occasionally cost as little as $450.

Many Victorian dressing tables and dressers are reasonably priced, selling for around $500. Victorian shaving stands are amusing although relatively expensive novelties, bringing between $400 and $1000. They may be good investments, especially those in Art Nouveau and Anglo-Japanese styles, which seem most likely to appreciate in value.

Art Deco pieces seem to become more expensive every year, and dressing tables are no exception. Although collectors occasionally pick them up in the country or in secondhand stores for only $100 to $200, in urban shops they may command $1000 or more, especially if they are the work of a well-known designer.

149 William and Mary lowboy $40,000–60,000
150 Queen Anne lowboy $25,000–40,000
151 Colonial Revival lowboy $300–500
152 Chippendale lowboy $30,000–60,000
153 Hepplewhite dressing table $3500–5000
154 Country Sheraton cabinet-top dressing table $1000–2000
155 Hepplewhite cabinet-top dressing table $3000–8500
156 Colonial Revival dressing table $200–400
157 Renaissance Revival shaving stand $600–750
158 Art Nouveau shaving stand $750–1000
159 Cottage-style dressing table $350–550
160 Late Sheraton dressing table $8000–12,000
161 Country Empire dressing table $450–750
162 Chinese export shaving stand $2000–3000
163 Eastlake tall chest with bonnet cupboard $750–1200
164 Late Victorian tall chest with bonnet cupboard $250–450
165 Late Victorian bowfront dresser $350–550
166 Empire dresser $1000–2000
167 Mission-style dresser $350–3000
168 Victorian marble-top dresser $450–650
169 Empire dressing mirror $3000–6000
170 Eastlake oak dresser $250–350
171 Eastlake drop-side dresser $275–650
172 Cottage-style dresser $450–700
173 Art Deco dressing table $750–1200
174 Art Deco pedestal dressing table $125–175
175 Lacquered Art Deco dressing table $400–800
176 Art Deco portable dressing table $250–400
177 Modern dressing table $500–900
178 Glass-top dressing table $700–1000

Mirrors

Mirrors come in every style, size, and price range, making them favorites with collectors. Age and condition largely determine value, with the presence of original glass sometimes doubling the worth of a piece. Among the most costly are rare Queen Anne and Chippendale examples, which often fetch as much as $15,000; some Federal mirrors may also bring many thousands of dollars. Most of the other pieces in this group are priced between $50 and $500.

Not all Federal pieces are extremely expensive. Some architectural mirrors with reverse painting range between $350 and $500, and Empire tabernacle examples cost even less. Later Victorian looking glasses are among the best buys, with many selling for as little as $125. Equally reasonable are some 20th-century mirrors, including Tramp Art and Art Deco examples. An elegant Federal dressing mirror may command as much as $1500, but 20th-century pieces can be bargains. Look for good Colonial Revival and Art Deco examples in out-of-the-way places, where they may cost as little as $50 or $100.

179 Shaker mirror $700–950
180 Stenciled mirror $300–500
181 Tramp Art mirror $75–125
182 Eastlake mirror $125–175
183 Late Victorian hall mirror $125–175
184 Eastlake pier glass $250–650
185 Sheraton architectural mirror $350–500
186 Empire tabernacle mirror $250–400
187 Empire ogee-frame mirror $100–200
188 Victorian oval mirror $75–250
189 Federal girandole mirror $1500–3000
190 Federal gilded mirror $2000–4000
191 Queen Anne fret-carved mirror $10,000–15,000
192 Chippendale fret-carved mirror $600–1000
193 Hepplewhite fret-carved mirror $7500–12,500
194 Art Deco mirror $150–250
195 Victorian cast-iron cheval glass $250–350
196 Queen Anne dressing glass $800–1200
197 Colonial Revival dressing mirror $85–135
198 Mission-style dressing mirror $125–625
199 Federal mirrored dressing box $1000–1500
200 Hepplewhite dressing glass $900–1300
201 Art Deco vanity mirror $65–125
202 Modern dressing-table mirror $50–90

Chests of Drawers

The least expensive chests of drawers are those produced in the past century. Sturdy, handcrafted Empire pieces are often ignored by collectors and consequently can be remarkable bargains. Occasionally fine examples with interesting veneer, such as bird's-eye maple, or grain-painting may bring only $300 to $500, and plainer pieces often cost much less. Victorian oak chests come in a variety of forms, with straight, bowed, or serpentine fronts, and often fetch between $300 and $500. At an even lower price level, look for Victorian Cottage-style pieces, which can sometimes be tracked down for only $200.

Colonial Revival chests vary substantially in style and quality. A Chippendale-style piece made in the late 19th century is a bargain at $200, while a poorly made Federal-style chest from the 1930s is overpriced at the same figure. Prices for other 20th-century pieces vary greatly. Unmarked Mission-style chests are fairly priced at around $150, but marked examples are highly desirable and consequently command much higher prices. Some Art Deco and 20th-century modern examples are reasonable, provided they do not have expensive lacquerwork, exotic woods, or the mark of a well-known maker.

Early period pieces are predictably expensive. Even a plain William and Mary example may bring $5000, and for a block-front Chippendale chest of drawers, the price may soar to more than $60,000.

203 William and Mary plain chest of drawers $3500–6500
204 Chippendale oxbow-front chest of drawers $10,000–15,000

205 Hepplewhite oxbow-front chest of drawers $8000–12,000
206 Colonial Revival block-front chest of drawers $400–700
207 Chippendale block-front chest of drawers $35,000–60,000
208 Chippendale bombé chest of drawers $150,000–200,000
209 Chippendale serpentine-front chest of drawers $20,000–40,000
210 Hepplewhite serpentine-front chest of drawers $4500–8500
211 Hepplewhite bowfront chest of drawers $3000–6000
212 Hepplewhite straight-front chest of drawers $2000–3000
213 Sheraton straight-front chest of drawers $1000–3000
214 Sheraton bowfront chest of drawers $3000–5000
215 Sheraton transitional bowfront chest of drawers $2500–4000
216 William and Mary paneled chest of drawers $20,000–60,000
217 Eastlake marble-top chest of drawers $250–450
218 Cottage-style chest of drawers $200–350
219 Pennsylvania painted chest of drawers $25,000–40,000
220 Country Sheraton chest of drawers $1000–1500
221 Victorian bowfront chest of drawers $300–525
222 Federal miniature chest of drawers $1000–1500
223 Country Hepplewhite chest of drawers $800–1200
224 Shaker chest of drawers $2500–3500
225 Miniature chest of drawers $400–700
226 Federal false-drawer blanket chest $1000–1900
227 Federal-Empire splashboard chest of drawers $650–950
228 Empire chest of drawers $800–1200
229 Art Deco chest of drawers $150–250
230 Modern chest of drawers $450–700

Chests and Blanket Chests

Chests were among the first pieces of furniture made in America and continued to be produced into the 20th century. For collectors, this means that they are abundant and available in a diversity of styles and price ranges. Age and decoration largely determine price. Plain pieces made in the 19th century may fetch as little as $100, but rare decorated chests from the Pilgrim century often command $50,000 or more. And with 19th-century pieces, good painted, carved, or molded decoration can raise prices to several thousand dollars. The price of a blanket chest depends on the same factors. Ordinary pieces may sell for around $500, but good grain- or sponge-painting may increase prices to more than $1000. Shaker blanket chests are particularly sought after today and often command as much as $5000.

231 Painted dome-top chest $300–600
232 Sea chest $1000–3500
233 Pennsylvania-type decorated box $500–2000
234 Miniature chest $1000–4000
235 Child's chest $250–500
236 Painted panel chest $350–650
237 Early 6-board chest $2500–4000
238 Pilgrim-century carved and painted chest-over-drawer $10,000–15,000
239 Storage chest $450–850
240 Empire 6-board chest $300–600
241 Dower chest $15,000–30,000
242 Chippendale chest-over-drawers $900–1200
243 Hepplewhite chest-over-drawers $900–1200
244 Hepplewhite blanket chest $1000–2000
245 Shaker blanket chest $3000–4000
246 3-drawer blanket chest $850–1650

247 Chippendale paneled chest-over-drawers $4000–6000
248 Hadley-type chest $30,000–45,000
249 Spindle-decorated chest $20,000–30,000
250 Colonial Revival paneled chest-over-drawers $1500–2500
251 Court cupboard $80,000–120,000
252 Pilgrim-century chest-on-frame $60,000–90,000

Small Storage Units

These small pieces are extremely popular with collectors and often command high prices, yet bargains can still be found. Look for attractive paint or inlays, or interesting drawer and shelf arrangements. Factory-made Victorian shelving units and cabinets are largely overlooked and tend to be underpriced. For example, at $200 to $400, ebonized Anglo-Japanese cabinets are good buys, as are Eastlake shelving units with scrollwork at $125. Some Victorian corner cabinets with mirrors cost as little as $75.

Small country cupboards and cabinets are much in demand. Spice cabinets are among the most popular types, and this has driven their price up to as much as $650. Simple tabletop cupboards often bear the more attractive price of $200 to $300.

Candle and pipe boxes, spoon racks, and pewter shelves made in the late 18th and early 19th centuries are among the most desirable of small collectibles. Well-decorated pieces may fetch as much as $3500, placing them out of the reach of many collectors. Plain examples, often selling for $200 to $300, are reasonable alternatives.

253 Hanging shelf-and-drawer unit $300–850
254 Pewter shelf $600–1000
255 Hanging double candle box $1000–1500
256 Hanging spoon rack $2000–3000
257 Decorated hanging candle box $2500–3500
258 Hanging pipe rack $1000–1500
259 Hanging shelves $900–1400
260 Victorian whatnot shelf $75–135
261 Fret-carved hanging corner cabinet $125–175
262 Victorian mirrored hanging corner cabinet $75–140
263 Eastlake mirrored hanging shelves $75–250
264 Eastlake hanging shelves $75–200
265 Anglo-Japanese hanging cabinet $250–450
266 Glazed hanging wall cabinet $400–700
267 Anglo-Japanese mirrored cabinet $250–350
268 Architectural tabletop cupboard $1500–3500
269 Victorian hanging file cabinet $75–150
270 Shaker tabletop cupboard $950–1200
271 Tabletop cupboard and drawers $175–275
272 Spice cabinet $150–650

Miscellaneous Furnishings

Because of their diversity, these objects vary greatly in price. More than half sell for less than $300, and many for less than $100 or $200. The most expensive pieces, such as an Art Nouveau cast-iron fish tank or a folk-art hall rack, may approach $4000; most of these are rare, one-of-a-kind objects. The less costly examples, including planters and umbrella stands, are appealing, creating as they do the look of a particular period or style for a relatively small price.

273 Hanging cattle-horn hat rack $45–250
274 Rustic gun rack $35–85
275 Bamboo magazine rack $75–135
276 Corner umbrella rack $60–120
277 Mission-style umbrella stand $75–250
278 Mission-style solid board umbrella stand $40–80
279 Victorian cast-iron umbrella stand $300–400
280 Rococo Revival cast-iron umbrella rack $175–250
281 Match holder and ashtray on stand $25–50
282 Wicker smoking stand $50–125
283 Art Deco smoking stand $100–175
284 Rustic smoking stand $85–150
285 Mission-style plant stand $50–300
286 Victorian double-shelf plant stand $70–120
287 Rustic plant stand $20–40
288 Bamboo planter $35–85
289 Modern abstract planter $20–100
290 Victorian wicker planter $75–150
291 Art Nouveau cast-iron fish tank $1500–3500
292 Victorian wicker planter $85–250
293 Art Deco planter $250–375
294 Arts and Crafts book trough $175–350
295 Art Deco liquor cabinet $275–700
296 Art Deco tobacco humidor $50–100
297 Dough box on stand $300–700
298 Colonial Revival tea cart $150–200
299 Modern tea cart $100–175
300 Victorian open shelves $95–185
301 Revolving book and magazine rack $175–300
302 Mission-style bookshelves $50–75
303 Victorian bamboo shelves $125–350
304 Victorian whatnot shelves $200–750
305 Mission-style magazine pedestal $600–1000
306 Semicircular stepped shelves $125–400
307 Art Deco wall shelves $125–750
308 20th-century mirror-back shelves $100–250
309 Art Deco shelves $100–200
310 Art Deco sofa-side shelves $50–75
311 Mission-style sectional bookcase $250–450
312 Art Deco skyscraper bookcase $150–300
313 Country bucket bench $250–650
314 Oak mirrored hall rack $550–800
315 Folk-art hall rack $2000–3000
316 Victorian cast-iron hall tree $450–950
317 Bamboo hall rack $350–600
318 Anglo-Japanese hall rack $300–850
319 Oak hall rack $250–450
320 Oak hall tree $50–125
321 Modern music stand $1800–2500
322 Display stand $125–250
323 Modern room divider $250–450
324 Bamboo bar $150–350
325 Steamer trunk $50–150
326 Federal knife box $2500–3500

Fire Screens

Made in a wide variety of styles, fire screens are popular with many collectors. Although some Colonial Revival examples may cost only $150, rare period pieces command extremely high prices. The most expensive screens are in the Chippendale mode; those with elaborately carved pedestals and legs and large panels displaying fine needlework may fetch as much as $20,000. Victorian examples are much less expensive, with most ranging from $400 to $700. And they are abundant, in styles reflecting the eclecticism of the second half of the 19th century. Original needlework or fabric is rare for any period fire screen. However, an appropriate replacement will not greatly lower the value.

327 Colonial Revival fire screen $150–250
328 Hepplewhite fire screen $2000–5000
329 Chippendale fire screen $5000–10,000
330 Chippendale fire screen $10,000–20,000
331 Empire fire screen $400–650
332 Eastlake-Renaissance Revival fire screen $500–700
333 Eastlake brass fire screen $400–675
334 Anglo-Japanese fire screen $450–700

Picture Credits

Photographers
All photographs were taken by Chun Y. Lai with the exception of the following: 41, 42, 111, 123, 133, 137, 162, 208, 251, and 321. Marvin Rand photographed 35 and 50.

Collections
The following individuals and institutions allowed us to reproduce objects from their collections:

Marna Anderson Gallery, New York City: 47, 154, 180, 226, 241.
The Bayou Bend Collection, The Museum of Fine Arts, Houston: 208 (Gift of Miss Ima Hogg).
Ruth Bigel Antiques, New York City: 17, 20, 24, 30, 77, 102, 153, 186, 187, 215, 223, 225, 272.
Bridge City–Collection of Peter Francese, Poughkeepsie, New York: 1, 79, 96, 107, 108, 112, 239, 254, 313.
The Brooklyn Museum: 41 (Gift of Israel Sack), 42 (Museum Purchase).
Wendell Castle, Inc., Scottsville, New York: 321.
China Trade Museum, Milton, Massachusetts: 162.
Christie's, New York: 18, 32, 40, 53, 69, 190, 204, 212, 233, 238, 242, 243, 248, 279, 326.
Nancy and Jim Clokey, Massapequa, New York: 15, 43, 100, 228, 240, 247.
Gary Davenport, New York City: 213.
Douglas Galleries, South Deerfield, Massachusetts: 9, 145, 184, 217, 301, 302, 304, 311, 333.
Richard and Eileen Dubrow Antiques, Whitestone, New York: 65, 90, 124, 199, 315.
Webb English, New York City: 174, 281, 296, 309, 310.
Samuel Herrup, Brooklyn, New York: 185, 231, 232, 237, 253.
Inglenook Antiques, New York City: 19, 22, 71, 72, 86, 146, 161, 170, 171, 172, 181, 182, 188, 195, 221, 260, 261, 262, 263, 264, 265, 273, 274, 275, 282, 284, 286, 287, 290, 292, 297, 317, 331.
Lareau-DeVleer Gallery, New York City: 49, 70, 144, 166, 167, 198, 277, 285, 294, 305, 314.
Bernard and S. Dean Levy, Inc., New York City: 28, 29, 33, 34, 46, 51, 52, 55, 57, 59, 66, 68, 78, 81, 82, 92, 104, 134, 135, 136, 139, 141, 149, 150, 152, 155, 160, 189, 191, 193, 200, 203, 207, 209, 210, 216, 249, 252, 328, 329.
The Metropolitan Museum of Art: 133 (Purchase, 1940, Joseph Pulitzer Bequest), 330 (Gift of Mrs. Russell Sage, 1909).
Judith and James Milne, Inc., New York City: 39, 64, 67, 85, 95, 98, 99, 101, 109, 110, 220, 222, 236, 246, 266, 271, 306.
Alan Moss Studios, New York City: 131, 148, 173, 176, 194, 201, 202, 283, 293.
Museum of American Folk Art, New York City: 26, 83, 219; formerly in the Museum's collection: 3, 16, 234, 255, 256, 257, 258.
Oak 'N' Stuff Antiques, New York City: 21, 63, 164, 276.
Private collections: 35, 50, 105, 224, 259, 268.
Pat Sales Antiques, New York City: 2, 45, 91, 93, 103, 142, 192, 196, 227, 235, 244.
Secondhand Rose, New York City: 38, 120, 132, 177, 178, 230, 288, 289, 307, 308, 312, 323, 324.
Shaker Community, Inc., Pittsfield, Massachusetts: 4, 14, 44, 60, 84, 179, 245, 270.
Sotheby Parke Bernet. Agent: Editorial Photocolor Archives: 137.
The Margaret Woodbury Strong Museum, Rochester, New
York: 5, 6, 7, 8, 10, 11, 12, 13, 23, 25, 27, 37, 58, 73, 74, 80, 87,

Index

Numbers in boldface refer to color plates. Numbers in italics refer to pages.

Staff

Prepared and produced by Chanticleer Press, Inc.
Publisher: Paul Steiner
Editor-in-Chief: Gudrun Buettner
Executive Editor: Susan Costello
Managing Editor: Jane Opper
Project Editor: Mary Beth Brewer
Assistant Editor: Cathy Peck
Art Director: Carol Nehring
Art Assistant: Ayn Svoboda
Production: Helga Lose
Picture Library: Edward Douglas
Drawings: Barbara Marcks and Dolores Santoliquido

Design: Massimo Vignelli

The Knopf Collectors' Guides to American Antiques

Also available in this unique full-color format: